Latino/a Rights and Justice in the United States

Second Edition

Latino/a Rights and Justice in the United States

Perspectives and Approaches

Second Edition

José Luis Morín
John Jay College of Criminal Justice
City University of New York

Carolina Academic Press
Durham, North Carolina

Library of Congress Cataloging-in-Publication Data

Morín, José Luis.
  Latino/a rights and justice in the United States : perspectives
and approaches / Jose Luis Morin. -- 2nd ed.
     p. cm.
  Includes bibliographical references and index.
  ISBN 978-1-59460-406-5 (alk. paper)
  1. Hispanic Americans--Civil rights. 2. United States--Race
relations. I. Title.
  E184.S75M675 2008
  323.1168'073--dc22

                                                                2007049074

CAROLINA ACADEMIC PRESS
700 Kent Street
Durham, North Carolina 27701
Telephone (919) 489-7486
Fax (919) 493-5668

Printed in the United States of America.

Sin dignidad no hay vida.

Without dignity there is no life.

—*Eugenio María de Hostos*

CONTENTS

TABLE OF CASES

FOREWORD

You are about to encounter a fine book on a much-neglected topic. *Latino/a Rights and Justice in the United States* brings history, theory, and case analysis to bear on the story of Latinos' efforts to obtain fair treatment from the American judicial system. With coverage of all the large national-origin groups, including Mexican Americans, Puerto Ricans, and Cubans, as well as each of the main areas in which they have come into contact with the justice system—immigration, media stereotypes, police profiling, and international law—it also considers issues that few other books do, such as economic, social, and political rights. It shows where and how Latino people have made gains and what remains to be done if they are to enjoy full legal recognition and respect. And it offers what few other books do, an entire chapter on how to achieve these goals through concrete action both at the domestic and the international levels.

THE BLACK-WHITE BINARY PARADIGM OF RACE

One obstacle confronting Latinos in their search for justice is the black-white binary paradigm of race. [See Juan Perea, The Black-White Binary Paradigm of Race: The "Normal Science" of American Racial Thought, 75 Calif. L. Rev. 1213 (1997)]. A common feature of mainstream civil rights thought, the binary paradigm selects two groups, generally blacks and whites, and pronounces their experiences and relations with each other central. Other groups, such as Latinos or Asian Americans, enter into the analysis only insofar as they succeed in analogizing their experience to that of one of the two key sets of actors.

For example, a Latino or Asian American beaten in a parking lot by a thug shouting obscenities would be able to draw upon a host of civil rights remedies in seeking relief. Authorities might even prosecute the perpetrator under a state or federal hate-crime law. Because an African American treated in similar fashion would be entitled to seek redress, most authorities would permit the Asian American or Latino to do so, as well.

But suppose that the Latino or Asian American instead suffers discrimination on account of a foreign-sounding name or accent, or because the attacker mistakenly believes him or her an unlawful alien or a member of a group that is responsible for destroying the American automobile industry?

Discrimination of these other kinds, based on language, accent, perceived foreignness, or even religion, rarely visits blacks. Consequently, legal remedies crafted with them in mind and based on the Reconstruction Amendments of the United States Constitution are of little use to the nonblack, even though his injury may be just as severe as that of a black family that awakens to find a cross burning in its front yard.

These incidents may not even strike us as civil rights problems, but as cases of patriotism carried to excess. Black and nonblack minorities, as this book shows, have different histories. For blacks, the formative event was slavery. For Latinos, it has been Conquest and, later, immigration. Because nonblack groups' search for justice has taken a different course from that of African Americans, understanding their current situation and remedying their wrongs must proceed in different terms. This book explains why.

THE DOUBLE PROXY PROBLEM

This book will also help the justice system avoid what one might call the "double proxy" trap. Deeply engrained in the American consciousness, the reigning black-white binary paradigm predisposes us to think of Latinos in terms of the black experience, as though they were blacks with slightly lighter skins. This approach makes it difficult to see many injuries to Latinos as discrimination at all. Latinos emerge as, at best, proxies or stand-ins for blacks, the central actors in civil rights discourse, sometimes able to secure relief, and sometimes not.

Our familiarity with African American history equips us with an appropriate degree of suspicion about many of the types of mistreatment they suffer. We stand ready to reject the most common disguises and excuses that racists use to cover their tracks, such as claiming that a hiring decision was based on a black applicant's discomfort during an interview or her inability to "communicate," not her dark skin.

With Latinos, rules requiring that employees speak only English at the job site, even during their lunch break, may not ring the same warning bells. Or a zoning ordinance, enacted in the wake of a surge in Latino immigration, forbidding more than five unrelated persons from occupying the same apartment, may not seem like discrimination, but a simple land-use measure. Or a school board's decision not to provide bilingual education may seem no more problematic than one not to offer wood shop.

In a 1991 decision (*Hernandez v. New York*, 500 U.S. 352), the United States Supreme Court saw no discrimination in a prosecutor's dismissal of jurors who spoke Spanish and hence could not be trusted to listen to the official, translated version of events. A rule that fell heavily on native Spanish speakers triggered no suspicion; Spanish speaking was not a sufficiently close proxy for race or national origin.

Could it be because the Supreme Court was not sufficiently attuned to discrimination against Latinos and found it difficult to think of them as objects of it in the same way the Court can easily think of blacks in that role? And when *Hernandez*, a decision nearly as perversely formalistic as *Plessy v. Ferguson,* caused little outcry, might it be because the public shared the Court's ignorance?

This book will make such mistakes more glaring. It paints in stark relief a social and legal history complete with Conquest, stolen lands, suppressed language and culture, lynching, and brutal or dismissive treatment at the hands of the justice system. Judges, law professors, and legislators ignorant of that history will now have little excuse.

Just as important, the book will contribute to a generation of students and readers equipped to recognize and understand examples of discrimination like those set out in the pages of this book. With effort and the kind of legal creativity contained in these pages, this generation will help bring justice for a group that has enjoyed precious little of it in a land that prides itself on the quality of it for all.

Richard Delgado
University Professor
Seattle University School of Law

Latino/a Rights and Justice in the United States

Second Edition

CHAPTER 1

INTRODUCTION: TOWARD AN UNDERSTANDING OF LATINOS/AS IN THE UNITED STATES AND THE U.S. JUSTICE SYSTEM

More than two-thirds of all persons arrested for all criminal offenses are White, leading prominent criminologists to conclude that the typical criminal offender in the United States is White (Walker, Spohn, and DeLone 2007, 48). Yet Latinos and Latinas, commonly perceived and treated as non-White, are more likely to be incarcerated than Whites (Villarruel et al. 2002) and more often depicted in the media as criminals than Whites (Dorfman and Schiraldi 2001).

What was long predicted has become a reality: In 2003, the U.S. Census Bureau officially announced that Latinos/as have become the "largest minority community" in the United States, surpassing African Americans in total numbers (Bureau of the Census 2003b; Cohn 2003, A1).[1] It is a population projected to continue to grow at a rapid pace well into the foreseeable future (Schaefer 2001, 3). Indeed, for many years now, Latinos/as have hardly been a "minority" in cities such as San Antonio, Texas, where persons of Mexican descent comprise a majority. In many other cities, such as New York or Los Angeles, Latinos/as are fast-growing segments of the population.

But in spite of their emerging demographic presence in the United States, Latinos and Latinas remain poorly understood. In the area of law enforcement

---

1. In May 2007, the U.S. Census Bureau (2007) reported that "Hispanics remained the largest minority group, with 44.3 million on July 1, 2006—14.8 percent of the total population."

and criminal justice policy, Latinos/as—commonly categorized with other "minority groups" or people of color—are generally understood to be a population that is overrepresented in incarceration rates, juvenile justice, and crime statistics (Walker, Senger, Villarruel, and Arboleda 2004).

Given the expanding presence of Latinos/as in the United States, it becomes more necessary than ever to increase our understanding of this population's relation to U.S. law and justice; the ways in which U.S. laws and the legal system have fallen short in protecting Latino/a rights; and the ways in which equality and justice may be advanced. As the italicized information at the head of this chapter suggests, unresolved questions persist as to whether Latinos/as are fairly perceived and treated within the criminal justice system, the media, and the society at large. There are ongoing concerns about their inequitable treatment in other areas, such as housing, voting rights, education and health care, raising questions as to whether the civil and human rights of Latinos/as are adequately and equally protected in the United States.

The Oxford English Dictionary defines justice as "a moral ideal that the law seeks to uphold in the protection of rights and punishment of wrongs" (Martin 2002, under "Justice") [an unpaginated electronic work]. *Latino/a Rights and Justice in the United States* examines justice issues in the context of rights that have not always been recognized or enforced in the United States. Thus, it looks at the many ways in which justice still remains elusive for most Latinos/as. Issues of justice and Latino/a communities in the United States are discussed not only in relation to the legal system and administration of criminal justice, but also in relation to the larger society and the economic, social and cultural inequities that inhibit the overall achievement of justice as well as equal access to the rights that allow for groups to advance within the United States.

Too often unfamiliar, misunderstood, and stereotyped within the U.S. context, Latinos/as have become synonymous with "the problem," and, consequently, they are vulnerable to bias and discrimination in the application of the law. This book challenges readers to examine what they know about Latinos/as and their history in the United States in order to promote understanding and changes in policies and in society that will promote greater equality and justice. It seeks to open a dialogue that deepens the understanding of the U.S. Latino/a experience within a broader legal, social, political, and economic context—an understanding that is essential if equality under the law for Latinos/as is to be achieved. Thus, race, class, and gender in the United States must be addressed in their historical context and in relation to Latinos/as, in particular. Finally, this book seeks to encourage the reader to look beyond the traditional and narrowly defined solutions to discrimination and to incorporate a broader concept of rights and justice that includes the fundamental economic, social, and cultural needs of all humanity in order to assure that society reaches its greatest level of justice for all groups.

This second edition not only updates information found in the first edition; it expands on the many topics covered in the first edition, including the prison and criminal justice systems and Latinos/as; matters related to citizenship and the ongoing immigration debate; Latinos/as in the evolving legal world of the post 9-11 era; the impact of power issues in relation to the country of origin of U.S. Latinos/as; and the prospects for new models for the implementation of international human rights standards in order to advance and protect Latinos/as rights in the United States.

What Do We Know about Latinos/as and How Do We Know It?

In tackling the numerous issues facing Latinos/as, it is appropriate that this introductory chapter begin with some fundamental questions about what we know about Latinos/as; the accuracy of what we "know"; and even what we should know about the terms "Latino" and "Hispanic."

Basic to any inquiry into a particular group's relationship to matters of justice is an appreciation and understanding of that population within the society it inhabits. Thus, an understanding of Latino/a populations in the United States— their history, their needs, and their experience—is indispensable. What we know about Latinos/as is largely a function of what is conveyed through the mass media and the educational system. As a result, it is fair to say that what the general population in the United States truly knows or understands about the single largest ethnic population in the country is less than adequate, and what that it sees, hears, and learns about Latinas and Latinos is often of questionable accuracy.

The popularity of certain Latino/a entertainers, foods, or music is unquestionable. However, one should not confuse familiarity with these trends with a true understanding of Latino/a populations, their culture, and their history in the United States. Studies reveal that what the general public in the United States sees, hears, or learns about Latinos/as in the United States is either very limited or all too often negative in content. A study conducted at UCLA points out that although Latinos/as make up more than 13 percent of the U.S. population, only 4 percent of regular characters on prime-time television shows are Latino or Latina and nearly nine out of ten series have no Latino/a characters (Hoffman 2003, 1). Moreover, the vast majority of characters on prime time are White (2). Similarly, a study on the portrayal of Latinos/as on network television news prepared for the National Association of

Hispanic Journalists finds that "Latino-related stories continue to make up less than one percent of all stories" (Méndez-Méndez and Alverio 2003, 3).

Latinos/as and their history in the United States are relegated to virtual invisibility (Perea 1995). They remain almost completely absent from books, school texts, and curricula throughout the United States. While it is common for Latinos/as to be absent from network news and prime time television, it is also true that when Latinos/as do appear their depiction is typically disparaging. The National Association of Hispanic Journalists (NAHJ) reports that 66 percent of network news stories about Latinos/as focused exclusively on three topics: crime, terrorism, or illegal immigration. In 2002, suspected terrorist José Padilla, who was suspected of, but not charged with, involvement in a plot to detonate a "dirty bomb," was found to occupy "a central role in the coverage of Latinos ... with 21 network stories or 18 percent of all stories aired on Latinos" (Méndez-Méndez and Alverio 2003, 3).

In its *Network Brownout Report, 2005*, NAHJ (2006) expressed frustration with the continuing absence of Latinas/os in news stories and the type of coverage rendered that year about Latinas/os by three major network evening newscasts, *ABC World News*, *CBS Evening News*, and *NBC Nightly News* (Montalvo 2006). The report notes that "Latinos make up 14.5 percent of the U.S. population but less than one percent of the stories on the network evening news" (5), and voices its dismay that "[i]n contrast to 2004, Latinos were more often portrayed in crime stories in 2005. For most of these stories, Latinos were the perpetrators, not the victims" (4).

The conclusions of the National Association of Hispanic Journalists studies are consistent with those of other research which shows that in local news coverage Latinos/as and African Americans are often overrepresented as criminals while Whites are usually underrepresented as such. In a report examining studies conducted on local television news, Dorfman and Schiraldi (2001, 13) found that nine out of twelve (75 percent) of the studies revealed that "minorities" were overrepresented as perpetrators of crime. With respect to Latinos/as, Dorfman and Schiraldi explain that

> Hispanics were 14% more likely to be depicted as committing violent crime than nonviolent crime, whereas Hispanics were 7% more likely to be arrested for a violent crime than a nonviolent crime. Some might argue that this is simply because violent crime is more newsworthy than nonviolent crime. But Whites were 31% more likely to be depicted committing a nonviolent crime than a violent crime, whereas Whites were in fact only 7% more likely to be arrested for a nonviolent crime. Thus, while Blacks and Hispanics were overrepre-

sented as violent offenders, Whites were underrepresented as violent offenders on the evening news. (15)

These and other studies raise serious concerns, not only about the invisibility of Latinos/as in the United States, but also about negative and one-sided representations that contribute to public misperceptions and the perpetuation of prejudice, discrimination, and injustice. The dearth of reliable information, data, and analyses about Latino/a communities invariably results in uninformed or misinformed policymakers as well as a misguided general public. It is a problem that cries out for attention. As the New Jersey State Troopers racial profiling scandal of recent years reminds us—a scandal in which the state governor and attorney general conceded that for at least a decade state troopers had engaged in systematic and illegal racial profiling of Latinos/as and African Americans—Latinos/as are among the groups most affected by police prejudice and discrimination (see New Jersey Black and Latino Caucus 2002). The lack of knowledge about Latinos/as, including their past and present reality, and the imbalance in how they are viewed, categorized, and treated are among the many dimensions of the problem that need to be studied and understood in the quest for fair and appropriate public policies toward Latino/a communities in the United States.

The perpetuation of misinformation about Latinos/as has been detrimental in many respects. In addition to advancing stereotypes about Latino/a communities, it has helped promote a false impression among Whites that the United States does all that it can for Latinos/as and their countries of origin.

Latino/a Populations in the United States

In the effort to fill the information gap and move toward a better understanding of Latino/a communities in the United States, present-day demographics can serve as a point of departure. As Table 1 indicates, Latinos/as do not comprise a homogeneous group. They originate from many countries and regions of Latin America and the Caribbean that differ in culture and experiences although they share points of commonality.

The U.S. Census Bureau uses the category "other Hispanic" to include persons who identify themselves with terms such as Dominican, Tejano, or Spaniard (Bureau of the Census 2003e). These categories must be examined carefully, as they can obscure what are increasingly significant and growing numbers of Latino/a communities. For instance, Dominicans—who are grouped with "other Hispanics" by the Census Bureau—represent a burgeoning segment of New York City's population and they are having a con-

Table 1. Latinos/as in the United States by Origin in 2002

Place of National Origin	Percentage
Mexican	66.9%
Puerto Ricans	8.6%
Central and South Americans	14.3%
Cubans	3.7%
Other Hispanic	6.5%

Source: U.S. Census Bureau, Demographic Supplement to the March 2002 Current Population Survey (Bureau of the Census 2002b, 1). The above figures do not include the islands of Puerto Rico, the U.S. Virgin Islands, American Samoa, and the Northern Mariana Islands.

siderable impact on the City's political, economic, and social dynamics. In 2001, the U.S. Census Bureau estimated the Dominican population in the United States at 765,000 persons or 2.2 percent of all Latinos/as (Bureau of the Census 2001b, 3). It is also essential to bear in mind that the comprehensiveness and accuracy of the census data collection process in Latino/a communities is often questioned and the undercounting of Latinos/as, especially with respect to the number of undocumented persons, is suspected.

Of persons from Central America, who represented 4.8 percent of the total Latino/a population in 2001, Salvadorans made up the largest group at 655,000 persons or 1.9 percent of all Latinos/as in 2001. They were followed by Guatemalans with 372,000 or 1.1 percent and Hondurans at 218,000 or 0.6 percent. Among South Americans—a group that comprised 3.8 percent of all Latinos/as in 2001—Colombians accounted for 471,000 persons or 1.3 of the total Latino/a population; 261,000 or 0.7 percent were Ecuadorians; and 234,000 or 0.7 percent were Peruvians (Bureau of the Census 2001b, 2).

Recent data reflect that the Latino/a population in the United States grows at a faster rate than the entire U.S. population. From April 1, 2000 to July 1, 2002, the number of U.S. Latinos/as increased from 35.3 million to 38.8 million, accounting for half of the U.S. population growth during that time period (Bureau of the Census 2003b). With a growth of 3.4 percent from July 1, 2005 to July 1, 2006, Latinos/as continue their trajectory as "the fastest-growing minority group" followed by Asians (Census Bureau 2007).

Given the marked expansion in the presence of Latinos/as in the United States revealed by the census data, it should be obvious that more should be known and understood about Latinos/as within the larger U.S. society. The absence of an informed general population in the United States provides fertile ground for the perpetuation of forms of prejudice and discrimination that inhibit the realization of full and equal rights for Latinos/as.

The federal government has grouped "Hispanics" or "Latinos" under an ethnic rather than a racial category for statistical purposes since Latinos/as encompass diverse racial backgrounds. As a result, certain data gathered by government agencies, such as the Uniform Crime Reports (UCR), only include four racial groups: Whites, African Americans, Native Americans, and Asians. In the daily workings of society and the justice system, however, Latinos/as have most often been perceived and treated in racial terms. As is the case with African Americans, they frequently experience discrimination in many aspects of their lives (see Pew Hispanic Center/Kaiser Family Foundation 2002, 69).

"LATINO" OR "HISPANIC"?

In any discussion of racial and ethnic groups, questions eventually arise about the proper nomenclature. Similar to the way that the term "African American" sparked debate but was accepted and adopted over time, the use of the term "Latino" over "Hispanic" has also triggered considerable discussion, while gradually gaining acceptance. The label traditionally used—and arguably imposed—by the U.S. government is "Hispanic," a general ethnic classification for a person of Latin American descent whose country of origin was a former colony of Spain, which serves as the term's point of reference. But the term "Hispanic" has undergone reexamination.

Increasingly, "Hispanic" is viewed as deficient and inaccurate. The term "Hispanic" has been deemed inappropriate, as an ethnic designator that homogenizes and subsumes millions of persons in the United States from diverse racial and ethnic origins and broad national and cultural experiences under one label (Oboler 1995, xiii–xiv). It also overemphasizes the legacy of European and Spanish colonial rule in Latin America and the Caribbean, rather than representing and validating their diverse racial and cultural characteristics, including the indigenous and African heritages of vast numbers of persons from Latin America and the Caribbean (Perea et al. 2000, 4; Flores, et al 2002, 83). As explored later in this volume, that Latinos/as often manifest strong African or indigenous roots racially and culturally becomes important in analyzing racial and ethnic prejudice and discriminatory treatment of Latinos/as in the United States under U.S. law and by U.S. law enforcement agencies.

"Hispanic" is also an "ahistorical" term that draws attention to the European colonial past while diverting attention away from the historical assertion of U.S. domination and control over Latin American countries as well as Latin Americans in the United States (Oboler 1995, 4). It is a term that obscures the political struggle for identity by Latin Americans in the United

States. In critically analyzing the term "Hispanic," some have even challenged its use as divisive within the social construction of race in the United States that places a premium on "White" over "Black." As such, Latinos/as are prompted to choose the term "Hispanic" in an attempt to avoid racially discriminatory treatment (Martínez 1993).

As Oboler explains, the label "Hispanic has been used to racialize and, through government sanction, officially "homogenize," which

> ... is undoubtedly an effective and time-honored method of social control. The label serves, on one hand, to divide those so designated from others in similar positions or from potential allies in the wider society. On the other, it serves to keep control over those who have not actually been conquered through a combination of the state-organized 'trickle down' strategy for distribution of social benefits and the simultaneous stimulation of competition for scarce social resources and legitimate positions among the group members. Through this 'ethnic' version of 'divide' and control, then, the perpetuation of racial stereotyping and the image of ineradicable foreignness are guaranteed. Thus, to the extent that Latino/as continue to be the one population that, whether formally citizens or not, is consistently considered 'alien' in their own land, they will continue to be an essential component of discussions on the changing meaning of citizenship in the US context, while also remaining central to US immigration policy and hemispheric power dynamics. (Oboler 2006, 10)

Because, as Oboler asserts, ethnic labels can be used to divide, racialize, and promote biases, the debate over the terms "Hispanic" or "Latino" cannot be trivialized as a question merely about semantics. Those disempowered by labels are challenged to take on the task of redefining and asserting their own authority to determine the terms that will prevail in the public sphere.

In contrast to the term "Hispanic," the term "Latino" has come to be used increasingly as a form of self-definition, re-thinking, and empowerment on the part of Latinos and Latinas, particularly in response to a government-imposed classification (Oquendo 1995). In this sense, embracing the term "Latino" is akin to the adoption of "Chicano" as an assertion of identity, culture, self-determination, and self-empowerment among Mexican Americans from the 1960s to the present (see, e.g., García 2001; Acuña 2007 266–270; 325–337). "Latino" has been employed as a more precise description of "a geographically derived national origin group, that has been constantly and consistently viewed and treated as a racial group, in both individual and institutional interaction while in the United States" (Hayes-Bautista and Chapa 1987,

66). It is difficult for one term to perfectly describe the multitude of persons from different Latin American countries who live in the United States today. But for those critically thinking and analyzing of the condition of persons of Latin American descent in the United States, "Latino" is a reflection of the struggle for self-identification and a more accurate and self-reaffirming term than "Hispanic" (see, e.g., Delgado and Stefancic 1998). Accordingly, its use has steadily increased. Indeed, because of its increased usage, new standards were issued by the Office of Management and Budget in 1997, and the U.S. Census Bureau has adopted the term "Latino" to be used interchangeably with "Hispanic" (Bureau of the Census 2001b, 1).

The term used primarily in this book is "Latino/a," rather than "Hispanic," in a form that also takes into account gender. "Hispanic" is used sparingly and cautiously, typically in instances where another source is quoted. As Latinos/as do not comprise a homogeneous group, they are referred to herein in the plural as Latino/a communities, populations, or groups.

Cultural and other differences among Latino/a groups also appear to be relevant to the manner in which Latinos/as tend to identify themselves. As a survey by the Pew Hispanic Center/Kaiser Family Foundation revealed (2002), most Latinos/as prefer to identify themselves first according to their countries of origin and second as either "Latino" or "Hispanic". The study describes that the "tie to home country is much more salient than any pan-ethnic or 'Latino/Hispanic' identity" (23). Nonetheless, a majority of Latinos/as also recognizes a "unified Latino culture" and prefers to identify their race as "Latino" or "Hispanic," feeling that they do not fit into any single racial category used by the U.S. government (23).

Another label often applied to Latinos/as is "minority." "Minority," when used most sensibly, attempts to describe a group that experiences a pattern of disadvantage or inequality whose members also share a visible trait(s) usually determined at birth (Healey 2006, 12). However, the term is frequently found to have offensive and belittling connotations (Walker et al. 2007, 12). Therefore, in this book, its use is avoided, except when quoting an outside source, such as the U.S. Census Bureau. "People of color" is preferred by this author and used instead of "minority."

Race, Racism, and Racialized "Others"

To help bridge the gap in understanding Latinos/as in relation to issues of justice, this book seeks to provide an examination of the history and evolution of law and justice issues as they affect Latino/a communities in the United

States. As Perea, Delgado, Harris, and Wildman stress (2000, 246), U.S. history insufficiently covers U.S. relations with Latin America and the history of Latinos/as in the United States. As these scholars point out, seldom is the history of the conquest of Latin America—not just by Spain, but by the United States—studied in U.S. schools. Even less attention is given to the underlying racial premises that have shaped U.S. government policies and practices (247–48). Absent is the history of the use of race as an instrument to suppress the rights of Latinos/as in ways similar to those of other people of color—Native Americans who endured cultural and physical genocide, the conquest of their lands, and forced assimilation; African Americans who suffered slavery, segregation, and the ongoing impact of these horrific institutions; Chinese immigrants who experienced discrimination and exploitation as cheap labor; persons of Japanese origin interned during World War II, who suffered great losses as a consequence, including the loss of their homes and property (Perea et al. 2000).

The history of conquests covered in Chapter 2 of this volume provides the background for understanding the long trajectory of U.S.-Latin American relations that have given rise to the presence of Latinos/as in the United States. From its earliest beginnings as a country, the United States' relationship with Latin America was grounded in an ideology that justified U.S. expansionism through military conquests. The legal framework constructed to delimit the rights of Mexicans and Puerto Ricans under U.S. territorial designation in the 1800s is, in great measure, a product of the hegemonic aspirations and racial assumptions of U.S. policymakers encompassed in the ideology known as "Manifest Destiny."

Mexicans and Puerto Ricans are the two largest and earliest Latin American peoples to have encounters with U.S. desires to realize its "destiny." Understanding the history of Mexicans and Puerto Ricans in relation to the United States is vital since its impact has set the course for the other Latino/a groups that followed. As Suzanne Oboler observes (1995, 16), "the experiences of more recent Latin American immigrants cannot be understood without serious consideration of the context of historical discrimination shaped in relation to Chicanos and Puerto Ricans." Hence, in this text, the experience of more recently arrived Latinos/as will be discussed in view of the events that preceded them and the legacy of discrimination derived from earlier actions taken to restrict the fundamental rights of Mexicans and Puerto Ricans.

In the attempt to present a more comprehensive picture of the current situation of Latinos/as in the United States than that generally available, *Latino/a Rights and Justice in the United States* singles out as crucial and influential to understanding the Latino/a experience, the pursuit of U.S. hemispheric dominance, the impact of a persistent undercurrent of racism in the development of U.S. law and foreign policy toward Latin America and Latin Americans historically, and the manner in which hegemony and racism have shaped the rights of Latinos/as in this country. Also explored is the historical link between U.S.-Latin America relations and the Latino/a presence within the territorial boundaries of the United States and the present-day flow of Latinos/as between Latin America and the United States. While this book cannot, nor does it purport to, cover all of these dimensions exhaustively, this author believes that some coverage is essential to providing a true and more complete understanding of Latinos/as in relation to their rights in the U.S. context.

In line with this approach, the central role that race has played historically cannot be underestimated and must be addressed. The issue of race helped set the pattern for the limitation of Latino/a rights in the United States, a pattern that resonates into the present. Upon close examination, the record is clear: Latino/a communities remain challenged by prejudice and discrimination in U.S. society and by problems that stem from institutionalized forms of inequality and injustice, of which racial profiling and police brutality are but two contemporary examples within the criminal justice system.

Based on the premise that Latinos/as may be of any race, the federal government's current ethnic and racial classification system categorizes Latinos/as (or using its usual terminology, "Hispanics") as an ethnic group. Nevertheless, Latinos/as are also regularly compared and grouped with racial "minority" groups in the United States, as demonstrated in Table 2 below. Derived from 2002 Census Bureau data, Table 2 presents estimates of the U.S. popu-

Table 2. U.S. Population by Race and Persons of Latino/a Origin: 2006

Race	Population	% of Population
Latino/a	44.3 million	14.80%
White	198.7 million	81.44%
African American	40.3 million	13.44%
Asian	14.9 million	4.98%
American Indian and Alaska Natives	4.5 million	1.50%
Native Hawaiian and Other Pacific Islanders	1 million	0.345%

Source: U.S. Bureau of the Census. 2007. Minority population tops 100 million (Press Release No. CB07-70). Washington, D.C.: Public Information Office, B. Bernstein, http://www.census.gov/Press-Release/www/releases/archives/population/010048.html (accessed July 15, 2007).

lation according to the number of people who identified with one race in the census, regardless of whether they reported any other races.

In discussing "race," it is important to note that it is well established that "race" has no basis in science and is merely a social construction (Ferrante and Browne 2001; Healey 2006, 18–19; Omi and Winant 1994).[2] If this is the case, why, then, do racial and ethnic prejudice and discrimination persist? As with other groups affected by racial and ethnic discrimination, the answer to this question for Latinos/as can be found in how "race" is socially constructed in U.S. society.

Latinos/as have and continue to occupy a "racialized" status within the United States. As described by historian Edward J. Escobar (1999, 7), the racialization of Latinos/as in the United States involves a process through which prevailing social assumptions preserve Latinos/as as racially "other" in relation to the dominant White society. The group considered to be "other" is consigned to a place of subordination in relation to those who dominate. As racialized "others," Latinos/as have and continue to be perceived as "foreign" and "less than" the White dominant population. Subordination, in turn, serves as the necessary prerequisite that justifies and explains the exercise of control and/or exploitation of the racialized group.

An overview of historical and contemporary forms of discrimination against Latino/a communities is incorporated into the discussion of race and the racialization of Latinos/as in Chapter 3. Indeed, discrimination—as manifested within the criminal justice system through the enduring problems of police brutality, corruption, racial profiling, and inequality in the courts, in sentencing, and incarceration—is a pressing concern among Latinos/as as are the issues of housing, employment, health care, and voting rights.

The lack of adequate representation in U.S. law enforcement and judicial institutions poses other obstacles for Latino/a communities. Yet, as described in Chapter 4, increases in numerical representation alone do not necessarily guarantee equal access to justice. Other inadequacies, such as the lack of Latino/a involvement in policymaking and the absence of culturally compe-

---

2. Healey (2006, 19) notes that "virtually the entire scientific community regards race as a biological triviality, a conclusion based on decades of research." Race has no significance beyond the amount of melanin in a person's skin, and as a result "who belongs to which racial group is largely a matter of social definitions and traditions, not biology" (19). There exists a similar agreement among social scientists (Feagin and Feagin 1996). Claims that race determines one's intelligence—as made by Herrnstein and Murray (1994)—have been resoundingly discredited and criticized by psychologists, sociologist, and anthropologists and organizations such as the American Anthropological Association—as unscientific and profoundly mistaken (Walker et al. 2007, 8–9).

tent services, cannot be overlooked. For Latinos/as, the ability to make decisions that promote meaningful change in the institutions that affect their lives and the ability to retain and assert their identity within institutions more inclined to promote conformity than diversity are essential to making society more responsive to the needs of Latino/a communities.

The Latino Officers Association represents an example of the many ways that Latinos/as have organized to advocate for change, reassert Latino/a identity, and open new opportunities. Indeed, examining the experience of Latino/a police officers in New York City also allows us to reflect on whether the level of Latino/a representation as legal professionals — lawyers, judges, and others working within the judicial system — is adequate, and on the consequences of an insufficient pool of Latino/a legal professionals on Latino/a communities.

Given the diversity of Latinas and Latinos in the United States — their many countries of origin, and even their cultural and linguistic differences — it is difficult for one book to cover the experiences of all Latinos/as in the United States. For this reason, New York City and Los Angeles — cities with significant and varied Latino/a populations — have been chosen for a specific discussion of justice issues in relation to the Latino/a groups that reside in these major urban centers. This discussion is found in Chapter 5. Highlighted in this chapter are police policies, practices, and scandals in New York City and Los Angeles, cities that have long been centers of police-Latino/a community tensions. The perspectives of two public figures, Alex Sánchez and Iris Báez, are provided to illustrate how their lives have been transformed in the midst of the harsh realities of life and justice in Los Angeles and New York City and how they, in turn, have acted to institute change.

BEYOND DEFINING THE PROBLEM: FINDING SOLUTIONS

The story of Latinos/as in the United States is a story of hope, struggle, and commitment to the realization of Latino/a identity and justice. In the search for solutions, Chapter 6 focuses on a program that seeks to address the needs of Latino/a youths and their families. The John Jay College-Family Life Center, *Palenque*, organized by members of the Puerto Rican/Latin American Studies Department of John Jay College of Criminal Justice in New York City, provides an alternative to traditional modes of viewing and assisting youths who are routinely labeled as "at risk."

Among Latinos/as, the conspicuous absence of Latinos/as in U.S. history books reinforces the notion that they have no history or culture worthy of being recorded. Stripped of the means through which to learn about themselves, Latinos/as become disconnected from their own history, culture, and identity. They are also made to feel that maintaining their heritage, language, and culture is futile and even counterproductive. For Latinos/as, the recurring message in the United States is usually that English, and only English, is worth learning; "speaking and learning your native Spanish will only set you back." Ubiquitous negative depictions of Latinos/as in the news and in the entertainment media only serve to instill a sense of being "other" and "less than" the dominant White society.

Palenque is a program that works with youth and families from the Washington Heights/Inwood community of New York City, comprised largely of Latinos/as from the Dominican Republic. The program approaches its work from a culture-based perspective in order to counteract the detrimental effects of marginalization and poor self-esteem common among Latino/a youths. The program attempts to fill the void left by a neighborhood rampant with deteriorating institutions—schools, medical facilities, and other public institutions and services unable to adequately serve the community. In this neighborhood, problems related to poverty combine with poor police-community relations and a myriad of structural problems that breed despair and undermine individual and collective advancement. By providing a range of academic, cultural, career, and personal and family development activities that emphasize the cultural background of the participants, *Palenque* helps these young people confront problems of personal and collective alienation.

In the search for alternative models and effective solutions to the problems faced by Latinos/as in the United States, Chapter 7 looks at the application of international human rights law, and its norms, principles, and standards oriented to protecting minority group rights, linguistic, cultural, economic, social, and other rights. Indeed, *Palenque* is itself an initiative consistent with the principles of international human rights law that provide for the respect and protection of persons not part of the majority group in the country.

Recognizing that the issues addressed in this book are not one-dimensional in nature, this book takes a multidisciplinary approach to present a more comprehensive picture of Latino/a groups in connection to the larger society, the law, and the legal system. Historical, sociological, political, ethnographic, and legal elements are integrated to provide the reader with an in-depth understanding. In this volume, knowledge of the past is considered essential to improving the present. For this reason, a premium is placed on providing the historical context of the subject matter. Equal importance is assigned to broadening the scope of inquiry to include advancements in the field of international human rights and, in particular, the development of economic, social, and cultural rights applicable to Latino/a groups in the United States.

As it is impossible for one book to represent all perspectives of the many diverse communities and people who make up Latino/a communities in the United States, this volume attempts to draw together information that is vital to understanding the general historical trajectory of Latinos/as. It explores contemporary patterns related to justice issues affecting substantial numbers of Latinos/as, and incorporates ethnographic data drawn from interviews of numerous U.S. Latinos and Latinas in order to delve into their lives, experiences, and perspectives. Latino/a perspectives are presented at various points in this book to allow sectors of the Latino/a communities to have their voices heard and their stories told in a society where Latinos and Latinas are often invisible and voiceless. Latino/a views are also presented to assist in the process of rethinking and challenging conventional wisdom on Latinos/as. Both quantitative and qualitative data have a place in this study of Latinos/as, with qualitative data providing insights that help explain why, rather than how much or how often.

Latino/a Rights and Justice in the United States seeks to advance a discussion for broadening our concept of rights, respect, and dignity. It endeavors to provide the means to re-envision the ways in which all persons—not just Latinos/as—can have access to educational, social, and economic progress. It also endeavors to deepen our understanding that we all have a stake in insuring progress for all persons in society and in the world. It is from this standpoint that the concluding chapter proposes to place in perspective the various experiences of Latinos/as and initiate a discussion about strategies to right wrongs and improve conditions for Latinos/as in their quest for equality and justice. While this book focuses on the elusiveness of equality and justice for Latinos/as in the United States, it also attempts to posit ideas, recommendations, and approaches to correct and reduce discrimination and inequality. In this sense, this book is meant to be a reflection about the absence of justice as well as the continuing quest for justice—recurring themes in the lives of Latinos and Latinas in the United States.

CHAPTER 2

THE ORIGINS OF LATINO/A PRESENCE IN THE UNITED STATES: AN ENCOUNTER WITH THE HISTORY OF U.S.-LATIN AMERICAN RELATIONS

Knowledge of the history of relations between the United States and Latin America and the Caribbean is indispensable to putting into focus the often forgotten events and circumstances that account for the Latino/a presence in the United States. In many instances, U.S. policies toward Latin America have been directly responsible for the influx of Latinos/as into the United States. But many today misconstrue that presence as solely based on immigration when, in fact, Latinos/as inhabited what now comprises the Southwestern and Western states of United States—approximately one-third of its continental territory—long before the existence of European settlements in North America (see Perea et al. 2000, 248).

Absent from the collective consciousness of the United States are the wars of territorial conquests that took place in the 1800s. At the end of the U.S.-Mexican War in 1848, Mexicans were subsumed into the United States along with the land that was previously sovereign Mexican territory. Following the United States' war with Spain in 1898, Puerto Ricans became subjects of the United States and their land a possession of the United States, even though in 1897 they had already obtained political autonomy from Spain. As elaborated upon further in this chapter, the colonization of Puerto Rico by the United States has played a direct role in causing Puerto Ricans to come the United States, not as "immigrants," but under a second-class form of citizenship. Thus, immigration alone does not account for the number of Latinos/as currently in the United States. In point of fact, recent census data reveals that three in five Latinos/as are U.S. born (Bureau of the Census 2002b, 3).

The conspicuous lack of awareness of this history provides fertile ground for the preservation of forms of prejudice and discrimination that inhibit the realization of full and equal rights and justice for Latinos/as. This chapter seeks to ground the discussion about rights and justice in its historical context to better inform our understanding of the present-day condition of Latinos/as in the United States.

U.S. Imperial Designs on Latin America

Before reviewing the early history of U.S. foreign policy toward Latin America, it is necessary to clarify that the United States, notwithstanding its anti-colonial beginnings, occupies a place in history as one of the world's greatest empires. Its ascent to this status was not accidental. By the end of the nineteenth century, the United States had successfully positioned itself as an imperial power with territorial possessions around the globe. It had also claimed a dominant role over all of the Americas—a role that it maintains to the present. It is well established that U.S. imperialism was not a passive endeavor or accidental, but a concerted effort to expand U.S. territorial reach for new markets and to secure other economic, social, and political gains (LaFeber [1963] 1998, xiv–xix; Smith 2000, 12; Schoultz 1998, 78–90; Morín 2000, 9).

However much it has been couched in benevolent terms or justified in the name of spreading democracy, acquiring territories through wars of conquest places the United States squarely in the league of other imperial powers in world history that have engaged in the systematic violation of the right of self-determination of peoples (LaFeber [1963] 1998, xiv–xix; Smith 2000, 11–12). Indeed, as with all other imperial powers, the United States has used war and the threat of war as indispensable instruments for the attainment of hegemony. Stated clearly, it was through military conquests that the United States was able to wrest approximately half of the lands of Mexico and gain control over a series of island nations—including Puerto Rico, Cuba, the Philippines, Guam, and Hawaii—by the end of the 1800s.

The conquests of the 1800s were rooted in the longstanding and deeply held desire of many founders of the United States to construct an empire. As early as 1767, Benjamin Franklin articulated aspirations for the expansion of U.S. territory, including intentions to make Mexico and Cuba part of the United States (Perea et al. 2000, 258). Thomas Jefferson contended that the United States "has a hemisphere to itself. It must have a separate system of interest which must not be subordinated to those of Europe" (quoted in Smith 2000, 17). By the 1780s, Jefferson avowed that the Spanish empire should be taken over by the United States "peice by peice [*sic*]" (18). These expansionist designs were not simply a whim of Franklin and Jefferson; they became an integral part of the ambitions of U.S. policymakers who followed. The goal of seizing other lands to advance U.S. global economic and political interests could not be clearer than in 1891 when Secretary of State James Blaine wrote in a letter to President Benjamin Harrison, "I think there are only three places that are of value enough to be taken that are not continental.... One is Hawaii and the others are Cuba and Porto Rico [*sic*]" (quoted in LaFeber [1963] 1998, 110).

Racial Justifications for U.S. Imperialism

U.S. domination over Latin American lands and peoples was made palatable and justifiable to the U.S public in large measure through the perpetuation of racist ideologies. "Manifest Destiny," a dominant and influential belief system boldly advanced in the 1800s, touted the divine right of Anglo-Saxon U.S. citizens to territorial expansion based on purported racial and cultural superiority (Cabán 1999, 83; Stephanson 1995; Horsman 1981). The influence of the racist assumptions inherent in the notion of the "White Man's Burden," together with "Manifest Destiny," provided the requisite justification for Anglo-American territorial conquests and domination (Stephanson 1995).[1]

Policymakers and the major news media combined to further the idea that the United States was governed by persons of a superior race, religion, and culture distinguishable from all others and that, therefore, the United States was uniquely and rightfully entitled to claim dominance over other lands and peoples. So deeply held were these beliefs that all non-Anglo Saxons, even those from Europe, were considered threats to the nation. By 1751, Benjamin Franklin (1959, 234) had already voiced his beliefs about the racial and cultural threat that non-Anglo Americans posed, including German immigrants, who in his words "will shortly be so numerous as to Germanize us instead of our Anglifying them, and will never adopt our Language and Customs, any

---

1. Taken from Rudyard Kipling's poem of the same name, the idea of the "White Man's Burden," like manifest destiny, helped justify the British colonial empire around the globe. The cynical and racist assumption underlying the "White Man's Burden" was that colonial rule over peoples who were not White and Christians would have a civilizing effect on them. Many in the United States gravitated toward this belief, incorporating it into the broader notion of Manifest Destiny. It was also understood that "by fulfilling one's duty to Christianity and civilization one would actually also profit, for 'with the obligations are associated recompense in the wide field of commercial development'" (Stephanson 1995, 88).

more than they can acquire our complexion" (see also Portes and Schauffler 1996, 433).

In spite of the diversity of people and races in the United States in its early years—Native Americans, Europeans of different countries of origin, and Africans—prominent leaders and founders of the United States regarded the country as one only of and for Anglo Americans. In *The Federalist Papers*, John Jay ([1788] 2003, 32) remarked that

> Providence has been pleased to give this one connected country to one united people—a people descended from the same ancestors, speaking the same language, professing the same religion, attached to the same principles of government, very similar in their manners and customs.

Very early in U.S. history, Latin Americans were singled out as racially inferior to Anglo-Saxon Americans. James Buchanan denounced "the imbecile and indolent Mexican race," and in the press, the *New York Evening Post* in the late 1840s categorized Mexicans as "*Indians*—Aboriginal Indians. Such Indians as Cortez conquered three thousand [*sic*] years ago, only rendered a little more mischievous by a bastard civilization.... They do not possess the elements of an *independent* national existence ... and they must share the destiny of their race" (quoted in Smith 2000, 47).

As historian Howard Zinn documents (2003, 154–55), major U.S. newspapers and political leaders repeatedly championed the idea of Anglo superiority as justification for the conquest of Mexico. In 1847, the *New York Herald* stated unequivocally: "The universal Yankee nation can regenerate and disenthrall the people of Mexico in a few years; and we believe it is part of our destiny to civilize that beautiful country" (155). Invoking God as further justification, Senator H. V. Johnson stated:

> I believe we should be recreant to our noble mission, if we refuse acquiescence in the high purposes of a wise Providence. War has its evils ... but however inscrutable to us, it has also made, by the All-wise Dispenser of events, the instrumentality of accomplishing the great end of human elevation and happiness.... It is in this view, that I subscribe to the doctrine of 'manifest destiny.' (155)

The notion that racial and cultural deficiencies rendered Latin American peoples unable to govern their own nations effectively laid the foundation for a foreign policy grounded on achieving and maintaining U.S. hegemony over the Americas. The foreign policy initiative that encapsulated the idea of U.S. hegemony over the Western Hemisphere was the Monroe Doctrine of 1823.

It is a policy statement that validated the establishment of a U.S. sphere of influence over the region—particularly over Latin America and the Caribbean—and it is a doctrine that many historians agree still remains influential in U.S.-Latin American relations (see, e.g., Schoultz 1999; Smith 2000; LaFeber 1993). In the 1800s, it was not only racially negative characterizations of Latin Americans that helped justify the wars of conquest against Mexico and Spain, these were complemented by U.S. government policies, practices, laws, and judicial decisions that relegated other Latin Americans subordinate to Anglo Americans.

The acceptance in the United States that Latin Americans were a separate and inferior "race" made numerous military interventions throughout Latin America unconvroversial. In the case of Cuba, Orville H. Platt, author of the notorious Platt Amendment, vehemently opposed Cuba's incorporation into the United States because "[t]he people of Cuba, by reason of their race and characteristic, cannot be easily assimilated by us.... Their presence in the American union, as a state, would be most disturbing" (quoted in Smith 2000, 49). Since under U.S. policy by virtue of their race Cubans were unworthy of incorporation into the union, they also could not be trusted with full political independence. As a result, the Platt Amendment of 1904 relegated Cuba to neocolonial status and insured complete U.S. authority to intervene in Cuba's internal affairs, including its economy and politics. While the Platt Amendment was in effect (1904–1932), U.S. military forces invaded and/or occupied Cuba from 1906–1909, in 1912, and from 1917–1922 (51).

Throughout the nineteenth century and into the twentieth century, in Washington and throughout the United States Latin Americans were openly and continually depicted as inferior and racialized "others," who were prone to uncivilized behavior, and undeserving of self-government. The U.S. public was fed a steady diet of news stories and media portrayals that vividly reinforced in their hearts and minds that in pursuing its colonial agenda the U.S. government was acting benevolently and justifiably (Gleach 2002; *Journal of el Centro de Estudios Puertorriqueños* 1998, 155–63).

In the 1800's, political cartoons in leading newspapers around the country reinforced demeaning and racist stereotypes of the peoples of Cuba, Puerto Rico, Hawaii, and the Philippines. Published in *Puck* magazine in 1899, the cartoon in Figure 1 conveys the idea that racial and cultural deficiencies rendered Latin American peoples unable to govern themselves. It depicts Uncle Sam (the United States) at the head of a classroom scolding Cuba, Puerto Rico, Hawaii, and the Philippines, represented by the dark-skinned, ugly, and unruly children. The caricature of Cuba, Puerto Rico, Hawaii, and the Philippines as revolting and ignorant children is consistent

Figure 1. "School Begins" cartoon

"School Begins," an illustration by Louis Dalrymple from January 25, 1899, published in *Puck* magazine. Image courtesy Bishop Museum.

The "lesson" on the chalkboard: "The consent of the governed is a good thing in theory, but very rare in fact. England has governed her colonies whether they consented or not. By not waiting for their consent, she has greatly advanced the world. The U.S. must govern its new territories with or without their consent until they can govern themselves."

The inscription on the sign at the rear of the classroom: "The Confederate States refused their consent to be governed, but the Union was preserved without their consent."

with racist images of African Americans, Native Americans, and Asians that were widespread at the time. The cartoon also depicts Alaska and other territories and states as having been "civilized" by Uncle Sam. The globe in front of the classroom alludes to the United States' mission of global territorial acquisition. Consistent with notions of "Manifest Destiny" and the "White Man's Burden," the cartoon contains the unambiguous message that U.S. imperial conquests were justified given the racial inferiority of the conquered.

Throughout the 1800s, cartoons and other images reinforced demeaning, negative stereotypes of the conquered peoples of Cuba, Puerto Rico, the Philippines, and Hawaii. An analysis of political cartoons of 1898 by Frederic W. Gleach of Cornell University pinpoints the purpose of the degrading images of the conquered peoples of these island nations around the world: "Racialization, infantilization, primitivization, and feminization were all used to construct our newly-interior Others as inferior to real Americans.... This was not a passing way of viewing them, but a persistent one—and a problematic one, even to the present" (Gleach 2002, 68). By casting Latin Americans as racialized "others," U.S. public opinion was galvanized in support of their government's actions around the globe. These powerful images offered a vision of a government carrying out a benign mission among inherently inept peoples. Thus, U.S. policies were not to be interpreted as those of a colonial power acting in contravention of its own founding democratic principles, but in furtherance of those ideals. Professor Peter H. Smith (2000, 38–39) explains that projecting the United States as a nation imbued with the higher goal of spreading democracy among these racially, culturally, and religiously backward peoples was vital not only to mobilize domestic support and resources for its imperial ventures, but also to justify its actions in the eyes of rival powers. In addition, he points out that the projection of lofty goals served to indoctrinate and thereby control the peoples of the subjugated societies.

Racism and a racialized vision of the peoples of the developing world also proved useful in the establishment of a framework for the unequal application of the law to Latinos/as in the United States. In the case of Puerto Ricans, U.S. Supreme Court decisions on the rights of Puerto Ricans have been compared to the separate and unequal treatment accorded to African Americans in the United States for more than half a century (Torruella 1988). Indeed, virtually the same group of Supreme Court justices responsible for *Plessy v. Ferguson*, 163 U.S. 537 (1896)—the case establishing the notorious legal doctrine of "separate but equal"—decided the *Insular Cases*, which, as explained further in this chapter, continue to delimit the rights of Puerto Ricans. As with the *Plessy* case, the restrictions the *Insular Cases* imposed on the rights of Puerto Ricans were grounded in the racist and racialized perceptions of Puerto Ricans and Latin Americans that prevailed throughout all branches of the U.S. government. Unlike *Plessy*, however, the *Insular Cases* have never been overturned. As a result, the most fundamental rights of the peoples of Puerto Rico are still significantly limited.

During the Congressional debate in 1900 about whether to extend constitutional protections to them, Puerto Ricans were characterized as follows:

> They are of the Latin race, and are of quick and excitable tempers, but they are at the same time patient, docile, frugal, and most of them industrious. (U.S. Senate 1900, 4875)

Given such characterizations, it is not surprising that Puerto Ricans were not extended full constitutional rights, and have not been to this very day. As persons perceived as collectively comprising a racially inferior group, the conclusion drawn was that Latin Americans present a danger to the dominant,

White U.S. population and its institutions (Torruella 1988). Therefore, to insure Anglo-American power and authority over the status and condition of Latinos/as in the United States it was imperative to restrict their rights through legislation and other legal obstacles (see Delgado and Stefancic 1998; Perea et al. 2000; Torruella 1988).

U.S. CONQUESTS IN MEXICO AND PUERTO RICO

At present, the two largest Latino/a populations in the United States, Mexicans and Puerto Ricans, share a history inexorably linked to the U.S. imperial expansion of the 1800s. As mentioned in Chapter 1, familiarity with the historical experiences of these two groups is essential to understanding the treatment of more recent Latin Americans arrivals to the United States and the contemporary situation of Latinos/as in this country.

Contrary to the depiction of Latinas and Latinos primarily as "illegal immigrants" to the United States, many Mexicans lived on the lands that presently comprise roughly one-third of the continental United States, including the present-day states of California, Texas, New Mexico, Arizona, Nevada, and parts of Colorado, Utah, and Kansas (Perea et al. 2000, 248). At the end of the U.S.-Mexican War in 1848, approximately 75,000 Mexicans living on the lands acquired by the United States through war were forced to decide whether to become U.S. citizens (Perea et al. 2000, 248; Acuña 2000, 50).

The conquest of these lands and the people who inhabited them was possible through the efforts of President James K. Polk. By stationing troops at its border, Polk intentionally instigated hostilities with Mexico (Smith 2000, 20–22; Zinn 2003, 149–69). In view of the vast territories and resources taken as part of the Treaty of Guadalupe Hidalgo that ended the U.S.-Mexican War, the $15 million payment to Mexico at the conclusion of this war has been shown to have been nothing more than a crude attempt to legitimize a patent land grab that violated the sovereignty of another nation (Zinn 2003, 169).

Drafted by a victorious U.S. government after Mexico's military defeat, the Treaty of Guadalupe Hidalgo of 1848 between the United States and Mexico failed to protect the rights of Mexicans who became U.S. citizens. Mexicans within the territories acquired by the United States were reduced to second-class citizenship, subjected to the loss of their lands in spite of preexisting land grants, and denied the right to vote and political representation (Perea et al. 2000, 260–91; Acuña 2000, 53–55).

Originally, consistent with international law, the Treaty of Guadalupe Hidalgo largely intended to extend full rights to Mexicans, but its final version was significantly modified. In order to appease concerns raised in Congress over the racial threat that Mexicans represented to Anglo-American rule (Perea et al. 2000, 263), article IX of the treaty was amended to grant Congress final say as to when Mexicans would be able to exercise full rights as U.S. citizens. As expressed in that article of the Treaty of Guadalupe Hidalgo (1848):

> The Mexicans who, in the territories aforesaid, shall not preserve the character of citizens of the Mexican Republic, conformably with what is stipulated in the preceding article, shall be incorporated into the Union of the United States and be admitted, *at the proper time (to be judged of by the Congress of the United States)* to the enjoyment of all the rights of citizens of the United States, according to the principles of the Constitution; and in the mean time, shall be maintained and protected in the free enjoyment of their liberty and property, and secured in the free exercise of their religion without restriction [emphasis added].

Any reference to the protection of the Mexicans' liberty and property in the treaty was disingenuous. Not only were full constitutional rights withheld in the amendment to article IX, article X of the Treaty of Guadalupe Hidalgo—expected to protect "[a]ll grants of land made by the Mexican government or by the competent authorities, in the territories previously appertaining to Mexico"—was completely stricken from the final version of the treaty (Perea et al. 2000, 261). As further discussed in Chapter 3 of this volume, this omission virtually guaranteed that Mexicans with valid land grants would eventually lose lands to White settlers who systematically challenged and won title over those lands in court (Perea et al. 2000, 270–92; Acuña 2000, 54–55; Ebright 1994, 45–50).

In 1898, the U.S. war with Spain—presented to the U.S. public by government officials and the news media as a crusade to end brutal Spanish colonial rule in Cuba—resulted in one colonial power substituting another. As with the Treaty of Guadalupe Hidalgo, the Treaty of Paris of 1898, which ended the war, fell short of granting equal rights to the peoples of the lands transferred to the United States as spoils of war. Article IX of the treaty states that the U.S. Congress shall determine the "civil rights and political status of the native inhabitants of the territories … ceded to the United States" (U.S. Department of State 1898). The ceded territories included the Philippines, Guam, and other Pacific islands, as well as Puerto Rico. At the time, fears about the "alien nations" that inhabited these territories and that incorporating so-called "mongrel" races into the United States might contaminate U.S. society were widespread. Hence, the language inserted in the Treaty of Paris by the U.S. government assured that the inhabitants of these conquered lands could not exercise full citizenship and constitutional rights (Torruella 1988).

Later in a series of decisions known as the *Insular Cases*, the U.S. Supreme Court determined it impossible to confer full constitutional rights to Puerto Rico because its "alien races" were not ready for "the blessings of a free government under the Constitution extended to them" (*Downes v. Bidwell*, 182 U.S. 244, 286 [1901]).[2] The Court based its decision in *Downes*, *inter alia*, on the Doctrine of Conquest set forth in *Johnson v. McIntosh*, 21 U.S. 543, 590 (1823)—a racially-charged doctrine that justified the granting of land titles in North America to persons the court deemed to be far superior, namely those from the "civilized" nations of Europe over Native Americans, who were no more than "fierce savages." Creating a legal rationale for U.S. colonial expansion was of such importance that in the *Downes* case Justice Henry Billings Brown conceded that any other decision could "be fatal to the development of … the American Empire" (*Downes v. Bidwell*, 182 U.S. 244, 286 [1901]).

As a result of the *Downes* case and subsequent U.S. Supreme Court decisions, the U.S. Congress has retained plenary (that is, absolute) power to determine the civil rights of Puerto Ricans and the political status of Puerto Rico. As an unincorporated territory, Puerto Rico is one of several territories that "belong to but are not a part of the United States" (*Downes v. Bidwell*, 182 U.S. 244, 287), and therefore, in accordance with the *Insular Cases*, full and equal constitutional protections need not apply to Puerto Ricans.[3] Further, as

---

2. In its narrowest sense, the term *Insular Cases* refers to the decisions of the U.S. Supreme Court dealing with the status of the territories the United States acquired pursuant to the Treaty of Paris of 1898, 30 Stat. 1754, T.S. 343, following the U.S. war with Spain (see Torruella 1988, 3). These cases include *De Lima v. Bidwell*, 182 U.S. 1 (1901); *Goetze v. United States* (*Crossman v. United States*), 182 U.S. 221 (1901); *Dooley v. United States*, 182 U.S. 222 (1901); *Armstrong v. United States*, 182 U.S. 243 (1901); *Downes v. Bidwell*, 182 U.S. 244 (1901) and *Huus v. New York & P. R. Steamship Co.*, 182 U.S. 392 (1901). More broadly defined, the term includes decisions that follow this original line of cases that also relate to the status of other U.S. colonies—such as Hawaii. Hence, the *Insular Cases* may also include *Fourteen Diamond Rings v. United States*, 183 U.S. 176 (1901); *Hawaii v. Mankichi*, 190 U.S. 197 (1903); *Gonzales v. Williams*, 192 U.S. 1 (1903); *Kepner v. United States*, 195 U.S. 100 (1904); *Dorr v. United States*, 195 U.S. 138 (1904); *Rassmussen v. United States*, 197 U.S. 516 (1905); *Dowdell v. United States*, 221 U.S. 325 (1911); *Ocampo v. United States*, 234 U.S. 91 (1914); *Balzac v. People of Porto Rico* [sic], 258 U.S. 298 (1922). For a further discussion of the *Insular Cases* as a part of U.S. imperial expansionism and their role in undermining self-determination, see Rivera Ramos (2001, 73–142).

3. As discussed further in this chapter, the unilateral decision to deny another "peoples" their rights—however much the United States has attempted to justify its actions through its own lawmaking—directly contravenes international law and standards that

pointed out by Professor Ediberto Román (2006), the Plenary Powers Doctrine—which posits that certain powers were inherent in the establishment of the country and is central to all the *Insular Cases*—was developed in the late nineteenth century as the United States sought to expand its colonial holdings. The exercise of inherent plenary powers by the U.S. government has continually been upheld by the U.S. Supreme Court and, in cases involving "the indigenous peoples of this land, inhabitants of the island colonies and immigrants in entry and exclusion proceedings," remains significant to this very day (Román 2006, 92).

In 1917, Puerto Ricans were made U.S. citizens with the adoption of the Jones Act by the U.S. Congress. Yet U.S. citizenship—imposed without the consent of the Puerto Rican people and in disregard for the unanimous vote of the Puerto Rican legislature to preserve Puerto Rican citizenship (Fernandez 1994, 67)—has not guaranteed full and equal protection under the U.S. constitution for the people of Puerto Rico and those residing there.[4] In *Balzac v. People of Porto Rico*[sic], 258 U.S. 298 (1922), the U.S. Supreme Court held that, unless expressly granted by the U.S. Congress, a jury trial and similar rights under the U.S. Constitution are not applicable to the inhabitants of Puerto Rico. The court's reasoning, still upheld today, is that, even after the enactment of the Jones Act, Puerto Rico remains an unincorporated territory of the United States, and thus the U.S. Congress retains plenary powers to determine the rights of Puerto Ricans under the Territorial Clause of the U.S. Constitution, article IV, section 3, paragraph 2.

As reflected in the legislative history of the Jones Act, Senator Foraker emphatically made clear that the "granting" of U.S. "citizenship" to Puerto Ricans from its inception was never intended to confer to them full rights as citizens:

> We considered very carefully what status in a political sense we would give to the people of [Puerto Rico], and we reported that provision not thoughtlessly.... We concluded ... that the inhabitants of that island must be either citizens or subjects or aliens. We did not want to treat our own as aliens, and we do not propose to have any subjects. Therefore, we adopted the term "citizens." *In adopting the term "citi-*

---

prohibit colonial rule over other countries and peoples. Arguably, it contradicts the letter and spirit of U.S. law, as well.

4. Some Puerto Ricans—most notably attorney Juan Mari Brás—continue to assert that Puerto Rican citizenship has never been extinguished, nor could it be, through the colonial policies of the United States. In 2007, the Department of State of Puerto Rico certified his Puerto Rican citizenship, and a process for obtaining a certificate of Puerto Rican citizenship has been established (Robles 2007).

zen" we did not understand, however, that we were giving to those people any right that the American people do not want them to have. "Citizens" is a word that indicates, according to Story's work on the Constitution of the United States, allegiance on the one hand and protection on the other. (Cabranes 1979, 37, quoting Sen. Foraker, 33 Cong. Rec. 2473–74 [1900]) [emphasis added]

Similar in the way that the U.S. government curtailed citizenship rights of Mexicans in the conquered territories in the post-1848 era and that the U.S. Supreme Court blocked African Americans from citizenship rights,[5] the United States has effectively subverted the right of Puerto Ricans to claim equal rights under the U.S. Constitution— a condition that Puerto Ricans living on their own homeland today continue to endure.

Notwithstanding Justice John Marshall Harlan's dissent in *Downes*, in which he maintained that holding colonies and colonial subjects runs contrary to the letter and spirit of the U.S. Constitution (*Downes v. Bidwell*, 182 U.S. 244, 380 [1901]), the *Insular Cases*, and even *Johnson v. McIntosh*, have never been overturned. They remain binding precedents in U.S. law that affirm Puerto Rico's colonial status and relegate Puerto Ricans to second-class legal status in contravention of the universal prohibition of colonialism under international law (see, e.g., United Nations 1960). Moreover, in recent years U.S. Supreme Court decisions have reaffirmed the exclusion of Puerto Ricans from equal protection under the U.S. Constitution by citing the *Insular Cases* as the legal precedent (see, e.g., *Califano v. Torres*, 435 U.S. 1 [1978]; *Harris v. Rosario*, 446 U.S. 651 [1980]; *United States v. Verdugo-Urquidez*, 494 U.S. 259 [1990]).

A review of its legislative history reveals that renaming Puerto Rico a "commonwealth" in the 1950s was never intended to end the colonial relationship between the United States and Puerto Rico. At the time, the House committee overseeing Puerto Rico acknowledged that

It is important that the nature and scope of S.3336 [the bill which allowed islanders to write a constitution] *be made absolutely clear.* The bill under consideration would not change Puerto Rico's fun-

---

5. In *Dred Scott v. Sandford*, 60 U.S. 393, 404 (1856), the U.S. Supreme Court determined that African Americans were racially inferior, "and can therefore claim none of the rights and privileges which that instrument [the U.S. Constitution] provides for and secures to citizens of the United States." In language virtually identical to that used in the *Insular Cases* to restrict the rights of Puerto Ricans to only those granted by Congress, in *Dred Scott* the Court made clear that African Americans "had no rights or privileges but such as those who held power and the Government might choose to grant them" (405).

damental political, social and economic relationship to the United States. (Fernandez 1994, 85, quoting House of Representatives, 82nd Congress, 2nd session, Report 1832, April 30, 1952, page 3). [emphasis added]

Not surprisingly, at present all political parties in Puerto Rico denounce Puerto Rico's ongoing colonial status (Trías Monge 1997, 138). They have also taken their dissatisfaction with the continuing U.S. colonial scheme to the United Nations. As a result, since its first substantive resolution on Puerto Rico in 1973, the United Nations Special Decolonization Committee responsible for the implementation of General Assembly Resolution 1514(XV) of 1960— commonly regarded as the decolonization Magna Carta—has repeatedly recognized the inalienable right of Puerto Ricans as "peoples" to the exercise of self-determination under U.N. standards for decolonization, standards that the United States has failed to recognize or meet (Trías Monge 1997, 138; Fernandez 1994; Gautier Mayoral and Del Pilar Arguelles 1978).[6]

Despite United Nations resolutions, U.S. Congressional authority over the island nation and its peoples continues, as it maintains Puerto Rico as a U.S.

---

6. The term "peoples" is used here in a manner consistent with its meaning under international law and with the manner in which the U.N. Special Committee on Decolonization uses the term upon asserting applicability of U.N. General Assembly Resolution 1514(XV) of 1960 to the case of Puerto Rico. That is, that "all peoples have the right to self-determination; by virtue of that right they freely determine their political status and freely pursue their economic, social and cultural development" (United Nations 1960, para. 1; 1966a, art. 1; 1966b, art. 1). The U.N. Decolonization Committee, formally known as the Special Committee on the Situation with regard to the Implementation of the Declaration on the Granting of Independence to Countries and Peoples, is mandated to implement U.N. General Assembly Resolution 1514(XV) of 1960, the Declaration on the Granting of Independence to Colonial Countries and Peoples (United Nations 1960; see Appendix B). Specifically with respect to the case of Puerto Rico, the Special Committee in 2003 adopted a resolution which echoed past resolutions, stating that it "*Reaffirms* the inalienable right of the people of Puerto Rico to self-determination and independence in conformity with General Assembly Resolution 1514(XV) and the applicability of the fundamental principles of that resolution concerning Puerto Rico." The resolution further called upon "the Government of the United States to assume its responsibility of expediting a process that will allow the Puerto Rican people fully to exercise their inalienable right to self-determination and independence, in conformity with General Assembly Resolution 1514(XV) and the resolutions and decisions of the Special Committee concerning Puerto Rico" (United Nations 2003b). As it has in the past, on June 14, 2007, the U.N. Special Committee reaffirmed "the inalienable right of the people of Puerto Rico to self-determination and independence" and also requested that the U.N. General Assembly "consider the question of Puerto Rico comprehensively in all its aspects" (United Nations 2007).

colony (Trías Monge 1997, 161–63; Rivera Ramos 2001, 225).[7] The United States has fashioned a legal framework that allows it to claim complete power to unilaterally nullify all or parts of the Puerto Rican Constitution.[8] In fact, the U.S. Congress actually eliminated Article 2, Section 20 on economic and social rights from the 1952 Commonwealth Constitution, thus overriding the work of the Puerto Rican Constitutional Convention (García Martínez 1989, 229).[9] Puerto Ricans do not share equal rights with U.S. citizens in the United States: They serve and die in U.S. wars, but cannot vote for the President who can send them into battle; U.S. laws apply to Puerto Rico without the consent of Puerto Ricans; Puerto Ricans have no say in treaties and foreign affairs that affect them; Puerto Ricans have no voting representation in the U.S. Congress; trade, maritime, immigration, and monetary policies in Puerto Rico are all controlled by the United States; the U.S. Federal Court is present in Puerto Rico and operates in English, rather than in the native language of Puerto Rico; and the "commonwealth" status continues out of compliance with United Nations decolonization requirements (Trías Monge 1997, 161-63; Rivera Ramos 2001, 130; Fernandez 1994, 61–94; Maldonado-Denis 1972, 189–208). This situation led former Chief Justice of Puerto Rico José Trías Monge to conclude that "[t]here is no known noncolonial relationship in the present world where one people exercises such vast, almost unbounded power over the government of another" (1997, 163).

---

7. Puerto Ricans are not the only ones over whom the U.S. Congress exerts plenary powers. Based on a U.S. Supreme Court decision that has never been reversed, the U.S. government has maintained that its relationship with Native Americans is one between a guardian and ward. In *Cherokee Nation v. Georgia*, 30 U.S. (5 Pet.) 1, 17 (1831), the U.S. Supreme Court declared that pursuant to the U.S. Constitution "Indian tribes" were "domestic dependent nations," whose relationship with the United States "resembles that of a ward to his guardian. They look to the U.S. government for protection; rely upon its kindness and its power; appeal to it for relief to their wants; and address the President as their great father." Consequently, to the present day this decision helps justify the U.S. government's claim of plenary or absolute power over Native Americans, their lands, and their federally recognized tribal status.

8. In December 2005, the White House released a report by the President's Task Force on Puerto Rico's Status (2005, 5), which reasserted the position that the U.S. Congress has unilateral authority to decide all questions with respect to Puerto Rico, including the power "to revise or revoke" the current system, "legislate directly on local matters or determine the island's governmental structure by statute." The report made no mention of any obligations under international law.

9. In certain cases where it assumes jurisdiction, the United States Federal Court in Puerto Rico has called for imposition of the death penalty, although this punishment is prohibited under Puerto Rico's Constitution.

Why the United States maintains colonies in the face of the worldwide repudiation of colonialism in the post-World War II era becomes apparent when
one considers the enormous benefits that accrue to the U.S. government and
U.S. corporate interests (Maldonado-Denis 1972, 151–88; Lewis 1963,
167–236).[10] Net profits from Puerto Rico to U.S. corporations surpass the
profits of all other industrial countries, including the United Kingdom, Germany and Japan (Gonzalez 2000, 249–50). Puerto Rico serves as a captive
market for U.S. goods; its population is a source of low-wage labor; 14 percent of the land is used for U.S. military bases; and Puerto Ricans can be readily drafted or they volunteer to serve and fight in the U.S. military (Gonzalez
2000, 251–53; Maldonado-Denis 1972).

Contrary to popular belief, Puerto Rico is not an example of U.S. magna-
nimity or a model for Third World development. Puerto Rico is an impoverished nation with 60 percent of its people living below the poverty line (Gonzalez 2000, 250). According to Trías Monge (1997, 2–3),

> [p]er capita income in Puerto Rico is still only about one-third of that
> of the United States and half of Mississippi. In the Caribbean, eleven
> other areas enjoy a higher per capita income: the Cayman Islands,
> Aruba, Montserrat, the Bahamas, Martinique, the American Virgin
> Islands, the British Virgin Islands, the Netherlands Antilles, Guade-
> loupe, French Guiana, and Barbados. The per capita income of the
> poorest of these areas is 20 percent higher than that of Puerto Rico.

As confirmed in a recent study, Puerto Rico's economy remains stagnant, with
living standards further apart "from the U.S. average today than they were in
1970, and a per capita income … only about half that of the poorest [U.S.]
state" (Collins, Bosworth, and Soto-Class 2006, 2).

The outcome of continuing U.S. colonial rule over Puerto Rico, masked
under the guise of a "commonwealth," is that it retains the economic benefits
for U.S. corporate interests, while simultaneously maintaining the Puerto
Rican population as a source of cheap and exploitable labor. Under "citizenship" as the U.S. government has determined it for Puerto Ricans under U.S.
law, true political and economic power is kept in check on the island nation,
but labor can migrate easily from Puerto Rico to the continental United States
in service of the U.S. economy. High rates of poverty in Puerto Rico assure

---

10. Today, the Decolonization Committee of the United Nations not only oversees the
case of Puerto Rico's status, but of other U.S. colonies—i.e., non-self-governing territories—including Guam, American Samoa, and the U.S. Virgin Islands (see, e.g., United Nations 2003a).

that Puerto Ricans will continue to be drawn to the United States in search of a better life. Once in the United States, their acceptance as real "citizens" or true "Americans" has yet to be fully realized, as succeeding chapters of this book will detail.

Consolidating U.S. Hemispheric Hegemony

Beyond its exercise of U.S. power over Mexico and Puerto Rico, the history of U.S. relations with Latin America abounds with examples in which the U.S. government has sought to extend its political, economic, and cultural domination through diverse means. The forms of racism and paternalism evident in the ideology of Manifest Destiny, in the *Insular Cases*, and the other examples cited, have also been discernible in U.S. actions toward other Latin American countries. In a seemingly endless number of cases, U.S. interventionism in Latin America's so-called "banana republics" reeks of condescension and paternalism (see LaFeber 1993).

The cornerstone of U.S. policy toward Latin America has been the Monroe Doctrine of 1823. After most of Latin America broke away from Spanish and Portuguese colonial rule by the 1820s, President James Monroe's administration moved quickly to stave off any additional intervention or colonization by other European powers, declaring such attempts "dangerous to our peace and safety" (Holden and Zolov 2000, 13). The Monroe Doctrine's silence on U.S. colonial aspirations opened the door for the use of force against any alleged outside threat to U.S. interests in the hemisphere, and consequently, to any obstacle in the way of achieving complete hegemony over the Americas.

To advance U.S. interests in the Americas, the 1904 Roosevelt Corollary to the Monroe Doctrine laid out the principles that justified U.S. military interventionism. In the words of Theodore Roosevelt:

> Chronic wrong-doing, or an impotence which results in a general loosening of the ties of civilized society, may in America, as elsewhere, ultimately require intervention by some civilized nation, and in the Western Hemisphere the adherence of the United States to the Monroe Doctrine may force the United States, however reluctantly, in flagrant cases of such wrongdoing or impotence, to the exercise of an international police power. (Department of State 1905, xli–xlii)

Of course, the "civilized nation" that was to oversee this extension of the Monroe Doctrine was the United States, and its desire to intervene in Latin America was far from reluctant. Commonly referred to as the "Big Stick" doctrine, the Roosevelt Corollary to the Monroe Doctrine legitimized the use of armed force by the United States. Thus, it did little to "civilize" or democratize the region. Between 1898 and 1934, the United States used its military forces to invade and/or occupied Latin American countries on more than thirty occasions and "despite high-minded rhetoric and ostensible nobility of purpose, not a single U.S. intervention led to installation of democracy" (Smith 2000, 60).

In the Dominican Republic, U.S. military interventions begun under President Theodore Roosevelt's administration spanned many decades and included the U.S. military invasions and occupations of 1903, 1904, 1914, 1916–1924, and 1965 (Smith 2000, 51, 169–172). These interventions provided direct control over the economy of the Dominican Republic for the benefit of U.S. banking and commercial interests. This was most clearly evident in U.S. seizure of the customhouses (Smith 2000, 54–56). Instead of spreading democracy, U.S. policies supported brutal dictators, as in the case of the Dominican Republic's Rafael Trujillo, who safeguarded U.S. business interests and profits until the early 1960s (Schmitz 1999; Roorda 1998). In the latter half of the twentieth century, the 1965 U.S. military occupation of the Dominican Republic guaranteed that the democratically elected government of Juan Bosch would never return, paving the way for Trujillo's right-hand man Joaquín Balaguer (Moya Pons 1995, 381–404; Smith 2000, 169–72).

At best, for the United States, adherence to the norms of international law has been an afterthought. As U.S. power and control over the region grew, justifying violations of international law became increasingly insignificant to U.S. government leaders. In a moment of complete candor in reference to his administration's intervention of Panama, Theodore Roosevelt offered no explanation other than "I took the Isthmus" (quoted in Schoultz 1998, 173). From as early as the 1850s, the U.S. government preferred to recognize William Walker—a North American "filibuster" who orchestrated an illegal coup to install himself as president, declare English the official language, and legalize slavery—as the legitimate president of Nicaragua rather than to respect the rights of Nicaraguans to self-determination (Holden and Zolov 2000, 39).[11] Well into the twentieth century, the United States abused its self-ordained "police power" to impose a brutally racist and autocratic U.S. military regime upon the people of Haiti during its occupation of the country from 1915–1934 (Schmidt 1995).

---

11. Filibuster is a term derived "from the Spanish *filibustero*, for freebooter or buccaneer" (Holden and Zolov 2000, 39). LaFeber describes the filibusters of the mid-1800s as "private adventurers who moved out of New Orleans, New York, and Baltimore to conquer the small countries [of Central America] for personal gain, the extension of slave territory, or usually both" (1993, 30).

After significantly consolidating its hegemony over Latin America and the Caribbean by the 1930s (Smith 2000, 64), the United States moved toward a "good neighbor" policy, adopting a noninterventionist stance, in words if not deeds. This shift was based, in part, on the implementation of international agreements, most notably the Convention on the Rights and Duties of States adopted at Montevideo in 1933. This international covenant reinforced the concept of equality among states. In article 8, it specifically declared that "[n]o state has the right to intervene in the internal or external affairs of another" (Convention on the Rights and Duties of States 1933). Although it was an effort to salvage its international reputation, the "good neighbor" policy, which ostensibly sought to demonstrate U.S. intentions to act in accordance with international law, did not actually result in a complete policy change. Instead of overt military interventionism, the United States resorted to installing and supporting puppet governments and military dictatorships responsible for egregious human rights violations throughout Latin America and the Caribbean (Schoultz 1998; Smith 2000).

In the name of fighting communism and at the expense of human rights in Latin America, U.S. policy took an especially brutal turn. Using methods similar to those for maintaining a neo-colonial relationship with the Dominican Republic, the United States propped up and sustained ruthless dictators and oligarchs throughout Latin America, such as the autocratic and ruthless regime of General Alfredo Stroessner in Paraguay (Smith 2000, 159). In Central America, support of the Somoza family dynasty (1934–1979) of Nicaragua which "seized most of the wealth, including a land area equal the size of Massachusetts," and of the infamous "Fourteen Families" of El Salvador who still control almost 60 percent of the land, are among the most notorious examples (LaFeber 1993, 10–11). In Cuba, the United States backed the government of Fulgencio Batista, a dictator who tolerated gross economic disparities, poverty, unemployment, illiteracy, and racial exclusion for the benefit of U.S. business interests (Pérez, Jr. 1995, 295–307). In these and other instances throughout Latin America, local repression became the means by which social unrest in the face of economic injustice was quelled. Latin American armies and police forces trained and financed by the United States became the surrogates for U.S. marines, who in earlier times were readily called upon to intervene.

Behind the Rhetoric of Democracy

It would seem inconceivable that the United States—a country founded after a war against colonialism—would seek to subjugate other peoples or undermine the very principles of democracy it developed and purports to spread. The juxtaposition of its stated principles and its hegemonic ambitions has been and continues to be a fundamental contradiction of U.S. foreign policy. However, a now familiar pattern was established early on in Latin America: U.S. global economic interests usually supersede even its best intentions. Smedley Darlington Butler, a U.S. marine in the 1930s, memorialized his recollection of decades of U.S. interventionism as follows:

> I spent thirty-three years, most of my time being a high-class muscle man for big business, for Wall Street and the bankers. In short, I was a racketeer for capitalism.... I helped make Mexico, especially Tampico, safe for American oil interests in 1916. I helped make Haiti and Cuba a decent place for the National City Bank boys to collect revenue in. I helped in the raping of half a dozen Central American republics for the benefits of Wall Street. The record of racketeering is long. I helped purify Nicaragua for the international banking house of Brown Brothers in 1909–1912. I brought light to the Dominican Republic for American sugar interests in 1916. (Butler [1935] 2003, 10)

But as Cornell University historian Walter LaFeber explains (1993), U.S. business interests were not alone in this venture. The U.S government worked ceaselessly to support U.S.-based commercial enterprises. By establishing and maintaining a system grounded in the Monroe Doctrine, it could always provide direct assistance—including the use of military force—to protect U.S. corporate interests in the region (81–85).

Hegemony over the Western Hemisphere translated into securing a perpetual source of cheap and exploitable land, raw materials, human labor, and other resources. This held true as much for the Cold War era (1947–1989) as it did in earlier periods in U.S.-Latin American relations. In 1950, George Kennan, chief State Department official responsible for the Cold War containment policy, outlined the goals of U.S. policy toward Latin America during this period in order of importance, as follows:

1. The protection of our [sic] raw materials;
2. The prevention of military exploitation of Latin America by the enemy; and
3. The prevention of the psychological mobilization of Latin America against us. (quoted in LaFeber 1993, 109)

To these ends, in 1954, the U.S. government, the C.I.A. and the United Fruit Company combined to topple the democratically elected government of

Jacobo Arbenz, who sought land reform for impoverished peasants in Guatemala. Although he was not a communist, the U.S. government considered Arbenz "soft" on communism, creating the necessary pretext for the coup. For decades, U.S.-backed, right-wing military juntas in Guatemala crushed the opposition and committed countless killings and other atrocities among civilians, peasants, and indigenous peoples (LaFeber 1993).

In El Salvador, the Salvadoran military engaged in bloody counterinsurgency operations backed by the U.S. government. Its mission to eliminate government opposition resulted in innumerable deaths, including the assassinations of three U.S. nuns, a Catholic layperson, and Archbishop Oscar Romero in 1980; the massacre at El Mozote, where hundreds of men, women and children were slaughtered in 1981; and the murder of six Jesuit scholars, their housekeeper and her daughter in El Salvador in 1989 (LaFeber 1993; Danner, 1993; LeoGrande 1998, 570–71). The U.S. government continued to provide military aid to the government of El Salvador even as the U.S.-trained Salvadoran soldiers, such as those in the Atlactl Battalion, were being implicated in these murders. In lieu of sending its own troops (that is, the use of the "Big Stick") to protect U.S. interests in the region, the U.S. government preferred a policy that allowed local armed forces to assume the role of assassins, saboteurs, and terrorists.

The 1975 Select Committee to Study Governmental Operations with Respect to Intelligence Activities, known as the Church Committee after Senator Frank Church, issued a report which revealed the extent of U.S. covert operations in Cuba, Chile, the Dominican Republic, and the Congo, including plots to kill Fidel Castro and Patrice Lumumba (Senate 1975a; Senate 1975b). The Church hearings and other disclosures established that the C.I.A.'s *Freedom Fighting Manual* and the School of the Americas' *Study Manual* were published and distributed to Latin American military personnel for the specific purpose of training in sabotage and torture (Holden and Zolov 2000, 297–99, 313–15).

In yet another successful attempt at "regime change" in Latin America, in 1973 the United States helped depose the democratically elected government of Salvador Allende in Chile. Recently declassified C.I.A. documents directly implicate President Nixon and then Secretary of State Henry Kissinger in the covert operations to destabilize the Allende government (Kornbluh 2003a, 2003b). In an exposé of Henry Kissinger's involvement in the events of 1973 in Chile, Christopher Hitchens (2001, 55) observed that "the very name of Allende was anathema to the extreme Right in Chile, to certain powerful corporations (notably ITT, Pepsi Cola and the Chase Manhattan Bank) which did business in Chile and the United States, and to the CIA." General Augusto

Pinochet—whose right-wing dictatorship unseated Allende's government and was recognized by the United States—has been accused of torture and other gross violations of human rights resulting in the deaths and disappearances of thousands persons following the 1973 coup (see, e.g., *Regina v. Bartle*, House of Lords, 24 March 1999 [1999] 2 All ER 97, [1999] 2 WLR 827). U.S. support for authoritarian regimes in Argentina, Paraguay, and Brazil had similar aims: violence—including torture, "disappearances," "dirty wars," and other violations of the most basic human rights—was deployed against anyone who opposed the established order of repressive, right-wing regimes that protected U.S. interests in the hemisphere.

In the case of Nicaragua, U.S. disregard for the human rights of Latin Americans under international law could not be more glaring. In 1986, the International Court of Justice (ICJ or the World Court) voted overwhelmingly to condemn U.S. support of the "contra war" and the mining of the Nicaraguan harbor as blatant violations of international law that, *inter alia*, endangered the lives and wellbeing of civilians and infringed upon Nicaragua's territorial sovereignty (Military and Paramilitary Activities (Nicar. v. U.S.), 1986 I.C.J. 14 (June 27)). By many criteria, actions condemned by the World Court could be categorized as state-sponsored terrorism. The seriousness of U.S. violations against Nicaragua left the ICJ no option but to rule that the United States was obligated to make reparations to the Republic of Nicaragua for all the injuries caused to the country and its people; damage claims had risen to $17 billion (Holden and Zolov 2000, 300). In defiance of the World Court's decision, the U.S. government refused to recognize the court's jurisdiction, shunning all accountability under international law (LaFeber 1993, 301; LeoGrande 1998, 333–34; Smith 2000).[12]

The resulting turmoil, death, and economic and social destruction left after decades of internal conflict in Central America cannot be underestimated:

> [T]he years from 1979–1991 turned out to be the bloodiest, most violent, and most destructive era in Central America's post-1820 history. The number of dead and 'disappeared' varies according to different sources. The minimum number is 200,000 (40,000 in Nicaragua, 75,000 in El Salvador, 75,000 in Guatemala, 10,000 in Honduras and the frontier fighting in Costa Rica), but this is only an

---

12. At the behest of the United States, the U.S.-backed government of Violeta Chamorro withdrew Nicaragua's case before the World Court on September 12, 2001, denying the country the opportunity to obtain court-ordered monetary compensation (Holden and Zolov 2000, 300).

estimate. Millions have been displaced or made refugees. If a similar catastrophe struck the United States in proportion, 2½ million North Americans would die and 10 to 20 million would be driven from their homes. (LaFeber 1993, 362)

Following this period of armed conflict in Central America, it was found that "[h]undreds of thousands of Central Americans (one out of four in the case of Salvadorans) have been uprooted by force, military pressure, or war destruction, becoming refugees either in their own countries or abroad" (Zea, Diehl and Porterfield 1997, 39). By the early 1990s, "more than a million Salvadorans and about 200,000 Guatemalan refugees resided in the United States alone ... most of them children or young adults" (39–40).

The connection between U.S. policy and many documented human rights atrocities of that era has been well established by authoritative entities, including the international commission of inquiry regarding Guatemala established under the Accord of Oslo of 1994 (United Nations 1994a). The commission of inquiry, officially named the Commission for Historical Clarification, concluded:

> Whilst anti-communism, promoted by the United States within the framework of its foreign policy, received firm support from right-wing political parties and from various other powerful actors in Guatemala, the United States demonstrated that it was willing to provide support for strong military regimes in its strategic backyard. (1999, 19)

Throughout the Cold War period, as Smith asserts, "[f]ear of the 'communist threat' may have been greatly exaggerated, as now appears in retrospect" (2000, 2). In support of this assessment, the Commission for Historical Clarification found that

> at no time during the internal armed confrontation did the guerilla groups have the military potential necessary to pose an imminent threat to the State. The number of insurgent combatants was too small to be able to compete in the military arena with the Guatemalan Army, which had more troops and superior weaponry, as well as better training and co-ordination ... the State deliberately magnified the military threat of the insurgency, a practise justified by the concept of the internal enemy. The inclusion of all opponents under one banner, democratic or otherwise, pacifist or guerrilla, legal or illegal,

communist or noncommunist, served to justify numerous and serious crimes. (1999, 22)

In hindsight it is entirely plausible to conclude that U.S. policies in Latin America had less to do with fighting communism and more to do with maintaining the old order in which U.S. economic interests could reign free to exploit Latin America's land, labor, and other resources. Certainly, U.S. support for brutal right-wing dictatorships belies the rhetoric about spreading freedom and democracy.

Globalization's Impact: Maintaining the System

Historically, the primary aim of U.S. policy toward Latin America has been to maintain its political and economic hegemony over the Americas. Tragically, this goal was pursued and met at the expense of the human rights, dignity, and lives of peoples of Latin America. But it is also argued that it is not only in the past that the United States reaped the benefits from its domination over Latin America, present policies also actively seek the power and hegemony that continue to reap benefits for the United States. After decades of consolidating its hegemony over the hemisphere, the United States in the post-Cold War era has developed new justifications for the use of military force; it has embarked on new strategies to consolidate its global economic interests and power over the region.

In its first military intervention in a Latin American country after the fall of the Soviet Union, the 1989 U.S. military invasion of Panama purported to fight the "war on drugs" by capturing the alleged drug-kingpin, Panamanian head of state Manuel Antonio Noriega, a former C.I.A. operative who had been paid upwards of $200,000 annually from U.S. tax dollars (Scott and Marshall 1991, 67). However, as an anti-drug initiative, this military invasion today is widely considered a failure. "Operation Just Cause had virtually no effect on drug trafficking," and in reality, Noriega turned out to be "a minor player in the narcotics business" (Smith 2000, 297; see also Scott and Marshall 1991, 72). Analysts have documented that the invasion had nothing to do with fighting a war against drugs and virtually everything to do with how Noriega became increasingly expendable to U.S. policy and interests by the late 1980s (Scott and Marshall 1991, 65–73). In fact, Panama's new President, Guillermo Endara, had ties to the banks implicated in drug-money laundering (72–73). Further belying President George H.W. Bush's justifications of the "war on drugs" for the invasion, the U.S. government's General Accounting Office reported increased drug activity in Panama two years after the invasion, noting that the country "continues to be a haven for money laundering" (General Accounting Office 1991, 1).

Along with other interventions, the U.S. invasion of Panama endures today, as another affront to human rights and international law. Critics charged that the U.S. military's use of excessive force caused the deaths of thousands of Panamanian civilians in violation of international law (see, e.g., Clark 1991). Numerous human rights groups reported that disproportionate numbers of Panamanian civilians were killed as a result of the invasion; at the United Nations, the U.N. General Assembly vehemently condemned the invasion as a "flagrant violation" of international law (Smith 2000, 297). In the post-Cold War era, the U.S. invasion of Panama became symbolic of U.S. intentions of consolidating its authority over the Americas. Past pretexts for U.S. interventionism—such as the fight against communism—have been replaced with new ones, including the war on drugs and the war on terrorism, along with some not so new justifications such as the need to spread democracy (see *NACLA Report on the Americas* 2007).

But it is crucial to note that direct military intervention—however much an option for U.S. policymakers—is superfluous in view of the United States' current global economic supremacy. The North American Free Trade Agreement (NAFTA) and other U.S. efforts to promote the neo-liberal agenda of free trade, open markets, privatization, and economic global integration have provided an international framework that facilitates and ensures the flow of economic bonanzas to the countries of the "North"—the United States, Western Europe, and Japan—often with diminishing returns and growing economic inequality for a vast number of developing nations of the "South"—Latin America, Africa, and Asia.

There is mounting evidence that the free trade policies promoted by the United States have actually perpetuated uneven development by favoring developed countries to the detriment of developing nations. "The income gap between the fifth of the world's people living in the richest countries and the fifth in the poorest was 74-to-1 in 1997, up from 60-to-1 in 1990 and 30-to-1 in 1960. By 1997, the richest 20% captured 86% of the world's income, with the poorest 20% capturing a mere 1%" (Wallach and Sforza 1999, 16). Throughout Latin America from the 1980s to the 1990s, "the absolute number of people living under conditions of poverty swelled from 125 million to 186 million, an increase of 61 million, or nearly 50 percent" (Smith 2000, 272).

With the globalization of U.S. corporate interests, the exploitation of Latin American human labor and resources by U.S. multinational corporations at the expense of human rights, labor rights, and environmental rights has become a growing concern. Over the last decade, U.S. companies have been accused of engaging in illegal child labor and sweatshop practices and creating gross environmental hazards in factories or *maquiladoras* that produce garments and other items for major U.S. corporations established throughout Mexico, Central America, and the Caribbean (Gonzalez 2000, 228–45; Rosen and McFayden 1995). Free trade zones that offer tax breaks to global corporations in developing countries have frequently been cited for using repressive means "to keep free trade zones free of labor unions, as well as health and safety regulations" (Sklar 1995, 46). In El Salvador, U.S. clothing manufacturers have been able to pay factory workers as little as 33 cents an hour (47).

As commented in a series of *New York Times* editorials, free trade, as it currently operates, provides an unfair advantage to U.S. business interests. Profits are harvested by developed countries on the backs of poverty-stricken nations. Huge government subsidies to the U.S. cotton and other industries virtually insure that developing nations will remain poor and unable to compete fairly with developed nations (*New York Times* 2003a, A18; 2003b, A14; 2003c, 10; 2003d, A20).

NAFTA has been the model for development in Latin America most often touted by U.S. presidents. Yet despite NAFTA's promise of economic development for Mexico, poverty stands roughly at the same rate today—just over 50 percent—as it did in the early 1980s. But if one factors in Mexico's population growth, from 70 million to 100 million over the same period, the country can be considered worse off today with "19 million more Mexicans living in poverty than 20 years ago, according to Mexican government and international organizations.... What has become painfully clear in Mexico is that free trade—most famously NAFTA—has failed to lift the country out of poverty" (Jordan and Sullivan 2003, A10).

Indeed, nearly ten years after NAFTA began, a study sponsored by the Carnegie Endowment for International Peace concludes that "NAFTA has not helped the Mexican economy keep pace with the growing demand for jobs." NAFTA's purported benefits to Mexico's poorest have not been realized. "Real wages for most Mexicans today are lower than they were when NAFTA took effect." Moreover, "NAFTA has not stemmed the flow of poor Mexicans into the United States in search of jobs; in fact there has been a dramatic rise in the number of migrants to the United States, despite an unprecedented increase in border control measures" (Audley et al. 2003, 6).

The Nobel laureate in economics, Joseph E. Stiglitz, has also voiced criticism about the course that globalization has taken, noting that even in instances where Mexico has experienced growth, "the benefits have accrued largely to the upper 30 percent, and have been even more concentrated in the top 10 percent. Those at the bottom have gained little; many are even worse off" (2002, 86). Stiglitz attributes the present-day attitude of developed countries to the persistence of the colonial mentality that presumes they know what is best for developing nations, and that the United States is still affected by the historical legacy of "Manifest Destiny" and expansionism, and to an even greater extent, "by the cold war, in which principles of democracy were compromised or ignored, in the all encompassing struggle against communism" (24–25).

In 2005, the United States entered into another free trade initiative with El Salvador, Costa Rica, Nicaragua, Honduras, Guatemala and the Dominican Republic, an initiative known as the Central American Free Trade Agreement or CAFTA. In reports commissioned by the U.S. Labor Department and released in 2005, the International Labor Rights Fund warned that "work conditions in the five Central American nations and the Dominican Republic were dismal, and that enforcement of labor laws was weak," which supported the argument by CAFTA opponents that the trade pact would have adverse consequences for workers (Forero 2005, C2). Nearly two years after the passage of CAFTA, it has become obvious that in spite of a provision requiring adherence to local labor laws, child labor runs rampant in Guatemala, with about a million Guatemalan children under age 18 working rather than attending school (Lacey 2007, A1). Even a 2007 U.S. State Department human rights report acknowledges that "'child labor was a widespread and serious problem' and that 'laws governing the employment of minors were not enforced effectively'" (Lacey 2007, A1). Back in 2005, CAFTA proponents stressed that jobs would be created for Central American workers and U.S. consumers would benefit greatly from "a 50-cent difference in the price of a T-shirt" (*New York Times* 2005a, A22). The question that must be asked now is whether the exploitation of children as cheap labor is worth the "50-cent difference in the price of a T-shirt."

CONCLUSIONS

As LaFaber explains (1993), the primary U.S. government objective in Latin America, past and present, has been to create and maintain a system that assures U.S. economic and political hegemony. The historical events outlined in this chapter, which have unfolded largely as a result of that objective, have had a profound impact in Latin America and the Caribbean and ultimately on Latinos and Latinas in the United States. This impact includes the establishment and fortification of a dominant-subordinate paradigm, the racialization of Latin Americans, U.S.-Latin American linkages and their consequences.

The Establishment and Fortification of a Dominant-Subordinate Paradigm

U.S. imperial conquests and interventionist policies have established a dominant-subordinate paradigm that persists to the present. The current global economic configuration maintains a system advantageous to U.S. government and corporate interests that had its origins in the hegemonic aspirations of the United States' earliest leaders. The consequences of U.S. hegemony over the Americas have been dramatic and lasting. Today, Latin American countries remain impoverished and, therefore, vulnerable to exploitation and subordination, nearly as easily today as they were in the 1800s. The pursuit of U.S. foreign policy goals and economic interests has too often blinded the U.S. government to the human suffering and the violations of sovereignty and other rights resulting from its actions. The covert and overt use of force and direct and indirect forms of intervention throughout the region have become so regular as to have become normalized as a matter of U.S. policy.

From Manifest Destiny to "free trade," U.S. policies toward Latin Americans have been repeatedly couched in benign terms, but its undercurrents of paternalism and its human, economic, social, and environmental costs to Latin America are undeniable. While Latin America's social and economic troubles are also attributable to widespread and unrelenting corruption in many Latin American countries (Rosenberg 2003), it is equally true that the United States has traditionally played a key role in undermining democracy in support of corrupt and brutal regimes that sustained inequalities and hardships in their respective countries.

For much of its 71-year rule, the Institutional Revolutionary Party (PRI) in Mexico, for instance, engaged in fraudulent elections and other kinds of illegal, corrupt, and undemocratic practices. Yet the United States government readily lent support for many of Mexico's leaders, including former President Carlos Salinas de Gotari, whose brother was implicated in illegal drug trafficking and who himself has been under a cloud of suspicion of corruption since the end of his term in office in 1994 (McKinley, Jr. 2004, A4).

Responsibility also rests with the United States for the many ruthless Latin American and Caribbean dictators it has sponsored over the years, including Somoza in Nicaragua, Trujillo in the Dominican Republic, Strossener in Paraguay, the Duvaliers in Haiti, Pinochet in Chile, and the military regimes in Argentina and Brazil. Given this record, it is no wonder that Latin America remains weak and impoverished, and a breeding ground for forced immigration.

The powerful forces of globalization, as they presently function, more often than not promote poverty and the unfair treatment of Latin American workers, peasants, and indigenous peoples, placing ever-increasing pressure on the poor of Latin America to immigrate to the United States in hope of a better life. U.S. free trade policies appear to be worsening conditions in Latin America and causing an increased flow of Latin American immigrants to the United States desperate for work (Audley et al. 2003). As Bacon (2004, 57) makes clear,

> Global inequality produces insecurity and economic desperation, which forces people from their countries of origin.... Migration from Mexico to the United States is a product of that inequality. No matter how many walls are built on the border, no matter how many National Guard troops or helicopters patrol it, workers will still cross, looking for a future. There's no more eloquent testimony to this than the deaths of 1,420 women and men—workers and farmers—who perished in the desert during the six years between 1996 and 2002, trying to make the journey from northern Mexico into the United States, according to the Mexican Foreign Relations Office.

The long-standing theory of "push and pull" factors—"[f]actors that cause population movement into an area" (push), and "[f]actors that cause population movement out of an area" (pull) (Healey 2006, 559) may be limited in explaining the immigration phenomenon from Mexico and Latin America. While dire economic conditions in their homelands may be a factor that "pushes" Mexicans to leave for the United States, it is also true, as Professor Gerald López (1981) explains, that substantial migration from Mexico to the United States did not exist until the United States began to promote and encourage the pattern Mexican migrant labor that we are witnessing today. López asserts that, as a result, a substantial level of responsibility for the current wave of undocumented immigration rests with the United States, a responsibility that morally, if not legally, obligates the United States to find a humane solution. Indeed, studies of the apparel industry in the United States show that U.S. companies continue to actively draw Latin American immigrants to the United States into industries where they serve as a source of cheap labor (Gereffi, Spener, and Bair 2002; Sassen 1998).

The dominate-subordinate paradigm that characterizes U.S.-Latin American relations fulfills two major functions: (1) it keeps Latin America and its peoples poor and vulnerable to exploitation by global corporate and financial interests, and (2) it provides for a steady stream of immigrants from Latin

America who feed the seemingly insatiable appetite of U.S. businesses for cheap labor. In view of the enormous benefits that accrue to the United States and its domestic economic interests, it is not likely that government policy-makers will pursue a reversal of U.S. policy in support of sustainable economic development in Latin America. Invariably, this will result in the continuation of undocumented Latino/a immigration into the country.

The Racialization of Latin Americans

Despite policy pronouncements on the promotion of democracy and human rights, U.S. foreign policy has mostly been indifferent to the human rights and well-being of Latin Americans. The United States has not been im-mune to the hubris common to previous imperial powers that believed they knew what was best for the world. Powerful ideas about race, including the grand allure of Manifest Destiny, shaped not only U.S. foreign policy, but how the United States was to view Latin Americans. The absence of concern for the human rights of Latin Americans by the U.S. government, as much as it is rooted in its hegemonic ambitions, is also rooted in racist and racialized per-ceptions of Latin Americans. The projection of Latin Americans as racially in-ferior not only served to justify U.S. conquests and policies, it helped ration-alize the subsequent subordination of Mexicans and Puerto Ricans in the United States, establishing the pattern of discriminatory treatment for Lati-nos/as who followed. As explored in the next chapter, this racialized image of Latin Americans established the foundation upon which prejudice and dis-crimination toward all other Latinas and Latinos was built.

U.S.-Latin American Linkages and their Consequences

Globalization and migratory patterns are likely to continue to strengthen linkages between Latinos/as in the United States and their native homelands. This phenomenon will make Latinos/as an ever-growing part of the future of the United States. U.S.-Latin American relations, thus, become an essential part of understanding the Latino/a experience in the United States today.

Latin Americans have endured an arduous historical trajectory. Centuries of colonialism, plunder, intervention, and exploitation have left an endur-ing legacy. Vast economic and social inequalities and injustices still mar the Latin American landscape, with the effect of globalized corporate power on Latin America being but one example of how foreign interests and profits supersede the needs and concerns of contemporary Latin Americans and U.S. Latinos/as.

In his classic work *Open Veins of Latin America*, Eduardo Galeano poignantly reminds us of the impact of U.S. colonialism and neocolonial policies over time:

> Along the way we [Latin Americans] even lost the right to call ourselves Americans, although the Haitians and the Cubans appeared in history as new people a century before the *Mayflower* pilgrims settled on the Plymouth coast. For the world today, America is just the United States; the region we inhabit is a sub-America, a second-class America of nebulous identity. ([1973] 1997, 2)

The possibility of Latin Americans fully exercising their right to chart their own historical course, to determine their own social and cultural identity, and to control their own economic development can appear as elusive as ever in view of the power of the North American behemoth. As the following chapter explores in further detail, this unequal power relationship presents equally difficult challenges for Latin Americans living within the United States.

CHAPTER 3

DISCRIMINATION AND LATINOS/AS IN THE UNITED STATES

"Racial Profiling is a tool we use, and don't let anyone say otherwise. Like up in the valley, I knew who the crack sellers were—they look like Hispanics who should be cutting your lawn."

—Deputy Bobby Harris,
Los Angeles County Sheriff's Department.
(Goldberg 1999, 57)

"Over eight in ten (82%) Latinos report that discrimination against Latinos is a problem in preventing Latinos from succeeding in the United States."

(Pew Hispanic Center/Kaiser Family Foundation
2002, 70)

The history of U.S.-Latin American relations can be summed up as unequal: one country wealthy and dominant, the others poor and vulnerable. This relationship has been, and in many ways, continues to be characterized by the inexorable drive of the United States to maintain a dominant-subordinate arrangement. To this end, racist ideologies, economic advantage, political power, and military might have all been deployed.

In the context of U.S.-Latin American relations, the concept of race as it has evolved in the United States has been an especially convenient device used for explaining and legitimizing the subordination of Latin American peoples. Racist and racialized categorizations in the United States have played a central role in justifying and unifying the country for the conquest of Latin American lands, the exploitation of Latin American workers, and unrestricted and unfair access to Latin America's natural resources and markets. The results have also been unfair commercial relations and other economic advantages at the expense of Latin Americans' right to self-determination, development, and well-being.

Over time, concerns over European recolonization of the Western Hemisphere, the fear of the spread of Soviet communism in the post-World War II era, the war on drugs, and currently the war on terror, have rationalized U.S. interventionism throughout Latin America. But an equally significant undercurrent of U.S. policy toward Latin America has been its racialized, condescending, and paternalistic aspects that question the capacity of Latin Americans to govern themselves. Then as now, the United States has exhibited an unwillingness to fully accept the exercise of the fundamental right of self-determination by Latin American peoples. Its actions demonstrate reluctance to treat Latin Americans as equals since in most instances that would impede the advance of U.S. commercial, political, and military interests. In the name of protecting those interests, the United States has not hesitated to stifle, rather than promote, human rights and democracy.

Latinos/as in the United States—the descendants of those who were conquered by the United States, as in the case of Mexicans after 1848 or Puerto Ricans after 1898, and those who followed, seeking to escape economic and/or political hardships in their homelands—have been no less subject to racialized characterizations. They have also been subject to unequal policies and practices within U.S. society that preserve economic, political, and social control in the hands of Anglo Americans. If one defines racial and ethnic discrimination as "the unequal or unfair treatment of a person or persons based on their group membership" (Healey 2006, 27), the history of Latinos/as in the United States makes plain that Latinos/as have not been treated as equals.

Similar to the use of race in U.S.-Latin American relations, race has been a powerful tool in shaping attitudes, policies, practices, and laws affecting Latinos/as in the United States. This chapter explores the Latino/a experience with discrimination in the United States and Latino/a resistance to the injustice rendered by prejudice and discrimination.[1]

---

1. In contrast to discrimination or the "the unequal treatment of a person or persons based on group membership" (Healey 2006, 27), prejudice can be defined as "the tendency to think about other groups in negative ways, to attach negative emotions to those groups, and to prejudge individuals on the basis of their group memberships" (26).

LATINOS/AS AND DISCRIMINATION: 1848–PRESENT

Understanding that U.S. policies toward Latin America have often been premised on the assumption of the racial inferiority of Latin Americans, it follows that in the United States Latinos/as would not likely be treated as equals any more than Latin Americans abroad would be. With respect to the earliest Latinos/as in the United States, Martha Menchaca explains that

> Most [U.S.] government officials argued that Mexicans of predominantly Indian descent should be extended the same legal status as the detribalized American Indians. Mexicans, on the other hand, argued that under the Treaty of Guadalupe Hidalgo and international laws, the U.S. Government agreed to extend [to] all Mexican citizens—regardless of their race—the political rights enjoyed by white citizens. These rights were accorded to them based on the international principle guaranteeing inhabitants of ceded territories the nationality of the successor state unless other provisions are made in the treaty of peace. (1993, 584)

Soon after the end of the U.S.-Mexican War in 1848, vast tracts of land inhabited by Mexicans pursuant to titles and land grants extended by the Spanish or Mexican governments were swiftly wrested by Anglo Americans. Whites forcibly removed Mexicans from their lands; married wealthy, landowning Mexican women; or used the courts and claims procedures established by Congress—including the California Land Claims Commission and the Court of Private Claims—to gain title to these lands (Perea et al. 2000, 270–71). Laws were created and the courts were used effectively to limit Latino/a rights and privilege Anglo Americans. Many land grants, for instance, were based on concepts of communal property, which conflicted with U.S. notions of private property. As a result, courts increasingly ruled in favor of Anglo claims over lands inhabited by Mexicans under the land grant system (Acuña 2007, 264; Ebright 1994). By 1897, the U.S. Supreme Court in *United States v. Sandoval*, 167 U.S. 278 (1897), ruled that property protected by article 8 of the Treaty of Guadalupe Hidalgo did not protect claims to communally held lands, as such lands had been under Spanish or Mexican government authority and, therefore, not subject to claims by individual claimants with no actual title.

The massive loss of land by Mexicans sparked resistance in the territories ceded to the United States. The insurgency movement led by Juan Cortina in 1859, known as the Cortina War, was among the earliest organized opposition efforts (Rosenbaum 1998). The fight over the seizure of land grants continued for many decades and included the organized resistance efforts of Reies López Tijerina's *La Alianza Federal de Mercedes* (the Federal Alliance of Land Grants) into the 1960s. The *Alianza's* protests "invoked the treaty of Guadalupe Hidalgo.... For them, it was problematic to force a defeated nation to 'sell' territory under duress" (Acuña 2007, 264). Unfortunately, a legacy of the Treaty of Guadalupe Hidalgo is its failure to adequately protect the most fundamental of rights: for Mexicans to remain on their own lands. The treaty did not effectively prevent lands from ending up in the hands of Anglo settlers; it simply provided the appearance of fair treatment of Mexicans in compliance with international law.

"Mexican Days" and the Indignities of Segregation and Discrimination

After 1848 in other areas of their lives, persons of Mexican and Latin American ancestry in the United States were denied full and equal rights as U.S. citizens. For generations, school segregation was as much a part of life for Latinos/as as it was for African Americans in the United States (Montoya 2001). The indignities associated with segregation were especially evident throughout the southwestern United States. As Christopher Arriola recounts, the solution to the growing Mexican presence in California post-1920s—or "the Mexican problem," as it was known—was segregation:

> Common reactions to the "problem" involved some form of segregation in practice, if not in law: housing on the "Mexican side of town"; "Mexican seats" in movie theaters and "Mexican days" at the public swimming pools—usually on the day the pool was to be drained and cleaned. However, perhaps the most tragic and painful form of segregation was in public education. (Arriola 1997)

It was not until 1940s, that segregation of Mexican school children was successfully challenged:

> In Orange County [California], Gonzalo Mendez, a tenant farmer in Westminster, and his wife Felicitas, a native of Puerto Rico, along with a group of Mexican American World War II veterans asked a fundamental question about their communities: If we are good enough to fight and die alongside Anglos, then why are my children not good enough to attend the same schools as their children? (Arriola 1997)

In *Mendez v. Westminster School District of Orange County*, 64 F. Supp. 544, 549 (S.D. Cal. 1946), *aff'd*, 161 F.2d 774 (9th Cir. 1947)—a precursor to the landmark 1954 Supreme Court decision in *Brown v. Board of Education*, 347 U.S. 483 (1954)—it was held that children of Mexican descent were being deprived of equal educational opportunities in the public school system through segregation. In *Mendez*, the court quite pointedly determined that "the methods of segregation prevalent in the defendant school districts foster antagonisms in the children and suggest inferiority among them where none exists" (*Mendez v. Westminster School District of Orange County*, 64 F. Supp. 544, 549).[2]

Along with African Americans, for decades Latinos/as in the United States endured general state-sanctioned segregation and exclusion. As the Supreme Court acknowledged in *Hernandez v. Texas*, 347 U.S. 475, 479–80 (1954), two weeks before delivering its decision in the *Brown* case, the segregation, exclusion, and subordination of persons of Mexican descent by Whites had been systematic for many years. In reviewing the evidence before it, the court confirmed that:

> The participation of persons of Mexican descent in business and community groups was shown to be slight. Until very recent times, children of Mexican descent were required to attend a segregated school for the first four grades. At least one restaurant in town prominently displayed a sign announcing 'No Mexicans Served.' On the courthouse grounds at the time of the hearing, there were two men's toilets, one unmarked, and the other marked 'Colored Men' and 'Hombres Aquí' ('Men Here').

Hernandez v. Texas—a case which struck down the practice of excluding persons of Mexican descent from service as jury commissioners, grand jurors, and petit jurors—marked the first instance in which a Latino/a group was recognized as a "cognizable minority group for equal protection purposes" under the Constitution's Fourteenth Amendment, transcending the commonly held Black/White paradigm characteristic of the common understanding of race and discrimination in the United States (Olivas 2006; Perea 1997b, 1248–49).

---

2. The absence of the *Mendez* case from most U.S. history books is symbolic of the invisibility of Latinos/as in this country. Fortunately, an Emmy Award-winning 2002 documentary, *Mendez v. Westminster: For All the Children, Para Todos los Niños*, tells the story of this groundbreaking legal victory. Although Gonzalo Méndez and his wife Felicitas are deceased, their daughter Sylvia Méndez and the filmmaker, Sandra Robbie, set out to tour the country in 2007 in a van to educate and impart information about the case (Hendricks 2007, A1). Their tour—well-received in many parts of the country—has also encountered its difficulties, and public pressure was necessary to ensure their participation in a California Fourth of July parade (*Los Angeles Times* 2007, B3).

Indeed, from the beginning discrimination and second-class citizenship for Latinos/as has existed and taken many forms. In the political sphere, California's first constitution granted voting rights only to "white" Mexicans, as Mexicans were generally considered an inferior race of indigenous ancestry (Perea et al. 2000, 265–70). The 1855 "Greaser Act"—an anti-vagrancy law enacted in California that defined vagrants as "all persons who are commonly known as 'Greasers' or the issue [children] of Spanish and Indian blood" (Act of April 30, 1855, ch. 175, §2, 1855, Cal. Stat. 217; quoted in Haney López, 1996, 145)—was a deliberate use of the criminal law to specifically target persons of Latin American descent for discriminatory treatment based on "racial" criteria. By the 1940s, Mexican Americans in Los Angeles had been relegated to the socioeconomic margins of society, as manifested by their poverty and segregation into the *barrio* or *colonia* in a city that was once a part of Mexico (Escobar 1999, Pagán 2003).

Later, from 1942–1964, the *Bracero* Program, a federal government initiative to compensate for labor shortages during World War II, represented another legal means through which Mexican workers could be brought to the United States to be exploited as cheap labor. Legal challenges to the unjust treatment received under this program have endured into recent years, with Mexican workers still seeking just compensation for wages never paid (Louima 2002, 5).

With the 1950s came a rise in anti-immigrant and anti-Mexican sentiment under another federal government program, "Operation Wetback." Under this program, growing nativist demands to stop Mexican migration were satisfied through a military operation that purported to deport undocumented Mexicans from the United States.[3] As its derogatory name implies, safeguarding human and civil rights of those targeted was not a concern. In fact, the program served as a smokescreen for illegal searches and seizures and resulted in the mass deportation of many Mexicans with U.S. citizenship (Mirandé 1987, 125–29; Acuña 2007, 225–26; Healey 2006, 310).

As with Mexicans after 1848, following the 1898 U.S. war with Spain the rights of Puerto Ricans were also severely circumscribed. With the U.S. occupation of Puerto Rico in 1898, the United States imposed martial rule on the

---

3. The term "nativist" is used in reference to "nativism," which, as described by Perea (1997a, 1), embodies "a preference for those deemed natives; simultaneous and intense opposition to those deemed strangers, foreigners." Nativism views White U.S. citizens as "real" Americans and casts non-Whites as representing that which is non-native and "un-American" (1). Deeply rooted in U.S. history and society, nativism's resurgence in recent years most often targets Latinos/as and Asians as persons who are foreign and "illegal" (2).

island nation. In 1900, a civilian government with a U.S. appointed governor was installed, disregarding Puerto Rico's own constitutional government and political autonomy as established in the 1897 Autonomous Charter. The United States also aggressively sought to undermine Puerto Rico's culture, linguistic heritage, and identity. In an attempt to force assimilation, the U.S. government banned Spanish as the language of instruction in public schools and imposed English as the official language of instruction from 1898 to 1948 (Zentella 1999).

Essentially, the same Supreme Court that decided the notorious case of *Plessy v. Ferguson*, 163 U.S. 537 (1896), also decided the cases that define Puerto Rico's present status and rights vis-à-vis the United States and U.S. law. Similar to *Plessy*, the Insular Cases were designed, in part, to protect the United States from "alien races" (see *Downes v. Bidwell*, 182 U.S. 244 (1901); Torruella 1988). In accordance with the *Insular Cases*, the U.S. Congress to the present day exerts absolute power over the civil rights of Puerto Ricans and the status of their homeland. Puerto Ricans benefit only from those rights that the U.S. Congress specifically grants them. Even though Puerto Ricans are U.S. citizens at birth, on their islands they cannot vote for the president of United States, they have no voting representation in the U.S. Congress, and they can be ordered by the U.S. government to fight and die in U.S. wars, as they have since World War I. Today, "unincorporated territorial status" under the Territorial Clause of the U.S. Constitution consigns Puerto Rico to colonial dependency and the rights of its peoples to a form of second-class citizenship (Trías Monge 1997; Fernandez 1994; Gonzalez 2000; Maldonado-Denis 1972).

The impact of second-class citizenship status on the rights of Puerto Ricans was felt over the years even among those who moved from their homeland to the United States. For example, although U.S. citizenship dates back to 1917, Puerto Ricans were excluded from participation in New York City elections if the language in which they were educated was not English. Even after the passage of the Voting Rights Act of 1965, there were still attempts to bar Puerto Ricans educated in Spanish in Puerto Rico from voting. It was not until 1966 in the case of *Katzenbach v. Morgan*, 384 U.S. 641 (1966), that Puerto Ricans were afforded greater access to the electoral process. In that case, the U.S. Supreme Court held that Section 4(e) of the Voting Rights Act—a provision that provided that no person be denied the right to vote in any election because of their inability to read or write English—was constitutional (658).

In addition to the delimitation of their citizenship and voting rights, Latinos/as have been subjected to discriminatory treatment in other significant areas of daily life. In some instances, as in the areas of education and hous-

ing, the effects of discrimination have been severe and have spanned generations. Even after the U.S. Supreme Court found school segregation to be unconstitutional, achieving equal educational opportunities for Latinos/as has
remained elusive.

In a case that combined housing and education discrimination claims, *U.S.
et al. v. Yonkers Board of Education, et al.*, 624 F. Supp. 1276 (S.D.N.Y. 1985);
aff'd, 837 F. 2d 1181 (2d Cir. 1987); *cert. denied* 486 U.S. 1055 (1988), stands
as a testament to the broad reach and span of discrimination as it affects
Latino/a communities in a U.S. city. The case examined three decades of housing development following World War II as well as school policies and practices in the City of Yonkers, New York. The trial alone—exclusive of appeals
and the remedy phase—lasted "nearly one hundred days ... during which
eighty-four witnesses testified and thirty-eight depositions, as well as thousands
of exhibits, were received in evidence" (1288). In its decision, the court held
the City of Yonkers and the Yonkers Board of Education liable for intentionally
creating and maintaining racial segregation in the City's housing and schools
by systematically isolating African Americans and Latinos/as from the City's
White population in violation of Title VIII of the Civil Rights Act of 1968 and
the Equal Protection Clause of the Fourteenth Amendment of the U.S. Constitution (1537, 1542). Years of discrimination in housing and schools were followed by years of litigation and many years of fashioning remedial steps and
monitoring to undo illegal segregation. Moreover, controversies surrounding
the court-ordered desegregation plans delayed the implementation of measures
to address the needs of the African American and Latino/a communities (see,
e.g., *Spallone v. United States et al.*, 493 U.S. 265 [1990]). Thus, the *Yonkers
Board of Education* case represents an example of long-term intentional discrimination across different and profoundly important areas of life in which
Latinos/as and African Americans endured its impact.

Latinos/as and Education: Left Behind Then and Now

Breaking the cycle of discriminatory treatment toward Latinos/as in education has been one of the most difficult hurdles for Latinos/as in their quest
for a better life nationwide. Dismantling inequalities in education has been
complicated by the inability of the courts to address and undo the discriminatory impact of certain education policies on Latino/a children. In the case
of *San Antonio Independent School District v. Rodriguez*, 411 U.S. 1 (1973),
Mexican-American parents, by way of a class action suit, sought to secure
equal educational resources for a poor school district with a student population 90 percent Mexican-American and more than 6 percent African-Ameri-

can. In rejecting any finding of racially discriminatory treatment in funding, the U.S. Supreme Court held that there was no explicit or implicit right to education under the Federal Constitution and deferred to local control decision-making over educational expenditures (35–38). The impact of a decision that no federal court action could be taken to insure adequate educational funding for a largely Latino/a school district cannot be more devastating. It closes the doors to equal educational opportunities and virtually condemns generations of Latino/a school children to a future of social and economic disadvantage. The court's decision also represents a disturbing acceptance of the normalization of egregious economic inequality in society.

In recent years, the focus on the problem of severe disparities in educational funding has shifted to the state level. In 2003, the highest court in New York State, the Court of Appeals, found the State of New York in violation of article XI, section 1, of the state's constitution which requires that the state legislature "provide for the maintenance and support of a system of free common schools, wherein all the children of this state may be educated" (*Campaign for Fiscal Equity, Inc., et al. v. State of New York, et al.*, 100 N.Y.2d 893, 901–02; 801 N.E.2d 326; 769 N.Y.S.2d 106 [2003]). The original trial court not only found the state in violation of the state constitution in this regard, but also held that the state was directly responsible for discrimination against students of color because the state's public school financing system had an adverse and disparate impact on New York City's public school children, in violation of Title VI of the Civil Rights Act of 1964, 42 USC §2000d (*Campaign for Fiscal Equity et al., v. State of New York et al.*, 187 Misc. 2d 1; 719 N.Y.S.2d 475 [2001]).

Agreeing with the trial court, the Court of Appeals found a "causal link" between the state's funding system and the provision of fewer resources to New York City public schools—precisely those schools in the state with the greatest need and attended overwhelmingly by students of color (*Campaign for Fiscal Equity v. New York*, 100 N.Y.2d 893 at 919).

A system with approximately 1200 schools and 1.1 million students, the court found that about 84 percent of the New York City public school system's children were "racial minorities," including Latinos/as and African Americans; "80 percent were born outside the United States; and 16 percent were classified as Limited English Proficient ('LEP'— persons who speak little or no English)—most of the State's students in each of these categories" (903–04). In addition, the schools' population was found to be largely poor or in economic need: "Upwards of 73 percent were eligible for the Federal free or reduced lunch program; 442,000 City schoolchildren came from families receiving Aid to Families with Dependent Children" (904). In spite of the obvious need for resources, "[p]er-pupil expenditures in the New York City public schools, at $8,171, were lower than in three-quarters of the State's districts, including all the other 'large city' districts, as classified by the SED [State Education Department]. The State's dollar contribution to this figure was also lower, at $3,562, than its average contribution to other districts; and the City's, at about $4,000, was likewise lower than the average local contribution in other districts" (905).

Former New York State Governor, George Pataki, insisted on pursuing this case to the highest court in the state at taxpayer expense, arguing that the state's obligation only extends to providing an eighth grade education, supposedly sufficient for a "sound basic education" (906). As a gubernatorial candidate, Pataki made great attempts to woo Latino/a voters to his candidacy and to the Republican Party. However, to the disappointment of many Latinos/as, it seems that under his leadership the state was willing to forego the education of a large number of its Latino/a children who rely on a public education.

In 2000–2001, close to 40 percent (37.8%) of New York City public school children were Latino/a (Citizens' Committee for Children 2002, 107). Yet the state's attorneys sought to sidestep the glaring problems of overcrowded classrooms, classes taught by unqualified teachers, and the lack of books and other necessary teaching instruments and facilities. In court, the state attorneys' argument, in large measure, amounted to blaming the victims: that educational failure was due to the students' poor socioeconomic situation, rather than any fault of the state (*Campaign for Fiscal Equity v. New York*, 100 N.Y.2d 893 at 920). Fortunately for the children of New York City, the governor's position did not prevail. Instead, the court held that regardless of the socioeconomic condition of the children, the state is obligated to meet the basic educational needs of all children. The "premise that children come to the New York City schools uneducable, unfit to learn" was deemed unacceptable to the court (921). Accordingly, it ordered that the State of New York implement a new funding scheme that would insure that a fair share of resources be allocated for the education of New York City's school children (947–48).

Although the lower court initially determined that as much as $6 billion was necessary, in 2006 New York State's Court of Appeals ruled that only $1.9 billion more each year could go to New York City. The $1.9 billion figure, derived from a commission created by former Governor Pataki, has raised concerns from the plaintiff organization, the Campaign for Fiscal Equity, and other advocacy organizations (Hakim 2006, B7). Controversy over how the funds that have been allocated will be spent has begun to stir, with advocacy groups criticizing the City for wanting to apportion disproportionately large amounts to already high-performing schools, instead of to the neediest schools with the lowest-performing students, which was the primary aim of the lawsuit (Medina 2007a, B4).

As is the case in many education decisions, the *Campaign for Fiscal Equity* decision brought to light the many years of unequal educational opportunities that Latino/a families and children have had to endure. It also demonstrated the great lengths that people of color have had to go to mount legal challenges against state officials indifferent to the discriminatory effects of their policies on Latinos/as and other communities of color. Taken in context, the *Campaign for Fiscal Equity* case, filed in the mid-1990s, was rapidly approaching a decade of litigation before the highest court of the state handed down its decision. As of the beginning of 2004, a corrective plan was not yet in place. For many years before, during, and after this case, vast numbers of Latino/a children in the New York City school system have been without schools that adequately meet their educational needs. The New York Court of Appeals itself cited examples of "systemic breakdown" that still plagues the system, including deplorable classroom conditions and a third of the city's third grade school children being "functionally illiterate" (*Campaign for Fiscal Equity v. New York*, 100 N.Y.2d 893 at 916).

In spite of reports of improvements in tests scores in New York City, school officials in 2003 were conceding that one out of two fourth-graders or "50 percent ... aren't making the grade" (Herszenhorn 2003, A1). Sizable gains in math scores from 2006 to 2007 have been reported, particularly in the lower grades, but "only 45.6 percent of eighth graders were proficient" in the subject (Medina 2007b, A1, B8).

In 2007, a sharp rise in reading scores for eighth graders—57 percent at or above grade level statewide, up from 49.3 percent in 2006—was reported (Herszenhorn 2007a, A1). However, this improvement was only possible when the statistics excluded children with limited English skills. "With those students included, the proportion of all New York City students meeting the standards remained essentially flat, moving to 50.8 percent from 50.7 percent" (Herszenhorn 2007a, A1). Indeed, English Language Learners in the New York City public schools—many of whom are Latina/o—are likely to be underserved, as Columbia journalism professor, Samuel G. Freedman, points out:

> An ELL, you need to know, is the abbreviation for English Language Learner. These students, immigrants or their children are legally entitled to special classes intended to make them fluent readers, writers and speakers of their new language. Another way of defining ELLs, though, is frequently as pawns in the overhaul of New York City's public schools. In addition, in repeated cases they have been moved

around, shunted aside and denied the very kind of instruction they
are due.… With the pressure of No Child Left Behind, which uses
standardized test scores to determine compliance with the law, what
school would seek out new immigrants who may not score well?
(Freedman 2007, B8)

For Latina/o public school students in New York City, the outlook remains
poor. Only half of the City's high school students overall graduated on time
in 2006 (Herszenhorn 2007b, B1), and the City's three best and most selective public high schools have experienced a decline in the percentage of African
American and Latina/o students (Gootman 2006, A1).

For Latino/a children nationally, educational prospects are equally grim.
The federal "No Child Left Behind" (NCLB) law, designed to raise national
educational standards by monitoring success through testing, has also received
substantial criticism. In February 2007, the National Assessment of Educational Progress, a national report card on educational achievement, showed
that 12th graders nationally are performing worse than in 1992 on similar tests
(*New York Times* 2007a, A18). A subsequent progress report indicates that
standards vary greatly national-wide, leading "[m]any educational experts to
criticize No Child Left Behind, saying it gives states an incentive to set low
standards to avoid sanctions for schools that do not increase the percentage
of students demonstrating proficiency each year" (Lewin 2007, A21). As a result, reports that have found some progress under NCLB, such as that of the
Center on Educational Policy, have been brought into question because the
progress is meaningless if the tests students take have been made easier (Lewin
2007, A21). Moreover, the absence of adequate funding for education continues to be central in the effort to provide educational opportunities, particularly for students of color. Ample funding for education remains an elusive
goal (Lewin and Herszenhorn 2007, A10).

As is the case with other people of color, Latinos/as continue to endure the
consequences of public policies that neglect their most basic of human needs.
Symptomatic of longstanding national trends to reduce or limit spending for
essential public services, for too long policymakers have placed education low
in their list of funding priorities. As reported by the National Criminal Justice
Commission, "[i]n 1991, for the first time in American history, several major
cities spent more on law enforcement than on secondary education. In 1994
and 1995, several governors—including George Pataki in New York—proposed building new prisons while cutting back on social services. These funding choices affect the quality of life and the degree of opportunity available to
all Americans" (Donziger 1996, 204). The Commission's findings beg the

question: Will Latinos/as and other communities of color ever be given the opportunity to advance as "Americans" in contemporary U.S. society? The ongoing lack of commitment to adequate funding for social services—such as housing, education, and health care—strongly suggests Latinos/as will continue to be relegated to a place of obscurity and inequity as a racialized "other" in U.S. society. While *de jure* segregation, as in the *Mendez* case, is no longer acceptable, it seems evident that U.S. society is still willing to tolerate *de facto* inequalities, which affect Latina/o communities around the country.

Racial Profiling and Bias in the Criminal Justice System

A discussion about discrimination against Latinos/as in the United States would not be complete without delving into the Latino/a experience with law enforcement and the criminal justice system. The racialization of Latinos/as as inferior, dangerous, and criminal manifests itself in the criminal justice system in many ways. Prejudice, stereotypes, and discrimination have taken many forms. According to studies of law enforcement behavior around the country (Walker et al. 2007, 135–36, Amnesty International 1998, 17–54), the use of abusive language and racial and ethnic slurs against people of color has been a regular occurrence. In many instances, the word "spic" has surfaced in police misconduct and brutality cases involving Latino/a victims (Morín and del Valle 1990). As a derogatory racial epithet and racial/ethnic identifier, the term "spic" differentiates Latinos/as from the dominant English-speaking society, reinforcing the idea of Latinos/as as "the other." Ostensibly, nothing more effectively drives home the message that Latinos/as are "the other" than abusive police behavior and brutality.[4]

The problem of police abuse and violence in Latino/a communities usually correlates with poor relations between police and Latino/a communities and prevailing attitudes on race and ethnicity, including that people of color are most often perceived as perpetrators of crime. However, contrary to the popular perception of people of color as society's criminal element, Walker, Spohn, and DeLone point out that the typical criminal offender is actually White:

---

4. The term "police brutality" is used herein in reference to the use of excessive force, which as defined by Walker, Spohn, and DeLone (2007, 121), is "any physical force that is more than reasonably necessary to accomplish a lawful police purpose."

Examination of arrest statistics for all offenses, for instance, reveals that the typical offender is white; over two-thirds (70.6 percent) of those arrested in 2003 were white, less than one-third (27.0 percent) were African American, and less than 3 percent were Native American or Asian. Similarly, over half of those arrested for violent crimes and nearly two-thirds of those arrested for property crimes were white. (2007, 48)[5]

The government's Uniform Crime Reports (UCR), upon which the foregoing statistics are based, do not include a category for Latinos/as since Latinos/as are classified as an ethnic rather than a racial group. The result is that the UCR data does not accurately account for Latinos/as, who are usually categorized as either "White" or "Black."[6]

It has been observed that in other instances Latinos/as are likely to be identified as "other," particularly in data collected based on the perception of the offender's race (Walker, Spohn, and DeLone 2007, 54). In statistics where an "other" category is used, again, Whites come up as the most common criminal offender. For instance, the Bureau of Justice Statistics (2000, 48) reports that for all crimes of violence in 1995, the breakdown in terms of the perceived race of offenders for a single-offender crime was: 63.1 percent were perceived

---

5. The data cited by Walker, Spohn, and DeLone for the year 2003 is derived from the U.S. Department of Justice Uniform Crime Reports (U.S. Department of Justice 2003). The arrests statistics cited here are not an aberration. In fact, arrest data by race are remarkably consistent. For the year 2000, arrest data by race show that 69.7 percent of those arrested for all criminal offenses were White, 27.9 percent were African American, and less than 3 percent were American Indian or Native Alaskan, or Asian or Pacific Islander (U.S. Department of Justice 2001). Figures on arrests by race for all criminal offenses for 2001 show that 69.5 percent of those arrested were White, 28.1 percent were Black, 1.3 percent were American Indian or Native Alaskan, and 1.1 percent were Asian or Pacific Islander (U.S. Department of Justice 2002, 252). Data on arrests by race for 2005 for all criminal offenses show that 69.8 percent were White, 27.8 percent were African American, 1.3 percent were American Indian or Native Alaskan, and 1.0 percent were Asian or Pacific Islander (U.S. Department of Justice 2005, Table 43).

6. Studies of Latinas/os and the U.S. criminal justice system criticize the failure of the system to maintain separate data on ethnicity in addition to race (Villarruel et al. 2002, 46–49). Data that does not keep track of Latinos/as, *inter alia*, masks the disparate treatment of Latino/a youths within the justice system (49). As Walker, Senger, Villarruel, and Arboleda (2004, v) indicate "Latinos are virtually invisible in the majority of key studies and publications in the field, and a number of states and federal agencies neither collect nor publish Latino criminal justice data. Thus, not surprisingly, with a few notable exceptions, until recently Hispanics were rarely included in policy debates in the criminal justice field."

as White, 27.3 percent as African American, and 8.0 percent as "other." In 2002, the breakdown of the perceived race of offenders for a single-offender crime for all crimes of violence was 63.3 percent White, 22.8 percent African American, and 13.0 percent "other" (Bureau of Justice Statistics 2003a, table 40). In 2005, the perceived race of offenders for a single-offender crime for all crimes of violence was 43.3 percent White, 21.0 percent African American, and 9.6 percent "other," with 26 percent unknown (Bureau of Justice Statistics 2006a, table 40).

In spite of the data suggesting that criminal activity is most frequent among Whites than any other group, law enforcement officers and the criminal justice system ostensibly continue to be influenced by prejudices present in the larger society based on the idea that those primarily responsible for crime are people of color. Thus, it is common for cases of police brutality and misconduct throughout the United States to be linked to problems of racial and ethnic prejudice and discrimination, including bias directed at Latinos/as (Amnesty International 1998; Human Rights Watch 1998; Mirandé 1987).

Systemic and institutionalized discrimination was most evident in the case of racial profiling by New Jersey State Troopers. After years of denial, New Jersey government officials were forced to concede that their state troopers had engaged in the racial profiling of African Americans and Latinos/as. During the decade of the 1990s, at least eight out of every ten automobiles singled out for searches on the New Jersey Turnpike were driven by African Americans and Latinos/as (Kocieniewski and Hanley 2000, A1). In the case of *State v. Pedro Soto*, 324 N.J. Super. 66, 85; 734 A.2d 350, 361 (1996), in which it was demonstrated that New Jersey State Police were engaged in unlawful racial profiling, the court concluded that "[t]he eradication of illegal drugs from our State is an obviously worthy goal, but not at the expense of individual rights." Despite this decision, Latinos/as and African Americans remain vulnerable to racial profiling by law enforcement agents because "get-tough" police tactics often garner support in a society conditioned to perceive that crime is more of a problem for certain groups than the empirical data suggests.

Claims of police misconduct and brutality are frequently countered with arguments that seek to justify tougher policing methods. Although some newer police strategies have been cited as responsible for the decline in the crime rate (Silverman 1999), certain aggressive "quality-of-life" and "zero tolerance" tactics have come under considerable criticism. "Stop-and-frisk" campaigns have been among the most controversial quality-of-life strategies employed by police officers. Presumably, it is a practice that operates under standards laid out in the 1968 U.S. Supreme Court decision in *Terry v. Ohio*, 392 U.S. 1 (1968). By adopting a lower standard than "probable cause" under the Constitution's Fourth Amendment, the U.S. Supreme Court in *Terry* expanded the authority of police officers to stop and search individuals based on a "reasonable suspicion" that a person has or is about to commit a crime (27–28). As critics contend, since then this lower standard has opened the door for abuses by law enforcement officers who use race and ethnicity as a basis for stopping and searching persons of color.

In 1996, the U.S. Supreme Court further extended the latitude available to police officers to use race in stopping persons. In *Whren v. United States*, 517 U.S. 806 (1996), two young African Americans in a car at a stop sign were stopped by plainclothes officers in an unmarked car under the pretext that the men were at the stop sign too long, which is a traffic violation. Even though it was shown in court that the officers had no interest in nor authority to enforce the traffic law, the Court held that the officers did not violate the constitutional rights of the two African American men so long as the officers observed a traffic violation. In a critique of the decision, Georgetown Law Professor David Cole points out:

> The Supreme Court unanimously upheld the stop, ruling that as long as an officer observes a traffic violation, a stop is constitutional, even if the officer has no authority to make the stop and no intention to enforce the law violated. The decision gives a green light to dishonest police work. It permits officers who lack probable cause or reasonable suspicion to manufacture a pretext for intervention. In addition, that allows officers who have no more basis for suspicion than the color of a driver's skin to make a constitution stop. Under *Whren*, a racially motivated pretext stop is "reasonable" under the Fourth Amendment. (Cole 1999, 39)

Because of the *Whren* decision, "pretext stops," as they are known, provide law enforcement officers additional cover and reason to take part in racial profiling, leaving Latina/o and African Americans open to pretexts for abuses of police authority not previously available even under *Terry v. Ohio*.

By the late 1990s, aggressive policing became increasingly associated with cases such as the 1997 torture and sodomizing of Haitian immigrant Abner Louima in a Brooklyn police station. Stops-and-frisks and other quality-of-life campaigns have prompted criticism that they have been used to routinely violate civil rights and liberties and to unfairly target those least able to negotiate the criminal justice system, in particular, communities of color (McArdle and Erzen 2001; Cole 1999; Human Rights Watch 1998; Amnesty International 1998).

A number of studies have now challenged the assertion that the drop in the crime rate in recent years is due solely or primarily to these new and aggressive law enforcement strategies. Indeed, a myriad of evidence has been amassed that points to other factors as accounting for the decline in the national crime rate. Improvements in the economy, a drop in the number of youth in the ages most prone to criminal activity, a decrease in the use of hard drugs, misperceptions about the murder rate in major cities such as New York, and other causes have been posited (see Blumstein and Wallman 2000; Karman 2000; Reiman 2001). In fact, crime has dropped in all parts of the country, including those that have turned to community policing, which focuses on building relationships and cooperation with communities, rather than "get tough" approaches.

Nevertheless, despite the precipitous decline in violent crime—54 percent from 1993 to 2002 (Bureau of Justice Statistics 2003a, 1)—polls reveal an increase in the fear of crime as well as an upsurge in media coverage of crime. As Dorfman and Schiraldi (2001, 3) point out, the National Crime Victimization Survey reported violent crime to be at its lowest in 25 years, yet 62 percent of those surveyed believed that juvenile crime was rising. Thus, aggressive policing to reduce crime appears to find support due to a sustained fear of crime that is in large part media driven. The exaggerated fear of crime appears to foster fear of youths of color in relation to crime, even though "Whites are actually three times more likely to be victimized by Whites than by minorities" (4).

The fear of crime, and more specifically fear of crime committed by people of color, has fed the drive to direct law enforcement strategies where crime is perceived to be most acute. In recent years, police tough-on-crime tactics, such as stop and frisks, have been most visible and controversial in communities of color. These tactics have even been called into question in government studies, especially in connection with the issue of racial profiling in Latino/a and African-American communities.

Reports by the New York State Attorney General and the U.S. Commission on Civil Rights confirm the gravity of the problem of using race as a sole criterion by law enforcement agents—or racial profiling—in New York City (Spitzer 1999; U.S. Commission on Civil Rights 2000).

Statistical data by the New York State Attorney General show that striking racial and ethnic disparities exist regarding who is likely to be subject to a "stop-and-frisk" and who is not (Tables 3 and 4). These disparities strongly suggest that New York City police officers engage in the illegal practice of racially profiling people of color. The data also contradicts the line of reasoning that Latinos/as and African Americans are stopped and frisked at higher rates than other racial groups because they live in high crime rate areas. The report finds that even after accounting for differences in crime rates in com-

Table 3. Street Searches ("Stops-and-Frisks") by Police in New York City

1998	Frisks	Arrests
	Of 27,061 people frisked, only 4,647 were arrested (22,414 persons searched were mistakenly thought to be armed.)	
1997	Frisks	Arrests
	Of 18,023 people frisked, 4,899 were arrested (13,124 persons searched were mistakenly thought to be armed.)	

munities of color and White communities, Latinos/as were still stopped 39% more often than Whites in New York City across all crime categories (Spitzer 1999, x).

The targeting of communities of color for aggressive police tactics and the use of racial profiles in communities of color has drawn criticism as harmful, ineffective, and counterproductive. As Table 3 shows, of 27,061 people frisked, only 4,647 were arrested, raising questions not only as to efficacy, but arbitrariness and whether an inordinate number of people were subject to harassment. Studies of police "stops" in other parts of the country present a similar pattern.

In a study conducted in Chicago, 80 percent of African American high school students and 62 percent of Latino/a high school students reported

Table 4. Rates of "Stops" of People of Color and Whites by Police in New York City (January 1, 1998 through March 31, 1999)

- Blacks comprise 25.6% of the City's population, yet 50.6% of all persons "stopped" were black.

- Hispanics comprise 23.7% of the City's population, yet 33.0% of all persons "stopped" were Hispanics.

- Blacks comprise 62.7% of all persons "stopped" by the NYPD's Street Crime Unit.

- The effect of differing crime rates in communities of color and white communities does not fully explain the increased rate of stops of people of color. After accounting for differences in crime rates:

- Blacks were stopped 23% more often than Whites across all crime categories.

- Hispanics were stopped 39% more often than Whites across all crime categories.

Source: Spitzer, Elliot. 1999. *The New York City Police Department's "Stop and Frisk" Practices: A Report to the People of the State of New York from the Attorney General.* New York: Civil Rights Bureau, vii–x.

being stopped by police, with 62 and 63 percent, respectively, reporting that they were treated disrespectfully by the police when stopped (Freidman and Hott 1995, 111).

In his examination of racial profiling, Professor David Harris (2002) shows that the notion of a particular profile for drug runners or other criminals has led law enforcement officials to draw very dangerous conclusions about what a drug crime suspect looks like. He finds that Latinos/as have been among the groups most often determined to fit the criminal profile (49–51). He also affirms that on a number of instances law enforcement personnel have been trained to identify narcotics dealers as "people wearing dreadlocks and cars with two Latino males traveling together," and that in 1999, a Drug Enforcement Agency (DEA) intelligence report identified top heroin traffickers as "Colombian, followed by Dominicans, Chinese, West African/Nigerian, Pakistani, Hispanic, and Indian. Midlevels are dominated by Dominicans, Colombians, Puerto Ricans, African Americans and Nigerians" (49). Indeed, profiles used by federal agents at airports to identify persons suspected of carrying drugs have included very long lists of seemingly odd and broadly-defined categories, such as someone who "made a local call after deplaning … made a long-distance call after deplaning … carried a small bag … carried a medium-size bag … carried two bulky garment bags … dressed casually … left the airport by taxi" (Cole 1999, 47–49). Federal drug-courier profiles specifically identify "Hispanics" as suspects (49).

Law enforcement agents assume that racial profiles used in anti-drug operations accurately determine which racial or ethnic groups are responsible for drug-related crimes. As Georgetown University Law Professor David Cole notes (2001, 248), "racial profiling studies … make clear that the war on drugs has largely been a war on minorities. It is, after all, drug enforcement that motivates most racial profiling." Racial profiles actually do not correctly reflect the racial makeup of illicit drug consumers or traffickers. In fact, U.S. government data about drug use indicate that Whites use drugs at much the same rate as persons from other racial or ethnic groups. The Substance Abuse and Mental Health Services Administration (2002, 1) finds that the "patterns of current use among major racial/ethnic groups in 2001 were similar to previous years. The rate among blacks was 7.4 percent, whites 7.2 percent, and Hispanics 6.4 percent."

In some instances, drug use among Whites is actually greater than among other racial and ethnic groups. Among youth ages 12-17, Whites were 6.8 percent more likely to use some form of hallucinogen in their lifetime, African Americans 1.7 percent, Asians 5.2 percent, and Latinos/as 4.1 percent (Substance Abuse and Mental Health Services Administration 2003, 2). Moreover, it has been discovered that Latino/a and African American youths have been "more likely than whites and Asians to perceive great risk in trying LSD" (2).

The notion that Latinos/as and African Americans are more likely to be involved in distributing illegal drugs may also be inaccurate. As Professor Cole explains (2001, 247), a "Justice Department study [Riley 1997, 1] found that most [illicit drug] users report getting their drugs from dealers of the same race, so the demographics of distribution likely reflect the demographics of drug use."

The staying power of prejudice and stereotypes of Latinos and Latinas as drug suspects have produced negative repercussions for them within the justice system. Prejudiced opinions have been found to permeate police departments throughout the country. In a 1999 cover story in the *New York Times Magazine*, police officers from different cities openly voiced an unwillingness to give up racial profiling in their day-to-day work, a reluctance principally grounded in bigoted attitudes about race and ethnicity (Goldberg 1999). With reference to Latinos/as specifically, Deputy Bobby Harris of the Los Angeles County Sheriff's Department unabashedly stated that "[r]acial profiling is a tool we use, and don't let anyone say otherwise. Like up in the valley, I knew who the crack sellers were—they look like Hispanics who should be cutting your lawn" (57). This statement is in keeping with existing research that demonstrates the pervasiveness of prejudiced attitudes among police officers (Walker et al. 2007, 136–37). In one study, for instance, 80 percent of Denver police officers were found to dislike persons with Spanish surnames (Bayley and Mendelsohn 1969). While holding prejudiced opinions does not necessarily mean that police officers will take discriminatory action, evidence regarding openness to bigotry and an inclination to use racial profiling has mounted over the years, suggesting that prejudice forms the fertile ground upon which discriminatory action develops. The high incidence of racial profiling and racial and ethnic bias in law enforcement throughout the country—as documented in many studies (see, e.g., Amnesty International 1998; Human Rights Watch 1998; Cole 1999; Harris 2002; Meeks 2000)—tends to support the position that prejudice frequently fosters discriminatory acts.

There has also been a growing body of evidence in cities such as New York and Los Angeles that police abuse and brutality is often directed against lesbians and gays (see Amnesty International 1998, 40–42). A report by the Audre Lorde Project (2000) finds that police misconduct and brutality has been particularly prevalent in lesbian, gay, bisexual, two spirit, and transgender communities of color in New York City. As no one in society should be subject to unfair police practices and brutality, what makes lesbian, gay, bisexual, two spirit, and transgender persons in Latino/a communities vulnerable to police abuse deserves further study and action.

For Latinos/as, racial and ethnic prejudice and discrimination in the courts appears to be a constant factor in the meting out of unequal justice. As one study in Los Angeles found, Latino males were regularly prosecuted to the fullest extent, with African American males, White males, and women of all ethnicities following in descending order (Spohn, Gruhl, and Welch 1987, 175–91). As further evidence of the impact of a criminal justice system prone to intentional and unintentional racial and ethnic discrimination, a major study conducted by Michigan State University/Building Blocks for Youth suggests that bias in the criminal justice system is a key factor in the high rates of incarceration among Latino/a youth (Villarruel et al. 2002). National data reveals that, as a result, Latino/a youth are charged with violent offenses at a rate five times higher than White youth and serve longer sentences than White youth—as much as 143 days longer for violent crimes (2–3). In Los Angeles, Latino/a youth are incarcerated at rates much higher than White youth—7.3 times as often from 1996–1998—and Latino/a youth are prosecuted as adults more often than White youth—2.4 times as often from 1996–1998 (2). A 2004 report sponsored by the National Council of La Raza, finds similarly that "Latinos are overrepresented and unfairly treated at every stage of the criminal justice system (Walker, Senger, Villarruel, and Arboleda 2004).[7]

The Enemy at the Border: Al Qaeda? No, Anyone Who Looks Mexican

Conflicts and controversy involving the U.S.-Mexican border have a long history. That history encompasses the militarization of the border by the U.S. government which provoked a war of territorial conquest in 1846 (Davis 2003, 189), the abuses levied on Mexicans at the hands of the U.S. Border Patrol (Mirandé 1987), and the recent surge of armed anti-immigrant vigilantes on the border, including Minutemen and white supremacists (Larsen 2007, 14–18). In recent years, the country has also been served a steady diet of fear-mongering at the hands of television news personalities, such as Lou Dobbs, further inflaming anti-immigrant sentiments. As reported in *The New York Times*, in the course of his relentless campaign to spread fear about the so-called "broken borders," Dobbs' has resorted to disseminating false information about immigrants at the Mexican border, including that they are linked to an outbreak of leprosy in the country when no such increase has occurred,

---

7. The topic of Latino/a overrepresentation in the prison system is more fully discussed in Chapter 4.

and that non-citizen immigrants constitute one-third of the federal prison population when they actually make up significantly less than that (Leonhardt 2007a; 2007b, C1). Given this level of fear-mongering, the threat of undocumented immigrants crossing the border is seemingly comparable only to another Al Qaeda attack.

However, the media is not alone in overextending itself when it comes to undocumented immigrants. The U.S. Supreme Court has also succumbed to concerns over immigration to such an extent that it has moved in the direction of eroding fundamental constitutional safeguards. In *United States v. Brignoni-Ponce*, 422 U.S. 873 (1975), the Court, in line with its decision in *Terry v. Ohio*, ruled that "probable cause" under the Fourth Amendment was not required for Border Patrol to stop an individual for questioning and that officers on roving patrol could only stop vehicles having specific articulable facts and rational inferences based on those facts that provide a reasonable suspicion that the vehicles contained persons who might be illegally entering the country. The Court also held that having a "Mexican appearance" could be a factor to justify stopping a vehicle by Border Patrol, although not the sole factor. The Court's acceptance of appearing similar to a particular group of persons as a factor in justifying a stop by Border Patrol has been denounced by Alfredo Mirandé as the "Mexican exception" to the Constitution's Fourth Amendment (Soltero 2006, 116). Yet, what is perhaps even more disconcerting is the Supreme Court decision that followed *Brignoni-Ponce*.

In 1976, in *United States v. Martinez-Fuerte*, 428 U.S. 543 (1976), the Supreme Court held that stopping vehicles at permanent checkpoints for brief questioning of its occupants, did not violate the Fourth Amendment, even though there was no reason to believe that the particular vehicle contained illegal aliens and the operation of a fixed checkpoint does not require judicial warrant in advance. In a strong rebuke of the majority opinion in *Martinez-Fuerte*, in his dissent Justice William Brennan made clear that the Court was undermining the Constitution's Fourth Amendment protections in ways never contemplated by the Court in *Terry v. Ohio* or *Brignoni-Ponce*:

> *Terry* ... made clear what common sense teaches: Conduct, to be reasonable, must pass muster under objective standards applied to specific facts. We are told today, however, that motorists without number may be individually stopped, questioned, visually inspected, and then further detained without even a showing of articulable suspicion, ... let alone the heretofore constitutional minimum of reasonable suspicion, a result that permits search and seizure to rest upon 'nothing more substantial than inarticulate hunches.' This defacement

of Fourth Amendment protections is arrived at by a balancing process that overwhelms the individual's protection against unwarranted official intrusion by a governmental interest said to justify the search and seizure. (428 U.S. 543, 569–570 [1976])

To Justice Brennan the danger that the *Martinez-Fuerte* decision poses for Mexicans and anyone who looks Mexican is clear:

Every American citizen of Mexican ancestry and every Mexican alien lawfully in this country must know after today's decision that he travels the fixed checkpoint highways at the risk of being subjected not only to a stop, but also to detention and interrogation, both prolonged and to an extent far more than for non-Mexican appearing motorists.... [F]or the arbitrarily selected motorists who must suffer the delay and humiliation of detention and interrogation, the experience can obviously be upsetting. In addition, that experience is particularly vexing for the motorist of Mexican ancestry who is selectively referred, knowing that the officers' target is the Mexican alien. That deep resentment will be stirred by a sense of unfair discrimination is not difficult to foresee. (428 U.S. 543, 572–573 [1976])

In a footnote to his dissent, Brennan adds the following:

Though today's decision would clearly permit detentions to be based solely on Mexican ancestry, the Court takes comfort in what appears to be the Border Patrol practice of not relying on Mexican ancestry standing alone in referring motorists for secondary detentions.... Good faith on the part of law enforcement officials, however, has never sufficed in this tribunal to substitute as a safeguard for personal freedoms or to remit our duty to effectuate constitutional guarantees. Indeed, with particular regard to the Fourth Amendment, *Terry* v. *Ohio*, 392 U.S. 1, 22 (1968), held that "simple' good faith on the part of the arresting officer is not enough.' ... If subjective good faith alone were the test, the protections of the Fourth Amendment would evaporate, and the people would be 'secure in their persons, houses, papers, and effects,' only in the discretion of the police. *Beck* v. *Ohio*, [379 U.S. 89,] 97 [1964]. (428 U.S. 543, 573 [1976], n4)

In spite of the concerns raised by Justice Brennan, the Supreme Court later continued on the path of diminishing Fourth Amendment protections against illegal searches and seizures when undocumented immigrants are apprehended. In 1984, the Court in *INS v. Lopez-Mendoza et al.*, 468 U.S. 1032

(1984), denied Adam Lopez-Mendoza the right under the Fourth Amendment to suppress evidence that was obtained in an illegal arrest by the Immigration and Naturalization Service (INS). In its 5-4 decision in *Lopez-Mendoza*, the Court reasoned that deportation proceedings are civil actions to determine a person's eligibility to remain in this country, and therefore Fourth Amendment protections that apply in criminal cases are not available in these hearings (468 U.S. 1032, 1038–1039). Additionally, the Court stated that the "social costs" were too great not to support INS's efforts to curb undocumented persons from entering the country (468 U.S. 1032, 1040–1045). In his dissent, Justice Brennan responded: "The Government of the United States bears an obligation to obey the Fourth Amendment; that obligation is not lifted simply because the law enforcement officers were agents of the Immigration and Naturalization Service, nor because the evidence obtained by those officers was to be used in civil deportation proceedings" (468 U.S. 1032, 1052; see also Hing 2004, 139–144).

A Pattern of Abuse

In the wake of these Supreme Court decisions, it should come as no surprise that African Americans and Latinos/as have experienced a disproportionate number of law enforcement stops and frisks. Recent data suggests a steady pattern of unequal treatment of African American and Latinas/os during police encounters. In New York City, complaints against police officers rose 13 percent in 2006 from the previous year—7,669 complaints in 2006 as compared to 6,785 in 2005 (New York City Civilian Complaint Review Board 2007, 1). When compared to 2002 figures, the number of complaints for 2006 escalated a striking 66 percent, up from 4,612 complaints in 2002). Even more disturbing is the abuse of authority complaints, which involve "such as allegations of improper stops, frisks, or searches" (1). Abuse of authority complaints rose more than any other type of complaint—a dramatic increase of 179 percent or 2,556 complaints in 2006, up from 925 in 2002 (1). These figures issued by the New York City Civilian Complaint Review Board in 2007 mark the sixth consecutive year of increases.

National data for 2007 on stops and searches by police raise concerns similar to that raised by data regarding the practice in New York City. In its report, *Contacts between Police and the Public, 2005*, the Bureau of Justice Statistics (2007a, 1) indicated that while their data show that Whites, African Americans and Latinos/as were stopped by police at similar rates, African Americans and Latinos/as were searched by police at higher rates than Whites. African Americans and Latinos/as are more likely than Whites to experience

Table 5. U.S. Poverty Rate According to Race and Ethnicity

Race/ethnic group	Percentage: 2001	Percentage: 2005
Latinos/as	21.4	21.8
African Americans	22.7	24.9
Asians & Pacific Islanders	10.2	11.1
Whites	7.8	8.3

Sources:

U.S. Bureau of the Census. 2002a. *Poverty in the United States: 2001.* Current Population Reports, Consumer Income, P60-219. Prepared by Bernadette D. Procter, and Joseph Dalaker, Bureau of the Census. Washington, D.C.

U.S. Bureau of the Census. 2006. *Income, Poverty, and Health Insurance Coverage in the United States: 2005.* Current Population Reports, Consumer Income, P60-219. Prepared by Carmen DeNavas-Walt and Bernadette D. Procter, Bureau of the Census. Washington, D.C.

use of force during contact with police (8). Approximately 80 percent of the contacts involved force initiated by police officers (8), and over half of the instances where the police used force involved physical force, as opposed to the use of threats, shouts, or cursing (9).

The Economic and Social Costs of Discrimination on Latinos/as

The troubling statistics cited above coincide with the thesis argued by many analysts, including Alfredo Mirandé (1987) and Rodolfo Acuña (2007): The pattern of abuse and discrimination experienced by Latinos/as in the United States is central to their political and economic subordination, exclusion, and exploitation. Discrimination results in economic, social, and cultural exclusion for those discriminated against, and discrimination provides the means through which the unequal distribution of opportunities and resources can be maintained. In many ways, the socioeconomic inequalities and injustices discernable in Latino/a communities today are products of past and present de *jure* and *de facto* discrimination (see Delgado and Stefancic 1998). For most Latinas and Latinos around the country, the effects of discrimination on their lives and on their ability to advance are very palpable. In their *2002 National Survey of Latinos,* the Pew Hispanic Center/Kaiser Family Foundation found that "[o]ver eight in ten (82%) Latinos report that discrimination against Latinos is a problem in preventing Latinos from succeeding in the United States" (2002, 70).

Table 6. U.S. Median Family Income for 2000 and 2005

Race/ethnic group	Median Income 2000	Median Income 2005
Latinos/as	$33,447	$35,967
African Americans	$30,439	$30,858
Asians & Pacific Islanders	$55,521	$61,094
Whites	$45,904	$50,784

Sources:

U.S. Bureau of the Census. 2001a. *Money Income in the United States: 2000.* Current Population Reports, Consumer Income, P60–213. Prepared by Carmen DeNavas-Walt, Robert W. Cleveland, and Marc I. Roemer, Bureau of the Census. Washington, D.C.

U.S. Bureau of the Census. 2006. *Income, Poverty, and Health Insurance Coverage in the United States: 2005.* Current Population Reports, Consumer Income, P60–219. Prepared by Carmen DeNavas-Walt and Bernadette D. Procter, Bureau of the Census. Washington, D.C.

Today, poverty and other forms of social and economic disadvantage in Latino/a communities are comparable to that of African Americans, a people of color that has been subjected to systemic exploitation, oppression, and discrimination throughout U.S. history. As Table 5 shows, the rate of poverty for Latinos/as, for instance, has been and continues to be nearest to that of African Americans. In 2001, Latinos/as and African Americans had poverty rates of 21.4 and 22.7 percent, respectively, while the poverty rate for Whites was 7.8 percent (Bureau of the Census 2002a, 4). By 2005, poverty rates had risen for all three groups, with Latino/a rates being closest to those of African Americans. In 2005, Latinos/as and African Americans had poverty rates of 21.8 and 24.9 percent, respectively, while the poverty rate for Whites was 8.3 percent (Bureau of the Census 2006, 14).

Table 6 identifies where Latinos/as stood in relation to income in comparison to African Americans and Whites in 2000 and 2005 (Bureau of the Census 2001a, 4; 2006, 5). Again, these statistics illustrate the proximity of income inequality between Latinos/as and African Americans.

Income increased overall from 2000 and 2005 (Bureau of the Census 2001a; 2006), but overall poverty rates also rose. In 2001, the poverty rate for all families was 9.2 percent (Bureau of the Census 2002a, 6–7), but in 2005 the official poverty rate had risen to 12.6 percent nationally, representing 37 million persons in the United States living in poverty (Bureau of the Census 2006, 13). From 2000 to 2001, the number of Latino/a families living in poverty rose from 1.5 million to 1.6 million (21.4 percent) (Bureau of the Census 2002a,

Table 7. U.S. Median Net Worth or Wealth for 2000

Race/ethnic group	Median Net Worth
Latinos/as	$9,750
African Americans	$7,500
Whites	$79,400

Source: U.S. Bureau of the Census. 2003c. *Net worth and asset ownership of households: 1998–2000.* Household Economic Studies, P70–88. Prepared by Shawna Orzechowski, and Peter Sepielli. Bureau of the Census, Washington, D.C. (Note: Asians and Pacific Islanders median net worth was not incorporated into this study.)

7). For 2005, the percentage of Latinos/as living in poverty was registered at 21.8 percent (Bureau of the Census 2006, 14).

Economic disparities along racial and ethnic lines become even more salient when one compares net worth or wealth depicted in Table 7 (Bureau of the Census 2003c, 12).

As Census Bureau analysts point out, "[w]hen ... considered alone, income—the resources a household or person receives from a job, transfer program, or other source—provides an incomplete picture of economic well-being. Only when wealth or net worth—the difference between assets and liabilities—a person or household has at any given time is considered in conjunction with income does a better understanding of economic health and well-being emerge" (Bureau of the Census. 2003c, 1). In fact, the net worth data show the persistence of economic inequality along racial and ethnic lines. Although Latinos/as and African Americans also experienced increases in net worth, in 2000, "White households in every income quintile had significantly higher levels of median net worth than their Black and Hispanic counterparts.... Between 1998 and 2000, the median net worth of non-Hispanic White households jumped by over $8,000" (12).

Census Bureau data and analysis reveal the severe socioeconomic emergency that exists in Latino/a communities. This crisis was spelled out further in a study on the health of Latino/a children published in the *Journal of the American Medical Association*:

> Latino children ... are 13 times more likely than whites to be infected by tuberculosis.... In 1999, 20% of Latino youth reported considering suicide, compared to 15% of black and 18% of white youth.... A half million Latino children have asthma; two thirds of them are Puerto Rican.... Children of migrant Latino farm-workers are particularly at risk for suboptimal health and use of services.... Latino youth

by far have the highest school dropout rate in the nation, 29%, compared with 13% for blacks and 7% for whites. Although 36% of Latino children live in poverty, only 26% attend Head Start programs…. Latinos are underrepresented at every level of the health care professions…. Latinos are more likely to be uninsured (27%) than any other ethnic group of US children. (Flores et al. 2002, 83–88)

A closer look at specific health problems reveals other very alarming facts about the condition of Latinos/as in the United States. For instance, Latino boys and Latina girls are the most overweight of any racial or ethnic group of children in the United States, which correlates with a precipitous rise in diabetes among Latino/a children (Flores et al. 2002, 86). Cross-border health statistics are also a major concern. One study on depression and suicide comparing Mexican American school children on the Texas border with Mexico with their cross-border counterparts "revealed that 48% of Mexican American students scored above the critical level for depression on a standardized scale compared with 39% of Mexican youths, and 23% of US [Mexican American] adolescents reported current suicidal ideation compared to 12% of Mexican students" (87). Hence, Latino/a children on the U.S. side of the border with Mexico were at greater risk for depression and suicide than Mexican youths. Because "Latinos are the largest minority group of children in the (11.6 million) United States" (82), the crisis they face now can have severe consequences, not just for their future, but for the entire United States.

Although persons of Cuban origin generally exhibit higher socioeconomic indicators than those of most other Latino groups, the more recent Cuban arrivals, particularly those who entered the U.S. during and after the Mariel exodus of 1980 and are more likely to be Black and working class, fall into socioeconomic patterns similar to those of most other Latino groups, in a clear trend unlike that of the first wave of Cubans that arrived soon after the 1959 revolution and were mostly from Cuba's light-skinned, economic elite. As Sylvia Pedraza points out (1996, 275), "when we consider Cubans by their race, we can see that while only 14 percent of White Cubans fall below the poverty line, 35 percent of Black Cubans and 23 percent of racially mixed Cubans fall below the poverty line—figures that compare most closely to the poverty rates among Black Americans and Puerto Ricans in the United States."

Moreover, other problems, including residential segregation, compound the difficulties Latinos/as face in obtaining equality of opportunity and advancement (Walker et al. 2007, 89). Recent census data reveal extremely high levels of group isolation and a marked increase in residential segregation over the last decade, with Latinos/as in cities such as New York among the groups experiencing the most separation (Scott 2001, B1). An analysis by the Mumford Center at the University at Albany in New York (2001, 1) found that an average White person in a U.S. metropolitan region "lives in a neighborhood that is 80% white and only 7% black." For equal distribution to occur between Whites and Latinos/as nationally, 51.5% of either Latinos/as or Whites would have to relocate (Mumford Center 2002, 7). Mexicans, Dominicans, Central Americans and Puerto Ricans, in particular tend to live in highly segregated communities (7). Physical separation along racial and ethnic lines thwarts contact and understanding among communities, exacerbating an already volatile situation in a society prone to prejudice and discrimination.

Prejudice and Popular Images: Have Latinos/as Really Made It?

As Madison Avenue and media outlets increasingly depict Latino/a images, food, and music—from salsa dancing to Jennifer López—as all the rage, it may appear incongruous that Latinos/as are still the objects of negative, racialized stereotypes and discrimination. But as Professor Arlene Dávila finds (2001, 217), it is still true that "U.S. minorities [including Latinos/as] are all subject to stereotyping as low income, unskilled, uneducated crime-ridden, unemployed, and, in some cases, as perpetual foreigners, and ... they are always required to prove their worth and compensate for their image." In her study of the current trend to market the "Latino" image, Dávila further explains:

> If Latinas are hot, does this mean that someone who is not "making it" is experiencing individual failure not social inequality? If the consumption indexes of blacks and Latinas are supposedly growing exponentially, does this mean that poverty, unemployment, or steady employment are no longer issues? After all, the people who are consuming must be making money; should we then care if they do so by holding three jobs, by working at the periphery of the informal economy? Alternatively, should we care that their income still lags behind that of whites? If the household incomes of Asian Americans are above the U.S. average, who cares if they are channeled into some professions, absent from others, or if their success comes at the cost of a greater human investment than whites make? Ultimately these questions bring to the fore that marketing discourse is not without political and economic repercussions. It prioritizes consumption over income, and spending over employment

or economic parity, veiling the ongoing segmentation between those with "real" jobs and income, and those who lack it. (Dávila 2001, 235)

Indeed, Dávila challenges us to examine whether popular Latino/a images are simply geared to reap large corporate profits while creating the image for U.S. Whites of the "ideal," non-threatening, successful Latino or Latina—*à la* Ricky Martin—supposedly a model for Latinos/as to emulate (234–36). Of course, as the previous discussion about current socioeconomic conditions illustrates, opportunities for upward mobility in Latino/a communities are actually very fleeting.

While many Latinos/as may be cognizant of the reality of discrimination, many—including those with a significant presence in the United States for some time—find the effects of discrimination in the United States nonetheless disconcerting and destabilizing. Based on research focused on Puerto Ricans, sociologist Joseph F. Healey observes:

> In the racially dichotomized U.S. culture [of Black and White], many Puerto Ricans feel they have no clear place. They are genuinely puzzled when they first encounter prejudice and discrimination based on skin color and are uncertain about their own identity and self-image. The racial perceptions of the dominant culture can be threatening to Puerto Ricans to the extent that they are victimized by the same web of discrimination and disadvantage that affects African Americans. There are still clear disadvantages to being classified as black in U.S. society. Institutionalized racial barriers can be extremely formidable, and in the case of Puerto Ricans, they may combine with cultural and linguistic differences to sharply limit opportunities and mobility. (2006, 318)

A *New York Times*/CBS poll suggests that because Puerto Ricans have been in the United States longer than some other Latino/a groups, they are less likely to be optimistic about their life circumstances (Navarro and Connelly 2003, B1, B4). Meanwhile Latin American newcomers escaping abject poverty and other economic, social, or political hardships are likely to be optimistic about starting a new life in the world's wealthiest country; they are often not prepared to confront the types of discrimination experienced by Latinos/as in the United States.

Responses to Inequalities and Injustices

The historical context of the Latino/a experience with discrimination reveals a long trajectory of overcoming formidable legal barriers as well as political and social limitations. As African Americans, Native Americans, and Asian Americans have done over decades, Latinos/as have responded to discrimination and unjust treatment by organizing efforts to protect and expand rights that should have protected them. Their response has often taken the form of grassroots organizing, as in the efforts of César Chávez and the United Farm Workers to unionize and protect exploited laborers of the 1960s and 1970s (Acuña 2007, 254–56). Others embraced more radical concepts for creating social, economic, and political change, as in the Chicano movement's Brown Berets on the West Coast (Haney López 2003) or the Puerto Rican activists in the Midwest and East who organized the Young Lords and the Puerto Rican Socialist Party (Torres and Velázquez 1998).

As discrimination frequently not only to marginalizes but also undermines a sense of identity, self-esteem, and ethnic solidarity, many organizing efforts in Latino/a communities past and present have made the reaffirmation of identity and culture an integral part of their mission. Latino/a communities gave rise to leaders, such as Bert Corona and Antonia Pantoja—who inspired cultural pride and unity and contributed to advancements in such areas as labor, education, and civil and political rights for Chicanos and Puerto Ricans (see García 1994; Pantoja 2002).

The specific means through which political, economic, and social change was to be effectuated also took many forms. Political activism by way of marches, sit-ins, protest rallies as well as community outreach and educational projects were undertaken to bring attention to the problems faced by Latino/a communities. Legal battles and other forms of political activism, including within the established political party system or on a more ad hoc community level, have been indispensable tools in the effort to bring about improvements in the lives of Latinos/as. In view of the social, economic and political realities Latinos/as have faced, it follows that Latinos/as would be active in the civil rights movements of the 1960s and 1970s and beyond (Gonzalez 2000; Healey 2006).

In spite of the best efforts of the past, Latino/a communities continue to confront inequalities and discrimination in areas, such as education, housing, and employment. To address issues of inequality and injustice, Latino/a legal and legislative efforts were often grounded in or complementary to community-based struggles. Over the years, the courts have been one of the most important venues of setbacks or victories for Latinos/as in the fight for bilingual education, affirmative action, and voting rights (Perea et al. 2000; Delgado and Stefancic 1998).

Since 1968, the Mexican American Legal Defense and Education Fund (MALDEF) has been a leading civil rights, legal advocacy, and educational outreach organization for Latinos/as in the United States. It has taken on many of the most pressing issues involving voting rights, immigrant rights, and discrimination in employment and education. In recent years, nativist sentiments have found expression through the Official English movement and legislation targeted at restricting immigrants' rights. California's propositions 187, 209, and 227—legislative initiatives geared to ending the provision of basic health and educational services to undocumented persons, affirmative action programs, and bilingual education, respectively—represent a backlash to the civil rights gains of the 1960s and 1970s (Acuña 2007, 316–18; Perea 1997a). In response, Latino/a communities have galvanized opposition to these legislative measures, and organizations, such as MALDEF, have been at the forefront of many of the legal challenges indispensable to protecting the rights of immigrants and Latinos/as in general.

MALDEF was one of the nonprofit legal organizations that successfully negotiated the settlement in which Governor Gray Davis and the state of California officially agreed to dismiss their appeal of the district court's decision in the case of *Gregorio T. v. Wilson*, 54 F.3d 599 (9th Cir. 1995). Through this settlement, nearly all of California's Proposition 187 provisions denying education, health care, and other social services to the state's undocumented immigrants were struck down. This legal victory also helped to preserve the right of immigrant children to public education in accordance with the U.S. Supreme Court's decision in *Plyler v. Doe*, 457 U.S. 202 (1982). This decision held that the Equal Protection Clause of the Constitution's Fourteenth Amendment prohibits states from denying a public education to undocumented children, and rejected, *inter alia*, the argument that such services impose a "special burden" on the state (226–30).

Puerto Ricans also formed their own legal organization to wage the fight for equal opportunity in the United States. Since the 1970s, the Puerto Rican Legal Defense and Education Fund (PRLDEF) has been at the forefront of legal battles to realize civil rights in housing, education, and voting for Puerto Ricans and other Latino/a groups. PRLDEF represented Aspira, a nonprofit organization founded to advance educational opportunities of Latinos/as, in securing the landmark 1974 Aspira consent decree, entitling Spanish-speaking Latino/a children in New York to bilingual education programs. Yet in spite of the success of their legal advocacy, the arduous task of enforcing compliance with the consent decree has been typical of the difficulties Latinos/as face preserving rights won over the long term. Indeed, PRLDEF was forced to institute further legal action to hold the New York City Board of Education in contempt for failing to fulfill its responsibilities under the consent decree (*Aspira of New York, Inc. et al. v. Board of Education of the City of New York, et al.*, 423 F. Supp. 647 (S.D.N.Y. 1976)).

On the question of discrimination within the law enforcement and criminal justice systems, Latino/a communities remain active in pursuing change and challenging racial profiling and laws, including draconian drug laws and mandatory sentencing laws that have been associated with the high rates of Latino/a incarceration (Villarruel et al. 2002). A recent project sponsored by Building Blocks for Youth places special emphasis on working with Latina and Latino youth and families in addressing bias in the criminal justice system (73–75). This project promotes a multifaceted approach to reach and organize Latino/a communities, emphasizing strategies for improving and increasing bilingual services within the justice system; advocacy to end racial and gang profiling; legislative reform to repeal or amend laws that have a disproportionate impact on Latinos/as, such as certain drug laws and "three-strikes laws"; and enhancing family and community involvement in monitoring the criminal justice system for bias and abuse against Latinos/as (27–80).[8]

Conclusion

The similarities in the experiences of people of color with issues of discrimination have led to the theoretical conclusion that colonization or conquest continue to be the reality of certain groups in the United States. Robert Blauner (1972), foremost in advancing this theory, viewed Latinos/as, Native Americans, African Americans and Asian Americans as "colonized minority groups" who have endured a process of colonization, conquest, or other forms of exploitation, domination and colonization not experienced by groups who came to the United States under circumstances that were more voluntary. Other social scientists have underscored that Latinos/as—along with African Americans, Native Americans and Asians—have continued to fall prey to the existing ethnocentrism, competition, and power dynamic within the United States leading to their disadvantaged or "minority" status in relation to the

---

8. "Three-strikes laws," in which a third criminal offense automatically results in a severe prison sentence, have not been proven effective against crime. A recent study by the Justice Policy Institute shows that other states without three-strikes law have experienced a greater decline in crime when compared to California, which has had the strictest "Three Strikes and You're Out" law in place for more than ten years (Ehlers, Schiraldi, and Ziedenberg 2004, 14–21). Rather than reduce crime, the three-strikes laws have contributed to the disproportionate incarceration of Latinos/as and African Americans (11–13). In California, the "Latino incarceration rate for a third strike (17 per 100,000 Latino residents) is *45 percent higher* than the third strike incarceration rate for Whites (12 per 100,000 White residents)" (emphasis in the original) (11).

dominant White society (Noel, 1968). But whether or not one subscribes to these theories to explain the current condition of Latinos/as in the United States, the unequal treatment of Latinos/as in the United States is unquestionable. From the Treaty of Guadalupe-Hidalgo and the Treaty of Paris to the rise of contemporary anti-immigrant and anti-bilingual movements, most Latinos/as have been affected by a long series of events and practices that have dehumanized them and de-legitimized their right to political, social, and economic advancement in relation to the dominant society.

Although the United States has seen progress away from some of the most virulent forms of oppression, including slavery and *de jure* segregation, prejudice and discrimination remain a part of the Latino/a experience in the United States (Healey 2006; Schaefer 2004). Media images of Latinos/as continue to be stereotypically negative (Berg 2002; Delgado and Stefancic 1992) or rare (Hoffman 2003). The plethora of negative images of Latinos and Latinas in U.S. films—such as the stereotypical "bandito" in Westerns or the incorrigible inner-city drug-user or criminal—has been difficult to overcome and still resonates in Hollywood and throughout U.S. society (Berg 2002, 270). The power of misrepresentations in the news and entertainment media assures that Latinos/as are likely to remain objects of prejudice and discrimination in the future.

Media images also serve to reinforce biases that surface in the operations of the criminal justice system. Racial biases, as discussed in this chapter, often surface in association with abuses of police authority and other racially-motivated practices. With respect to the criminal justice system, criminologists Samuel Walker, Miriam DeLone, and Cassia C. Spohn find in their "analysis of race and crime in the United States ... that those who conclude that 'the criminal justice system is not racist' are misinformed ... the U.S. criminal justice system has never been, and is not now, color-blind" (2007, 423).[9] As other scholars have also shown, this conclusion holds true for Latinos/as, not only in the area of criminal justice, but in virtually all aspects of U.S. society (Delgado and Stefancic 1998; Perea et al. 2000; Haney López 2003; Mirandé 1987).

Understanding that racial and ethnic bias persists, the question becomes one of how to create a more just society for all. With more than one in eight people in the United States being of Latin American descent and with that segment of the population continuing to grow (Bureau of the Census 2002b, 1), it is more urgent than ever that access to justice and equality be made available for Latinos/as and other people of color. If not, Latinos/as run the risk

---

9. Specifically, Samuel Walker, Miriam Delone, and Cassia C. Spohn (2007) refute the assertions of William Wilbanks (1987).

of being permanently condemned to marginalization, discrimination, and injustice, and forced to engage in an unending struggle for their rights.

CHAPTER 4

Latinos/as and the U.S. Justice System: Present and Absent

Beyond the problems identified previously, this chapter delves further directly into issues related to the quality of justice afforded Latinos/as in the United States. This probe not only looks into Latino/a representation in the prison system, but it also considers the impact that the lack of meaningful Latino/a representation has on the administration of justice. The potential that an increased presence of Latino/a professionals within the justice system has to enhance the system's ability to afford greater equality and access to justice is also discussed.

To further the discussion on the Latino/a experience of the justice system, this chapter contains a case study of the Latino Officers Association (LOA), a group actively engaged in the criminal justice system. While the presentation of this group's position here does not purport to be representative of all Latinos/as in law enforcement, LOA represents a contemporary wave of Latino/a activism and advocacy within the justice system. LOA speaks for a sizable and visible group among Latinos/as inside law enforcement agencies. As such, its stance on and their insights into the justice system have become invaluable for the broadening of our understanding and addressing the pressing concerns of Latino/a communities regarding the administration of justice. Its views allow us to reflect on the ways law enforcement currently functions and assist in envisioning ways that may make the justice system more effective and just.

Latinos/as and Over-Representation in the Criminal Justice System

Statistics routinely reflect the alarming racial and ethnic disparity that exists in incarceration rates in the United States. The United States is considered the country with the highest rate of incarceration in the world. The Bureau of Justice Statistics reported that by 2002 one in every 143 U.S. residents was in prison or in jail (2003d, 2), and that incarceration rates continue to climb. In analyzing U.S. census data for 2000, Human Rights Watch (2002) indicated that "[o]ut of a total population of 1,976,019 incarcerated in adult facilities, 1,239,946 or 63 percent are black or Latino, though these groups combined constitute only 25 percent of the national population" (1). In 2002, of a total of 1,291,326 prisoners sentenced under state or federal jurisdiction, 235,000 were Latino and 15,000 were Latina, with Latino men representing 18.1 percent of prisoners under state or federal incarceration (Bureau of Justice Statistics 2003d, 9). By midyear 2006, persons incarcerated in state or federal prisons or local jails totaled 2,042,100, and of these prisoners, Latinos/as comprised 426,000 or 20.9 percent at a time when the total Latino/a population in the entire country is estimated at 14.8 percent (Bureau of Justice Statistics 2007b, 9; Bureau of the Census 2007).

According to the Bureau of Justice Statistics (1997, 9), Latinos/as represent "the fastest growing minority group being imprisoned". From 1985 to 1995, "the number of Hispanics in prison rose by 219%, with an average 12.3% increase each year" (9). In 1985, Latinos/as represented 10.9% of all state and federal inmates, and by 1995 the percentage had grown to 15.5% (9). Since then, annual growth in the Latino/a prisoner population has continued. The total percentage of Latino/a prisoners in state and federal jurisdictions by yearend 2004 had grown to 19.2 % (Bureau of Justice Statistics, 2005, 8).

In 2004, the rate of Latino/a incarceration in State and Federal prisons was 2.6 times greater than for Whites (1,220 per 100,000 compared to 463 per 100,000) (Bureau of Justice Statistics, 2005). As Walker, Senger, Villarruel, and Arboleda point out (2004, 105), "[o]ne in four federal prison inmates is Latino, even though fewer than one in eight U.S. residents is Latino." However grave these statistics appear, the severity of the problem of Latino/a incarceration becomes evermore evident when one considers its exponential growth over the last two decades.

A closer look at the incarceration rates of Latinos/as reveals an extremely disturbing picture:

- In ten states, Latino men are incarcerated at rates between five and nine times greater than those of white men.
- In eight states, Latina women are incarcerated at rates that are between four and seven times greater than those of white women.
- In four states, Hispanic youths under age eighteen are incarcerated in adult facilities at rates between seven and seventeen times greater than those of white youth. (Human Rights Watch 2002, 2)

At first glance, these statistics can lead one to conclude that Latinos/as are simply committing more crimes than Whites. However, contrary to the impression left by incarceration data, empirical and other evidence suggest a more complex situation and point to other factors that need to be taken into account in any analysis. Like African Americans, Latinos/as emerge as trapped by the phenomenon known as *mass imprisonment* (Garland 2001a). Many factors appear to converge to produce the increasing number of Latino/a prisoners. As with African Americans, the construction of race in the United States provides fertile ground for the unequal treatment of Latinos/as within the criminal justice system and elsewhere. While not identical, the Latino/a experience in the United States tends to mirror the many patterns of domination and subordination endured by African Americans. Adverse perceptions of and policies toward anyone considered non-white have been prevalent throughout U.S. history. It is an ignominious past that has had a lasting and negative impact on many groups, including Latinos/as. Similar to African Americans, Latinos/as have also suffered indignities of *de jure* segregation in the past, and in the present, they endure high levels of *de facto* segregation throughout the United States. Arguably, Latinos/as are also affected by "hyper-incarceration" and the symbiotic relationship between prison and the ghetto identified by Wacquant (2001) when examining the mass incarceration of African Americans.

Influential in producing high incarceration rates that disproportionately impact on persons of color is the manner by which policy on public safety is formulated around crime and the fear of crime, and the role of the media in promoting fear and negative images (Simon, 2007; Beckett and Sasson, 2004; Western, 2006). As many analysts suggest (e.g., Haney López, 2003; Harris, 2002; Garland, 2001a, 2001b; Beckett, 1997), examining the conventional operation of the court, law enforcement, and the criminal justice systems provides insights into the development of the racial and ethnic disparities evident in the penal system.

The considerable disparities in race and ethnicity are not just due to the incidence of crime in communities of color but also correlate with biases that have an impact on the operations of the justice system. Of course, disparities *per se* do not prove discrimination, but when controlling for numerous factors other than bias, discrimination often appears as one that explains the differences found between the treatment of people of color and that of Whites within the criminal justice system. After accounting for differences in crime rates in communities (Spitzer 1999, x) or varying levels of respect for police (Walker et al. 2007, 125), the only factor left that accounts for the disparities in treatment in the justice system appears to be discrimination.

Regarding their disproportionate rate of incarceration specifically, common misperceptions about Latinos/as and crime seemingly contribute to their over-representation in prison populations. As shown in various studies (see, e.g., Office of National Drug Control Policy 2003; Hagan and Palloni 1999), Latinos/as are not necessarily any more prone to illicit drug activity than Whites nor are Latino/a immigrants more inclined to engage in criminal conduct than any other group. Nevertheless, Latinos/as are visibly overrepresented in federal prisons among those convicted of drug and immigration-related offenses (Walker et al. 2007, 346). Similarly, despite strong evidence in support for the contrary conclusion, the Latino/a immigrants are typically assumed linked to increases in criminal activity. Thus, racial and ethnic biases serve to make Latino/a immigrants vulnerable to law enforcement crackdowns.

The Mass Imprisonment Phenomenon and Latino/a Prisoners

A major factor in Latino/a imprisonment rates is the phenomenon of *mass imprisonment*. As defined by Garland (2001a, 1, 2), mass imprisonment is characterized by unprecedented high rates of incarceration that are "markedly above the historical and comparative norm for all societies of this type," and by the incarceration not of individuals but "the systematic imprisonment of whole groups of the population." With an incarceration rate six to ten times higher, the United States far surpasses other comparable European and Scandinavian countries (1). Additionally, Latinos/as increasingly appear to meet the criterion of a group systematically subjected to disproportionately high levels of imprisonment.

Citing LaFree et al. (1992) and Sampson and Lauritsen (1997), Loïc Wacquant (2001, 82) points out that racial inequality in the penal system becomes most discernible when one considers how the ethnic composition of prisoners in the United States was dramatically reversed, "turning over from 70 percent white at the mid-century point to nearly 70 percent black and Latino today, although ethnic patterns of criminal activity have not been fundamentally altered during that period." Focusing on the African American experience, Wacquant (2001) posits that the current ethno racial makeup of the prisons is part of a continuum that can be traced to the institutions that have historically provided the means for dominating and dividing persons based on race and ethnicity. Wacquant (2001, 83–84) argues that just as the institutions of slavery and Jim Crow provided the means to keep "African Americans 'in their place,' i.e., in a subordinate and confined position in physical, social, and symbolic space" in earlier times, the ghetto and the ever-expanding prison system in the United States in the post-Civil Rights era form "a *carceral continuum* that ensnares a supernumerary population of younger black men, who either reject or are rejected by the deregulated low-wage labor market, in a never-ending circulus between the two institutions." He states that a symbiotic relationship between ghetto and prison "enforces and perpetuates the socioeconomic marginality and symbolic taint of the urban black sub proletariat, feeding the runaway growth of the penal system that has become a major component of the post-Keynesian state" (84). Wacquant further asserts that this symbiosis "plays a pivotal role in the remaking of 'race' and the redefinition of the citizenry via the production of a racialized public culture of vilification of criminals" (84).

If applied to Latinos/as in the United States, Wacquant's thesis resonates as similarly applicable, given the historical and present-day Latino/a experience and place in U.S. society. Regarding the question as to which groups are most vulnerable to incarceration at present, it is worth noting that, in addition to African Americans, other groups considered "non-white" were typically subordinated and targeted for discrimination throughout U.S. history. As early as 1740, the South Carolina Slave Code, identified "the people commonly called negroes, Indians, mulattos and mestizos have [been] deemed absolute slaves, and the subjects of property in the hands of particular persons the extent of whose power over slaves ought to be settled and limited by positive laws so that the slaves may be kept in due subjection and obedience" (quoted in Hall, Wiecek, and Finkelman, 1996, 37). Indeed, as the institution of slavery evolved in the United States, a person considered a mulatto or a person "of mixed race" was presumed to be a slave (191). This history provides insight into to how Latinos/as would be regarded in later years, since persons of mixed racial backgrounds, as many Latinos/as are, have been and often continue to be viewed with disdain and subject to discrimination by the dominant "White" social structure. Consonant with Wacquant's analysis about African Americans, Latinos/as are perceived as a class of poor people of color that pose a threat to the social order, and thus must be controlled and dominated.

As discussed in earlier chapters, throughout history race has played a central role in defining U.S. laws and policies toward Latin Americans and subsequently toward Latinos/as in the United States. The notion of Latin Americans as racially "other," and therefore inferior to Anglo Americans, was key to justifying the U.S. imperial enterprise of the 1800s, including U.S. conquests in Mexico and the colonization of Puerto Rico and of other islands and peoples. Racism was also at the core of laws that discriminated against Latinos/as, such as the 1855 "Greaser Act;" it was at the heart of a system of schools that segregated "Mexican" children from White children; and it is at the center of controversies involving police-Latino/a community relations and the general treatment of Latinos/as in U.S. society at present.

Consistent with Wacquant's hypothesis, many Latinos/as in the United States have experienced patterns of ghettoization similar to those of African Americans in the post-1960s Civil Rights period. Many often live in highly segregated and mostly poor areas of cities, such as Los Angeles and New York, where they have been susceptible to abuse by law enforcement officers and the criminal justice system (see Chapter 5). Indeed, Wacquant (2001, 101), citing Ellis (1993), observes that by "the late 1980s, three of every four inmates serving a sentence in the prisons of the entire state of the New York came from only *seven* black and Latino neighborhoods of New York City which also happen to be the poorest areas of the metropolis, chief among them Harlem, the South Bronx, East New York, and Brownsville."

The experience of Latinos/as who have lived under *de facto* segregation since the middle of the twentieth century is similar to that described by Wacquant (2001, 84), having gone from living in ghettos that resemble prisons to prisons that are now like ghettos. It should not come as a surprise, then, that analysts have concluded that Latino/a dissatisfaction and disillusionment with the criminal justice system was manifested through their participation in the unrest that followed the acquittal of the White police officers involved in the Rodney King verdict in 1992, with a majority of those arrested during the disturbances being Latino/a and a considerable amount of damage occurring in areas where Latinos/as live (Martínez, 1993; Pastor, 1993).

CRIME POLICIES
AND THEIR IMPACT ON LATINOS/AS

Given that national data show a decline in the number of crimes committed since the 1990s, it appears that "[c]rime rates themselves may not have driven the prison boom, but long-standing fears about crime and other social anxieties may form the backdrop for the growth in imprisonment" (Western 2006, 48). As Beckett (1997) notes, since the 1960s politics and policymaking shifted from the "war on poverty" to the "war on crime" and the "war on drugs," often linking poverty with crime, especially in "minority" communities. Notions about rehabilitation through the penal system gave way to a bourgeoning "culture of control" with fear-mongering images of criminals as virtually irredeemable " 'career criminals', 'drug addicts', 'thugs' and 'yobs' " (Garland 2001b, 135). Coupled with this imagery is the profound racialization of the victims, "not all victims, but primarily white, suburban, middle-class victims, whose exposure has driven waves of crime legislation" (Simon 2007, 76). Moreover, modern crime legislation has come to represent victims in many powerfully symbolic ways, even when victims may not be referenced in the legislation, and thus

> police are often portrayed in such legislation as victims themselves, not only of criminals, but of defense lawyers, soft-on-crime judges, misguided parole and probation officers, and so on. Prison cells, meanwhile, are the purest expression of the public's embrace of and promise to protect the victims, and potential victims, of crime. (Simon 2007, 76)

Although crime dropped by almost one-third between 1993 and 2000, crime continues to dominate both the news and entertainment media (Beckett and Sasson 2004, 43, 100). To the extent that the media's influence on public policy can be measured, it appears to "encourage punitive attitudes, especially when the offenders depicted are African American" (101). Hence, the power of the media lies not only in its ability to project fear but also in its capacity to convey a highly racialized picture of crime to the public.

Latinos/as and Drugs

Fear of violent crime has been a primary reason for adopting stiffer penalties that aim to incarcerate violent offenders. However, it has not generally been the case that those in prison are there primarily for having committed violent offenses. Over the last decade, more than half of the prison population consists of nonviolent drug offenders (Human Rights Watch 2003, 1). Persons sentenced for nonviolent drug offenses constituted the largest group of federal prisoners at 55 percent in 2003 and 60 percent in 2002 (Bureau of Justice Statistics 2006b, 10).[1] From 1995 to 2003, of the prisoners held in state facilities, violent offenders have most often constituted only half of those incarcerated: 46.5 percent in 1995, 49 percent in 2001, and 51.8 in 2003 (Bureau of Justice Statistics 2003b, 1; 2006b, 9).

The "get-tough" strategy commonly referred to as the "war on drugs" is now "the single greatest force behind the growth of the prison population" (Human

---

1. The Bureau of Justice Statistics (2001, 12, table 19) distinguishes between violent crimes, such as homicides and robbery, and nonviolent crimes, such as property offenses (e.g., burglary and fraud), drug offenses, and public-order offenses (e.g., immigration and weapons violations).

Rights Watch 2003, 1). This is a strategy that has been increasingly recognized as a "war" that is being fought almost entirely in Latino/a and African-American communities. It is based largely on an assumption that communities of color bear most of the responsibility for drug-related crime in the country (Cole 2001; Donziger 1996; Human Rights Watch 2003; Walker et al. 2007).

However, as pointed out in Chapter 3, Latinos/as are no more inclined to engage in illegal drug activity than Whites. In fact, the White House's own Office of National Drug Control Policy (2003, 1) cites the 2002 National Survey on Drug Use and Health to show that 54 percent of Whites report having used illicit drugs over a lifetime, followed by African Americans at 43.8 percent. As for Latinos/as, "[t]he lowest rate of lifetime illicit drug use was among Hispanics (38.9%) and Asians (25.6%)" (1). In addition, the Office of National Drug Control Policy found that "[o]f 12th graders, whites tended to have the highest rates of use for a number of drugs, including inhalants, hallucinogens, LSD, ecstasy, heroin without a needle, amphetamines, sedatives (barbiturates), tranquilizers, and narcotics other than heroin" (2).[2]

In stark contrast to these statistics reflecting a lower illicit drug use by Latinos/as as compared to Whites, the "collateral effects" of the war on drugs on communities of color have been "devastating," with arrests of Latinos/as and African Americans for drug offenses skyrocketing (Donziger 1996, 116). For instance, of a total of 23,784 federal offenders charged with drug trafficking in 2001, most were Latino/a (44.7%) while only about a quarter (26.2%) were White and 28.4 percent were African American (U.S. Sentencing Commission 2001, 14, table 4).

For state prisons, the statistics are similarly dire. In 1996, 40 percent of Latinos/as sentenced to state prisons were serving time for drug-related crimes (Bureau of Justice Statistics 1999, 6). In considering available evidence of high drug use among Whites, in some instances higher, than other groups, it seems inconceivable that Latinos/as and African Americans comprised 92 percent of drug arrests in New York City in 1991 (Donziger 1996, 116). The disproportionately high rate of incarceration of people of color has brought severe criticism of strict drug laws, such as the Rockefeller drug laws in New York State that require mandatory minimum sentencing. The impact of these drug laws on communities of color has been so extreme that it has even become popular for politicians, including New York's Governor George Pataki, to call for

---

2. The Office of National Drug Control Policy cites the results of a National Institute on Drug Abuse and University of Michigan study entitled *Monitoring the Future, National Survey Results on Drug Use, 1975–2002, Volume II: College Students & Adults Ages 19–40* (U.S. Department of Health and Human Services 2003).

changes in the Rockefeller drug laws (25). Nevertheless, the "tough-on-crime" narrative remains a staple of political campaigns, as no politician wants to look weak on the crime issue. Politics plays a significant role in the push for toward longer sentences and more prisons (Donziger 1996; Jacobson 2005; Beckett and Sasson 2004; Simon 2007).

Prisoner Disenfranchisement and "Phantom Constituents"

There are many political advantages to be garnered from mass incarceration. Felony disenfranchisement laws greatly diminish the political power of communities of color in relation to dominant power structure (Fellner and Mauer 1998; McLeod, White and Gavin 2003). Currently, almost all U.S. states (48 states and the District of Columbia) have laws that restrict prisoners' voting rights. With the striking growth of the penal complex over the last 30 years, these laws have had a significant impact on the level and the type of political participation throughout the country (Sentencing Project 2007). The Sentencing Project (2007) estimates that "5.3 million Americans, or one in forty-one adults, have currently or permanently lost their voting rights as a result of a felony conviction"; "1.4 million African American men, or 13% of black men, are disenfranchised, at a rate seven times the national average"; "[g]iven current rates of incarceration, three in ten of the next generation of black men can expect to be disenfranchised at some point in their lifetime"; and [i]n states that disenfranchise ex-offenders, as many as 40% of black men may permanently lose their right to vote."

As is the case with African Americans, Latino/a political power is diminished by felony disenfranchisement. Latinos/as are incarcerated at a rate that is almost double (1.8 times more) that of Whites—742 per 100,000 for Latinos/as as compared to 412 per 100,000 for Whites (Sentencing Project 2007b, 14). However, incarceration rates vary among states, and in some states the Latino/a-to-White ratio reaches a high of 6.6 (14).[3] Compared to the White population, the impact of voter disenfranchisement is greater in relation to Latinos/as in states with sizable Latino/a populations, and their political voice is diminished as a consequence.

Along with felony disenfranchisement, the fact that the federal Census counts state and federal prisoners as part of the local population can further

---

3. Sixteen states have a higher Latino/a-to-White ratio than the national average of 1.8. Some of these states include Massachusetts with a 6.1 ratio; Pennsylvania at 5.6; the District of Columbia at 4.8; and New York at 4.5 (Sentencing Project 2007b, 14).

exacerbate the problem of unequal political power. A report by the Prison Policy Initiative (2007), *Phantom Constituents in the Empire State: How Outdated Census Bureau Methodology Burdens New York Counties*, explains that prisoners are counted as residents, even though they are unable to vote or be politically active in the communities where they are imprisoned. This results in an unequal distribution of political power in New York State. As the Executive Director of the non-profit Prison Policy Initiative, Peter Wagner, explains:

> The Prison Policy Initiative identified 15 counties, plus New York City, that rely on census counts of prison populations when they draw lines for county legislative districts or weigh the votes for county boards of supervisors. The report finds five counties—Chautauqua, Livingston, Oneida, Madison, and St. Lawrence—where relying on faulty Census data created districts that were at least 20% prisoners. In such a district, every group of eight residents has the same voting power as 10 residents in other districts. Some counties have even larger vote dilution problems. For example, 62% of the people counted by the Census in Groveland are incarcerated, giving every group of four residents in Groveland the same say over county affairs as 10 residents elsewhere in the county. (Wagner 2007)

Although not a subject addressed in the Prison Policy Initiative report, it is equally important to note that in New York City African Americans and Latinos/as convicted of crimes most often serve their sentences in upstate prison facilities where they are counted as part of the population. This further tips political power upstate where there is a larger White population and away from New York City, where persons of color comprise a majority of the population.

Legal and public advocacy challenges to felony disenfranchisement laws are being made by a broad range of organizations based on violations of constitutional, state and federal law, and international human rights standards. The Prison Policy Initiative, the Sentencing Project and Human Rights Watch are among the many groups addressing this problem.

Selective Prosecutions

A number of studies point out that contributing to the problem of the disproportionate rate of incarcerated people of color is the link between the operations of the criminal justice system—and the courts in particular—with racial and ethnic bias and selective prosecutions. As Walker, Spohn and Delone have found:

> There is evidence that defendant race/ethnicity continues to affect de-
> cisions regarding bail, charging and plea bargaining.... If racial mi-
> norities are more likely than whites to be represented by incompetent
> attorneys or detained in jail prior to trial, they may, as a result of
> these differences, face greater odds of conviction and harsher sen-
> tences. Racially discriminatory charging decisions have similar
> "spillover" effects at trial. (2007, 194)

One study conducted in Los Angeles revealed that Latino males were most likely to be prosecuted fully (42 percent), followed by African American (26 percent) and White males (39 percent) (Spohn, Gruhl, and Welch 1987). In another study, a similar pattern of prosecutorial decisions was discovered and attributed to indirect and subtle forms of discrimination against people of color (Crutchfield et al. 1995). Other studies show that Whites are more often given reduced sentences or plea bargains and more frequently granted larger reductions of sentences than people of color (Bernstein et al. 1977; Albonetti 1997; Maxfield and Kramer 1998). Thus, evidence of selectiveness in prose-cutorial practices and other forms of unequal treatment in the courts com-bined with policies that exaggerate the occurrence of drug-related crimes among Latinos/as contribute to unequal and unfair outcomes in the justice system and, in particular, higher rates of incarceration of Latinos/as and other people of color.

Other studies have found that some policies and practices of the criminal justice system have a negative impact on Latinos/as and their rates of impris-onment. Pretrial detentions, for instance, have been found to increase the probability of a prison sentence after trial (Hood 1992; Petersilia and Turner 1986). Further, research has shown that bail, which is extended to persons still under the presumption of innocence before trial, is less likely to be granted to Latinos/as, making them more vulnerable to pretrial detention (Walker et al. 2007, 174–84). Although the lack of financial resources to make bail certainly accounts, in part, for pretrial detentions, researchers have also concluded that race and ethnicity may influence judges' decisions regarding bail (182–84). Given these circumstances, Latinos/as are more at risk than Whites of being denied bail, and thus of pretrial detention, which in turn results in the dis-proportionate rates of incarceration.

The Discriminatory Impact of Sentencing Laws and Practices

The disproportionately high rate of incarceration of people of color has provoked criticism of laws that have brought changes in sentencing policies and practices—including strict mandatory minimum sentencing laws, "three-strikes" legislation, and so-called "truth in sentencing" laws, designed to replace indeterminate sentences with clearly defined penalties without the possibility of early release on parole (Jacobson 2005, 45). The possibility that stricter state and federal sentencing policies have had a discriminatory impact on people of color has been a subject of considerable study (Walker et al., 2007, 231–80). Some prominent analysts affirm that changes in sentencing guidelines may have worsened the racial divide within the criminal justice system (e.g., Tonry 1995). Others conclude that, on balance, discrimination occurs and harsher penalties are imposed, but within certain contexts, as when a person of color is accused of a crime against a White person as opposed to when the crime is against another person of color (Walker et al. 2007, 280).

Studies that specifically look at bias against Latinos/as in sentencing reveal a consistent pattern. In analyzing sentencing data collected by the State Court Processing Statistics program of the Bureau of Justice Statistics for the years 1990, 1992, 1994, and 1996, Demuth and Steffensmeier (2004, 1008) found that "in general, Hispanic defendants were sentenced more similarly to black defendants than white defendants. Both black and Hispanic defendants tended to receive harsher sentences than white defendants."

In an earlier study that examines ethnicity as well as race as a factor in sentencing using quantitative and qualitative data gathered on Pennsylvania sentencing practices, Steffensmeier and Demuth (2001) show that Latinos/as are susceptible to harsher penalties because of the prevalence of negative stereotypes and biases that associate Latinos/as with illegal drugs activities, low intelligence, and the rise in neighborhood crime. Their qualitative data reinforces this conclusion, with one particular Pennsylvania judge from a county with an expanding Latino/a population stating:

> We shouldn't kid ourselves. I have always prided myself for not being prejudiced but it is hard not to be affected by what is taking place. The whole area has changed with the influx of Hispanics and especially Puerto Ricans. You'd hardly recognize the downtown from what it was a few years ago. There's more dope, more crime, more people on welfare, more problems in school. (Steffensmeier and Demuth, 2001, 168)

A comprehensive review of bias in the courts confirms a familiar pattern: Both Latinos/as and African Americans experience bias in sentencing practices and policies, and as a result, they receive harsher sentences than Whites. An examination of forty recent and methodologically sophisticated studies on the effects of race and ethnicity on sentencing—including 32 studies of state court decisions and eight studies of federal court decisions—concluded that

> Black and Hispanic offenders—and particularly those who are young, male, or unemployed—are more likely than their white counterparts to be sentenced to prison; they also may receive longer sentences than similarly situated white offenders. Other categories of racial minorities—those convicted of drug offenses, those who victimize whites, those who accumulate more serious prior criminal records, or those who refuse to plead guilty or are unable to secure pretrial release—also may be singled out for more punitive treatment. (Spohn 2000, 481–82)

The Sentencing Reform Act of 1984, 28 U.S.C. 991 (b)(1)(B) (Supp. 1993), designed to prevent "unwarranted sentencing disparity among defendants with similar records who had been found guilty of similar criminal conduct" does not appear to have eliminated the influence of legally irrelevant factors, such as racial and ethnic characteristics and immigrant status, on sentencing decisions. Based on data regarding 14,189 defendants convicted of drug offenses, Albonetti (1997, 817) points out that in spite of the new federal sentencing guidelines adopted as a result of the Sentencing Reform Act of 1984 "judges impose significantly more severe sentences on defendants who are not U.S. citizens and on defendants who are black or Hispanic."

It is also important to note that biased sentencing is possible because federal judges can circumvent strict sentencing guidelines:

> Although the federal sentencing guidelines severely constrain judges' discretion in deciding between prison and probation and in determining the length of the sentence, they place only minimal restrictions on the ability of judges (and prosecutors) to reduce sentences for substantial assistance or acceptance of responsibility. Mandatory minimum sentences also can be avoided through charge manipulation. (Walker et al. 2007, 273)

However, the studies on the effects of judicial and prosecutorial discretion on federal sentencing overwhelmingly show that African Americans and Latinos/as are treated more harshly in sentencing than Whites (Walker et al. 2007, 273). Most notably, in examining federal court data gathered by the U.S. Sentencing Commission from 1993–1996, Steffensmeier and Demuth (2000) found that the ability under the federal sentencing statute to "depart downward" from the sentencing guidelines resulted in leniency towards White defendants and harsher sentences for Latino/a and African American defendants (722).

Latino/a Immigrants and Crime

In recent years, the immigration issue has prompted considerable debate and controversy. In the course of this debate, fear and anti-immigrant sentiments have been stirred up. The false assumption that Latino/a immigrants are a significant source of crime in the country has gained ground, contributing to Latino/a vulnerability vis-à-vis law enforcement policies and practices fueled by this assumption. However, the purported link between crime and Latino/a immigrants has been shown to be more a product of the criminal justice and immigration laws, policies, and practices than anything based in reality (Hagan and Palloni 1999). In fact, research has shown that "recent immigration generally does not increase community levels of homicide" and that "immigration can be a stabilizing force that suppresses criminal violence" (Lee 2003, 80).

Perhaps no one in the national media has been as effective and persistent in the proliferation fear and false information about immigrants as CNN's Lou Dobbs. In a recent *New York Times* exposé, David Leonhardt (2007a) revealed that Lou Dobbs had falsely stated on one of his 2003 broadcasts that "One-third of the inmates now serving time in federal prisons come from some other country—one-third." Contrary to Dobb's assertions, at midyear 2005, non-citizens actually comprise less than one-fifth (19 percent) of all prisoners in federal custody—well below one-third—and non-citizens in federal and state facilities combined comprised only 6.4 percent (Bureau of Justice Statistics, 2006c, 5). As Butcher and Piehl (2005) point out, immigrants to the United States actually have lower incarceration rates than other groups in the population. While it is assumed that factors, such as low education levels and low average wages, would predispose immigrants to engage in criminal conduct, immigrants to the United States, in the main, tend to come to the country highly motivated to use their skills in forging a better life and not interested in run-ins with the law that would thwart their goal of social and economic advancement. Butcher and Piehl find that immigrants are typically self-selecting, not typical of the general population, and thus less inclined to engage in criminal behavior.

The presumed link between crime and Latino/a immigrants specifically has been shown not to be substantiated. An empirical study of Mexican immigrants revealed that "it is currently the case that immigration and criminal justice policies which appear neutral in relation to Hispanic immigrants actually

bias and distort public perceptions of immigration and crime by inflating Hispanic rates of imprisonment" (Hagan and Palloni 1999, 617). In a comparison of non-citizen immigrants and citizens in state prisons, Hagan and Palloni found that after taking into consideration factors such as age and
vulnerability to pre-trial detention, non-citizen Latino/a immigrants are actually *less* likely to be involved in crime than citizens. The study notes that
non-citizen Latino/a immigrants come to the United States with strong cultural and family traditions that are incompatible with criminal behavior
(630–31). They also noted that, not only are non-citizen Latino/a immigrants
not more involved in criminal activity, "by other measures of well-being—including smoking, alcohol consumption, drug use, and pregnancy outcomes—
Mexican immigrants are generally found to do well and sometimes better than
citizens" (630-31). To the extent that Latino/a cultural strengths serve to deter
crime, the study's authors recommend that "we may wish to place the priority in policy formation on ways to preserve, protect, and promote the social
and cultural capital that Mexican immigrants bring to their experience in the
United States. The increasing reliance on imprisonment detracts from this goal
by banishing immigrant males from their families and communities" (631).

Latino/a immigrants are generally recognized as underserved by law enforcement agencies and susceptible to negative experiences with the criminal
justice system because they face numerous obstacles to establishing good relations with police and other law enforcement agencies—including language
barriers and fear of being subject to immigration law enforcement (Walker et
al. 2007, 107). In the period following the events of September 11, 2001,
heightened enforcement of federal immigration laws has rendered Latino/a
immigrants increasingly vulnerable. Not surprisingly, the number of persons
detained by the U.S. Immigration and Customs Enforcement (ICE) agency
"more than doubled between 1995 and 2005" (Bureau of Justice Statistics,
2006b, 10). At yearend 2005, 19,562 persons were being held for immigration
violations (10). Moreover, as Mark Dow (2004) has documented, those in the
U.S. immigration prison system are subject to horrific arbitrariness and many
forms of abuse by officials and guards, for which they are unable to seek adequate redress due to their non-citizen status.

Although organizations, such as the Mexican American Legal Defense and
Education Fund, have vehemently objected to new legislation that would further threaten the rights of immigrants, including proposed laws that would
empower state and local police to enforce federal immigration laws (Walker
et al. 2007, 117), in the current climate of anti-immigrant hostility, it is likely
that undocumented immigrants will continue to confront new efforts to criminalize their status. As Rumbaut, Gonzales, Komaie, Morgan and Tafoya-

Estrada (2006, 84) indicate, the driving forces behind the rates of incarceration of immigrants are the "myths and stereotypes about immigrants and crime [that] often provide the underpinnings for public policies and practices and shape public opinion and political behavior."

The belief that Whites are more likely to be victimized by a person of color is similar to the myths about Latino/a drug use or Latino/a immigrant crime. Data for 2000 indicate that the Latino/a rate of victimization for all forms of violent crimes was 27.9 per 1,000 while the rate of White victimization was 26.5 per 1,000 (Bureau of Justice Statistics 2002, 2). The 2002 National Crime Victimization Survey of the Bureau of Justice Statistics reports that of all persons young African American males are most likely to be victims of violence (Bureau of Justice Statistics 2003b). "Hispanics and non-Hispanics were victims of violence at similar rates during 2002, with one exception: Hispanics were more likely than non-Hispanics to be victims of aggravated assault" (8). As for hate crimes, FBI statistics reveal that African Americans and Latinos/as are most often the victims of hate crime along with Asians and persons identified as being of "mixed race" (Walker et al. 2007, 61).

Latinos/as and Under-Representation in the Justice System

The deeply-rooted and often mistaken concerns about Latinos/as in relation to crime tend to overshadow the need for Latinos/as to become part of the justice system as lawyers, judges, jurors, and other professionals, lending their skills and services to make the system more effective and equitable. Given the disproportionate Latino/a presence within the prison system, the absence of Latina and Latino professionals in the legal process becomes even more conspicuous and necessary to address. Moreover, since our legal system is based on the principle of trial by one's peers, it is also important to address the difficulties Latinos/as face being chosen as jurors.

The Lack of Latino/a Lawyers and Judges

The under-representation of Latinos/as in the justice system is most evident in the lack of Latino/a lawyers and judges. Many studies identify Latinos/as as having high rates of involvement in the judicial system, either as defendants or plaintiffs (Moore and Pachon 1985; Reynoso 2000; Falcón 2002, 2). In stark contrast, however, the number of Latina and Latino attorneys and judges in the United States remains extremely low. The American Bar Association (ABA)

Commission on Racial and Ethnic Diversity in the Profession reports that in 1999 only 5.7 percent of all those enrolled in law schools nationwide were Latino/a while African Americans were 7.4 percent, Asians were 6.3 percent, and Native Americans were less than 1 percent (Chambliss 2000, 3). In 1998, people of color made up 7 percent of all lawyers and only 3 percent of all partners in law firms (1, 9). More specifically, only 2.8 percent of all lawyers are Latino/a while Whites comprise 92.6 percent (U.S. News and World Report 2003).

Further, as the number of people of color in law school decreases, the number of people of color entering the profession will continue to drop. The ABA's Commission on Racial and Ethnic Diversity in the Profession (n.d.) points out that from the academic years of 2001–02 to 2003–04, the representation of students of color among law students dropped from 20.6 percent to 20.3 percent.[4]

The ABA also posits that increasing the number of people of color entering the legal profession has been hindered by efforts to abolish affirmative action in recent years (Chambliss 2000, 2, 3). After many years of controversy, in the case of *Grutter v. Bollinger*, 539 U.S. 306 (2003), the U.S. Supreme Court in 2003 ruled in favor of affirmative action programs similar to that of the University of Michigan Law School. But, despite this important victory in favor of diversity, attacks against affirmative action over the last decade have been proven to have set back law school enrollment of people of color, especially in states that banned affirmative action (Chambliss 2000, 1).[5]

---

4. Professor Leonard Baynes, who has been examining trends in New York State, finds that "[b]etween 2000 and 2005, African-American enrollment in the 15 New York State laws schools dropped approximately 20 percent, from 7.7 percent of all New York States law students in 2000 to 6.2 percent of law students in 2005. Latino/a enrollment dropped approximately 6 percent during the same period, from 6.4 percent of New York State Law students in 2000 to 6 percent in 2005" (Roach 2007, 18). Among the factors contributing to this decline is the overuse and misuse of the Law School Admission Test (LSAT) by law schools that have raised their admissions test scores to increase their U.S. News and World Report ranking (Baynes 2006).

5. In a case involving two public school districts (*Parents Involved in Community Schools v. Seattle School District No. 1*; *Meredith v. Jefferson County Board of Education*, 127 S. Ct. 2738; 168 L. Ed. 2d 508 [2007]), the U.S. Supreme Court in a 5-4 decision struck down the use of race in making school assignments to promote integration. Although the Court sought to distinguish this decision from the one in *Grutter v. Bollinger*, 539 U.S. 306 (2003), some legal analysts, including noted legal scholar Derrick Bell, contend that the decision portends a dim future for diversity in higher education (Bell 2007, B11). Moreover, Professor Leonard Baynes asserts that the Supreme Court's decision could result in the abandonment of the main goal of the 1954 *Brown v. Board of Education* decision to create a system of integrated schools. He notes that the decision may leave "few avenues for local and

The scarcity of people of color in law school is so acute that even the ABA concedes that the legal profession has one of the lowest levels of representation of people of color among all professions:

> Minority representation among lawyers lags well behind minority representation in most other professions. In 1998, African Americans and Hispanics made up 12.5 percent of all professionals, including 14.3 percent of accountants, 9.7 percent of physicians, 9.4 percent of college and university teachers, and 7.9 percent of engineers but only 7 percent of lawyers. The professions with lower levels of minority representation were dentists (4.8 percent) and natural scientists (6.9 percent). (Chambliss 2000, 2)

In a study sponsored by the Puerto Rican Legal Defense and Education Fund, Angelo Falcón (2002) reports that the degree of Latino/a under-representation in the judiciary is extraordinarily high. Moreover, given the ever-increasing Latino/a population he projects an almost insurmountable gap in the future. Using disparity ratios to examine levels of representation, Falcón found a significant gap between the percentage of Latinos/as in the population and Latinos/as on the bench:

> The percentage of Hispanic-Americans holding federal judgeships was 3.7 percent in 2000, compared to 3.8 percent of those holding state judgeships.... Dividing these percentages by the Hispanic percentage of the total U.S. population (12.5 percent) yields Hispanic judgeship disparity ratios of −70.4 percent at the federal level and −69.7 percent at the state level. (Falcón 2002, 3)

Raising grave concerns about fairness in the judicial system, Falcón warns that if current trends persist an even larger disparity will result, with the percentage of Latino/a judges only growing slightly over time. "[B]y the year 2050 (when the Census conservatively projects the Hispanic-American population to reach 24.3 percent of the total population), the number of Hispanic-American judges would have grown to 4.7 percent in the federal courts and 5.3 percent in the state courts" (4).

Whether or not the judicial system would function more fairly simply with an increase in the number of Latino/a judges may be open to some debate. Nonetheless, with regard to African American judges, some scholars view

---

state governments to legally equalize educational opportunities or eliminate the racial isolation of K-12 students" (Baynes 2007).

African American judges as more capable of understanding poor defendants and the experience of communities of color, resulting in decisions that may be more conducive to fairness (Welch, Combs, and Gruhl 1988). Regarding sentencing decisions, other scholars have found few differences between White judges and African American judges (Engle 1971; Uhlman 1978; Spohn 1990; Spears 1999).

However, in a study comparing White judges and Latino/a judges, Holmes, Hosch, Daudistel, Perez, and Graves (1993) found that Latino/a judges sentenced White and Latino/a offenders alike, but White judges levied harsher sentences on Latinos/as. Thus, this study suggests that Latino/a judges produce fairer decisions than White judges. Interestingly, the researchers rationalize that "Anglo judges are not so much discriminating against Hispanic defendants as they are favoring members of their ethnic group" (502). Of course, if White judges were treating groups unequally based on race or ethnicity, they would, by definition, be acting in a discriminatory manner.

Many scholars readily contend that prejudice and discrimination persistent in today's society are manifested in ways that are more subtle and indirect, with Whites tending to regard their behavior and attitudes as untainted by prejudice (Healey 2006, 125–26). How Latinos/as have been treated in the courts has also been found to reflect nuanced forms of prejudice and discrimination.

In his study of late 1960s and 1970s cases involving Chicanos in Los Angeles, Professor Ian F. Haney López (2003, 6) argues that simply acknowledging that race is a social construct is not sufficient. Instead, he points out that it is important to understand what makes racism operational. He sees racism functioning as a form of common sense informing and engendering discriminatory behavior and "rendering such behavior as normal and legitimate" (7). In describing discrimination in jury selection as experienced by Chicanos in Los Angeles, Haney López explains:

> Called upon to pick grand juries from a cross-section of Los Angeles County, the judges ... consistently nominated their friends and neighbors ... insisted that they desired only to pick qualified persons for the grand jury. But as became clear in their testimony, patterns of social, educational, residential, and workplace segregation ensured that the judges had few Mexican acquaintances, save perhaps their gardeners, and that they regarded Mexicans as unqualified to serve on the grand jury. The judges assumed that persons like themselves white, older, affluent, and male, or married to someone like that deserve that honor. For the judges, it was simply indisputable that people like themselves were dependable, competent, and qualified, mer-

iting not only a seat on the grand jury but the esteem accorded friends. Likewise, it was common knowledge to the judges that Mexicans were, well, inferior. Intentional discrimination was unnecessary. To systematically exclude Mexicans from the Los Angeles grand jury, the judges only had to rely on what seemed to them common sense. (Haney López 2003, 78)

In this context, Haney López further asserts that the normative aspects of discriminatory behavior continue to play a major part in society today (7).

In this same vein, the legal profession and the justice system tend to norm and homogenize certain behavior and to chastise any deviation from the norm. Judges, regardless of race, are influenced by the system and are probably not likely to rule much differently than the norms and practices followed within the institution that has selected them, a court system that tends to be conservative and to reinforce the middle and upper-class values and experiences of those who predominate in the judiciary (Uhlman 1978, 893; Walker et al. 2007, 262). Indeed, to buck the system can come at a great cost for a professional person of color within the justice system (Wright 1987).

Nevertheless, federal appellate court judge Sonia Sotomayor (2002) provides an important perspective on the significance of Latina and Latino representation within the judiciary. She reminds us that the experience and understanding that many venerated jurists brought to the bench were not usually brought into question, as in the cases of Oliver Wendell Holmes and Benjamin Cardozo, judges who voted on certain cases upholding gender and race discrimination. As a Latina member of the judiciary, Judge Sotomayor maintains that Latino and Latina judges must retain their identity and be able to use their experience and background, not to curry favor for their own, but to make the system fair for all: "[W]e who judge must not deny the differences resulting from experience or heritage but attempt ... continuously to judge when those opinions, sympathies and prejudices are appropriate" (92).

Latino/a Representation on Juries

The right to a jury of one's peers is a fundamental principle of the U.S. system of law. However, for many years it has also been the case that people of color have had to endure decisions made by all-White juries (see Cole 1999; Haney López 2003; Walker et al. 2007). *Hernández v. Texas*, 347 U.S. 475 (1954), stands as a testament to the historical exclusion of Latinos/as from juries in the United States. Even today, potential Latino/a jurors still encounter barriers to serving on juries. Rather than being deemed an asset, their proficiency in a second language (Spanish), may be treated as a potential liability, leading to their exclusion from a jury.

In its six-to-three decision in *Hernandez v. New York*, 500 U.S. 352 (1991), the U.S. Supreme Court held that a criminal defendant's Fourteenth Amendment right to equal protection was not violated when a prosecutor used a peremptory challenge to exclude from a jury Latino/a candidates who understood Spanish on the basis that they might not accept as the final arbiter in the case the court interpreter's version.[6] The defendant had argued that the elimination of potential Latino/a jurors violated his right to a trial by his peers which, in turn, violated his constitutional rights. But the majority in *Hernandez* explained that the prosecutor's reason for excluding Latino/a jurors was "race-neutral" because anyone, regardless of race, may be fluent in a language other than English (361–62).

In *Hernandez v. New York*, the court dodges the most obvious issue in the case: the overwhelming number of the persons in the jury pool who speak Spanish in a city like New York are going to be Latino or Latina and their exclusion through the peremptory challenge process will have an adverse impact on the make up of juries and the outcome of cases, particularly in cases where the defendant is Latino/a. The flawed reasoning of the majority opinion in *Hernandez* is exposed in Justice Stevens' dissent:

> First, the [prosecutor's] justification [for the use of the peremptory challenge] would inevitably result in a disproportionate disqualification of Spanish-speaking venire persons [prospective jurors]. An explanation that is "race neutral" on its face is nonetheless unacceptable if it is merely a proxy for a discriminatory practice. Second, the prosecutor's concern could easily have been accommodated by less drastic means. As is the practice in many jurisdictions, the jury could have been instructed that the official translation alone is evidence; bilin-

---

6. In *Batson v. Kentucky*, 476 U.S. 79 (1986), the U.S. Supreme Court held that the use of a peremptory challenge (the exclusion of a potential juror without the need to show cause) is permissible except in cases of race-based exclusions which violate the Constitution's Fourteenth Amendment Equal Protection Clause. As Del Valle notes (2003, 196), the Supreme Court in *Hernandez* did not give serious consideration to the "sociological link between race and language" critical to understanding how this situation amounted to violation of the equal protection rights of Latinos/as. She explains that the *Hernandez* Court looked narrowly at the issue of race, relying on *Batson*, and applied an intent standard that focused on the "subjective intent" of the prosecutor, rather than a disparate impact standard, which would have been more appropriate given the impact peremptory challenges have on the exclusion of Latinos/as from juries (196–98).

gual jurors could have been instructed to bring to the attention of the judge any disagreements they might have with the translation so that any disputes could be resolved by the court. See, e.g., *United States v. Perez*, 658 F.2d 654, 662–663 (CA9 1981). Third, if the prosecutor's concern was valid and substantiated by the record, it would have supported a challenge for cause. The fact that the prosecutor did not make any challenge ... should disqualify him from advancing the concern as a justification for a peremptory challenge. (*Hernandez v. New York*, 500 U.S. 352, 379 [1991])

Justice Stevens further posits that the use of peremptory challenges to disqualify Spanish-speaking venire persons is completely unnecessary: "An even more effective solution would be to employ a translator, who is the only person who hears the witness' words and who simultaneously translates them into English, thus permitting the jury to hear only the official translation" (379n2).

As the law stands today, potential Latino/a jurors may be disproportionately rejected through the use of peremptory challenges virtually anytime a prosecutor claims that he or she feels that a bilingual person would not abide by the court's official translation (Méndez 1993). In fact, in the *Hernandez* trial, prospective jurors with Latino/a surnames were systematically excluded from the jury, and no Latinos/as served on the jury (Del Valle 2003, 190–91). The *Hernandez* decision has been singled out as an example of the inability of the U.S. justice system to properly address discrimination that bilingual Latinos/as encounter in their attempt to participate in the system as jurors (Méndez 1993; Del Valle 2003).

Latinos/as in Law Enforcement

Increasing Latino/a representation in the administration of judicial and law enforcement processes should be regarded as a partial solution. It is evident that to be effective, Latino/a participation in the justice system must also be made meaningful. In line with the view expressed by Judge Sotomayor, the cultural knowledge and experience of Latino/a judges, lawyers, law enforcement personnel and jurors can and should be utilized to advance an effective and fair system of justice throughout, from local police precincts to the highest courts in the land. But this can only be made a reality if the opportunities to do so are made available.

Historically, the first obstacle communities of color have had to overcome has been that, largely because of racial and ethnic discrimination, careers in law enforcement were closed to them. Progress toward equal opportunity in employment in law enforcement began only after legal action was taken by civil rights organizations. It was the lawsuit against the City of New York and the New York Police Department (NYPD) by the Puerto Rican Legal Defense and Education Fund, for example, that eliminated at least some of the barriers Latino/a officers faced in seeking promotions. The suit successfully challenged non-job related examinations that had a disparate impact on the ability of Latino/a offices to move up the ranks in the department (*Hispanic Society of the New York City Police Department et al. v. New York City Police Department*, 42 Fair Empl. Prac. Cas. (BNA) 905, 40 Empl. Prac. Dec. (CCH) P36, 385 [S.D.N.Y. 1986], aff'd, 806 F.2d 1147 [2d Cir. 1986]).

Although nationally the percentage of Latinos/as city police officers rose from 5.2 percent in 1990 to 8.3 percent in 2000 (Bureau of Justice Statistics 2003a, 4), as police officers, Latinos/as, generally, continue to be under-represented in many cities. Under-representation is especially marked in the upper echelons of police departments, particularly from the rank of sergeant on up, with Latina women "almost completely unrepresented in the rank of sergeant and above" (Walker et al. 2007, 152).

Augmenting the number of police officers of color, while often cited as a remedy for strained police-community relations, falls short of a satisfactory remedy for the deeply entrenched problems of bias in law enforcement and problems related to a police culture predisposed to shield officers from accountability in cases of misconduct or excessive use of force.

Consistent with previously mentioned studies regarding judges, it has been found that having people of color represented among police officers alone does not necessarily bring changes in police behavior. No significant differences have been reflected in the ways that police officers of color do their jobs as compared to White officers in research involving the use of deadly force (Fyfe 1981) and arrest patterns (Black 1980). These results seem to show that officers of color are not likely to veer away from established patterns of behavior within the police force. Familiar practices and behaviors engrained in police culture appear likely to be replicated by officers of color. With few persons of color in supervisory and decision-making positions able or willing to break with traditional patterns and practices, it stands to reason that officers of color are less inclined to establish new modes of working with or viewing the communities they serve; such is their training as described further in this chapter.

Perhaps the aspect of police culture most resistant to change has been the unwritten "code of silence," by which officers refuse to provide honest testimony in order to protect their colleagues from allegations of wrongdoing (see Amnesty International 1998; Human Rights Watch 1998). Accounts of instances where an officer fails to observe the code of silence show that such behavior can exact a heavy price. Such was the case involving Latina police officer Daisy Boria of the New York City Police Department (NYPD). Officer Boria, who witnessed the death of Anthony Báez at the hands of a White police officer using a chokehold prohibited under department rules, testified about what she witnessed during police perjury and obstruction of justice testimony in the Báez case (Weiser 1998, B1). In retaliation for her honesty, Boria was reportedly harassed by fellow officers, left without back-up in dangerous situations, and eventually forced to resign (Gonzalez 1996, 21). This case serves as a cruel lesson for those Latino/a officers who defy the code of silence which rigorously protects police ranks even in egregious cases of misconduct and abuse.

Activism in Law Enforcement: The Latino Officers Association

Aside from contract disputes, rarely do police officers organize opposition to policies and practices within their police departments. However, over the years the one consistent exception has been the organizational efforts of African American and Latino/a officers, who have often challenged discriminatory department policies and practices. Indeed, as with the court case cited above, the Hispanic Society of the New York City Police Department was a lead organization in the early lawsuits that helped open opportunities for Latinos/as in the department. Further, in recent years, the emergence of the Latino Officers Association (LOA) has sparked new activism among Latino and Latina officers in the New York City Police Department. Its expansion into a national entity has given rise to its new name, the National Latino Officers Association, and its expanded role.

Founded in 1996, LOA immediately attracted headlines as a Latino/a advocacy group that successfully challenged in federal court attempts by the City and the NYPD to block the group from marching in parades while wearing their police uniforms (Weiser 1999b, B5). LOA has also backed numerous discrimination cases against the City and the NYPD on behalf of Latino/a officers. In addition to class action-oriented litigation, LOA has supported individual cases, including the case of William L. Acosta who filed suit against New York City for having wrongfully dismissed him from the police force in retaliation for uncovering police corruption (*New York Times* 1999, B7).

One of LOA's largest lawsuits involved the disproportionate number of disciplinary cases against officers of color within the NYPD. In 1997, when NYPD internal police data for 1996 revealed that 31.7 percent of the force were police officers of color, but that 54.8 percent of all departmental disciplinary charges were against officers of color, LOA and an African American officers group filed a complaint with the federal Equal Employment Opportunity Commission (*New York Times* 1997, B4). Subsequently, a lawsuit filed in 1999 charged that Latino/a and African American officers are more harshly disciplined than White officers (Weiser 1999a, B3). On February 1, 2004, the National Latino Officers Association announced that New York City agreed to settle the lawsuit filed against the New York City Police Department, former mayor Rudolph W. Giuliani, and former Police Commissioner Howard Safir for $26.8 million (Moynihan 2004, 33). While the City admitted no wrongdoing, the settlement required it to pay compensation to Latino/a and African American officers who experienced discriminatory treatment, including hostile work conditions and reprisals (33). In addition, the settlement included changes in the department's disciplinary process and compliance monitoring (Pérez 2004, A12). At its press conference, the LOA proclaimed that after a four-year court battle this settlement served as an acknowledgement of the type of internal discrimination and retaliation prevalent in the NYPD (Moynihan 2004, 33).

The spokesperson and executive director of the National Latino Officers Association is 45-year-old Anthony Miranda, a retired NYPD sergeant who served on the force for 20 years. Born to Puerto Rican parents, Miranda grew up in New York's Bedford Stuyvesant community in Brooklyn, where he still resides. Passionate and outspoken, Miranda states that the organization's mission is to promote racial and ethnic tolerance and equality and to end all forms of discrimination, sexual harassment, and retaliation against people of color in law enforcement agencies. He asserts that, to that end, LOA has successfully supported a series of legal actions. Its accomplishments have spurred the organization's growth to thousands of members. At present, its membership includes not only police officers, but law enforcement agents in corrections, probation, customs, hospitals, and other agencies. According to Miranda, LOA has established chapters outside of New York in places such as Florida, Maryland, Alaska, and Puerto Rico (Miranda 2002).

Despite LOA's achievements, Miranda considers that from the perspective of Latinos and Latinas in law enforcement many changes are still necessary. In response to the issue of increasing Latino/a representation in law enforcement, he emphasizes that a growth in the number of Latino/a officers alone does not automatically result in a police force that is sufficiently sensitive and fair toward Latino/a communities. Miranda describes how police training promotes the idea that one's sense of self should revolve exclusively around the police force over and above one's own family ties and cultural identity:

At the academy, you go through what I call a 'brainwashing period,' when they get you to stop identifying with anything else that you had outside the police department. The mentality they teach you: 'there's us and there's them.' Nobody else is going to be there for you except for us. You have to depend on us. 'We're the Blue,' and that's how we identify and you get the whole blue wall of silence thing that comes up. (Miranda 2002)

Miranda further explains that after intense and rigorous physical training, Latino/a police officers are exposed to ideas that have an enormous psychological impact. He states that officers in training are told:

we have to stick together ... these officers have gotten killed in the line of duty, and you have to understand how officers are in danger all of the time, and you're going to be a target, and people are always going to be looking at us, and that type of thing. So you grow into that identity that you have to stick together. You have to depend on each other. You can't depend on somebody outside of our group. And that is when you start losing your people of color and the impact that they can have. That starts off with an intense six months and then you're off to your field training period, which is probably another six months to another year. (Miranda 2002)

Speaking from his experiences and that of other members of LOA, Miranda asserts that success in law enforcement depends greatly on how well one adapts to the police culture:

You want to get this job and want to be successful, and you want to go home and say I did something. So you're going to strive to adhere to as much of their rules because you want to be successful. We're driven by a desire to be successful in what we do, so when we get in there, we're going to give it all. And in order for me to be a part of it, I have to be in it. That's when we start adapting those mentalities—a very limited perception of things—and you lose contact with your friends, and your neighbors, and the people that you used to play basketball with or the people that you went to college with. And they'll do that. You're going to lose your friends, get a new group. (Miranda 2002)

Miranda recounts that, as part of the pressure he felt to conform to the police culture, when he was on the force he was chastised by White officers for continuing to live in the Bedford-Stuyvesant community, a neighborhood that has for decades consisted largely of people of color. He notes that many White officers in the NYPD do not live in the city and "have never seen or interacted with Hispanics or Black people.... They used to ask me why I still live in Bedford-Stuyvesant. Why don't I move out? Because, I don't have to.... Why am I still in Bedford-Stuyvesant with all these things going on? This is where I grew up. I feel comfortable. I'm not scared" (Miranda 2002). Consistent with Sergeant Miranda's claim that the residency of officers matters, the New York City Civilian Complaint Review Board (2003, 70) reported that, during the period of January to June of 2003, of the officers against whom allegations of brutality or other misconduct were *substantiated*, 52.8 percent were non-New York City residents.

The New York Chapter of the Latino Officers Association has been especially vocal in cases of police misconduct and brutality. It has been forthright in supporting the families of police violence victims, including the family of Anthony Báez. Miranda avows that police misconduct operates in the larger context of racial profiling and police practices that specifically single out Latino/a neighborhoods and communities of color for arrests.

The unwritten rule, according to Miranda, is to "get the numbers" (arrests) in areas where African Americans and Latinos/as live because it is assumed that "we're the ones [Latinos/as] committing the crimes, which is not the case." He asserts that in his experience throughout his career this assumption, this perception of Latinos/as, was present within the precinct house as much as it was on the streets. Miranda states that it is taken as a given "that most cops that get disciplined happen to be people of color" because it is believed that they are the most deserving of discipline in as much as communities of color are targeted because it is thought that they commit most of the crime (Miranda 2002).

However, Miranda says that in his experience the perception that people of color were mostly responsible for crime was mistaken, noting that wherever police officers were assigned that is where arrests were made: "When I worked in a predominately White community, then I would be arresting White people." Miranda also clarifies that, in spite of the many claims by the department that a quota system does not exist, quotas do exist, informally and unofficially, to selectively "get the numbers" from the areas of the precinct where people of color live. He distinctly recalls being ordered by his superiors to conduct arrests in certain predominantly Latino/a or African American neighborhoods: "In this neighborhood, we want numbers. Whereas, if we ended up on Avenue U and Avenue X, down that side, we were told you can't give out any summonses" (Miranda 2002). On the subject of police treating people of color differently from Whites, Miranda's statements find some support in criminal justice literature. Regarding police practices on the streets, criminologists have written about the *racial halo effect*, "a dynamic whereby being white American, in and of itself, reduces the odds of being viewed with suspicion or being questioned by an officer" (Weitzer and Tuch, 2006, 19; see also Weitzer, 1999).

Miranda and other officers state that their own experiences confirm that racial profiling is often practiced within the department. As an example of racial and ethnic profiling, Miranda claims that while driving his car he has been stopped by fellow officers for no reason (Miranda 2002). Another Latino officer, who asked to be identified only as Police Officer David (2002), stated that in 2001 alone he was stopped on the road four times, asserting that fitting the racial/ethnic profile could be the only explanation for being stopped.

Reinforcing Miranda's contention that Latino/a officers are discouraged from relating to their own community, Officer David related an experience in which he was disparaged by another officer for engaging in conversation with a "perp" (a Latino male) while on duty. He stated that it is not unusual to hear officers casually refer to young Latino males on the streets as "perps" (perpetrators), even when they are not under arrest or suspicion. According to Officer David, baggy pants and a baseball cap are usually sufficient for a Latino male to be labeled a "perp" (Police Officer David 2002).

As do many other law enforcement agencies, the NYPD contests the assertion that its practice is to target people and communities of color. Police departments typically argue that they deploy officers to areas from which they have received the most complaints. But in an extensive study of racial profiling Professor David A. Harris notes that "police do not get reports on all crime, and for those not reported police will make no arrests" (2002, 76). Professor Harris cites the 1999 National Crime Victimization Survey which shows that

> victims of violent offenses did not report these crimes to the police *more than half of the time—54.3 percent.* Almost three-quarters of all sexual assaults, more than a third of all robberies, and more than 40 percent of all aggravated assaults go unreported; almost 75 percent of all purse snatchings and nearly half of all household burglaries never make it into police files. (Harris 2002, 76)

Professor Harris recognizes, of course, that police departments regularly receive complaints about drugs incidents and crimes that occur on the streets and in neighborhoods. But he also explains that

> the great bulk of drug activity, including the transport of larger quantities of drugs by couriers, goes unreported, unseen, and undetected. Police officers may have general knowledge of drug activity, its loca-

tions, or the people involved. But this tells them little about any specific patterns or instances of offending. Weapons possession offenses work much the same way.... So if police want to enforce laws against illegal guns, they must seek out the offenders—that is, they must go find these otherwise hidden activities. (77)

He also cautions against the use of incarceration rates as an indicator of who is actually committing crime, noting that "incarceration rates measure not crime but the activity of people and institutions responsible for determining criminal sentences, primarily legislatures (the bodies that make the law that determines sentences) and judges (the people who do the actual sentencing)" (78). Consistent with former Police Sergeant Miranda's experience, Harris found that statistics that show a disproportionate number of drug-related arrests of African Americans, for instance, reflect the "decisions made by someone in the police department, the chief, lieutenants, street-level supervisors, or even the individual officer themselves to concentrate enforcement activity on these individuals" (78).

Professor Harris explains that the assertion by police officials that Latinos/as and African Americans are stopped more often than Whites because the police "go where crime is" is not borne out by the most dependable data currently available. An examination of data regarding hit rates, that is, "the rates at which police actually find contraband or other evidence of crime when they perform stops and searches" repeatedly show that Latinos/as and African Americans were disproportionately stopped compared to Whites, who were in fact more often found with contraband or otherwise engaged in criminal conduct (79). Indeed, hit rates from Maryland, New Jersey, North Carolina, and New York all reveal the same pattern (79, 82). Hit data from New Jersey, for example, showed that even though police targeted African Americans and Latinos/as for stops at a higher rate, Whites who were stopped "were almost twice as likely to be found with contraband as blacks, and five times as likely to be found with contraband as Latinos, clearly not what the advocates of racial profiling would predict" (80).

Moreover, although Latinos/as and Africans Americans are disproportionately stopped by customs agents at airports (43 percent in 1998), the Customs Service data for 1998 reveals that the hit rates for White passengers was actually higher at 6.7 percent than for African Americans at 6.2 percent. For Latinos/as, who are specifically and most frequently profiled as drug couriers, the hit rate was the lowest at 2.8 percent (Harris 2002, 84).

In view of this information about racial profiling, LOA has been attuned to the subtle manner in which profiling occurs. An especially trying aspect of policing for Miranda and LOA members has been the common practice of identifying a suspect solely as "Hispanic" with very few, if any, other details or descriptive information: "What does a Puerto Rican look like? When they start putting these descriptions out like that, using that terminology, there's no justification for that. So, they say a male, Hispanic, 5'9". What does a male Hispanic look like?" (Miranda 2002).

Miranda and the LOA have raised numerous concerns about racial and ethnic bias throughout the justice system, including instances of racial and ethnic prejudice directed at Latino/a officers. He cites instances when Latino officers were placed on wanted posters and when racial and ethnic slurs were used in police stations:

> LOA did a whole big thing on the wanted posters, because they started putting the names of Latino cops on the wanted posters ... in the precincts. It was 'a joke.' But it wasn't a joke to us. So, we have been fighting them on a number of issues just like the racial profiling, the slurs that go on in the commands ... they're so comfortable in doing it to us, and we're in uniform. And that's why I used to tell officers, you know, sometimes people say it's a joke. Don't let it be a joke, because that's how they think about you. (Miranda 2002)

LOA has also been concerned with the treatment of Latina women officers in different agencies and has lent support to Latinas who have filed discrimination claims. Miranda declares that Latina women officers are often treated unfairly and are given the worst assignments. Miranda complains that the attitude that "[t]hey shouldn't be here'" is not uncommon among male officers (Miranda 2002).

Miranda and LOA find sensitivity and racial/ethnic diversity training offered to police officers to be superficial and ineffective. For this reason, they opine that it is critical for Latino/a officers to stay in touch with who they are and where they come from:

> In terms of changing the mentality, we just have to be stronger, as people, and we cannot afford to have separation in Latino law enforcement and in our Latino communities, and that's part of what we [LOA] push. We stress that in the new officers. And the old officers who are already indoctrinated, re-acclimate yourself to your family, and every time you see them out there doing something make believe that's your brother or sister, that's potentially your family member that they're messing with. Have a different approach and that's what we teach them. We teach the newer cops: stay with the people you

came out with, the guys you went to school with, your neighbors. Don't lose touch with them, because they are … keeping you balanced. They prevent you from saying 'us-and-them.' Because the moment the police department gets you to identify with the us-and-them mentality, they make it easy for you to abuse the other people because you separate yourself in that way…. If you can separate a person from their community and their family, then you're more inclined to do something that's wrong with them or allow something to be done to them and turn the other way. (Miranda 2002)

Conclusion

The views held by former Police Sergeant Miranda and the Latino Officers Association presented here do not necessarily represent the position or experience of all Latinos/as in law enforcement. Indeed, positions of the Latino Officers Association have been and continue to be disputed by the NYPD and the City of New York. However, that the profound sense of inequality and injustice has given rise to organizations, such as LOA, is instructive about the Latino/a experience.

The disconcerting fact remains that Latinos and Latinas are too often absent from the ranks of officials in law enforcement, judges, and lawyers in the courts. Even in a city like New York, where approximately a quarter of the 8 million people who reside there are Latino/a, their numbers are still wanting in these institutions, especially at the higher levels of authority. It is also evident that the law enforcement and judicial systems are still insufficiently open to change and to the positive contributions that a diverse group of officers, judges, and other professionals rooted in their own culture, language, and heritage can make toward a more effective system. Within the justice system, Latino/a identity and culture are still looked upon with suspicion. It is a suspicion grounded in societal norms and perceptions that more often than not associate Latinos/as with crime rather than decency and hard work. As a result, Latino/a officers, judges, and other professionals often grapple with pressure to give up their culture, identity, and, conceivably, their dignity. Like most other Latinos/as, they too are conditioned to believe that only by distinguishing and separating themselves from the "other" can they expect to achieve acceptance or advancement within the system.

It is also significant to observe that whenever change has occurred to improve law enforcement agencies and the justice system it is because dissenting voices have been at the forefront, communities have organized, lawsuits filed, and other steps have been taken to address grievances and inequities. At different times, organizations, such as the Hispanic Society and the Latino Officers Association, have taken the lead in identifying problems that need attention, thus representing the interests of Latinas and Latinos, who often have had no one else to turn to for support. Civil rights institutions, such as the MALDEF and PRLDEF, have played an equally important role in taking action to confront injustices in the courts and elsewhere.

Latinas and Latinos must make a concerted effort to retain their identity in the face of powerful institutions deeply entrenched in their ways, especially in the ways they exclude Latinos/as. Only by forging a sense of community and identity have many Latinos/as, professionals and nonprofessionals, been able to survive and take steps toward improving their lives and the lives of other Latinos/as.

Ultimately, one does not need to look far to find disturbing patterns of racial and ethnic disparities in the U.S. justice system: the persistent history of complaints, lawsuits, and grievances by Latinos/as and other people of color speaks to the need to effectively address the problem of discrimination based on race, ethnicity, gender, and linguistic heritage. To address these and other problems, mere numbers are insufficient. The justice system and society will need to look beyond numbers, and ensure that representation is meaningful and effective—representation that is capable of providing relevant input and insights; that is able to incorporate cultural and linguistic knowledge and experience to better serve Latino/a communities; that can provide culturally competent services; that can to stand up to biases when they arise; and able and willing to help make the system work equitably for all.

Meanwhile, Latino/a over-representation in the prison system will require greater efforts to understand and address the forces and factors behind the mass imprisonment phenomenon that drive up incarceration rates in this country and that disproportionately harm and disempower communities of color. If we are to forge a more equitable system of justice, efforts must be made and supported to disengage the society from long-held stereotypes that wrongly link Latinos/as with illegal drugs, that falsely associate Latino/a immigrants with criminal conduct, and that reinforce biases within the criminal justice system and the courts.

CHAPTER 5

A TALE OF TWO CITIES: LATINOS/AS IN LOS ANGELES AND NEW YORK

In a press release announcing that the Latino/a population had reached an "all-time high of 38.8 million" in June 2003, the U.S. Census Bureau (2003e) described Latinos/as as "young, diverse, [and] urban." Los Angeles and New York City are two cities that in many ways represent the dynamic Latino/a presence in the United States. Indeed, Latinos/as in both cities are young, diverse, and urban. Latino/a groups in these two major metropolitan areas come from very distinct regions of Latin America—Mexico, the Caribbean, and Central and South America—and they are diverse in their cultures, linguistic differences, and historical experiences.

At the same time, Latinos/as in the United States also share much in common. Economic and social marginalization is common to the experience of most Latinos/as. Their ability to garner adequate local and state government assistance in response to their community needs is often complicated and a source of frustration and disappointment. Their relations with law enforcement are also typically strained. Los Angeles and New York, in particular, are cities with deep economic divisions, with Latinos/as primarily inhabiting the areas of these cities most underserved by public services, and deprived of basic health care, education, housing, and jobs. In both cities, Latinos/as are part of those groups most affected by poverty, economic inequality, and residential segregation, and most entangled in controversies arising from their desire for fair and equal justice in their interactions with the police and the judicial system. Both cities share a long history of ethnic and racial tensions. Both cities have been marred by police scandals, corruption, and misconduct—problems that have adversely affected people of color and Latinos/as, in particular.

This chapter takes a look at the experience of Latinos/as in Los Angeles and New York and their struggle for economic and social justice. It is the story of communities striving to make better lives for themselves under circumstances that continually fall short of the mythical "American dream." It is also a story of perseverance and activism in response to conditions that Latinos/as face in these cities. Highlighted in this chapter are the lives of two members of these Latino/a communities—Alex Sánchez in Los Angeles and Iris Báez in New York—and their struggles for justice. These two individuals—of different age groups and national origin—call our attention to some of the most pressing questions about justice that Latinos/as face today.

Los Angeles and New York City

In 2000, New York City and Los Angeles had the largest Latino/a populations in the United States—New York with 2,160,554 and Los Angeles with 1,719,073 (Bureau of the Census 2001b, 7, table 3). In both cities, Latino/a communities generally live under highly segregated circumstances. Both cities also continue to experience new waves of immigrants from Latin America and have Latino/a populations that are relatively young.

Nationally, the largest concentration of Latinos/as reside in urban centers, and of all urban areas, the highest concentration of Latinos/as live in East Los Angeles where 96.8 percent of the population (120,000) is Latino/a (Bureau of the Census 2001b, 7).[1] As in East Los Angeles, New York City exhibits very high levels of residential segregation, with Latino/a communities among the groups most isolated from Whites (Scott 2001, B1, B5).

Besides living largely separated from Whites, Latino/a communities in both cities continue to experience an influx of new groups from Latin America. Indeed, in Los Angeles, where the largest group of Latinos/as are of Mexican descent, and in New York City, where Puerto Ricans still make up the single largest Latino/a group, new immigrants from Latin America have been steadily arriving and settling into the *barrios* of these cities. In the Washington Heights/Inwood section of Manhattan, for instance, by the 1990's, almost one out of every two persons was of Dominican descent and "78 percent of all new immigrants who settled in the neighborhood came from the Dominican Republic" (Hernández 2002, 112). Along with Dominicans, new immigrants from Mexico have also been arriving in New York City and settling in places such as East Harlem (*El Barrio*), a longstanding Puerto Rican neighborhood. With a population estimated at 200,000, Mexicans are now the third-largest Latino/a group in New York City after Puerto Ricans and Dominicans (Feuer

---

1. The cities of El Paso and San Antonio, Texas, also had majority Latino/a populations, with 76.6 percent and 58.7 percent, respectively (Bureau of the Census 2001b, 7).

2003, B1). Similarly, Los Angeles has seen noticeable increases in new immigrants, including arrivals from Central America. Nationally, the largest group of Central Americans is Salvadoran, comprising 655,000 persons or 1.9 percent of the total Latino/a population in 2000 (Bureau of the Census 2001b, 2).

These new arrivals settle in already existing Latino/a communities that are exceedingly poor and underserved. The natural consequence of this is a perennial "fight over crumbs"—that is, Latino/a groups find themselves pitted against each other in competition over limited resources and services in such areas as employment, education, business opportunities, housing, health care, and other public services. A study by the Urban Institute shows that (2002, 1), "[d]espite their strong attachment to the labor force, many immigrants in Los Angeles County and New York City are experiencing a substantial unmet need for health care, food assistance, and other social services." The Urban Institute also found that "[p]overty rates for immigrant families are more than twice as high as rates for native citizen families in California and New York state" and that "[i]mmigrants tend to have lower incomes despite high labor force attachment, largely because they are more likely than native citizens to work in low wage jobs" (2).

There is an extreme polarization that exists in the midst of the world's wealthiest country. *New York Times* columnist Bob Herbert poignantly describes the growing economic divide as it manifests itself in New York City:

> A lot of New Yorkers are doing awfully well. There are 8 million residents of New York City, and roughly 700,000 are worth a million dollars or more. The average price of a Manhattan apartment is $1.3 million. The annual earnings of the average hedge fund manager is $363 million. The estimated worth of the mayor, Michael Bloomberg, ranges from $5.5 billion to upwards of $20 billion. You want a gilded age? This is it. The elite of the Roaring Twenties would be stunned by the wealth of the current era. Now the flip side, which is the side those public school students are on. One of the city's five counties, the Bronx, is the poorest urban county in the nation. The number of families in the city's homeless shelters is the highest it has been in a quarter of a century. Twenty-five percent of all families with children in New York City—that's 1.5 million New Yorkers—are trying to make it on incomes that are below the poverty threshold established by the federal government. The streets that are paved with gold for some are covered with ash for many others. There are few better illustrations of the increasingly disturbing divide between rich and poor than New York City. (Herbert 2007, A23)

In the situation described above, Latinos/as most often find themselves on the lower end of the socioeconomic ladder, and it is to cities like New York and Los Angeles—where the dividing line between rich and poor can be quite sharp—that many Latin American immigrants are drawn.

Factors that are internal and external to Latin American countries help explain recent migratory patterns (see Hernández 2002, 25–26). In the United States, U.S. business enterprises continue to act as a force attracting immigrants from Latin America who are desperate for jobs. In spite of the movement of many industries outside the United States in the past decade, Los Angeles and New York remain centers of commercial and industrial activity that lure workers from Latin America. Both cities still play an especially pivotal role in the U.S. apparel industry, an industry notorious for its exploitation of Latino/a and Asian immigrant laborers (Gereffi, Spener, and Bair 2002).

Among New York City's Latino/a sweatshop workers, Dominicans predominate (Palpacuer 2002, 61). In Los Angeles, Mexican and Central American workers are most commonly exploited as cheap labor (Kessler 2002, 75). Notwithstanding campaigns to rid these cities of sweatshops, including the Department of Labor's "No Sweat Initiative," the illegal practice of hiring workers to work under substandard conditions and below the minimum wage thrives as employers count on immigrant workers reluctant to unionize for fear of retaliation or termination (90).

Economic turmoil and despair cast a long shadow over most of Latin America, causing many workers to flee, often to the United States, in the hope of finding jobs. Countries in Central America have been particularly hard hit, unable to compete in an unfair global market in which the world's richest nations—the United States, Japan, and the developed nations of Europe—subsidize their farmers and maintain protective tariffs on agricultural products (see New York Times 2003d). In the United States, the government spends $19 million annually to support U.S. agri-businesses that, in turn, dump their surplus grain on the world market, hurting farmers in developing countries unable to compete with cheaper U.S. grain (Pollan 2003, 41–48).

The failure of globalization and free trade to remedy the economic plight of Latin American countries has also left many Latin Americans with few choices other than to leave their homelands in search of employment in the United States. Working people in countries such as El Salvador have grown desperate, unable to weather economic hard times. Falling coffee prices in 2003, caused by a worldwide surplus of coffee beans, sparked a surge in migration out of El Salvador. Many Salvadorans and other Latin Americans risk their lives to make the dangerous trek through the Sonora Desert to reach the United States (Hadden 2003b).

Immigrant Latino/a populations have tended to be relatively young compared to the rest of the U.S. population. In 2000, thirty-five percent of Latinos/as were under the age of 18, in contrast to 25.7 percent nationally (Bureau of the Census 2001b, 7). The median age for Latinos/as in the United States was 25.9 years, as compared to 35.3 years for the whole U.S. population (7).[2] Further, adolescent Latinos/as, whose families fled war and/or poverty in Central America, have been joining the ranks of marginalized youth finding a sense of identity and family in street gangs in the United States. Central American countries, such as El Salvador, Guatemala, and Honduras, have had to contend with this issue internally, particularly as youth return to their countries.

In a report from El Salvador aired on *National Public Radio*, young Salvadoran gang members who called a press conference held in 2003 provided their perspective on the current situation facing youths in their country:

> We, the saddest children in the world, were never children. We never had toys, kisses or hugs. The most important thing has always been to survive in this crazy, savage and disorderly world. Why bother learning to read and write when our parents sacrificed us for the illusion of a better life, fleeing the country? (Hadden 2003a)

In the 1990s, with the worst of the Central American wars over, many youths were deported back to their homelands, including youths who had adopted gang lifestyles. Central American societies have proven intolerant of gangs, adopting harsh laws that specifically target youth gangs. In Honduras, for example, a young person can be sentenced to as much as 12 years for merely having a gang tattoo, and similar crackdowns on youths are underway in El Salvador and Guatemala (Hadden 2003a). Thus, Latino/a youths report feeling trapped between two worlds: marginalized in the United States and equally unwelcome in their countries of origin (see, e.g., DeCesare 2003).

Their economic predicament and the effects of decades of internal armed conflicts lead many Central American youths to travel north, to cities such as Los Angeles. Once in the United States, the financial, social, familial, and cultural dislocation they encounter cause many of them to turn to street organizations—or "gangs" as they are most commonly referred to—in search of cohesion, self-worth, identity, and dignity (see Kontos, Brotherton and Barrios 2003). Further complicating an already complex set of circumstances for

---

2. The U.S. Bureau of the Census reported in 2001 that "Mexicans had a median age of 24.2 years, Puerto Ricans 27.3 years, Central Americans 29.2 years, Dominicans 29.5 years, South Americans 33.1 years, Spaniards 36.4 years, Cubans 40.7 years, and all other Hispanics had a median age of 24.7 years" (2001b, 7).

Latino/a youth are the many popular misconceptions about gangs in urban centers, such as Los Angeles and New York City, as well as nationwide.

Gangs: Misperceptions and Public Policy

Very few issues raise fear among people like news about crimes committed by youth gangs. As a report sponsored by the Justice Policy Institute (JPI) and authored by Greene and Pranis (2007, 3) notes, "public concern and media coverage of gang activity has skyrocketed since 2000" even though "[y]outh crime in the United States remains near the lowest levels seen in the past three decades." In fact, "there are fewer gang members in the United States today than there were a decade ago, and there is no indication that gang activity is growing" (4). Based on the most complete and up-to-date law enforcement data, "youth gang membership fell from 850,000 in 1996 to 760,000 in 2004 and … the proportion of jurisdictions reporting gang problems has dropped substantially" (4).

In stark contrast to prevailing ideas about gangs in the United States, Greene and Pranis (2007, 3), in their comprehensive examination of gangs, make clear that the get-tough policies that typically garner strong support are actually misplaced. Los Angeles, a city known for aggressive anti-gang tactics, is actually a case study in the many failures of hard line responses to gang activity:

> Los Angeles taxpayers have not seen a return on their massive investments over the past quarter century: law enforcement agencies report that there are now six times as many gangs and at least double the number of gang members in the region. In the undisputed gang capital of the U.S., more police, more prisons, and more punitive measures haven't stopped the cycle of gang violence. Los Angeles is losing the war on gangs.… Absent better information, lawmakers in the nation's capital and across the country risk blindly following in Los Angeles' troubled footsteps.… Federal proposals—such as S. 456, the 'Gang Abatement and Prevention Act of 2007'—promise more of the kinds of punitive approaches that have failed to curb the violence in Los Angeles. (Greene and Pranis 2007, 3)

In highlighting the major findings of experts in the field, the Justice Policy Institute (J.P.I.) debunks many popular misconceptions about gangs. The Institute's report points out the following:

- **Gang members account for a relatively small share of crime in most jurisdictions.** The available evidence indicates that gang members play a relatively small role in the national crime problem. Further, analysis of state-level data shows no consistent relationship between crime rates and reports of gang activity.[3]

· **The public face of the gang problem is black and Latino, but whites make up the largest group of adolescent gang members.** Law enforcement sources report that over 90 percent of gang members are non-white, but youth survey data show that whites account for 40 percent of gang members between the ages of 12 and 16. The disparity raises troubling questions about how gang members are identified by law enforcement.

· **Gang control policies make the process of leaving more difficult by continuing to target former members after their gang affiliation has ended.** Most young people who enter gangs will leave the gang within a year. But law enforcement practices can target former gang members long after their active participation in the gang has ended, and may dissuade employers from offering jobs to former gang members or youth who merely look like gang members.

· **Heavy-handed suppression efforts can increase gang cohesion and police-community tensions, and they have a poor track record when it comes to reducing crime and violence.** In Chicago, a cycle of police suppression and incarceration combined with a legacy of segregation to *sustain* unacceptably high levels of gang violence. Results from the Department of Justice-funded interventions in the three major cities of Dallas, Detroit, and St. Louis show no evidence of a positive impact on target neighborhoods. The picture is little better for gang enforcement strategies that seek to combine suppression with social service interventions: evaluations of Operation Ceasefire and the 'Comprehensive Gang Program Model' show that neither was able to replicate the apparent success of the pilot programs, or to achieve a 'balance' between law enforcement and community stakeholders. (Justice Policy Institute 2007)

Based on its findings, the JPI report endorses "positive pubic safety strategies" to reduce youth violence (Greene and Pranis 2007, 6–7). Its main pub-

---

3. "National estimates and local research findings suggest that gang members may be responsible for fewer than one in 10 homicides; fewer than one in 16 violent offenses; and fewer than one in 20 serious (index) crimes" (Greene and Pranis 2007, 4). The Uniform Crime Reports list as serious index crimes: rape, robbery, murder, aggravated assault, burglary, larceny, theft of a motor vehicle, and arson. Factoring in that many of the crimes committed by gangs are against themselves, their impact on crime affecting the general public is diminished further (Greene and Pranis 2007, 4).

lic policy recommendations draw from "lessons of the past and results from recent innovations in juvenile justice policy," including the following:

- **Expand the use of evidenced-based practice to reduce youth crime.** Instead of devoting more resources to the already heavily funded and ineffective gang enforcement tactics, policy makers should expand the use of "evidenced-based" interventions that are scientifically proven to reduce juvenile recidivism.
- **Promote jobs, education, and healthy communities, and lower barriers to the reintegration into society of former gang members.** Gang researchers observe that employment and family formation help draw youth away from gangs. Creating positive opportunities through which gang members can leave their past, as opposed to ineffective policies that lock people into gangs or strengthen their attachments, can help to improve public safety.
- **Redirect resources from failed gang enforcement efforts to proven public safety strategies.** Gang injunctions, gang sweeps, and various ineffective enforcement initiatives reinforce negative images of whole communities and run counter to best practices in youth development. JPI suggests that, instead, localities should end practices that can make the youth violence problem worse, and refocus funds on effective public safety strategies. (Justice Policy Institute 2007)

Adopting these approaches is no easy feat. Indeed, the JPI report acknowledges the enormous "political, public, and media pressure" that sustains the belief that only aggressive gang unit suppression efforts are effective in reducing gang-related problems (Greene and Pranis 2007, 5). Forging effective solutions is further complicated by longstanding, poor police-community relations in many communities around the country, especially in communities of color.

POLICE-LATINO/A COMMUNITY RELATIONS IN BOTH CITIES

In 1988, twenty years after race riots broke out in major U.S. cities, such as Los Angeles and New York, and twenty years after the Kerner Commission concluded that racism and inequality were dividing the country, it was determined that discrimination and inequality was worsening an already difficult economic and social situation (National Advisory Commission on Civil Disorder [1968] 1988; Harris and Wilkins 1988). At present, nearly forty years since the Kerner Report, both Los Angeles and New York City can still be considered cities reflecting two separate and unequal societies, where the schism in society is not simply between Blacks and Whites, but more generally between people of color and Whites. Discrimination, segregation, "frustrated hopes," the "legitimization of violence," and "powerlessness"—terms used by the Kerner Commission to identify the basic causes for the disturbances of the 1960s in places such as Los Angeles and New York (National Advisory Commission on Civil Disorder [1968] 1988)—are words that, in many ways, are still applicable to the circumstances under which many Latinos/as, African Americans, and other people of color live within U.S. society.

Frustration among Latinos/as with longstanding inequality and discrimination has been cited as a major factor in the sizeable Latino/a participation in the 1992 Los Angeles disturbances following the Rodney King verdict. As a result of this expression of Latino/a disillusionment, 49 percent of the damage was caused in Latino/a communities, and a majority of those arrested were Latino/a (Martínez 1993, 469; Pastor 1993). It is not coincidental that Latino/a dissatisfaction would be expressed in relation to a case largely considered a travesty of justice in which it appeared to communities of color that White police officers would once again walk free after committing a heinous act of brutality. The 1968 Kerner Commission report singled out the perception of "the existence of police brutality and corruption, and of a 'double standard' of justice and protection" (National Advisory Commission on Civil Disorder. [1968] 1988, 206)—a perception of many Latinos/as and people of color today. The dissatisfaction among people of color with the double standard of justice they experience is present in the many reports issued that examine police-community tensions in Los Angeles and around the country (see, e.g., Amnesty International 1998; Human Rights Watch 1998). Citing a *NY1* local television news poll in 1997, Human Rights Watch (1998, 275) reported that 81 percent of African Americans and 73 percent of Latinos/as in New York City indicated that police brutality was a severe problem.

In Los Angeles, the 1943 zoot-suit riots—in which police officers in combination with White military servicemen rampaged through the Latino/a *barrio* for several days, brutalizing Mexican Americans and other people of color—remain emblematic of the extended history of strained relations between the police and Latino/a communities (see Escobar 1999; Págan 2003). Strained relations continue today, as the police and law enforcement establishment are persistently criticized for their tactics, corruption, and brutality in both Los Angeles and New York.

New York City and Los Angeles, without question, have long histories of police misconduct and abuse that have directly affected Latinos/as and other people of color. In both cities, investigative commissions have repeatedly linked corruption with brutality (Chevingny 1995; Human Rights Watch 1998). In New York, the 1972 Knapp Commission and the 1993–1994 Mollen Commission examined issues of corruption and excessive use of force following revelations of major police scandals. Both called for major reforms in the NYPD.

Indeed, the link between police corruption and brutality in New York City policing could not have been established more clearly than through the Mollen Commission testimony presented by NYPD officers Bernard Cawley and Michael Dowd. Officer Bernard Cawley, nicknamed "The Mechanic," whose job it was to "tune people up," testified: "We'd just beat people in general … to show who was in charge" (quoted in Human Rights Watch 1998, 268). Officer Dowd epitomized the extent to which the police department had corrupted. Through his testimony it was proven that brutality was not only tolerated, it was considered a necessary part of the job if an officer wanted to be accepted in the police force. Dowd acknowledged that "[Brutality] is a form of acceptance. It's not just simply giving a beating. It's [sic] the other officers begin to accept you more" (quoted in Human Rights Watch 1998, 273). Crawley and Dowd presented evidence that this behavior was endemic, testifying to "hundreds of acts of brutality they engaged in; yet apparently no fellow officer had filed a complaint about either of them" (273–74).

Scandals continue to mar the reputation of the NYPD. Forms of so-called "quality of life" and "zero tolerance" anti-crime tactics adopted by Mayor Rudolph Giuliani, so highly acclaimed at first, exacerbated racial tension and brought on numerous protests and claims of discrimination as the number of innocent people of color killed at the hands of White police officers climbed. The 1999 case of the African immigrant Amadou Diallo killed in a hail of 41 bullets outside his Bronx home by members of the now infamous Street Crimes Unit and the 1997 case of Abner Louima who was tortured and sodomized with a stick by police officers in a Brooklyn precinct house were among the cases that received national attention and helped galvanize a movement calling for an end to police violence against communities of color (see McArdle and Erzen 2001; Human Rights Watch 1998; Amnesty International 1998).

New York City communities of color point to other cases as characteristic of a pattern of police violence directed at them. The 1995 shooting death of a sixteen-year-old Chinese boy Yong Xin Huang and the 1994 chokehold death of Anthony Báez were among the cases in the Asian and Latino/a communities that aroused opposition to Mayor Rudolph Giuliani and NYPD (McArdle and Erzen 2001). Most recently, two separate police killings of unarmed men—Sean Bell, an African American who died in a hail of police gunfire in 2006, and Fermin Arzu, a Honduran immigrant shot to death in a police encounter in 2007—have reignited protests and claims of police brutality in the City (Fernandez 2007, 29).

In the wake of the precipitous rise in cases of alleged police brutality during the Giuliani years, the Street Crimes Unit—the specialized unit that engaged in stop-and-frisk tactics in search of guns or drugs and which was often implicated in brutality cases—was dismantled. Nevertheless, stop-and-frisk practices have not ended, but were transferred to the NYPD's Anti-Crime Units. Further, although the events of September 11, 2001 have largely drawn attention away from problems in police-community relations, controversies surrounding deployment of police and their tactics in communities of color have not subsided. They continue to be raised by the Latino Officers Association and by numerous organizations based in communities of color in New York City (McArdle and Erzen 2001).

In Los Angeles, the videotaped beating of Rodney King by police officers served as the catalyst for an investigation by the Independent Commission on the Los Angeles Police Department, known as the Christopher Commission. As in New York's Mollen Commission findings, the Christopher Commission reported that police violence had become the norm throughout the department. According to the Commission, race was inexorably tied to the unlawful and excessive use of force against persons of color because "an officer's prejudice towards the suspect's race may lead to the use of excessive force" (Independent Commission on the Los Angeles Police Department 1991, 69). The Christopher Commission also discovered a pattern of police conduct that adhered to the "code of silence," the unwritten vow of secrecy among police officers responsible for inhibiting the proper investigation and prosecution of police abuse and excessive force cases (170). Unfortunately, as with the inquiries into corruption and brutality in New York, the heightened awareness of the crisis in law enforcement in Los Angeles did not lead to fundamental changes in police culture needed to prevent future abuse and corruption.

In a scandal similar to that which tarnished the NYPD's reputation and led to the dissolution of its Street Crimes Unit, the LAPD's CRASH (Community Resources Against Street Hoodlums) unit had also adopted corrupt and brutal police tactics and was eventually disbanded. The CRASH unit, which focused its operations in the section of town known as Rampart, ended in disgrace and controversy. The infamous Rampart CRASH scandal shocked Los Angeles and the nation with revelations that while engaging in "[p]olice work targeting predominantly Latinos/as and Latino/a 'suspected gang members' in Los Angeles … [it] framed thousands of innocent people by planting evidence on them, committed perjury in court to gain convictions, and physically brutalized innocent youth and adults" (Villarruel et al. 2002, 64). Also, police brutality was shown to be linked to illegal conduct, including drug-related activities, on the part of police officers (Cannon 2000).

As news of the CRASH scandal broke, it became inescapable that the police were implicated in abuse and corruption within Latino/a communities. It was disclosed that an officer planted false evidence on a Latino man who was left paralyzed in a police attack and wrongfully charged and convicted (Cannon 2000, 32; see also Chemerinsky et al. 2000). At the center of the Rampart CRASH scandal was a Puerto Rican police officer, Rafael Pérez, who at his sentencing characterized his actions as having become "consumed by the 'us-against-them ethos of the overzealous cop' after he transferred to Rampart Crash" (Cannon 2000, 32).

Disturbingly, CRASH became a mirror image of the unlawful "hoodlums" that it was supposed to have been placing under control. Its members brandished gang-styled patches and logos, and its motto, "We intimidate those who intimidate others," was proudly hung over on the unit's door (Cannon 2000, 32). In his testimony Pérez revealed that the CRASH culture and behavior was encouraged and protected by his own supervisors who "specifically instructed him to lie on police reports in order to have a more successful prosecution" (Chimerinsky 2001, 637n183).

Most significantly, the Rampart CRASH scandal made it clear that not just the LAPD but the entire criminal justice system bears responsibility. In interviews for a *New York Times Magazine* article, several Los Angeles county judges readily admitted presiding in cases where they suspected police officers of committing perjury. One judge conceded that:

> It's said that we need to change the police culture…. But we have to change the judicial culture too. The judicial culture is hostile to the defense. You'll hear judges talking at lunch about some stupid thing a defense attorney did—they rarely talk that way about a prosecutor. I don't think they're aware how biased they sound. (Cannon 2000, 32)

The CRASH unit debacle brought to the fore the ease with which the criminal justice system convicts Latino/a youths. When the arresting officer is Latino/a or a person of color, the system can pretend not to be biased against certain racial or ethnic groups and thereby buffer itself from criticism.

In Los Angeles, the heightened fear of gang-related crime and violence has led to the enactment of a series of laws that are increasingly being viewed as reinforcing negative stereotypes about Latinos/as and contributing to unfair and discriminatory results. In a joint report by the Institute for Children, Youth, and Families of Michigan State University and the organization Building Blocks for Youth assessed California's anti-gang efforts:

Anti-gang laws, such as California's ballot initiative, Proposition 21, have converted a broad range of youth offenses, including misdemeanors, into adult felonies.... In practice, anti-gang laws have caused significant numbers of Latino/a youth across the country—only some of whom are actually members of gangs—to receive harsh treatment by police, detention facilities staff, prosecutors and the courts.... Under California's Proposition 21, by merely alleging that an offense is 'gang-related,' prosecutors may have the power to file charges against a youth as young as 14 years old directly in adult court, without the generally required 'fitness' hearing before a judge (Cal. Pen. Code §186.22(b); Cal. Wef. & Inst. Code §707 (d)(2)). (Villarruel et al. 2002, 62)

The "gang databases," which list anyone deemed to have gang associations have grown and are maintained in California and other states. New anti-gang laws tend to reinforce stereotypes of Latino/a youths as criminal elements in society by systematically labeling Latino/a youths as gang members. The consequence, as the previously-mentioned report finds, is that "Latino/a and other youth of color who merely have a tattoo, wear hip-hop clothing or live in low income, high crime neighborhoods are sometimes presumed to be 'gang affiliated' by police and, therefore, stopped, questioned, and physically threatened or assaulted" (8). Other scholars support these findings and conclude that anti-gang laws have helped to legalize "gang profiling" and have encouraged the use of police stops and other aggressive strategies against Latino/a youths (Chemerinsky 2001).

As happened with the bold zoot suits worn by Latino youths in the 1940s, law enforcement officers too often view the hip-hop fashions, tattoos, and other forms of expression currently in vogue among young Latino/a youth—whether or not they actually belong to a gang—as synonymous with crime. Thus, as they were in the early 1940s Latino/a youths in the main continue to be a racialized group of criminal "others," who "may be penalized for suspected gang involvement, based on appearance, neighborhood, clothing, or other factors not related to alleged unlawful behavior" (Villarruel et al. 2002, 7). As further proof that Latino/a youth were systematically treated as foreign "others," Rampart CRASH officers were known to collaborate with the Immigration and Naturalization Service (INS) in the deportation of Latino/a youths, an activity which is illegal as immigration is a federal matter falling outside the authority of local police (64).

In spite of many attempts to study the problem and recommend change, the high number of people of color who have fallen prey to police brutality, mistreatment, or other forms of misconduct has generally remained a constant part of life in New York and Los Angeles (Chevingny 1995, 38–57, 72; Human Rights Watch 1998; Amnesty International 1998). In New York, for instance, evidence of consistent complaints against police officers has been made available by the city's Civilian Complaint Review Board (CCRB). In fact, the CCRB reports that "[c]omplaint activity has increased during every six-month period since the last half of 2001" (2003, 1). "For the first half of 2003, the CCRB received 2,758 complaints—21% more than the same six months last year (2,274), and 18% more than the last six months of 2002 (2,338)" (1). The race of alleged victims has remained constant over the period of January 2002 through June 2003, with 78.4 percent of alleged victims being African American and Latino/a (53.3 percent and 25.1 percent, respectively) while 64.0 percent of the officers subject to complaints for the same period were White (15–16). Indeed, a study of police violence in New York City by Marilynn S. Johnson (2003, 277–305) not only documents the racialized nature of present-day police brutality cases—violence directed primarily at African Americans and Latinos/as—but also the historical inertia of the police department in making effective changes in their policies and practices.

Policing the Police in New York and Los Angeles

How incidents of police corruption and abuse in Latino/a communities in Los Angeles and New York are investigated and prosecuted has been a subject of much scrutiny and debate. In New York, a 1999 investigation by the City's Office of the Public Advocate was critical of the NYPD's Internal Affairs Division and the ineffectiveness of the Civilian Complaint Review Board (CCRB). The Public Advocate's interim report noted that "*only 2% of officers who CCRB substantiated a complaint against were actually disciplined*" and that in 90% of the times when the Police Department did not impose discipline, "*the Police department rejected out of hand the CCRB's conclusion that legally sufficient evidence existed to demonstrate that the officer had engaged in misconduct without conducting its own investigation. Moreover, the Department never even explained why it reached the opposite conclusion from the CCRB to the CCRB, the victim or the public*" (Green 1999, i, iii) [emphasis in the original].

In New York and elsewhere around the country, the lack of efficacious complaint processes continue plague Latinos/as in particular as language and other cultural barriers exacerbate already largely ineffective complaint procedures (see Villarruel et al. 2002; Amnesty International 1998, 43–54). However, when greater priority is given to allocating adequate resources for civilian over-sight of the police better outcomes tend to appear. The New York City Civil-ian Complaint Review Board has stated that the Board was previously "[u]nderfunded, understaffed, and under fire" (2003, xix). But with im-provements in staffing and resources, it reported being able to conduct more rigorous investigations, and "[a]s a result, of the officers the CCRB found committed misconduct in 2001, the department has disciplined 79%; by con-trast, of the officers against whom the CCRB substantiated allegations from 1994 though 1996, the department imposed discipline against 34% or less" (xx). This marked improvement gives credence to the claim that throughout the administration of Mayor Rudolph Giuliani there was lax enforcement of the mechanisms designed to rein in rogue cops. It also emphasizes the point made by many human rights groups and analysts that more and better re-sources are needed to supervise criminal justice agencies to prevent unlawful abuses (see Amnesty International 1998; Human Rights Watch 1998; Villar-ruel et al. 2002; Donziger 1996).

An additional remedy available in cases of police brutality is a civil action under the 1871 Ku Klux Klan Act, commonly referred to as Section 1983 liti-gation for the section where it is found in the federal code (42 U.S.C.A. §1983). In many instances, Section 1983 civil rights actions have been used to obtain monetary compensation from municipalities but they also often fall short of affording an opportunity for redress to those affected by police violence or abuse. As Harvard law professor Randall Kennedy maintains (1997, 121), these lawsuits frequently do not serve as a useful alternative for persons because of the expense, delay, and legal intricacies involved. It is conceivable that as a re-sult many Latinos/as and people of color do not mount legal actions.

It is also questionable whether such civil rights lawsuits are truly effective at changing the conduct of local police departments and governments. De-spite the fact that in 1998 New York City spent a record $40 million to settle police misconduct claims (Flynn 1999, B1), many doubt that such huge set-tlements have provoked fundamental change in the city and its police depart-ment. Hefty monetary damages paid to victims are so common that local mu-nicipalities seem to simply absorb the expense as part of the cost of doing business, rather than seeing it as an urgent call for change.

In reference to the situation in Los Angeles, New York University law pro-fessor Paul Chevingny comments that "[p]olice brutality litigation has become a cottage industry" (1995, 52). He points out that, in spite of the abundance of cases brought, law enforcement agencies have proven to be resilient against change. In 1992, for instance, New York City's police union, the Patrolman's Benevolent Association, sponsored an angry protest rally against reforms designed to better manage police corruption and abuse (64–65). Chevingny notes that officers yelled out racial slurs, leading the police commissioner at the time to conclude that there were "serious questions about the department's willingness and ability to police itself" (65). Thus, even though police abuse cases may be effectively litigated through the courts, achieving fundamental change in police conduct and policies still appears to be a distant goal.

Activism, Protests, and Resistance

The long trajectory of discrimination and prejudice against Latinas and Latinos in Los Angeles and New York has given rise to a shared history of activism, protest, and resistance. From the zoot suit—worn by Latinos as a symbol of identity and defiance in the 1940s (Escobar 1999)—to the early formation of organizations that addressed unfair treatment of Mexican Americans, to the militancy of young Chicanos and Puerto Ricans in the 1960s and 1970s, to the immigrant rights movement of the present, Latinos/as have understood the significance of organizing opposition to oppression, inequality, and injustice. Responding to the need for services and equal rights, the G.I. Forum of the 1940s and later the League of United Latin American Citizens (LULAC) were precursors of many future organizations. In fact, LULAC was instrumental in supporting the earliest court battles to desegregate schools, including the case of *Mendez, et al. v. Westminster School District*, 64 F. Supp. 544 (1946) (Gómez Quiñones 1990, 63).

By the 1960s, the frustration with the continued oppression of Mexican farm workers and the continuing injustices and deprivations experienced among all Latinos/as nationwide prompted new kinds of activism, self-awareness, and militancy. César Chávez and the United Farm Workers of America ignited a struggle to defend Mexican agricultural workers and brought national attention to the plight of laborers working under inhuman conditions. Groups with more radical agendas that called Latino/a youths and students to take action also formed in the 1960s. In Los Angeles and the West Coast, through their many organizing activities, the Brown Berets and the United Mexican American Students (UMAS) developed agendas for political change (Gómez Quiñones 1990, 101–153). They also struggled with questions of race and identity in the face of the dominant White society that had effectively racialized Mexican Americans as non-White "others" who were, therefore, not entitled to equality and justice as real "Americans" (see Haney López 2003). The need to assert racial and cultural identity in the face of racism pushed many Mexican American youths toward Chicanismo, "a politically charged *Mexicanidad*" (Gómez Quiñones 1990, 104).

In Chicago, New York, and other parts of the East Coast, Puerto Rican youths and students became active in such groups as the Young Lords in response to the forms of discrimination Puerto Rican communities faced in housing, schools, and health care, and the need to address the issues of Puerto Rican identity in the context of Puerto Rico's ongoing colonial status in relation to the United States (Morales 1998; Meléndez 2003). Both the Chicano and Puerto Rican movements in the 1970s clashed with law enforcement and were subject to the FBI's counter intelligence operations (COINTELPRO), which sought to disrupt nationalist movements in communities of color regardless of whether their activities were constitutionally protected under freedom of expression and association clauses (see, e.g., Haney López 2003, 34; Morales 1998).

On the legal front, the Mexican American Legal Defense and Education Fund, with offices in Los Angeles, Sacramento, Chicago, Washington, D.C., San Antonio, and Houston, and the Puerto Rican Legal Defense and Education Fund in New York City have used legal strategies and advocacy to safeguard the rights of Latinos/as in the courts and in communities. Over the years, other civil rights groups have also served as legal advocates for the rights of Latinos/as; these include the Center for Constitutional Rights, the American Civil Liberties Union Foundation of Southern California, the New York Civil Liberties Union, and other public interest legal groups. A myriad of private attorneys nationwide—Latinos/as and non-Latinos/as—have also been instrumental in protecting Latino/a rights and access to justice.

Latino/a Activism Today

Today, Latino/a activism takes many forms. A very prominent form is activism to protect the rights of immigrants and to offer solutions to the plight of Latino/a immigrants who work and contribute to the United States, but remain isolated, exploited, and marginalized as "aliens." The 2003 Immigrant Workers Freedom Ride across the United States, reminiscent of the Freedom Rides for African American civil rights of the 1960s, brought together numerous community-based groups, labor unions, and churches of numerous religious denominations, including the Catholic Church, in a call for an end to the harassment and exploitation of immigrants and the granting of legal status to immigrants upon whose work and services the United States depends economically (Greenhouse 2003a, 33).

The backbone of social change for Latino/a communities, however, has been the activism of community-based groups and Latino/a communities themselves. Over the years, many community-based projects have worked on a daily basis to organize, protect, and educate Latinos/as across a broad spectrum of issues such as workers' rights, immigrants' rights, literacy, police misconduct, and education. Organizations such as the *Instituto de Educación Popular del Sur de California* and the *Asociación Tepeyac de New York* work with many Latino/a immigrants, providing needed advocacy and services to their constituents. Police Watch and the Coalition against Police Abuse in California, the National Congress of Puerto Rican Rights (now commonly referred to as the Justice Committee) and other groups have played significant roles in responding to police brutality in Latino/a communities. Indeed, community-based organizing, education, and mobilization have been central to the progress made.

Characteristic of Latino/a activism is its emergence from events that have directly touched the lives of Latino/a community members. What follows are the stories of two activists. In Los Angeles, Alex Sánchez, a Salvadoran and former gang member, helps to lead a group created to assist Latino/a youths out of the gang lifestyle. In New York, Iris Báez, whose son Anthony was killed by a police officer in 1994, became an advocate and activist for Latino/a communities after the tragedy that befell her family.

Alex Sánchez

Founded in 1996, Homies Unidos, a non-profit gang violence prevention and intervention organization, provides crisis intervention and support for transnational, gang-affected families in San Salvador, El Salvador and Los Angeles, California. In Los Angeles, Homies Unidos works closely with street gang members, creating alternatives to violence and drugs by making available alternative education, leadership development, and health education programs, and building the self-esteem of the program participants. One of its founders, Alex Sánchez, is a former gang member, whose early life story has become all too common in the City of Los Angeles, one of the main destinations for Salvadorans seeking to escape the horror that engulfed their homeland. It is the story of families from Central America fleeing the seemingly endless and brutal armed conflicts in their countries during the 1980s.

Under the banner of its anti-communist Cold War effort, the U.S. government spent billions of taxpayer dollars to support governments favorable to U.S. interests in places such as El Salvador and Guatemala. Central America was rendered a bloody battlefield, where right-wing death squads razed villages, massacred innocent civilians, and even U.S. priests and nuns were targeted for politically-motivated killings (LaFeber 1993; LeoGrande 1998).

The Salvadoran Peace Accords of 1992—ostensibly marking an end to the war in El Salvador—and the wave of anti-immigrant sentiment sweeping the United States at the time led to thousands of Salvadorans being deported back to El Salvador. After decades of war, El Salvador was a country left in economic and social ruin. With numerous broken families and the social fabric of society in decay, death squad activity, drugs, gang rivalry, and violence reemerged (DeCesare 2003).

Alex Sánchez was among the youths caught between the war in El Salvador and the harsh realities of Los Angeles street life. An impetus for establishing Homies Unidos, initially founded in El Salvador, was his interest in addressing the transnational character of the gang problem. Sánchez explains that upon their return to El Salvador, gang members from the United States became role models for youths who, after the war, had little hope for the future and even fewer role models to look up to:

> All of a sudden they see these guys coming down there all tough macho, bigger, you know, because the way they were bred here, I guess, … we're going down there and to see the skinny kids over there with big bellies … and these kids are out there running loose, they analyzed us when we got down there. They saw us and … they idolized us and they did everything that we did. They wanted to get tattoos … they wanted to get into the gangs … they started copying everything that we did. (Sánchez 2001)

Sánchez has come across similar patterns in Guatemala, Honduras, and Nicaragua, where disaffected youth from these war-torn nations have sought refuge in the gang lifestyle, either in the United States or in their countries of origin. Throughout Central America and in the United States, these youths have found themselves subject to harassment, intimidation, and, eventually, imprisonment at the hands of the authorities. In Central America, remnants of the right-wing death squads of the 1980s now prey on youth gangs, such as the Eighteenth Street gang or the Mara Salvatruchas (MS) gang (DeCesare 2003). Sánchez himself explains that if he had been deported back to El Salvador, he is certain that he would have been killed:

> If I were to be sent to my country I was facing death. I had been outspoken about the death squads, I had been about the … gangs really killing each other down there, … I had been outspoken … talking about the LAPD. So I was speaking out against a lot of people, you know, which put me in a situation where I could have gotten killed.… I had enemies down there already that were coming over to my auntie's place and asking for me. (Sánchez 2001)

As reflected above, death squads who kept surveillance on his aunt's home were among the enemies that Sánchez faced. Based on the imminent danger of persecution awaiting him in El Salvador and with the support of former U.S. Senator Tom Hayden, a campaign to garner national and international support and attention for Alex Sánchez was successful in preventing his deportation. His cause now is the work of Homies Unidos.

Spearheading the coordination of Homies Unidos today are Salvadoran-born Silvia Beltrán, a former staff member to Sen. Hayden and now the Executive Director of Homies Unidos, and Alex Sánchez, who serves as Homies Unidos' Program Director. Their focus, as explained by Sánchez, is to convey a message about alternatives to the gang lifestyle, not by lecturing to Latino/a youths and gang members, but through education (Sánchez 2001). Their program encompasses these specific areas: violence prevention and intervention, creating alternative educational opportunities, strengthening families, artistic expression, and health care education. Thus, the program provides participants with the tools to improve their lives. It helps them advance educationally, by tapping into their creativity and potential, and by orienting them toward healthy and productive lives. Homies Unidos' educational programs have expanded under the Epiphany Project, a project encompassing a variety of skills and self-development components, including personal coping skills, health awareness, leadership, and other educational programs.

While many have come to believe that Homies Unidos is a beacon of hope in the sea of neglected *barrios* in Los Angeles, others are skeptical and often hostile toward the group's work. The Los Angeles police have often been cited as treating Homies Unidos as a criminal enterprise, rather than a source for constructive change and peace (Rappleye 2000). Nevertheless, Homies Unidos has persevered, growing in its importance and its impact on the problems of youth alienation and gang violence (Hayden 2000, B11).

Iris Báez

Since his death at the hands of a New York City police officer, Anthony Báez has become symbolic of the problem of police brutality in Latino/a communities. Angered because a football accidentally hit his police car as Anthony and his brothers played in the street, New York City Police Officer Francis Livoti used a chokehold, prohibited under department regulations, that killed Anthony Báez in 1994 (McArdle 2001). Even though the judge recognized that the police department engaged in "a nest of perjury," officer Livoti was acquitted at trial in state court (Human Rights Watch 1998, 290). International human rights organizations that studied the case have concluded that it represents an unmistakable case of police racism and brutality (Human Rights Watch 1998; Amnesty International 1998). Left to contend with what was widely considered a travesty of justice was Anthony's mother, Iris Báez.

Born in Ponce, Puerto Rico in 1942, at an early age Mrs. Báez came to New York, where she lived and raised six of her own children and adopted another six. She is a woman who has worked all her life—as a home attendant, as a teachers aide, and as a medical assistant in several hospitals. She was active in the local Parents Teachers Association (PTA) in the Bronx and had even become PTA president. From her perspective, until 1994 her life had not been affected directly by discrimination:

> I didn't know what racism was until, really, this happened. Though before I saw it, but I didn't know what that was.... So I didn't know there was a problem. I didn't know what I was, as a Latina, running into.... Why do they treat you different? I never really focused on those issues. I ... worked, I brought my kids home, made sure they were okay. And my husband, you know, and I, we did everything like we were supposed to, you know, and we go to church and that's it. (Báez 2002)

She recalls that the day that her husband was called to go to Union Hospital, where he received the news that their son Anthony was dead, there was still uncertainty about the magnitude of the problem. It was only after the autopsy results and the disclosure of evidence at trial that Mrs. Báez came to fully appreciate that a heinous offense had been committed against her son.

After the initial dismissal of the cases against Officer Livoti in state court, the testimony of Latina Police Officer Daisy Boria proved to be crucial in a subsequent federal court case for civil damages. Through that court proceeding, it was disclosed that Livoti had a history of brutality complaints. Livoti "had been subject of at least eleven brutality complaints over an eleven-year period" (Human Rights Watch 1998, 290). The trial convinced Iris Báez that her son's death was linked to racial and ethnic discrimination: "it was because my son was Latino. They said, 'no, don't put race into this right now.' But I say that was part of it, because afterwards, I started finding out stuff about Lavoti. Livoti didn't get along with Latinos" (Báez 2002).

The federal civil case against the City and NYPD resulted in a damage award of three million dollars, which Mrs. Báez has used to establish a foundation in her son's name. The Anthony Báez Foundation provides her with the basis for continuing to work in support of others affected by police misconduct and abuse. She has also participated in the formation of Parents Against Police Brutality, a community organizing and support group for family members whose children have died or suffered during encounters with New York City police officers (Hsiao 2001; Johnson 2003, 292).

Her son's death created a sense of awareness of her community's relationship to the law and law enforcement, which was previously nonexistent. She finds solace that her son's case "gave the people something to say: 'Hey, we've got to put a stop to this—this abuse in the neighborhood'.... When I used to walk around, everybody used to come out and tell me: 'You know that cop, that cop did this to me.' So I'd say: 'Why didn't you do something?' You know, maybe if we would have stopped them back then, he would have never murdered my son!" (Báez 2002).

Like Alex Sánchez, her life and understanding of the larger society were transformed—a transformation that led her to work for social change. In 2002, Iris Báez ran for District Leader for the 86th District in the Bronx. Though unsuccessful in her bid for political office, she remains committed to a life of community service.

Conclusion

Los Angeles and New York City exemplify the diversity of Latinos and Latinas in the United States who arrive here from Mexico, the Caribbean, and Central and South America. They represent the past and future struggles, hopes and aspirations of Latinas and Latinos in the United States. To this very day, the stark realities of discrimination, residential segregation, and political and economic marginalization among Latinos/as in Los Angeles and New York City are readily discernible. Present-day social deprivation and dislocation experienced by Latinos/as are rooted in the colonial conquests of the past and the colonial and neocolonial relationship maintained between the United States and the Latin American countries from which Latino/a migration derives. Prejudices and stereotypes of the past manifest themselves in the policies and practices of the present that preserve the image of Latinos/as as "foreign," even if they are U.S. citizens. Latino/a youth, in particular, are viewed with suspicion—too often perceived by the dominant White society not as young people with potential, but rather as potential criminals.

Tragically, for most Latinos/as the promise of escaping the poverty and despair of their respective homelands in the hope of a better life in the United States never materializes. Many Latino/a youths find themselves in search of identity, caught between the homelands their parents left and a new society which is often not welcoming and sometimes overtly hostile. As with Alex Sánchez, many Latino/a youth have sought to find their sense of self within the collective bonds they create for themselves in the form of street organizations, commonly referred to as gangs (Kontos, Brotherton, and Barrios 2003; Bourgois 1995). While gang-related violence and crime is, indeed, a major concern, it behooves us to ensure that not all youth of color on the street are labeled as gang members. As Walker, Spohn, and DeLone warn (2004), myths about gangs abound. Stereotypes that all gangs are involved in illicit drug activity, that they exist only in large urban areas and that they are mostly made up of youth of color are popular misperceptions that ignore the complexities of this phenomenon (54–59).

Efforts to improve the lives of our society's youths should not be summarily substituted in favor of the narrow focus on incarcerating as many gang members as possible. As Alex Sánchez did, many other young Latinos/as have tried to change their personal circumstances. They have taken the initiative to work within their communities and among Latino/a youth in constructive ways. Wisely, Sánchez heavily emphasizes his work and the work of Homies Unidos on education—one of the basic public services most neglected in Latino/a communities. The work of Homies Unidos, thus, entails making up for that which the greater society has consistently defined as a low priority: the education of children in the United States, and especially those in poor communities of color.

Like Alex Sánchez, Iris Báez is also worried about the future. At 65, her concern is not about her own future, but that of Latino and Latina youths. It is a concern fixed on preventing another tragic and needless death at the hands of a police officer whose biases are expressed through violence. Iris Baez's personal loss was due to the insensitivity and illegal practices of a law enforcement agent, something that has become all too frequent in cities like New York City and Los Angeles. To her credit, Iris Baez did not allow the loss of her son to be simply a personal tragedy. The events that led to and followed her son's death transformed her life. They made her more aware of the world around her; they politicized her and gave her life a different purpose: to serve the community and others; to bring about change.

The lives of both Alex Sánchez and Iris Báez are now dedicated to issues related to justice. As Alex expresses it, he struggles with a society that has sought to criminalize youths and immigrants through its stereotypes, its laws, and its legal system: "All these laws that are just against the youth. You know, they're criminalizing everybody. They're criminalizing the youth, they're criminalizing the immigrants, they're criminalizing just about anything that they don't want in this country anymore" (Sánchez 2001). The rejection of Latinos/as as rightful members of U.S. society and the dehumanizing effect of unjust and discriminatory treatment is an experience generations of Latinos/as in Los Angeles, New York City, and many other parts of the United States recount. It is also part of a larger narrative of resistance and social change.

Alex Sánchez analogizes his work to that of planting seeds: "You've got these seeds and … and maybe it won't happen the next week or maybe it won't happen that year, but that seed is there and it will grow" (Sánchez 2001). In their own ways and in their own work, both Alex Sánchez and Iris Báez seek to plant seeds—seeds of change for a more just society; seeds of hope for future Latino/a youth and communities in the United States.

CHAPTER 6

A CULTURE-BASED APPROACH TO WORKING WITH LATINO/A COMMUNITIES: A CASE STUDY

Reaffirmation of culture and identity has been integral to Latino/a responses to marginalization and disempowerment. Just as racism and other forms of colonial oppression have aided the United States in maintaining its dominance over Latin America, within the U.S. domestic context control over Latinos/as has been exercised by institutions that reinforce the racialized, structural inequalities that maintain Latinos/as as a subordinate group. Indeed, the racialized and unequal treatment of Latinos/as mirrors colonial modes of domination that Latin Americans have experienced abroad.

This chapter addresses the common problems faced by Latino/a youth and families in their efforts to negotiate structural inequalities in the provision of basic health care, education, and other human needs and services that impede their attainment of full and equal human rights in the United States. It looks at strengthening the cultural identity and ethnic solidarity within Latino/a communities as a model and a means for reversing the effects of marginalization, racialization, and disempowerment. To this end, this chapter's main focus is a specific project designed to address these problems, using a culture-based approach to working with Latino/a youths and families.[1]

Palenque—a project of the Puerto Rican/Latin American Studies Department at John Jay College of Criminal Justice—aims to decolonize on personal and collective levels by addressing the problems of alienation and disempowerment frequently observed among Latino/a youths and families. Low self-esteem is a recurring indicator among the participants in the program, as the

---

1. I extend my appreciation to Prof. Luis Barrios of the Puerto Rican/Latin American Studies Department (recently renamed "Latin American and Latina/o Studies Department) of John Jay College of Criminal Justice for his dedication and vital contributions in conceptualizing and implementing the John Jay College-Family Life Center/*Palenque* described in this chapter.

youths and families are chosen on the basis of being considered "at risk" of being unable to cope with a gamut of social problems. Inverting the popular notions about at risk youth and families, *Palenque* views the lack of community services and the neglect of public institutions as institutions at risk which then adversely affect youth and families. It focuses on the many positive elements of Latino/a families and culture as a means of building self-confidence and achievement. Its culturally-oriented approach fills the void among Latino/a youths and families who typically experience an absence of respect for and protection of their human rights both within the criminal justice system and in attaining equal access or opportunities in other areas of daily life, such as education or housing. In a society where Latino/a cultural identities and social and linguistic attributes are often devalued, the validation of culture, heritage, and traditions within Latino/a families becomes an essential part of working with Latino/a communities. Professor Luis Barrios and this author, both from the Puerto Rican/Latin American Studies Department at John Jay College of Criminal Justice, serve, respectively, as the program's principal investigator/director and co-principal investigator/summer program coordinator. It is from this hands-on research perspective that this chapter is written, highlighting three years of the program's operation (2000–2003).

Reaffirming Culture and Identity

Throughout their history, Latino/a community-based initiatives to organize and mobilize for social change in the United States have typically involved a process of reengaging with cultural roots and reaffirming a sense of self and identity within their culture. Indeed, the rejoinder to the prevailing White/Black racial paradigm facing many Mexicans in the United States in the 1960s and 1970s was to embrace "Brown" as part of a self-aware Chicano identity grounded in the culture and history of *La Raza* (see, e.g., McWilliams 1990, 285–308; Haney López 2003). Music, art, language, theatre, and literature have and continue to be expressions of cultural reaffirmation and vehicles for organizing within communities (see McWilliams 1990, 297–304). Indeed, *Teatro Campesino* used theater as an important organizing tool for the Chicano/a movement of the 1960s and 1970s (see Broyles-González 1994). Among Puerto Ricans in the United States from the 1960s to the present, reconnecting to their music and cultural identity has played an important part in the process of developing their understanding of Puerto Rico, from its colonial status to the destructive effects of the U.S. Navy's bombing of the island of Vieques, Puerto Rico (see Meléndez 2003). Indeed, there are projects throughout the United States today that seek to connect community and culture as a strategy to work with Latinos/as. One such program is the *"Aquí se Puede"* Youth Violence Prevention Program at New Mexico State University in Las Cruces, New Mexico. Another, located in Chicago, is *Batey Urbano*, which has used hip-hop to develop social and cultural awareness among youth in a largely Puerto Rican community (Flores-González, Rodríguez and Rodríguez-Muñiz 2006).

Palenque continues in this long tradition of reestablishing and reaffirming cultural awareness and identity among Latinos/as by incorporating cultural elements throughout its curriculum. Formally known as the John Jay College-Family Life Center (JJC-FLC), *Palenque* was founded in 2000. It operates during the academic year and the summer, with the objective to promote Latino/a cultural identity as a means of reducing violence in the lives of urban youths and their families. The program's name is derived from the term self-liberated slaves (*Cimarrones*) in the Caribbean used to identify zones that they created to protect their personal and collective identities. As such, the program is an alternative to traditional approaches that merely seek to keep youth off the streets and out of trouble. Thus, it is designed to create a safe haven, symbolic of that created by *Cimarrones* for their own protection. Within this safe space, *Palenque* provides a wide range of academic, cultural, career, and personal and family development activities that emphasize the community's cultural knowledge and ethnic solidarity while addressing problems of alienation, low self-esteem, and marginalization among Latino/a youth and families.

Drawing from Paulo Freire's work with the poor and oppressed (1994), *Palenque* attempts to make young people more conscious of their world and aims to transform and empower them. Freire pointed to a problem present among the most disadvantaged in society: the internalization of the judgment of those who are dominant in that society (24). He noted that

> [s]o often do they hear that they are good for nothing, know nothing and are incapable of learning anything—that they are sick, lazy, and unproductive—that in the end they become convinced of their own unfitness. (45)

Moreover, Freire considered "the fundamental theme of our epoch to be that of *domination*—which implies its opposite, the theme of *liberation*, as the objective to be achieved" (84). The data analysis showing low self-esteem among the *Palenque* participants is consistent with findings that Latinos/as and other youths of color experience cultural alienation and marginalization, requiring intervention for empowerment (Freire 1994; see also Cummins 1993). Indeed, Freire held that "intervention in reality" was basic—that is, that learning to think critically and understand the world in which one lives is an essential part of becoming empowered and thereby able to transform and improve one's life circumstances (Freire 1994, 90).

Palenque's focus on strengthening cultural identity and forging greater ethnic and cultural solidarity among the youths and their families is also grounded in research that indicates that traditional Latino/a cultural values and norms appear to deter delinquency and other socially counterproductive behavior (Rodriguez 1996; see also Hagan and Palloni 1999). A recent study focusing on Latino/a homicide rates in five major U.S. cities—Chicago, El Paso, Houston, Miami, and San Diego—reveals that strong social networks within Latino/a communities help deter criminal activity (Martinez, Jr. 2002). These findings reinforce the call for greater "cultural competency" within public institutions (Villarruel et al. 2002) and greater efforts to work with Latino/a youths within their cultural contexts (Koss-Chioino and Vargas 1999). Thus, *Palenque's* culture-based approach, while addressing a population of largely Dominican youths, has implications for assisting other Latinos/as and can be adapted to various specific cultural needs.

Palenque's methods and goals also find support in international human rights standards intended to protect minority group rights; economic, social, and cultural rights; and linguistic human rights (see, e.g., Skutnabb-Kangas and Phillipson 1995),[2] as they are geared toward promoting the social, cultural, and economic advancement of all sectors of society. It is an approach that is culturally relevant and specifically designed to provide tools for empowering Latino/a youths and families. Considering the marginality and social dislocation experienced by Latino/a communities, it is an approach that is appropriate to the situation of Latinos/as in the United States.

PALENQUE AND THE WASHINGTON HEIGHTS/INWOOD COMMUNITY

The target area for *Palenque* is the Washington Heights/Inwood area (Community District 12), a densely populated urban neighborhood located in Manhattan. At any given time, the program participants consist of a cohort of 30

---

2. The term human rights, as used in this chapter, encompasses the broadest concepts of economic, social, and cultural rights recognized internationally in addition to the political and civil rights commonly acknowledged under U.S. law. The use of international human rights law, norms, and principles in the context of Latinos/as in the United States is further explored in Chapter 7.

to 40 youths who are commonly categorized as "at risk" because of the lack of educational, health or other basic services in their neighborhood and their vulnerability to being exposed to or involved in violence in the community where they live (Hernández and Torres-Saillant 1996). The project attracted Latino/a participants who are primarily, but not exclusively, new arrivals from the Dominican Republic who have settled in the area and are among the largest, youngest, and most disadvantaged groups in New York City.

In world history, nations engaged in imperial conquests have usually imposed their own cultural norms and have dominated other peoples at the expense of native identity and culture. In response to such domination, different forms of resistance have typically taken shape to counter the impact of cultural imperialism (Said 1993; Memmi [1965] 1991; Fanon [1963] 1986). Within Latino/a communities in the United States, a similar phenomenon has been observed as Latinos/as have clashed with assimilationist modes of addressing Latino/a cultural differences (see Chapman 2002, 179–84). This has especially been the case in *Palenque's* target area of Washington Heights/Inwood, a community where many come from the Dominican Republic, a country repeatedly invaded by the United States and historically subject to U.S. hegemonic power and influence. The dominant-subordinate relations between the United States and the Dominican Republic are often replicated in the relationship between Dominicans and other Latinos/as in the Washington Heights/Inwood area and the public institutions in that community which have for too long failed to meet the most basic needs of the people there.

The Washington Heights/Inwood area can be characterized as a poor, working-class community, consisting primarily of Dominican immigrants (Hernández 2002, 112–17; Grasmuck and Pessar 1991), but with a growing population of immigrants from Mexico (Smith 1996, 65). The area is a vibrant ethnic enclave, with streets and avenues lined with thousands of businesses that provide cultural goods, services, and job opportunities (Grasmuck and Pessar 1996). At the same time, many of its residents strive to overcome poverty and marginalization (Hernández 2002, 117–19).

Poverty rates in the area are reported at over 80 percent, and it is the area with the largest number of children receiving public assistance in Manhattan, and the fourth largest in New York City (Citizens' Committee for Children 2000). Schools in the district (District Six) are overcrowded and characterized by severely deficient educational facilities and resources. The long-term implications of a substandard education are clear and alarming. Longitudinal research points to the role of school under-achievement as a critical risk factor for child and youth violence (Hirschi and Hindelang 1977; Eron and Huesmann 1990). Students who are low achievers will be more likely to start skipping school or dropping out altogether. Patterson, Reid, and Dishion (1997) find that truants usually begin to hang out with each other when not attending school, thus creating peer associations that make more likely the possibility of engaging in delinquent and/or violent activities. Therefore, academic development is an important component of *Palenque's* program design.

As has been the case with Mexicans, Puerto Ricans, and other Latinos/as throughout the United States, the Dominican community in Washington Heights/Inwood has been vulnerable to incidents of bias attacks, racial profiling, and police brutality. Examples of police brutality in Latino/a communities abound (Morín, and del Valle 1990). Along with many other people of color, Dominicans have joined the ranks of those killed at the hands of police officers. The protest rallies organized in response to the death of 40-year-old Juan Rodríguez in 1988 (Lyall 1988, 40) and the controversial and deadly confrontation between the police and José "Kiko" García that led to three days of unrest in Washington Heights in 1992 (Hernández and Torres-Saillant 1996, 49–50) are among the cases vividly remembered in the Dominican community as examples of the use of excessive police force. In both of these examples the police officers were acquitted of wrongdoing, much to the community's dismay. Thus, discriminatory treatment and poor police-community relations are among the many problems that Dominicans face in the community.

CONNECTING WITH LATINO/A YOUTHS AND FAMILIES

The deeply entrenched problems of poverty, inadequate social services, poor police-community relations, and the subordination of the community in relation to the dominant culture invariably manifest themselves in the alienation of Latino/a youths and families. Indeed, one of *Palenque's* major findings within its first year of operation was the low self-esteem prevalent among the youths in the program. Consequently, in the second year of the program, *Palenque* placed greater emphasis on connecting culturally with these youths. Its curriculum not only linked activities to the history and cultural traditions of the youths in the program, but it also addressed the social and cultural realities present in the lives of contemporary Latino/a youth. These realities encompass the question of Latino/a identity in the diaspora and cultural phenomena that are generational and expressed these days through hip-hop music and styles (see Flores 2000; Rivera 2003). Thus, *Palenque* takes into account current forms of youth expression, such as rap, within the framework of a curriculum that guides participants in their academic and personal development.

By encouraging youths to channel their creative talents through the arts and performance, *Palenque* assists them in developing a greater sense of identity, independence, discipline, and self-worth. One of the strong underpinnings of the program is the use of culture to understand oneself within one's historical and social context. The program also promotes understanding personal violence and its relation to street and structural violence. More specifically, the program examines how different forms of exploitation and exclusion— both local and global—affect communities and individuals.

As previously mentioned, unlike traditional youth and education programs that merely attempt to keep young people occupied in recreational and other activities, *Palenque* uses cultural awareness as a source of personal and community empowerment. Learning and interacting with Latino/a culture—its values, customs, language, and artistic forms—help forge solidarity among youths, which in turn is used to deliver messages of self-worth and non-violence and promote peaceful solutions to problems. Cultural knowledge and ethnic solidarity are used as tools to overcome structural barriers and constraints, such as poorly funded schools, deteriorating neighborhoods, racism, discrimination, and violence. Specifically, certain elements of culture—any culture—can be used to create unity as well as a sense of pride and community, and can serve as a means to reduce violence in the neighborhood, the household, and among youths themselves. Thus, the program addresses violence in the community through culturally specific activities, such as workshops on music, drama, dance, and the visual arts.

To further enhance its ability to connect with the community it serves, the program is facilitated by an experienced bilingual staff of artists, writers, professors, poets, photographers, and administrators—many of them Latinos/as who come from the program's target neighborhood. The participants are also exposed to current Latino/a John Jay College students who assist in the program's operation and serve as mentors, role models, and inspiration for the youths. As an incentive to the participants, after-school and summer youth employment programs pay the youths a stipend.

A key component of *Palenque's* design is its partnership and collaboration with Latino/a community-based organizations for the purpose of effective outreach and service. Attracting enrollees into *Palenque* is coordinated through one of the program's community partnership agencies, *Alianza Dominicana*, the largest multi-service youth program in the Washington Heights community. *Alianza Dominicana* and other community-based partnership organizations, including the Dominican Women's Development Center, also provide support in the areas of individual and family counseling, crisis intervention, and other services when needed.

The program's curriculum focuses on five specific developmental areas:

Academic Development: This component incorporates a variety of activities that promote greater interest and improved attitudes toward schooling. Given the harsh conditions, such as overcrowding, unqualified teachers, lack of resources and other problems that plague the New York City public schools, most of the program participants experience high levels of alienation within the educational process. To address this problem, *Palenque* uses innovative, nontraditional approaches, including a computer-based mathematics instruction program that was effective in keeping the participants engaged in an academic activity they formerly rejected. Computers were also used to create web pages that promote peaceful resolutions to disputes and tension. Other academically-oriented activities include poetry writing. Latino/a poets and writers help participants improve their writing and language skills.

Personal Development: Conflict resolution and problem-solving workshops have been conducted by the City University of New York Dispute Resolution Consortium and/or the *Palenque* staff. These workshops include weekly life skills training workshops on a wide range of areas, including motivation, self-discipline; frustration tolerance; habits and attitudes; decision-making; problem-solving; and peer influences. In relation to personal development, the poetry workshops play another role: They help in the development of critical thinking and awareness of self in relation to the environment and community. Participants have also held meetings with police officers from their own community to discuss each other's role in producing and preventing violence in the community.

Cultural Development: *Palenque* participants have engaged in a variety of Latino/a cultural activities involving music, dance, and painting. For instance, the summer 2001 participants were taught the art of Dominican-style ceremonial mask-making. In these classes, the youths learned how culture varied by region and the socio-political meanings of the colors and designs of the masks. The participants also learned how to paint their own works of art, to appreciate various forms of Latino/Dominican music, and to understand how various forms of Caribbean musical expression—merengue, bachata, salsa, classic, rap, reggae, rock, hip-hop, modern, and others—are linked to history and culture. These workshops helped promote socio-cultural awareness and pride in their culture, families and community.

Career Development: The *Palenque* staff have offered photography workshops to present the youths with a concrete example of a career option. The youths were equipped a 35-millimeter, disposable camera and assigned to photograph conditions within their neighborhood. Their photographs captured the symbols or evidence of violence in the community as well as the struggles of everyday life. Deadlines and other requirements were established to help participants develop work skills involving meeting deadlines, managing time and resources, and working with others. The participants not only acquired important skills, through their assignments they also grew in their knowledge and understanding of the world around them.

Recreational Enrichment: A recreational component—that includes playing dominoes, basketball, and dancing—has been integrated into the program to teach the youths how to relax and enjoy themselves while abiding by rules, working collectively, improving concentration and memory, and in some instances, as with playing dominoes, developing their mathematical skills.

Each of the program's components covers many issues in every session, providing for enriching discussions that advance personal, educational, and developmental objectives. For instance, poetry sessions encompass multiple levels of personal development—including constructive discussions about sex, love, gender roles, and relationships—while engaging in academic development activities that improve grammar, spelling, vocabulary, and writing skills in both English and Spanish. The variety of culture-based components have provided the occasion for each participant to choose activities in which they are able to excel and generate interest in areas not usually attractive to youths.

Palenque's Impact on Latino/a Youths

Palenque's impact has been assessed through an array of quantitative and qualitative data gathered throughout the academic year and the summer program. To measure academic development through quantitative means, the Wide Range Achievement Test, Third Edition (WRAT-3) and the School Bonding Index-Revised (SBI-R) have been administered. To gauge personal, cultural, and career development, the program has used the Youth Self-Report Inventory (YSR), the Multigroup Ethnic Identity Measure (MEIM), and the Career Maturity Inventory (CMI). Finally, the participants complete the Violence Risk Assessment Inventory (VRAI) to assess the level of violent behavior in the lives of youth participants. Over the three years (2000–2003), the academic year participants and the summer participants, separately, were given pre-and post-tests to measure change. Control groups were similarly tested for comparison.

Qualitative data have also been collected—life history interviews, photos, poems, drawings and paintings. Field observations have been conducted on all participants, focusing on various themes, such as community violence, immigration, education, employment, experiences with delinquency, conflict resolution, relationships with parents, and ethnic identity. Field observations have centered on recording classroom interaction and dialogues between youths and police officers. Other data of a qualitative nature include other writing projects and art work by participants.

In the relatively short period in which the funder's guidelines[3] required the program to work with 30 to 40 youths—Mondays through Thursdays for four to seven weeks during the summer, and after school Mondays through Thursdays from 4:00 p.m. to 8:00 p.m. during the academic year—it was predictable that some results of the quantitative tests would be mixed, with some youth still requiring greater improvement in such areas as academics and self-esteem. In addition, the quantitative instruments required by the funding source did not always produce the most valid and reliable results. For instance, the tests were written in English, a language in which some participants were not proficient. Test results also suggested the need for greater long-term cultural reaffirmation to improve self-esteem. A study spanning a longer period of time in which to observe the participants' progress is also needed. While there are still areas requiring improvement, the program has succeeded in meeting its overall goals, evidence of which was most visible in the qualitative data.

It must be noted that since the first year of the program (2000–2001) did not emphasize culture, there was greater reliance on traditional methods of quantifying progress. The program's initial inability to effectively engage the participants required the shift to a culturally-oriented approach based on the work of Prof. Luis Barrios (Barrios 1998; Kontos, Brotherton, and Barrios 2003). The refocusing of the program to center on culture and the inclusion of qualitative measurements has dramatically enhanced the program's effectiveness and reinforced the thesis that culture matters. The program, thus, has begun to reach the youths more successfully on multiple levels—personal, academic, social, and developmental—in ways not easily measured by the quantitative tests.

---

3. Funding for *Palenque*/John Jay College-Family life Center (2000-2003) was provided by the Family and Community Violence Prevention (FCVP) Program of Central State University, Wilberforce, Ohio, which administers funds from the Office of Minority Health, Department of Health and Human Services.

The most compelling evidence of the program's success comes from the qualitative data gathered, post-program interviews, and focus groups. In the academic sphere, non-traditional approaches, such as specialized computer-based math instruction, increased the overall enthusiasm and motivation of the summer participants toward academic achievement. Summer 2001 participants, for example, reported math to be one of the activities they most enjoyed.

Many elements of the program in combination have produced positive results. Cultural-orientation plus the program's efforts to expose the youths to a college environment and to worlds beyond their community have provided an enriching experience for the program participants. Each year, the artistic works produced by the youths—including photographs, poetry, and paintings—have been publicly exhibited at John Jay College of Criminal Justice and at other institutions, including *La Casa de la Cultura Dominicana*, a cultural center in the Washington Heights community, and *El Museo del Barrio*. These exhibits have reinforced positive self-image and enhanced the participants' sense of accomplishment. Additional positive results were garnered through the use of John Jay College student mentors who served as examples of persons from similar backgrounds pursuing educational and career options unfamiliar to many of the youths and their families. Moreover, components of *Palenque*'s academic development curriculum which foster a positive cultural and linguistic identity (e.g., through poetry writing in the students' native Spanish) are consistent with calls for greater language diversity in schools attended by Latino/a children (Delpit 1995).

Reactions solicited from the participants reflect a remarkable improvement in attitude and academic performance. Formerly reserved youths exuded confidence in being able to interact in the classroom. Below, for example, are two former participants' comments after returning to school in the fall of 2004:

> What I learned was to have guts; to say what's on my mind in front of everybody [in the group], not to hold anything back ... that's helping me in school, like in my class participation rate. Now I participate more. (15-year-old male, Summer 2003 participant)

> I learned how to communicate better, to have self-esteem; I learned to listen better, like, it [the program] helped me in English class. I thought English was boring but now I listen more. It helped [me with] my listening skills. (17-year-old male, Summer 2003 participant)

Our qualitative findings also confirm that the conflict resolution/peer mediation workshops have been successful in helping participants recognize anger; accept and manage it in constructive ways; and articulate negative emotions that the youths have identified as previously unrecognized or normalized in everyday life. The participants' journal entries indicate success in learning skills to cope with conflict in their daily lives and in their communities, and to articulate the interrelation between personal anger and the structural oppression and exclusion experienced in school and other areas of their lives. Among the typical entries in their journals are notes of a particular session in which strategies to deal with conflicts were discussed. One participant's outline was characteristic of most of the youths' notations:

"J.," male, 14 years old:[4]

Alternatives to violence

- Resolving conflicts
- Negotiation for win/win situation
- Listening to each other
- (not imposing your ideas)
- Need patience in order to listen/to resolve conflict
- Seek peaceful solution to violence or negative situation
- There are always two sides to a story

Negotiation process

- Use mediator if possible
- Go to a neutral place where both parties feel safe
- Both parties must want to resolve situation
- Listen, Listen, Listen
- Help deciper [*sic*] fact from gossip

As the following examples show, however, the most telling positive results were the journal entries that expressed how well they learned and articulated the ways they could incorporate the lesson in their personal lives:

"I.," female, 14 years old:

The way that I'm going to use the alternatives to violence and the negotion [*sic*] process is by listening more because most of the time I really don't listen to what people have to say I just asume [*sic*] that I'm right and there [*sic*] wrong and today I learned that that is not correct.

---

4. Names have been withheld to preserve the participants' confidentiality.

"J.," female, 15 years old:

I feel that I can use this in my life in any future confrontations that I may have. Also discussing negotiation between people and gangs leads me to learn that not everything is what you think. I learned that assumptions can cause a lot of issues and looking at both sides is a key struggle.

"I.," female, 16 years old:

I want to use this in my life in the way that when I'm stuck in a conflict I can find a better way to solve without violence. I also want to take this [sic] skills and knowledge to improve the way I think about certain things. Besides this is a good learning experience that I can carry throughout myself and motivated to successed [sic] in the future.

Of course, the harsh realities of life for these youths have found expression in their work. Painting, photographs, and poems have often focused on the themes of police brutality, rape, and other forms of violence. However, *Palenque's* curriculum has focused on positive messages, encouraging the participants to be proactive in promoting peace as a response to the negative depiction that their community is marred by violence.[5] In fact, "keeping the peace" was the motto created and adopted by summer 2003 participants. Discussions on conflict resolution and about how to "keep the peace" were subsequently reflected in many of the forms of artistic expression the participants engaged in throughout the program that summer. Below are two of many examples of poetry on the topic of peace:

What Eye See
by Brain Heredia,[6] age 16

Life through my unique eyes
I see the true lies
Violence, and the people who would light you up like fireflies
They don't be seeing what life is worth

---

5. Other programs have also taken steps to move youth toward positive and peaceful solutions. Homies Unidos in Los Angeles is one such example, where "peace" is emphasized as a central theme.

6. Consent was obtained to publish the poems of the participants whose names appear in this chapter. These poems were also displayed and presented publicly as a way for participants to contribute to each other and to the community.

You wanna keep killing yourself, go back to birth
I don't want to see violence
This chaos, on my block or yours
I'll bet them bullets wound shots would hurt like soars
This whole world is crazy, believe it or not
Just for pulling out your wallet you get stopped by crooked cops
So I leave you these rhymes until you see the light
If this poem was the opposite this world would be tight

P-E-A-C-E
by Manuela Núñez, age 14

P eace is everything we need to make the world a better place
E veryone has to get along in order to make peace
A nswers to questions will be found if everyone gets along very well
C are and love will bring us happiness
E verything will be alright if we make peace

The program's emphasis on peace is significant as a response to violence. As pointed out by Noguera (2001) [an unpaginated electronic work], violence in the United States has become so common that it has become normalized, and therefore, it is important "to challenge and critique the normalization of violence" through educational initiatives.

The participants' paintings, photography, poetry and other written work speak directly to the positive impact the program has had on them, as evidenced by this poem written for and recited at the 2003 summer program's closing reception and celebration:

Palenque
by Jennifer Rodríguez, age 15

There is a time when you need to be guided, through the tough times of our age, and you don't know what the answers are, of the questions we have today.

Yet there were places we had not experienced, people who made sure we were different, angels that gave us options, and friends who were there often.

All this we found here as we opened the knob, And that's why: Palenque is much more than a job, it's an opportunity to grow and learn with each other, to help our community and especially one another. It's a place where we sought knowledge, fortune and goodwill, not for a check for basically staying still.

We learned to work together against one of our enemies, "violence," which in our community has become an identity. We learned to find solutions to most of our problems and also to learn to talk, listen and follow. And all this we'll take with us in our lives and it will help us to finally put down some knives.

Yes, I'll admit we had had some issues but like any united group we stepped on and continued because mistakes in life lead to growth and it led Palenque to this dance and show, but we have to say the staff helped us a lot because every lecture we had to stand made us a rock, a rock with steepness and power to endorse and to help us in this greedy cruel world.

Yet that's not all we went through here in Palenque, we had learned a lot but we were also tremendous. We met so many people that made us laugh like Reynaldo's crazy style and Claudio's way to act.

We also listened to Isamilli's funny laugh and heard Jeffrey's sarcastic way to react. And we can't leave Oscar's dance for last, I mean I had never seen pants fall that fast. We can't forget the train dance the guys did or when Guillermo almost turned into Tyson, but these are memories we won't forget cause we'll remember them every time we take a rest.

So as you can see we have been through a lot, I mean we hadn't noticed we sounded this hot. We found friendship, talent, knowledge and more it has been a summer like never before. And as I finish this poem it hits me direct, that Palenque is not a memory but a life time effect.

The above poem attests as to the effectiveness and success of the program at achieving its objectives.

The end of the summer of 2003 marked the program's third year of operation. While largely Dominican, the program also attracted other Latinos/as, such as Puerto Ricans, and other growing Latino/a populations in the city, such as Ecuadorians. It has also included members of other racial and ethnic groups. The 2001 *Palenque* Summer Enrichment Program, for example, targeted a cohort of 39 youths between the ages of 14 and 18 and consisted of 32 Latino/a participants (82 percent), six African Americans (15.4 percent), and one youth (2.6 percent), who identified her/himself as being of "mixed race." Sixteen were females (41 percent) and 23 were males (59 percent). The qualitative evidence suggests that non-Dominican participants in *Palenque* (such as Haitian and Ecuadorian youths) also benefited from its approach since they were able to relate to and participate in cultural activities, such as music and art.

Palenque's goal of promoting personal and collective identities within Latino/a communities is an integral component of a multi-faceted approach to assisting Latino/a communities with their harsh historical and present-day realities in the United States (see Barrios 1998; Kontos et al. 2003). The program's approach is also consistent with a series of established and burgeoning norms and principles of international human rights law that seek to protect the rights of all persons to their culture, language, heritage and identity as fundamental rights for those persons who do not constitute a majority of the population (see, e.g., Skutnabb-Kangas and Phillipson 1995). A discussion of the intersection between the culture-based model presented here and norms and principles of international human rights law is more extensively addressed in the next chapter.

Conclusion

Past and current injustices demand responses that validate the existence of Latinos/as as human beings — persons whose social, cultural, and economic well being are deserving of respect and protection in addition to equality of civil and political rights. The culture-based approach of *Palenque* is one of many methodologies that can be employed to address injustices experienced by Latinos/as at a grassroots, community level. It does not seek to be a mere diversion for Latino/a youths, but to help empower them through the use of their own cultural knowledge, identity, and solidarity. Empowerment and a critical perspective is needed in all Latino/a communities. A cultural experience that creates a critical consciousness among the participants about the society in which they live — including an awareness of the dynamics of race, class, and gender that affect their lives — can help transform and mobilize them to change their realities for their own individual as well as their community's collective advancement.

Palenque offers a model that reaffirms Latino/a culture, linguistic heritage, and identity among Latino/a youth and families — a model that has the potential to improve the status of Latinos/as in U.S. society. It is also an example of an effective university-community partnership that brings together talent and resources from both. The qualitative data show that Latino/a youth understand the message society sends when their communities are the recipients of the worst schools, educational instruction, health care, and other social services available in the society, and when they are the objects of discrimination based on race and ethnicity, as manifested by their treatment within the legal system, and the poor conditions in their communities. As evidenced by our data and experience with the participants in the *Palenque* program, Latino/a youth receive a loud message that in the context of U.S. society "they are less than." It is inconceivable that Latino/a youth and families will ever be able to advance in the United States if the conditions that reinforce low self-esteem and marginalization are not addressed. However, the lesson to be drawn from *Palenque* is that, when given the opportunity and the tools to excel, Latino/a youth hold great promise. Like all young people, Latino/a youth aspire to a better future. Their sense, and the reality, that a better life is remote presents a seemingly insurmountable obstacle in their paths. Thus, breaking down barriers to allow positive perspectives to grow is a quintessential challenge that must be faced. *Palenque* attempts to meet that challenge.

Palenque's preliminary success makes it worthy of additional study, along with other programs with similar goals, strategies, curricula, and focus. The non-traditional approach to teaching academic subjects, coupled with an environment that accepts and reaffirms the participants' cultural background, has yielded promising initial results that bode well for the continued success of programs such as this. *Palenque* offers an approach to working with Latino/a communities that reinforces the essence of all humanity: dignity, culture, language, and identity. It addresses economic, social and cultural needs acknowledged under international human rights law standards, as discussed in the next chapter.

In spite of its success, funding for *Palenque*—as is the case with many community-based initiatives—depends on resources being made available over the long term. The Puerto Rican/Latin American Studies Department at John Jay College of Criminal Justice hopes to secure funding to resume the program and expand its components and services in order to have a greater impact on the community.

CHAPTER 7

INTERNATIONAL HUMAN RIGHTS STANDARDS AND LATINO/A COMMUNITIES IN THE UNITED STATES

The culture-based community project model presented in the previous chapter finds support in international human right standards that espouse the idea of cultural rights as human rights. The forms of cultural domination and marginalization experienced by Latinos/as in the United States require the implementation of strategies to advance the promotion of equality and justice, including on a cultural level. International human rights law and principles provide guidance on issues of cultural domination, marginalization, and equality on both international and domestic fronts. Adherence to international standards would not only help make U.S. foreign policies toward Latin America and Latin Americans more sound, but international human rights principles and standards on economic, social, and cultural rights also would provide direction on how to address the condition of Latinos/as in the United States.

This chapter highlights aspects of international human rights law and principles that may help effectuate positive changes for Latino/a communities in the United States and enhance their possibility of achieving equality and justice. Moreover, the benefits of recognizing and implementing international human rights laws and principles in the United States—particularly calling for an expansion of economic, social, and cultural rights—would have positive ramifications for the broader U.S. society by augmenting opportunities and rights for everyone and improving social stability.

CULTURAL SUBORDINATION IN THE
INTERNATIONAL AND U.S. DOMESTIC CONTEXTS

A variety of mechanisms—military, economic, political, social, and cultural—have been employed by the United Sates to subordinate Latin America and marginalize Latin Americans in the United States. As described by Smith (2000, 6), the United States today "wields unilateral hegemony." Over time, the subordination of Latin American identity and culture has been as important as the use of U.S. military, economic, and political might in establishing and maintaining U.S. control and domination. Implicit in the racialization of Latin Americans as "other" to justify U.S. conquests and domination of the hemisphere is the notion that Latin Americans lack any redeeming cultural, social, religious, or linguistic traditions. U.S. policies and practices toward Latin America not only presume U.S. cultural as well as racial superiority but also affect social and cultural changes that disempower and dominate Latin American societies.

In the Latin American context, Puerto Rico serves as an example of the methods used to dominate social and cultural life. Policies and practices regarding language and religion, which the United States instituted in Puerto Rico after assuming jurisdiction over it 1898, are especially illustrative of the subordination of the language and culture of Latin American peoples. From 1898 to 1948, the United States imposed the use of English as the language of instruction in public schools in Puerto Rico, banning Spanish, the native language of Puerto Rico, from the educational process of Puerto Rican children. A 1929 study by the International Institute of Teachers College, Columbia University revealed the school dropout rate in Puerto Rico to be more than 80 percent as a result of this language policy, the impact of which scholars have found is still being felt today (Zentella 1999, 158). Similarly, with the U.S. military intervention in 1898 came a concerted effort by the U.S. military and U.S. religious organizations to "Americanize" Puerto Ricans by promoting Protestantism—a religion considered by the North American victors of the war with Spain to be a more "modern" or "enlightened" religion than Catholicism and, therefore, superior (Díaz-Stevens 1996, 156–61).

As was the case regarding the colonial conquest of Puerto Rico, in the territories wrested by the United States following the U.S.-Mexican War of 1846–1848, such as California and New Mexico, the Spanish language was also systematically suppressed (Hernández-Chávez 1995, 146–48). Indeed, the widespread use of Spanish in New Mexico became a factor in delaying statehood for this former part of Mexico. Only when the English language became dominant and the Anglo-American population exceeded the Mexican population was statehood granted to New Mexico, a process that took sixty-four years (147).

In later years, the imposition of U.S. views and cultural values took other forms. In the early 1940s, under President Franklin Delano Roosevelt the U.S. government established the Office of the Coordinator of Inter-American Affairs (OCIAA), an agency headed by Nelson Rockefeller to disseminate pro-U.S. positions and information in order to counteract a growing fear of Nazi influence in Latin America (Smith 2000, 80–83). As part of this endeavor, Hollywood's cooperation was secured to produce of films for distribution in Latin America that presented the United States in a favorable light. In a 1942 memorandum, the U.S. State Department reported the success of the OCIAA, concluding that "[i]t was the greatest outpouring of propagandistic material by a state ever" (quoted in Smith 2000, 83).

Throughout contemporary Latin America, U.S. corporate interests continue to project their cultural, linguistic, and commercial ideas and standards. In a now famous work entitled *How to read Donald Duck: Imperialist ideology in the Disney Comic*, Ariel Dorfman and Armand Mattelart (1984) drew attention to the impact of Disney, Coca Cola, and other powerful U.S. companies in fostering a cultural atmosphere in Latin America favorable to its continued exploitation for the benefit of U.S. commercial and corporate interests, including dependence on the consumption of U.S. products. The result, as Dorfman and Mattelart assert, has been the stifling of Latin America's economic development and the deterioration of social conditions for most Latin Americans. Hence, in the 1980s, Dorfman and Mattellart's book became a central document in the study of "cultural imperialism' (Holden and Zolov 2000, 272)—a term used in reference to direct and indirect ways the United States imposed and disseminated its values, language, ideas, beliefs and positions in order to advance its policy goals and business interests and dominate Latin American and other societies (see Tomlinson 1991).

As discussed previously in this volume, racialized structural inequalities and marginalization are perpetuated throughout U.S. society—education, housing, healthcare, and the criminal justice system included—reflecting the prevailing norms of the dominant culture. The application of a culture-based approach to addressing the problems faced by Latino/a communities in the United States is derived from an understanding of the ways in which Latinos/as are affected by the dominant perspectives that position them as "less than" within the society, leading to disempowerment and alienation. For this reason, a culture-based approach, such as *Palenque's*, emphasizes the community's cultural knowledge and ethnic solidarity to address problems of alienation, low self-esteem, and marginalization among Latino/a youth and families. But it is essential to know that this approach recognizes that the economic, social, and cultural contexts in which Latinos/as live undermine equality, justice, and progress for many of them.

A key dimension of *Palenque* is that it addresses the problems Latino/a youths and families face by opening up the opportunity for personal and collective decolonization to the U.S. context. *Palenque* helps participants and their families exercise a form of self-determination analogous—though not strictly identical—to the international law principle that recognizes the right of "peoples" to "freely pursue their economic, social and cultural development" (United Nations 1960, para. 2; United Nations 1966a, art. 1; United Nations 1966b, art. 1; see Appendices B and C).

Under international law, "peoples" are those who can exercise full rights to determine their own political status, including their right to establish an independent nation, as well as the right to determine their economic, social, and cultural development (see United Nations 1960; Appendix B; see also, Cassese 1996). It is not argued here that Latino/a communities in the United States are entitled to rights as "peoples" to establish independent nations, as defined in international law, but rather that they comprise a group entitled to minority rights under international law (see United Nations 1992; Appendix D). Nevertheless, as set forth by Robert Blauner (1972), the experience of Latinos/as in the United States, along with that of Native Americans, African Americans, and Asians, has been compared to that of people subject to imperial conquests and control and, thus, treated as "colonized minority groups" within the United States, as opposed to European immigrants who relocated to the United States on a more voluntary basis.

While some have critiqued Blauner's theory as too limited in its approach to the issue of race in the United States because of its reliance on a nation-based paradigm, it provides a useful framework, for analyzing the experience of Latino/a groups in the United States (see Omi and Winant 1994, 46–47). The conquest of Puerto Rico and its continuing colonial status; the conquests of Mexican territories; U.S. interventions and occupations of Caribbean and Central American countries, such as the Dominican Republic and Nicaragua; and U.S. economic hegemony over Latin America all speak to forms of colonialism relevant in shaping the Latino/a experience in the United States.

Certainly one of the most abhorrent facets of colonialism is its tendency to deny peoples not merely their right to political self-determination, but also their right to determine their own economic, social, and cultural development. Indeed, seizing control over the culture and identity of those under colonial or neocolonial status has been identified as indispensable to maintaining peoples under subjugation (Césaire 2000; Fanon [1963] 1986; Memmi [1965] 1991; Ngũgĩ 1986). The need to address the economic, social, and cultural impact of colonialism and neocolonialism on the peoples of Latin America is comparable to the need of Latino/a communities in the United States to confront impediments to their pursuit of their political, economic, social, and cultural development. Failing schools, poor housing and health care, and lack of employment in Latino/a communities tend to reinforce the idea that Latinos/as are "less than" and, therefore, undeserving of the most basic of human needs and equal opportunities.

By providing youths and families the tools to gain control over their individual and collective right to determine their future, *Palenque* seeks to make attainable a form of decolonization. It is a program that attends to the issues of culture and identity at the heart of the problems of the low self-esteem that many Latino/a youths experience. It mirrors the decolonization process on an international level, which addresses the need to dismantle institutions that subvert the culture and identity of those under domination. *Palenque* assists Latino/a youths and their families in regaining and reaffirming their own cultural, social, and economic development through its educational and career development components. Its culture-based approach attempts to fill a void among Latino/a youths and families who typically experience disrespect and disavowal of their Latino/a cultural identities and their social and linguistic attributes.

Palenque's goals reaffirm that culture matters, particularly in its work with people who experience high levels of alienation in society (Barrios 1998; Kontos et al. 2003). Its methods mirror legal rights paradigms found in international human rights standards intended to protect minority group rights, economic, social, and cultural rights, and linguistic rights (see Skutnabb-Kangas and Phillipson 1995). It is consistent with an international human rights framework that acknowledges as legitimate the right of persons who do not constitute a majority of the population to maintain their own culture, language, heritage, and identity, parting from the premise that these are basic to the human rights of all persons. Moreover, the protection of these rights should not be viewed simply as a matter of respecting excluded or marginalized groups in their own countries, but an essential part of providing for the overall well-being and advancement of society as a whole (see Goldewijk, Baspineiro, and Carbonari 2002).

Although often maligned in the United States, bilingual education, for instance, is an integral part of the educational system of many countries around the world where instruction in minority languages takes place as a matter of right and as a benefit for the larger society. Many countries—including Norway, England, the Netherlands, Sweden, Australia, Mexico, and China—help insure equal educational opportunity for linguistic minority groups through bilingual education programs (Krashen 1999). In turn, these programs have been shown to be successful in assisting students acquire the national language while subjects are taught in their native tongue (22–48). Such educational systems are premised on the basic concept that bilingual educational programs are not only pedagogically sound, but also valuable because they serve the greater good by advancing the education of all and upholding the right of linguistic minority groups to retain their cultural identity, a right that is basic to the dignity of all persons.

International Recognition of Economic, Social, and Cultural Rights

In the post-World War I period, the League of Nations recognized the importance of protecting the rights of ethnic, linguistic, and religious minorities. Various ethnic, linguistic, and religious minority groups were threatened by changes in the political configuration of certain states after the war. Hence, an effort to protect their rights was initiated (Buergenthal, Shelton, and Stewart 2002, 10; Sohn and Buergenthal 1974, 213). These efforts culminated in the development of special treaties for the protection of the human rights of ethnic minorities (see Hannum 1990, 50–55; Buergenthal, Shelton, and Stewart 2002, 11; Lauren 1998, 95).

Since its inception in 1945, the United Nations has made the development of international standards for the protection of human rights a central part of its mission. To that end, human rights principles and norms developed over the years have been codified to require states to respect and enforce various human rights provisions. The International Bill of Human Rights is a central component of the U.N. system for the protection and promotion of human rights. This instrument consists of the Universal Declaration of Human Rights (United Nations 1948; Appendix A), the International Covenant on Economic, Social and Cultural Rights (United Nations 1966b; Appendix C), and the International Covenant on Civil and Political Rights (United Nations 1966a) and its two optional protocols.[1]

---

1. The two protocols to the International Covenant on Civil and Political Rights of 1966 include the Optional Protocol to the International Covenant on Civil and Political Rights of 1966 and the Second Optional Protocol to the International Covenant on Civil and Po-

In consideration of the fact that the human dignity of all persons rests not just on their ability to exercise civil and political rights, the United Nations has established that human rights protections extend to a broad array of economic, social, and cultural rights:

> International human rights law has been designed to protect the full range of human rights required for people to have a full, free, safe, secure and healthy life. The right to live a dignified life can never be attained unless all basic necessities of life—work, food, housing, health care, education and culture—are adequately and equitably available to everyone. Based squarely on this fundamental principle of the global human rights system, international human rights law has established individual and group rights relating to the civil, cultural, economic, political and social spheres. (United Nations 1991) [an unpaginated electronic work]

Most importantly, the United Nations has emphasized that economic, social, and cultural rights are not secondary to civil and political rights, but stand on equal footing, as stated in paragraph 1 of the United Nations General Assembly resolution 32/130 of 16 December 1977:

> (a) All human rights and fundamental freedoms are indivisible and interdependent; equal attention and urgent consideration should be given to the implementation, promotion and protection of both civil and political, and economic, social and cultural rights;
> (b) The full realization of civil and political rights without the enjoyment of economic, social and cultural rights is impossible; the achievement of lasting progress in the implementation of human rights is dependent upon sound and effective national and international policies of economic and social development, as recognized by the Proclamation of Teheran of 1968. (United Nations 1977)

The United States is obligated to comply with a number of human rights conventions it has ratified, including the International Covenant on Civil and Political Rights (United Nations 1966a), the Convention against Torture and Other Cruel, Inhuman or Degrading Treatment or Punishment (United Nations 1984), the International Convention on the Elimination of All Forms of Racial Discrimination (United Nations 1966c), and the Convention Relating

---

litical Rights of 1989, which promotes the abolition of the death penalty (United Nations 1994).

to the Status of Refugees (United Nations 1951). Other human rights documents, such as the Universal Declaration of Human Rights (United Nations 1948; Appendix A), which may not establish binding obligations as treaties under international law, are still believed to carry "the moral force of having been negotiated by governments, and of having been adopted by political bodies such as the UN General Assembly" (Amnesty International 1998, 15).

The United States has been one of the most reluctant nations in the world to recognize economic, social and cultural rights or obligate itself to observe and enforce human rights agreements that incorporate these rights, despite their broad acceptance worldwide. In fact, the United States stands with a minority of U.N. member states that have not ratified the International Covenant on Economic, Social and Cultural Rights (ICESCR) (United Nations 1966b; Appendix C).[2] The ICESCR recognizes a broad range of rights for everyone in society to enjoy, including the right to work (art. 6), the right to an adequate standard of living (art. 11) and to the "highest attainable standard of physical and mental health" (art. 12), the right to an education (art. 13), and the right to take part in cultural life (art. 15). While not all nations, and in particular developing nations, are expected to realize these rights immediately given the level of the resources required (Trubeck 1984), ICESCR does establish that basic rights extend beyond the realm of the civil and political, and that human rights cannot be fully realized without insuring the adequate conditions fundamental to human life and society. Certainly, the economic, social and cultural conditions endured by most Latino/a communities in the United States, as described in this book, are an impediment to their development and advancement in society.

Within the framework of international human rights law, economic, social, and cultural rights have special relevance for Latinos/as in the United States. Cultural rights, in particular, encompass aspects of ethnic identity, including language, that have been at the core of many Latino/a struggles. Upholding the rights to culture, language, and other forms of ethnic identity under international standards is consonant with a culture-based approach to working with U.S. Latino/a communities, like that of the *Palenque* program.

One United Nations document that incorporates the right to one's culture, language, and other forms of ethnic identity is the Declaration on the Rights of Persons Belonging to National or Ethnic, Religious and Linguistic Minorities, adopted by the U.N. General Assembly in 1992 (United Nations 1992;

---

2. As of 20 July 2007, the total number of state parties to the International Covenant on Economic, Social and Cultural Rights was 156. In 2007, membership in the United Nations totaled 192 member states.

Appendix D). This declaration declares that "States shall protect the existence and the national or ethnic, cultural, religious and linguistic identity of minorities within their respective territories and shall encourage conditions for the promotion of that identity" (art. 1). The same declaration affirms that "States should take appropriate measures so that, wherever possible, persons belonging to minorities have adequate opportunities to learn their mother tongue or to have instruction in their mother tongue" (art. 4, para. 3). In furtherance of these and other rights, the declaration calls for "[n]ational policies and programmes ... [to] be planned and implemented with due regard for the legitimate interests of persons belonging to minorities" (art. 5, para.1).

Along the same lines, the Convention on the Rights of the Child provides that "States Parties agree that the education of the child shall be directed to ... the development of respect for the child's parents, his or her own cultural identity, language and values, for the national values of the country in which the child is living, the country from which he or she may originate, and for civilizations different from his or her own" (United Nations 1989, art. 29, para. 1(c); Appendix E). It also provides that "[i]n those States in which ethnic, religious or linguistic minorities or persons of indigenous origin exist, a child belonging to such a minority or who is indigenous shall not be denied the right, in community with other members of his or her group, to enjoy his or her own culture, to profess and practice his or her own religion, or to use his or her own language" (art. 30).

These principles of international human rights recognize the importance and value of language, culture, and identity to the education and overall advancement of persons not from the dominant group in a society. *Palenque's* efforts to use the native language and culture of the participants to build self-esteem and improve academic achievement are in keeping with these standards and universally acknowledged rights. The practices of initiatives such as *Palenque* coincide and find support with established international human rights principles. Thus, *Palenque* serves as a model for other culture-based community efforts striving for the recognition of cultural rights as a human right within the United States.

The Relevance of International Human Rights Standards for Latinos/as in the United States

As can be concluded from the above, international human rights standards have particular relevance and applicability to the situation of Latinos/as in the

United States. Below is a summary of the significance of international human rights to Latinos/as and matters of justice affecting them in such areas as discrimination, immigrants' rights, Latina women, criminal justice, the death penalty, and economic and social rights:

Discrimination

The International Convention on the Elimination of All Forms of Racial Discrimination (United Nations 1966c), ratified by the United States in 1994, obligates the U.S. government to eradicate discrimination. The Convention defines "racial discrimination" as "any distinction, exclusion, restriction or preference based on race, colour, descent, or national or ethnic origin which has the purpose or effect of nullifying or impairing the recognition, enjoyment or exercise, on an equal footing, of human rights and fundamental freedoms in the political, economic, social, cultural or any other field of public life" (art. 1, para. 1). The Convention not only requires that State Parties take action to prohibit and enact appropriate action to eliminate racial discrimination (art. 2), but also calls for "special measures to be taken for the sole purpose of securing adequate advancement of certain racial or ethnic groups or individuals requiring such protection as may be necessary" (art. 4).

The implications of the effective implementation of the International Convention on the Elimination of All Forms of Racial Discrimination for Latino/a communities may be far reaching. The Convention is designed to address discrimination against persons based on national or ethnic origin, and to have an impact on the larger issues of economic, social and cultural matters. Its application has been viewed by human rights organizations as also being vital to addressing the problem of discrimination within the judicial system in the United States and, in particular, racial discrimination by law enforcement personnel (see, e.g., Amnesty International 1998; Human Rights Watch 1998).

Immigrants' Rights

Despite the many misconceptions about immigrants as a burden on the U.S. economy and society, most immigrants to the United States are in the country legally; documented and undocumented immigrants alike make significant contributions to government revenues; and immigrants make significant contributions to the growth of the economy. For instance, 84 percent of all immigrants in New York—the state with the largest foreign-born population—are legal (Passel and Clark 1998, 2). These immigrants include naturalized citizens, documented permanent residents, and refugees. Urban Institute analysts who have studied New York's immigrant population have also found that "legal immigrants pay roughly the same percentage of their income in taxes as natives do—about 30 percent" (2). Undocumented immigrants were also found to make sizable contributions in the form of federal, state, and local taxes—including Social Security, residential property, general sales and unemployment taxes—and while the percentage of their income going to pay taxes is lower (15 percent), that is attributable in part to their lower wages and lower tax brackets (5).

Moreover, the Bureau of Labor Statistics' *Monthly Labor Review* reports that "[f]oreign-born workers have come to play an increasingly important role in the U.S. economy; between 1996 and 2000, they constituted nearly half of the net increase in the U.S. labor force" (Mosisa 2002, 3). In fact, contrary to popular misconceptions of foreign-born persons in the United States, it was "white, non-Hispanics" that had a lower labor force participation rate "than any other race/ethnic group" (6).

The true facts about immigrants notwithstanding, misperceptions and discrimination against immigrants persist in the United States. Bias crimes, such as the attacks against Latino day-laborers and the firebombing of the home of a Latino/a immigrant family in Farmingville, New York, exemplify the level of hostility and violence to which anti-immigrant sentiment can rise (Gootman 2003, B1).

Throughout the United States, local governments have also sought to usurp federal authority over immigration policy by attempting to enact anti-immigrant laws. One case in point is the City of Hazleton, Pennsylvania, where Mayor Louis J. Barletta vowed to make his city "one of the toughest places in the United States" for undocumented immigrants, thus making Hazleton one of an estimated 100 municipalities seeking to clamp down on undocumented immigrants (Preston 2007, A14). The Hazleton ordinances, which endeavored to prohibit undocumented immigrants from working or renting homes in the city, was struck down by a federal court in July 2007, making the decision "the most resounding legal blow so far to local efforts across the country to crack down" on undocumented immigrants (Preston 2007, A14).

In *Lozano et al. v. City of Hazleton*, 496 F. Supp. 2d 477, 554–555 (M.D. Pa. 2007), the United States District Court for the Middle District of Pennsylvania ruled that

> Federal law prohibits Hazleton from enforcing any of the provisions of its ordinances.... The ordinances disrupt a well-established federal scheme for regulating the presence and employment of immigrants in the United States. They violate the Supremacy Clause of the United

States Constitution and are unconstitutional.... The Hazleton ordinances [also] violate the procedural due process protections of the Fourteenth Amendment to the United States Constitution. They penalize landlords, tenants, employers and employees without providing them the procedural protections required by federal law, including notice and an opportunity to be heard. Our analysis applies to illegal aliens as well as to legal residents and citizens. The United States Constitution provides due process protections to *all* persons.... Whatever frustrations officials of the City of Hazleton may feel about the current state of federal immigration enforcement, the nature of the political system in the United States prohibits the City from enacting ordinances that disrupt a carefully drawn federal statutory scheme. Even if federal law did not conflict with Hazleton's measures, the City could not enact an ordinance that violates rights the Constitution guarantees to every person in the United States, whether legal resident or not. The genius of our Constitution is that it provides rights even to those who evoke the least sympathy from the general public. In that way, all in this nation can be confident of equal justice under its laws. Hazleton, in its zeal to control the presence of a group deemed undesirable, violated the rights of such people, as well as others within the community. Since the United States Constitution protects even the disfavored, the ordinances cannot be enforced.

The Puerto Rican Legal Defense and Education Fund (PRLDEF), one of the civil rights organizations representing the Hazleton plaintiffs[3], issued a statement after the court's decision, quoting one of its attorneys, Foster Maer, who commented that

'Walking while Latino' has become a crime in many of these towns.... Local elected officials blame all of the town's ailments on the most vulnerable group: undocumented immigrants. Their solution is to push immigrants and their children out of their homes and jobs. This

---

3. The challenge to the Hazleton ordinances was led by PRLDEF, the American Civil Liberties Union, the ACLU of Pennsylvania, the PA Community Justice Project, the law firm of Cozen O'Connor, and local lawyers David Vaida and George Barron. Their efforts to defend the rights of immigrants received support from the U.S. Chamber of Commerce and the U.S. Council of Catholic Bishops (Puerto Rican Legal Defense and Education Fund 2007).

is the worst form of political scapegoating as it appeals to racial bias. If the Ordinances had survived, no one would want to hire or rent to our Latino clients for fear of breaking the law. Our clients became nervous about walking the streets of Hazleton for fear of being blamed for anything that goes wrong. (Puerto Rican Legal Defense and Education Fund 2007)

PRLDEF further asserts that the Mayor of Hazleton Louis J. Barletta was unable to prove in court many of the assertions he made in his campaign to rally support for what are ostensibly ordinances targeting, not just immigrants, but Latino/a immigrants, in particular:

- Mayor Barletta admitted that he cut the police force in half in his first few years as mayor, but then blamed Latino immigrants for an alleged rise in crime.... [H]is own police records indicated that undocumented people only committed 20 crimes in five years out of over 8,000 offenses.[4]
- Mayor Barletta took credit for the city's revitalization, which had been spurred by a population growth of almost 40% driven by the arrival of Latino immigrants over five years. Then he blamed these newcomers for all the increased costs of managing a bigger city. He provided no evidence that Latino immigrants were responsible for increased costs.
- Mayor Barletta blamed Latino immigrants for increased waiting times in hospitals even though this came at a time when two main hospitals were consolidated. He provided no statistics that Latino immigrants were responsible for this increase.
- Mayor Barletta blames Latino immigrants for a crime wave, yet testimony showed that Latino immigrants have the lowest crime rate of any demographic group. He provided no evidence to back up his claims.
- Mayor Barletta blames Latino immigrants for a rise in overtime due to a murder allegedly committed by an undocumented immigrant. Yet his own records reveal that only 15% of the overtime was due to that crime and the rest was due to the chronic understaffing stemming from the layoffs he earlier imposed. He provided no evidence to back up his claims. (Puerto Rican Legal Defense and Education Fund 2007)

---

4. The court in *Lozano*, took note of the plaintiff's argument that crime actually decreased during the years when the number of immigrants increased, but did not rule on that issue, as the legal issues of the case did not require the court to do so (496 F. Supp 2d 477, 542 [2007]).

Consonant with PRLDEF's position on the case, *The New York Times* published an editorial condemning Mayor Barletta and efforts like his as "vigilantism":

> A federal judge has dealt what we can only hope is a decisive blow against a dangerous trend of freelance immigration policies by local governments.... It is not yet clear when or whether Hazleton's vigilantism will finally be stifled. Mr. Barletta says he will appeal. He and others across the country can be expected to keep concocting ever-more-inventive strategies to deliver pain to immigrants. But that is a legal and moral dead end. As long as people like Mr. Barletta persist in misusing the law to serve their prejudices, they will make the immigration system an ever more incoherent muddle. They will thwart reasonable efforts to grapple with the opportunities and problems borne in with the influx of newcomers. And they will continue to dehumanize not only their victims, but themselves. (*New York Times* 2007b, A14)

The *Hazleton* decision stands as an important decision, but, as *The New York Times* predicts, it will not hinder other attempts to push for other equally objectionable laws. Those efforts could also come at the federal level, which will require that other legal actions be taken to ensure that legal precedents, laws, and constitutional safeguards are maintained which protect the rights of all persons in the United States, not just citizens. In this respect, Professor Kevin R. Johnson advocates that federal class actions on be half of immigrants—particularly in relation to cross-border issues—include violation of international human rights claims in support of protecting immigrant rights (Johnson 2004). The value of implementing and enforcing international human rights principles and laws for Latinos/as generally—and especially vulnerable communities, such as Latino/a immigrants—has gained increased importance. In addition to anti-discrimination provisions in human rights treaties and principles, international human rights instruments specifically address other human rights issues of immigrants and migrant workers.

The International Convention on the Protection of the Rights of All Migrant Workers and Members of their Families calls for the protection of the health, safety, and well-being of all migrant workers and their families, including the provision of fair and equal conditions of employment, freedom from slavery or servitude and child labor, and other basic rights and treatment (United Nations 1990; Appendix G). Implementation of this instrument along with the enforcement of national laws can help promote protections for many Latino/a workers in the United States. In light of California's Proposition 187 and similar legislative attempts to curtail basic health, education and other public services to immigrants, legal scholars have sought to use international human rights law to promote standards that protect immigrants from legislative actions and policies, such as those being promoted in California, that seek to blame immigrants for the economic woes of states (see Hernández-Truyol 1997).

Consistent with international standards are measures that protect the human rights of immigrant workers from exploitation by U.S. companies seeking workers from Latin America as a cheap source of labor. Trafficking in human beings has become an industry onto itself, one that preys on immigrants desperately seeking jobs in the United States, often with deadly consequences. In May and June of 2003 charges were brought against approximately 100 persons accused of participating in a smuggling ring that brought Latin American immigrants into the United States (Zernike 2003, A18). The indictments were initiated after 19 of 74 immigrants from Mexico and Central America were found dead, apparently of suffocation, in a crowded truck (A18).

Nevertheless, trafficking in human beings for low wage employment and other purposes, such as prostitution, has become a lucrative business in the United States. In October 2003, federal agents in 21 states raided 60 stores of the world's largest retailer, Wal-Mart, which had been illegally employing undocumented workers (Greenhouse 2003b, A1). The exploitation of undocumented workers was in violation of labor laws, and thus, in 2003 the Mexican American Legal Defense and Education Fund filed suit against Wal-Mart for paying workers below the minimum wage and for failing to pay overtime (A1).

Human trafficking has been identified and condemned by the United Nations as a contemporary form of slavery and is prohibited under international human rights law, including the International Covenant on Civil and Political Rights (United Nations 1966a, art. 8). Greater awareness and enforcement of these and other international standards, such as those that protect workers rights under the International Labor Organization (ILO), could provide broader safeguards for immigrant and migrant workers.

Sensible strategies that provide immigrant workers with protections are possible. For instance, farmers in Napa County in California, who run a $4 billion wine industry primarily using immigrant labor, have begun to tax themselves to provide humane living conditions for their workers and to support legislative efforts to legalize the immigration status of their farm workers (Sánchez 2003). These steps are being taken in view of the fact that these immigrant workers benefit the U.S. economy and that it is only just that their plight be ameliorated.

In contrast, however, recent proposals for a new guest-worker program in the United States raises legitimate concerns about the exploitation of laborers from Mexico. Such a program may replicate the worst exploitative practices of the infamous *Bracero* Program (1942–1964) and, of course, would be contrary to international standards for the protection of the human rights of migrants. The Mexican Labor Program, or the *Bracero* Program as it has become known, was an agreement entered into between the United States and Mexico during World War II, ostensibly to assuage a labor shortage in the United States. Mexico, for its part, signed an agreement for a temporary guest-worker program in the United States that supposedly protected its citizens from abuse and discrimination. The accord specified that immigrant workers from Mexico would receive decent health care, wages, housing, food, and other conditions and treatment. But, as Gilbert Paul Carrasco notes, the rights and protections built into the agreement were ignored by both the U.S. government and the U.S. agriculture industry:

> The upshot of the *Bracero* Program was that the U.S. government provided [U.S.] growers with cheap labor.... *Braceros* across the country were compelled to endure poor food, excessive charges for board, substandard housing, discrimination, physical mistreatment, inappropriate deductions from their wages, and exposure to pesticides and other dangerous chemicals. (Carrasco 1997, 195)

Considering the track record of guest-worker programs in the United States, it is imperative that immigrants and immigrant workers be protected in a manner consistent with international human rights standards.

The Rights of Latinas

The advancement of women's rights has been an area of concern and action in the United States since women have and continue to face economic, social, and political inequalities and discrimination. In this regard, Latinas have not been an exception. They often endure inequalities and discrimination even more severe than those experienced by White women.

The socioeconomic condition of Latinas has been exceptionally alarming. In comparison to African American and White girls, school-age Latinas are more likely to drop out of school (Canedy 2001). The Census Bureau confirms that 26 percent of Latinas leave school without a diploma, compared to 13 percent of African American girls and 6.9 percent of White girls (1). Among all students, only Latino boys drop out at a higher rate, with 31 percent Latino boys dropping out compared to 12.1 percent of African American boys and 7.7 percent of White boys (1). Vulnerability to mixed cultural messages and the lack of viable career prospects are among the factors that the American Institute for Research and other prominent observers attribute to this disturbing trend among Latinas. As Rossana Rosado, publisher of the New York Spanish-language newspaper *El Diario-La Prensa*, explains, too few options and opportunities are available to Latinas. Consequently, at age "12 or 13 you pretty much realize you're not going to be Jennifer and if you're not going to be Jennifer López then what is there?" (24).

Within the criminal justice system, the situation of Latinas in prison is similarly disconcerting, as evidenced by the statistics compiled in a report by the Sentencing Project:

- In state prisons and jails Hispanic females are incarcerated at almost twice the rate of white females (117 persons to 63 persons per 100,000 [persons in the] population).
- Hispanic women are three times as likely to go to prison in their lifetime as compared to white women (1.5% vs. 0.5%).
- In the U.S. general population, 9.7% of women are Hispanic. In the U.S. prison population, 15% of women state prisoners and 32% of women Federal prisoners are Hispanic.
- Between 1990 and 1996, the number of Hispanic female prisoners rose 71%.
- In New York, Hispanic women are 14% of the state's prison population but constitute 44% of women sentenced to prison for drug offenses. (2003, 2)

Undoubtedly, these disturbing statistics speak to the need to address the economic, social, and cultural conditions, and discrimination Latinas face in the United States. Attention to these areas would undoubtedly be helpful in preventing Latinas from becoming entangled in the criminal justice and prison systems. In addition to the implementation of the aforementioned human rights provisions, the Convention on the Elimination of all Forms of Discrimination against Women (CEDAW) provides specific human rights protections for women (United Nations 1979b; Appendix F). CEDAW requires State Parties to prohibit discrimination against women and to take measures, including legislative action, to advance the rights of women in all areas of political, economic, social, and cultural life (arts. 1, 3, and 5). All aspects of family, work, security, education, and health and safety, in which women have been subject to unequal treatment, are addressed by the Convention. The benefits for Latinas, whose particular economic and social circumstances leave them susceptible to inequities and discrimination, would likely be profound if CEDAW were to be ratified and enforced in the United States. Indeed these benefits would extend to many other women of color and women in general.

Disturbingly, the United States that stands virtually alone in the world as not having ratified this important treaty.[5]

Language Rights

The United States, which often takes pride in being a country of immigrants, is also a country deeply torn by the issue of language diversity. The contentiousness of the language debate too often sidetracks a dispassionate look at the issues involved. That the controversy is fueled by xenophobic, nativists forces that seek to incite anti-immigrant sentiments makes it even more difficult to discern the facts concerning language issues (Hernández-Chávez 1995).

Few opinions on language are as popular as the belief that immigrants— and especially Latinos/as—refuse to learn English. In her book, *"Why don't they learn English?": Separating Fact from Fallacy in the U.S. Language Debate,* Professor Lucy Tse (2001, 14) addresses the question empirically, citing research that shows that, in fact, "the large majority of immigrants *are learning English and learning it well."* Data for all immigrants—as well as data on Latinos/as based on geographic areas, such as Florida, where they are concentrated, and data on specific groups, such as Colombians, Dominicans, Guatemalans, and Salvadorans—point to remarkable progress in English-language acquisition (12–21). Contrary to popularly held beliefs about the influence of culture, differences in social class affect the rate of English language acquisition much more than cultural heritage. Therefore, a child from a higher social class who benefited from better quality education in his/her home country is likely to have better educational achievement in the United States (21–24). Tse concludes that

> [d]espite public perception to the contrary, children of immigrants are by and large learning English rapidly and succeeding in school. Important to note is that these achievements are being made in spite of formidable economic and social obstacles, including a high level of poverty and inadequate publicly supported English-language programs. It is clear, then, that the question ..."Why don't they learn English?" is based on an unsupported assumption that immigrants are not learning the language and are resistant to becoming English proficient. The language restrictionism advocated by policy makers and members of the public is, in fact, unnecessary. (2001, 21)

---

5. As of 19 April 2007, 185 parties among the United Nations' 192 member states have ratified of CEDAW.

Tse's conclusion strikes at the fallacy of much of what the "English-only" and "Official English" movements since the 1980s have attempted to convince the public of, essentially that other languages pose a threat to English as the unifying language of the country. She points out that English is not threatened, and that "[c]hildren of immigrants, in fact, favor English over their heritage language, which has spelled the systematic loss and eventual death of heritage language in immigrant families" (Tse 2001, 71). Immigrants also feel the powerful pull of the English language. They understand the importance of English to participation in the political, social, and economic life in the country and in the world (Tse 2001, 32). As James Crawford (1992, 3) notes, a major argument of the proponents of English as an official language is that immigrants today are not learning English as rapidly as their predecessors, an assertion Tse refutes. Crawford also makes clear that much of the Official English's "thrust was not only *for* English, but *against* bilingualism" (Crawford 1992, 1). There, too, Tse and others show that bilingualism can actually serve as an effective strategy in English language learning to the benefit of the individual and the society (Tse 2001, 44–51; see also Portes and Rumbaut (2006, 241–43).[6]

Researchers Alejandro Portes and Rubén G. Rumbaut (2006, 229) report findings similar to Tse's. English language acquisition follows a consistent pattern. Most first-generation immigrants who come to the United States as children speak English well, bilingualism is most common among second-generation immigrants and by the third generation English is predominant. Portes and Rumbaut (2006, 242) find that when one controls for social class, "fluent or 'true' bilingual children actually outperformed monolinguals on a variety of achievement tests."

The Pew Hispanic Center (2006) also finds little validity to the claim that many Latinos/as do not wish to learn English. To the contrary, the Center's research shows that "[b]y overwhelming margins, Latinos say it is very important that English be taught to children of immigrant families" and that on this issue "Hispanics hold stronger views than either non-Hispanic whites or blacks (92%, 87% and 83% respectively)" (Pew Hispanic Center 2006, 2). Indeed, one of the greatest obstacles to learning English is not the lack of desire

---

6. Tse indicates that the individual benefits have been shown in a number of studies. In one study, bilingual students of Latino "heritage were better readers in English and had higher academic aspirations" than their monolingual counterparts, while other studies showed similar results (Tse 2001, 48). In the United States, the benefits of knowing other languages are many, including advantage in the fields of international business and commerce (48–51).

to learn it, but the lack of programs. As reported in *The New York Times*, the demand far outstrips the supply:

> A survey last year by the National Association of Latino Elected and Appointed Officials found that in 12 states, 60 percent of the free English programs had waiting lists, ranging from a few months in Colorado and Nevada to as long as two years in New Mexico and Massachusetts, where the statewide list has about 16,000 names.... Luis Sanchez, 47, ... has been ... on the waiting list for English classes in Perth Amboy five months. "You live from day to day, waiting to get the call that you can come to class," Mr. Sanchez said in Spanish, explaining that he knew a little English but wanted to improve his writing skills so he could apply for better jobs. "I keep on waiting." (Santos 2007, A1)

Given the prevailing view, garnering support for English-language programs has been difficult. It was Senator Lamar Alexander, a Republican and education secretary under President George H.W. Bush, who took a reasonable stance on the issue of federal funding for English-language programs: "If we make it easier for people to learn English, they will learn it. I think that ought to be a priority of our government, and I don't think it has been." (Santos 2007, A1)

Despite Senator Alexander's view, the language question continues to be skewed in favor of a restrictive and even punitive approach, rather than one that recognizes the diverse linguistic heritages in the country as a strength, instead of a deficit, and the willingness of immigrants to learn English. Several court decisions have perpetuated this restrictive and punitive approach. For instance, the Fifth and Ninth Federal Court Circuits have ruled in favor of employers who impose English-only rules in the workplace (*Garcia v. Gloor*, 618 F.2d 264 [5th Cir. 1980]; *cert. denied* 449 U.S. 1113 [1981]; *Garcia v. Spun Steak Co.*, 998 F.2d 1480 [9th Cir. 1993]; *cert. denied* 512 U.S. 1228 [1994]). In *Gloor*, the court allowed the policy without requiring a show of any business purpose for prohibiting its employees from speaking Spanish (618 F.2d 264, 267–69). In *Spun Steak*, the court explicitly rejected a guideline by the Equal Employment Opportunity Commission (EEOC) against English-only workplace policies. Grounded on its experience and judgment as an administrative agency specifically mandated to oversee employment discrimination cases, the EEOC promulgated a guideline allowing for a *prima facie* case for discrimination where an English-only policy exists because such policy may "create an atmosphere of inferiority, isolation and intimidation based on national origin which could result in a discriminatory working environment" 29

C.F.R. §1606.7(a). Scholars have questioned whether, in spite of the growth of the Latino/a population in the United States, the society—and the courts by extension—fully appreciate the adverse impact that such workplace policies can have on language minority groups (see, e.g., Perea 1990; Perea et al. 2000, 548–51).

The United States is inhabited by persons with many types of accents. Workplace discrimination based on accents is another area of controversy. In this respect, the Ninth Circuit concurred with the EEOC guidelines in recognizing that equal employment opportunities should not be denied " 'because an individual has the ... linguistic characteristics of a national origin group' 29 C.F.R. §1606.1 (1988)" (*Fragante v. City and County Of Honolulu*, 888 F.2d 591 [9th Cir. 1989]). Nevertheless, the court ruled against the Filipino plaintiff, Manuel Fragante, finding that the business had shown a reasonable business necessity in selecting a person with "superior qualifications" (888 F.2d 591, 599). In her critique of the case, Professor Mari Matsuda raises the question about how the distribution of power in society determines how accents are evaluated, including which are valued and which are denigrated (Matsuda 1991).

Yet, of all the issues involving language rights in the United States, bilingual education remains perhaps the most debated and misunderstood (Crawford 1992). In spite of the strong, if not overwhelming, scholarly evidence about the soundness of bilingual education (see Romaine [1989] 1992; Krashen 1996; Krashen 1999; Crawford 2000; Cummins 2000), the controversy about bilingualism in schools continues. Unfortunately, anti-immigrant sentiments, xenophobia, and ethnic/racial hatred feed misconceptions about bilingualism and bilingual education (see, e.g., Crawford 2000; Cummins 2000). In stark contrast to the United States, in many parts of the world the use of native language instruction in schools and multilingualism are common because of their pedagogical soundness and as a matter of human rights (Skutnabb-Kangas and Phillipson 1995; Kontra et al. 1999; Skutnabb-Kangas 2000).

Nonetheless, the merits of programs that address the needs of non-English speaking persons in the United States have not gone unrecognized. As a matter of law, U.S. Supreme Court decisions still stand as precedents in support of the basic concept of bilingual education for children whose native language is not English (see *Meyers v. Nebraska*, 262 U.S. 390 [1923]; *Lau v. Nichols*, 414 U.S. 563 [1974]). Moreover, a substantial body of research on bilingual education conducted in the United States, including studies sponsored by the federal government, speaks to the effectiveness of bilingual education programs when properly organized and funded (Del Valle 2003, 223–224; see also

Romaine [1989] 1992; Krashen 1996; Krashen 1999; Crawford 2000; Cummins 2000).[7]

Language Rights in the Courts

Beyond controversies about bilingual education, it would seem only reasonable for courts to protect persons whose language is not English from being convicted simply because they did not understand the charges, the testimony, or the legal proceedings against them. But in fact, no Supreme Court decision has recognized a constitutional right to an interpreter in court; no national standards for interpreters in state courts exist; and in civil or administrative proceedings courts have routinely refused to recognize a constitutional right to an interpreter (Piatt 1990). Taken together, for many Latinos/as, these present formidable obstacles to equal justice.

The Court Interpreters Act, 28 U.S.C. §1827 (1994), does extend the right to an interpreter within the federal court system, but it also requires astute and persistent advocacy on the part of legal counsel to insure full and proper exercise of this right (Piatt 1990). Given the difficulty that a poor, limited-English Latina or Latino is likely to have in securing adequate counsel, this federal right is not a sure safeguard.

Problems even arise in state courts that provide assistance for those who speak a language other than English. Although in 1970 in *United States ex rel. Negron v. New York*, 434 F.2d 386 (2d Cir. 1970), the Second Circuit Court of Appeals held that non-English-speaking defendants had a right to simultaneous interpreters at the government's expense, in cases where a defendant's lawyer can interpret, courts have placed the burden of translating on the attorney, presenting obstacles for both the attorney whose advocacy may be impaired and the client whose case may suffer from not having simultaneous translation. In instances where an interpreter is provided, attorneys may still have to insist on a simultaneous translation (Piatt 1990).

With respect to interpreter services for witnesses, they are not necessarily provided interpreters even when requested. Legal scholars point to the case of *Gonzalez v. United States*, 33 F. 3d 1047 (9th Cir. 1994), as an example where

---

7. A longitudinal study of bilingual education conducted by J. David Ramírez at the request of the federal government found that bilingual education had positive results, supporting the theory posited by Jim Cummins that development of the first language increases the development of the second (Del Valle 2003, 223). Other extensive studies support the validity of long-term developmental bilingual programs for language-minority children, including that of Drs. Virginia Collier and Wayne Thomas (224).

the denial of an interpreter may have caused the defendant to inadvertently plead guilty (Méndez 1997; Del Valle 2003). A reading of the court transcript in the *Gonzalez* case ostensibly shows that the defendant with limited English proficiency was confused by the questions asked by the judge, yet the guilty plea was upheld on appeal (Méndez 1997). In spite of a request for a certified court appointed interpreter, the court denied the request and ruled that Gonzalez's wife could assist as an interpreter, even though there was no proof that she could translate accurately and impartially, as required by the Court Interpreters Act (93).

The results of the *Gonzalez* case appear to support the assertion of some legal scholars that courts commonly take a cavalier and ethnocentric approach in cases involving Latinos/as where interpreters are required (see, e.g., Haney López 2003; Bender 2003). Examples of inconsistency or nonexistent standards for the use of interpreters stand as a testament for the need to establish uniform nationwide guidelines that address the linguistic and cultural needs of a diverse population. In this area, international human rights principles and standards may prove effective in the development and implementation of appropriate safeguards for language minority groups in the United States.

In the provision of bilingual services, it is also important to take into account the linguistic variations that exist among Latinos/as in the United States. Latinos/as generally share certain cultural characteristics, but they should not be assumed to have identical linguistic needs, particularly within the criminal justice context. The meaning of words and the use of expressions in Spanish vary from one Latin American country to another in ways that may be significant in a court proceeding. To produce a system that adequately addresses the linguistic needs of all persons who enter into the judicial process, providing culturally competent and appropriate services, such as qualified bilingual interpreters familiar with the linguistic differences between persons of specific Latin American countries, must be among the measures that are adopted. Researchers and policy reform advocates alike have reported on the detrimental effects of not providing culturally competent services in the criminal justice system, prompting urgent calls for the creation of such services (see Villarruel et al. 2002).

Criminal Justice

International human rights groups have campaigned strongly for expanded use of international human rights standards to help ensure accountability for police misconduct and brutality cases in the United States (Amnesty International 1998; Human Rights Watch 1998). In response to the many cases of excessive use of police force against Latinos/as and African Americans in the United States, human rights groups have supported the implementation of international standards for the conduct of law enforcement officials, especially the rules found in the Code of Conduct for Law Enforcement Officials (United Nations 1979a). The provision of the Code most basic to protecting human rights maintains that "[l]aw enforcement officials may use force only when strictly necessary and to the extent required for the performance of their duty" (art. 3).

Additional guidance to law enforcement personnel is found under article 5 of the Code, which instructs that "[n]o law enforcement official may inflict, instigate or tolerate any act of torture or other cruel, inhuman or degrading treatment or punishment, nor may any law enforcement official invoke superior orders or exceptional circumstances such as a state of war, threat to national security, internal political instability or any other public emergency as a justification of torture or other cruel, inhuman or degrading treatment or punishment." This provision has drawn particular attention in recent years as a result of the highly publicized case of Abner Louima, the Haitian immigrant who was sodomized with a stick by a police officer in a Brooklyn police station in 1997.

As a matter of international law, torture or cruel, inhuman or degrading treatment or punishment are prohibited pursuant to many international human rights treaties, including the International Covenant on Civil and Political Rights (United Nations 1966a, art. 7) and the Convention against Torture and other Cruel, Inhuman or Degrading Treatment or Punishment (United Nations 1984). Having ratified both treaties, the United States is obligated to observe their provisions. Human rights groups have urged adherence to the requirements of these treaties in order to provide additional protection to communities of color, including Latino/a communities, from police violence (see Johnson 2003, 293).

The Death Penalty

The United States is the only industrialized nation that maintains the institution of capital punishment. The world community has widely adopted the policy of abolishing the death penalty as a matter of upholding the fundamental human right to life. Human rights groups not only condemn the U.S. government's reluctance to end capital punishment, but denounce its disproportionate effect on people of color. The racial impact of the death penalty has been widely documented, with Whites representing 48 percent of all death row inmates and all other groups representing 52 percent of death row inmates, including African Americans at 42 percent, Latinos/as at 8 percent, and "others" at 3 percent in 1990 (Amnesty International 1998, 111). Although Latinos/as are not affected to the extent African Americans are, there is still reason for concern. Race continues to loom large in how the death penalty is applied (Amnesty International 2003). As history shows, whenever race has been an issue, Latinos/as have usually been affected. Moreover, as Amnesty International reports (2003), there are a significant number of documented death penalty cases involving Latinos where race appears to have been a decisive factor.

One indicator of racial and ethnic bias in the criminal justice system's handling of death penalty cases is the data that show that the race of the victims in almost all capital punishment cases tends to be White. From 1976 to 1990, 83 percent of the victims in capital cases were White while only 12 percent were African American and 4 percent were Latino/a. However, for the same period only 50 percent of murder victims in capital cases were White (Amnesty International 1998, 111). Thus, a person of color was more likely to be sentenced to death for killing a White person than a White person for killing a person of color.

Another significant issue that has gained considerable attention in recent years is the mounting number of persons on death row proven to have been wrongly convicted and sentenced to death. With the increased use of DNA tests and other methods to prove their innocence, an ever-increasing number of death row inmates have gone free. From 1973 to 1998, approximately 75 people sentenced to death were found to be innocent (Amnesty International 1998, 118). Moreover, a number of states have looked into the possibility of imposing moratoriums on the death penalty as the number persons on death row who are found to be innocent grows. In fact, Governor George Ryan of Illinois, a Republican, not only took the dramatic step of imposing a moratorium after 13 individuals sentenced to death were found innocent, in January 2003 he also commuted the sentences of all death row inmates based in large part on the racially discriminatory impact of the capital punishment process. In doing so, Governor Ryan singled out that over two thirds of the death row inmates were African American, and that at least 35 of them had been sentenced to death by all-White juries (Amnesty International 2003).

The growing body of evidence linking racial and ethnic bias to the death penalty process coupled with the history of racial and ethnic bias against Latinos/as in the U.S. criminal justice system and their ever-increasing numbers in prisons should make capital punishment an issue of enormous concern for Latino/a communities. The death penalty becomes another area of the justice system where Latinos/as are exposed to unfair and unequal treatment. In his study of the death penalty, Professor Martin G. Urbina (2003, 233) found that Latinos/as "do not receive the same type of treatment by the criminal justice system." He confirmed that Latinos faced severe difficulties in California, Florida, and Texas between 1975 and 1995 in having their death sentences overturned or declared unconstitutional on appeal and that Latinos face a myriad of obstacles—including linguistic and financial limitations—that impede them from securing equal justice in death penalty cases (227-38).

Adding to the perils faced by Latinos/as with regard to the death penalty, there have been many instances in which the United States has been willing to defy international law in order to try and execute persons from Latin America. Amnesty International (1998) and other human rights groups have repeatedly condemned the U.S. government's actions in violation of the Vienna Convention on Consular Relations, a treaty that the United Sates is obligated to observe. In 1998, in defiance of a decision by the International Court of Justice, the United States allowed the execution of Ángel Francisco Breard, a Paraguayan who was never allowed to exercise his right to secure assistance from the Paraguayan consular office as provided for under Vienna Convention on Consular Relations (125). Similarly, the case of Humberto Álvarez Machaín—a Mexican citizen kidnapped from his country by the U.S. Drug Enforcement Agency, then tried and executed in the United States—sparked an international incident as he, too, had been denied the right to assistance from the Mexican consul in an egregious violation of international law (124–25).

U.S. violations of the basic sovereignty rights of Latin American countries and the Vienna Convention on Consular Relations signal a continuation of the paternalistic and condescending patterns and policies of the past, which need to change. Adherence to international law standards would be an essential first step. To that end, the United States should not only join the vast community of nations that prohibit the death penalty, but also respect the basic principles of international law that pertain to the equal rights and sovereignty of nations. (see, e.g., United Nations 1945, arts. 1 and 2).

A glimmer of hope that the United States may be moving in a direction consistent with the rest of the world on the death penalty was raised by Justice Anthony Kennedy's opinion in *Roper v. Simmons*, 543 U.S. 551 (2005), which brought to an end the application of capital punishment against minors in the United States:

> Our determination that the death penalty is disproportionate punishment for offenders under 18 finds confirmation in the stark reality that the United States is the only country in the world that con-

tinues to give official sanction to the juvenile death penalty. This reality does not become controlling, for the task of interpreting the Eighth Amendment remains our responsibility. Yet ... the Court has referred to the laws of other countries and to international authorities as instructive for its interpretation of the Eighth Amendment's prohibition of "cruel and unusual punishments." ... Article 37 of the United Nations Convention on the Rights of the Child, which every country in the world has ratified save for the United States and Somalia, contains an express prohibition on capital punishment for crimes committed by juveniles under 18.... Respondent and his *amici* have submitted, and petitioner does not contest, that only seven countries other than the United States have executed juvenile offenders since 1990: Iran, Pakistan, Saudi Arabia, Yemen, Nigeria, the Democratic Republic of Congo, and China. Since then each of these countries has either abolished capital punishment for juveniles or made public disavowal of the practice.... In sum, it is fair to say that the United States now stands alone in a world that has turned its face against the juvenile death penalty. (543 U.S. 551, 556–557)

Economic, Social, and Cultural Rights: Rights for All

International human rights laws and principles protect the human rights of all members of society. These international protections extend into the realm of economic, social, and cultural rights as well as civil and political rights. In this regard, the International Covenant on Economic, Social and Cultural Rights seeks to ensure that the right to work, to fair wages, to equality of remuneration, to adequate health care, to education, and to maintain one's linguistic and cultural heritage are protected for everyone without discrimination based on race, color, sex, language, religion, political or other opinion, national or social origin, property, birth, or other status (United Nations 1966b). The realization of these principles stands to benefit everyone since they are intended to provide a basic standard of living, and thereby serve as a preventive measure against crime and other social problems.

Unfortunately, it is widely assumed that people of color in the United States comprise the vast majority of the poor and persons receiving public assistance in some form. Just as the culprits of crime have been racialized, so has poverty. A study of news stories by the media found that the news media often present a distorted image of the racial and ethnic make up of the poor in the

United States. Professor Martin Gilens (1999) at Yale University discovered that 65 percent of television news and 62 percent of newsmagazine stories depicted the poor as African Americans when in reality African Americans make up only 29 percent of the poor. His study concluded that welfare and poverty have been "racialized" as demonstrated by public attitudes toward welfare and poverty that are heavily influenced by negative stereotypes of African Americans in particular, including the perception that they are lazy (70–71). Although not to the same degree as the depiction of African Americans, the study shows that Latinos/as are also negatively perceived as "lazy," and predicts that "[a]s the country's Hispanic population continues to grow, attitudes toward welfare may become as strongly associated with perceptions of Hispanics as they are now with perceptions of blacks" (71). This conclusion is consistent with the analysis of other scholars who have examined the problem of Latino/a stereotypes in the United States and have shown that "laziness" is among the most omnipresent stereotypes attributed to Latinos/as (see, e.g., Bender 2003; Haney López 2003).

The persistence of stereotypes of Latinos/as as "lazy" obfuscates the reality that Whites comprise the single largest group living in poverty in the United States, according to the latest census data (Bureau of the Census 2003d, 2).[8] Welfare reform in the 1990s dramatically reduced the number of persons on public assistance, from 5 million to 2 million persons (Rainwater and Smeeding 2003, 141), but it did little to reduce poverty. In fact, poverty rates have actually been on the rise. In the United States, it rose from 11.7 percent in 2001 to 12.1 percent in 2002 (Bureau of the Census 2003d, 1). Accordingly, more benefits would probably accrue to Whites than any other group if the United States were to embrace international human rights standards that promote economic, social, and cultural rights.

Indeed, recent studies indicate that it is increasingly difficult to argue that economic and social conditions in the United States are better than in most other advanced nations. Recent census data show that about 43.6 million people (15.2 percent of the population) in the United States were without health coverage in 2002, an increase of 2.4 million (14.6 percent) from 2001 (Bureau of the Census 2003a, 1). The United States is the only developed nation without some form of universal health care, something that in many countries has long been deemed vital to the economic and social wellbeing of a nation.

---

8. The Bureau of the Census (2003d, 2, table 1) indicates that 15,271,000 persons under the category of "White, not Hispanic" fall below the poverty level while 7,997,000 of those categorized as "Hispanic (of any race)" and 8,136,000 of those categorized as "Black" fall below the poverty level.

In its call for universal health coverage in the United States by the year 2010, the Institute of Medicine of the National Academy of Sciences (2004b, 1) not only drew attention to the nation's appalling lack of health coverage, but pointed out that "[a]bout 18,000 unnecessary deaths occur each year because of lack of health insurance." The Institute of Medicine report further explains that:

- The number of uninsured individuals under age 65 is large, growing, and has persisted even during periods of strong economic growth.
- Uninsured children and adults do not receive the care they need; they suffer from poorer health and development, and are more likely to die early than are those with coverage.
- Even one uninsured person in a family can put the financial stability and health of the whole family at risk.
- A community's high uninsured rate can adversely affect the overall health status of the community, its health care institutions and providers, and the access of its residents to certain services. (Institute of Medicine of the National Academy of Sciences 2004a, 2)

Although the United States is the wealthiest country in the world, the United Nations Development Programme (2003, 249) reports that according to its Human Poverty Index (HPI), which measures national levels of poverty, illiteracy, unemployment, and life-expectancy among the world's richest countries, Sweden ranked first and the United States last (with more people living in the mentioned conditions and a lower life expectancy). While Sweden has a lower per capita income, the United States, on average, has more adults who are functionally illiterate and more who are living in poverty (248–49).

In an analysis comparing the United States and 14 other developed countries of the world, researchers of the Luxembourg Income Study, Lee Rainwater and Timothy M. Smeeding (2003, 21), found that the United States has the highest percentage of children (20.3 percent) living in poverty.[9] Their study also addresses the issue of economic inequality in the United States, noting that the poor in the United States are not necessarily better off:

A comforting belief in the United States is that while we may have more inequality than European countries, decades of economic

---

9. Rainwater and Smeeding (2003, 21) found the United States to have the highest rate of child poverty followed by (in descending order) Italy, United Kingdom, Canada, Australia, Spain, Germany, France, the Netherlands, Switzerland, Belgium, Denmark, Norway, Finland, and Sweden.

growth have lifted even the worst-off Americans to a higher standard of living than the marginal economic classes of Europe. Rather surprisingly, this turns out not to be the case. In half of our comparison countries roughly the lowest income third of children are better off in real terms than their American peers. And in the others (except for Australia, Spain, the United Kingdom, and Italy) the children in the same rank as the poor American children who make up the bottom income child quintile are as well or better off. (48)

Rainwater and Smeeding also found that children in the United States are likely to be poorer longer and are less able to move out of poverty than in other countries they studied. In comparing the United States to Germany, they state that "[n]ot only are more children poor for a longer period of time than in Germany, but American children are much more likely than German children, if they have been economically marginal as adolescents, to also experience poverty when they grow up" (67).

As for the impact of immigration on poverty, their study showed roughly that "while in most (or perhaps all) countries recent arrivals have elevated child poverty rates compared with rates for natives, these differences nowhere approach those in the United States between minorities and whites. And it is not clear that the differences that do exist are likely to persist over the decades in the same way they have in the United States" (31).

The hope for children in the United States, as Rainwater and Smeeding conclude, lies in the implementation of a comprehensive plan that invests in the following societal needs: job creation (employment), parental leave, child care, child-related tax policy, child support, and education (132–41). These areas are, in fact, among the areas that pertain to economic, social, and cultural rights under international human right law, including the Convention on the Rights of the Child (Appendix E).

Resolving problems of poverty and other forms of economic and social deprivation will require more than an effort to address a presumed lack of family values. Sweden, with a much lower percentage of children born into poverty than the United States, has proportionately a larger number of children born out of wedlock (Donziger 1996, 215). Why other developed countries fare better has much to do with the social safety net that is available in those countries (Donziger 1996; Rainwater and Smeeding 2003).

Ultimately, the United States must also come to terms with the social costs of the enormous number of persons without health insurance and with other problems related to high levels of economic inequality. Poor health and low economic status are associated with long-term problems and consequences to society in the form of social dislocation and increases in criminal behavior (see Walker et al. 2004, 65–89). Thus, it becomes incumbent on society to adopt measures that address the economic, social, and cultural rights of all persons as recognized under international human rights standards. As international law scholar Louis Henkin asserts (1990, 10), a commitment to human rights implies that societies must take responsibility for meeting the basic needs of all:

> We are all members of a community that benefits all. Community and communality imply obligations, and high among them is the obligation to assure basic human needs for those who cannot satisfy their own.

Conclusion

The United States still lags behind most nations of the world in ratifying many human rights agreements. Although U.S. presidents have signed the International Covenant on Economic, Social and Cultural Rights, the Convention on the Elimination of all forms of Discrimination against Women, and the Convention on the Rights of the Child, there is negligible interest in the U.S. Senate for the ratification of these international instruments. Having ratified several major international human rights treaties, however, the United States is obligated to observe and protect human rights pursuant to these international agreements. It is also obligated to observe article VI of the U.S. Constitution, which requires that "all Treaties made, or which shall be made under the Authority of the United States, shall be the supreme Law of the Land."

But, the United States has been reticent to enforce the international human rights documents it has ratified. Its ratification of human rights treaties, such as the International Covenant on Civil and Political Rights or the Convention against Torture and Other Cruel, Inhuman or Degrading Treatment or Punishment, was accompanied by reservations that limited their application and enforceability within the United States. Its reservations regarding international law and standards on the death penalty and cruel and unusual punishment, for instance, have been the subject of controversy and objections at the international level since such reservations have been deemed to undermine the meaning and purpose of human rights treaties. The U.N. Human Rights Committee (1994) has declared that these types of reservations are detrimental to the implementation and effectiveness of human rights treaties. Nevertheless, the Human Rights Committee's admonitions have fallen on deaf ears in the United States.

One of the major obstacles to the enforcement of international human rights law in the United States is the requirement of an enabling federal law granting jurisdiction to U.S. courts to hear cases brought pursuant to human right treaties. Indeed, even provisions of the U.N. Charter regarding human rights (arts. 55 and 56) have been found to be non-self-executing (that is, lacking an enabling federal statute) and therefore unenforceable in U.S. courts (*Sei Fujii v. California*, 38 Cal.2d 718, 242 P.2d 617 [1952]).

In a some instances, gross violations of human rights so universally condemned by the world community, as in the case of torture, have successfully proceeded through U.S. courts as matters falling under the Alien Tort Claims Act and customary international law (see, e.g., *Filartiga v. Peña-Irala*, 630 F.2d 876 [2d Cir. 1980]).[10] However, with the exception of the limited cases in which U.S. courts have had to confront issues of international human rights, the United States has generally avoided full compliance with international law, either in the courts or as a matter of government policy.

U.S. observance of international law and standards has implications for all of Latin America. Respect for the sovereignty of Latin American nations, in instances such as the case of Álvarez Machaín, have an impact on matters of justice in both Mexico and the United States. Similarly, the United States is obligated to eradicate colonialism in all its forms pursuant to the universal repudiation of colonialism under the United Nations Charter and other authoritative documents, but in the case of Puerto Rico, it has refused to do so (see Trías Monge 1997; Fernandez 1994; Maldonado Denis 1972). Puerto Rico's continuing colonial status deserves immediate attention since it represents an affront to international law affecting the lives of millions of persons. U.S. adherence to international law and the U.N. decolonization standards delineated in the Declaration on the Granting of Independence to Colonial Countries and Peoples (United Nations 1960; Appendix B) is, therefore, paramount.

Given their potential to expand human rights for the benefit of all society, the relevance of international human rights standards becomes ever more salient in the United States. Major international human rights organizations, such as Amnesty International and Human Rights Watch, stress the need for the United States to abide by international standards it has already ratified and

---

10. In *Filartiga v. Peña-Irala*, 630 F.2d 876 (2d Cir. 1980), the court relied on the Alien Tort Claims Act, 28 U.S.C. §1350 (1982), a law with origins in the Judiciary Act of 1789. Similar to the Alien Tort Claims Act, a subsequent law passed in 1992, the Torture Victims Protection Act, 28 U.S.C. §1331 (1992), provides for the right to bring before a U.S. federal court an action for civil damages against individuals who commit acts of torture outside the United States.

to begin to join the many other countries of the world that have expanded their concept of human rights principles and standards (Amnesty International, 1998; Human Rights Watch, 1998).

For Latinos/as, who continue to experience deprivation of rights, existing standards serve as a model for their protection, not in the form of preferential treatment, but in observance of human rights principles increasingly grounded in worldwide acceptance. Increased knowledge and familiarity with international human rights principles and their applicability to local struggles can help champion respect for and the protection of cultural, linguistic, social and economic rights, opening the possibility of advancing Latino/a rights throughout the United States.

To protect the economic, social, and cultural rights of every person is to protect that which is most essential to the dignity of all human beings (Goldewijk, Baspineiro, and Carbonari 2002). Thus, an expansion of the concept of human rights within the United States to include economic, social, and cultural rights would do more than assist those who are marginalized in the society. Based on the discussion above, large benefits could accrue to all sectors of society. Greater economic and social stability would also go far in reducing crime and other social ills. Thus, advocating for the implementation of broader human rights standards not only serves to extend protection to Latino/a communities, but to further the cause in favor of equal rights and human rights for all.

CHAPTER 8

THE QUEST FOR JUSTICE

The past and current injustices, social and economic disadvantage, and racialization of Latinos/as in the United States discussed in this book beg the question about how best to engage in effective and meaningful action to right these wrongs. A central thesis of this book has been that a response is needed that validates the rights of Latinos/as as human beings—that is, as persons whose social, cultural, and economic wellbeing is as deserving of respect and protection as their civil and political rights. Moreover, this book posits responses that assist not only Latino/a communities, but all communities, expanding rights and protections for all persons and broadening opportunities for economic and social justice throughout society.

There are many approaches used to address the panoply of justice issues Latinos/as face in the United States. This book has mentioned many strategies used by Latinos/as over the years in their struggle against discrimination and injustice, including litigation, community advocacy and organizing, protest politics, and legislative initiatives. These strategies are as relevant for Latino/a communities today as they were in decades past. However, this book has focused purposefully on aspects of justice and rights that find resonance in the realm of international human rights law and principles. Although others have advocated for the application of international law in the U.S. context (e.g., Amnesty International 1998; Human Rights Watch 1998) and some have specifically endorsed its application to address Latino/a issues (see, e.g., Hernández-Truyol 1997, 1998; Johnson 2004), this book has placed special emphasis on the facets of international human rights that can provide a point of departure for seeking justice in areas of economic, social, and cultural rights as well as civil and political rights. It is this author's premise that without economic and social rights and respect for cultural differences in society, equality in the areas of civil and political rights will be difficult to achieve. Economic and social disadvantage undermine the civil and political progress of a community. As such, the future advancement of Latinos/as rests on progress made toward guaranteeing economic, social, and cultural rights.

LATINO/AS AND JUSTICE: RECOMMENDATIONS

This book encompasses many of the most pressing rights and justice issues Latinos/as face in contemporary United States. It does not—nor could it possibly—cover every aspects of the Latina/o rights experience. However, the following recommendations can be made, based on the overall issues discussed:

Implement sensible and humane policies toward immigrants

The United States has experienced periods in its history in which anti-immigrant policies and practices burgeoned (see, e.g., Hing 2004; Zinn 2003; Healey 2006). The modern era of increased militarization of the border with Mexico has become another bleak period in that history (Hing 2004).

> Heightened immigration enforcement in the 1990s has taken a terrible human toll. The measures have racially disparate impacts. Military forces are massed almost exclusively on the southern border with Mexico, with the most likely casualties being Mexican citizens. The fact that it is Mexican, not white, persons being killed has tended to dampen any public outcry over the thousands of deaths. Military-style operations on the Southwest border have channeled immigrants into remote, desolate locations where thousands have died agonizing deaths from heat, cold, and thirst. A week rarely goes by without press reports of undocumented Mexican immigrants who have died on the long, treacherous journey to the United States. The title of one November 2002 New York Times article tells it all: 'Skeletons Tell Tale of Gamble by Immigrants.'[1] Despite the growing death toll, the U.S. government continues to pursue enforcement operations with vigor. The California Rural Legal Assistance Foundation attributes over 2,000 deaths in the last decade to one southern California operation known as Operation Gatekeeper. (Johnson 2003, 221–223)

Current U.S. policy has not deterred the flow of immigrants into the United States; rather, it has caused vast human suffering.[2] As Princeton Professors Pa-

---

1. See Fountain with Yardley (2002, A1).
2. Immigration and Customs Enforcement (ICE) officials have continued to aggressively pursue and arrest undocumented immigrants. In one year, "Operation Return to Sender," which purports to target undocumented immigrants with criminal records, has resulted in the doubling of arrests in New Jersey (Schweber 2007, 14NJ2). Recent tactics employed by agents around the country, including the raid on a meat processing plant in

tricia Fernandez-Kelly and Douglas S. Massey (2007) have found, the U.S.-Mexico free trade agreement, NAFTA, has not reaped the type of economic benefits that would keep Mexicans in their country. Instead, they found that "the most important but unexpected effect of current immigration policies was to decrease the likelihood that unauthorized workers will return home.... Beefing up the Border Patrol may not have reduced the inflow of unauthorized immigrants but it has substantially increased the probability that they will stay longer in areas of destination" (112). Additionally, Johnson (2003) has found that aggressive border enforcement tactics since the 1990s appear to have encouraged the permanent settlement of undocumented immigrants in the United States.

Any resolution of the current immigration impasse must take into consideration deep underlying humanitarian issues. U.S. policies should not recreate the exploitative guest-worker practices reminiscent of the *Bracero* program, nor should they pursue further militarization of the border, which has been found to be futile and a source of profound human misery. As Johnson (2003) points out, the current scheme lends itself to racial discrimination, the criminalization of all immigrants and the unraveling of the close familial, economic, and social ties that many Mexicans have across the two borders.

The United States should strive for a policy based on humane and rational means to integrate immigrants into U.S. society, rather than look to additional punitive measures as the solution. To that end, innumerable recommendations that would lead to just treatment of immigrants, undocumented and documented, should be considered. As Fernandez-Kelly and Massey (2007) recommend, a starting point may be to create a more reasonable and coherent visa policy:

> it is imperative to increase the number of permanent resident visas available to Mexicans to one hundred thousand. Mexico is a country of 105 million people with a one-trillion-dollar economy that shares a two-thousand-mile border with the United States, to which it is linked by a free trade agreement that has increasingly integrated the North American economy to make Mexico and the United States one another's largest trading partners. Yet despite these intimate linkages, Mexico has the same immigration quota as Nepal or Botswana. Maintaining a quota of twenty thousand visas per year for a nation to which the United States is so closely bound by history, geography, and

---

Colorado, have been characterized as heavy-handed, and have been said to have terrorized entire communities (Cooper 2007).

free trade is unrealistically low, bringing about waiting periods that
surpass ten years, creating frustration among qualified applicants,
and making it all but certain that illegal migration will continue. (Fernandez-Kelly and Massey 2007, 115)

Of the estimated 10–12 million undocumented immigrants in the United
States, it is unrealistic that they will or could all return to their countries of origin. Therefore, organizations, such as the Mexican American Legal Defense and
Education Fund, have backed legislative proposals to create paths toward legal
status, such as the "DREAM Act."[3] Other recommendations, such as those proposed by Johnson (2003), go further by addressing a range of social, economic,
and human rights issues by reasonably opening the border in such a way as to
reduce the human toll of current policy and promoting economic benefits on
both its sides. U.S. policy decisions should veer toward recognizing and preserving the human rights and dignity of immigrants rather than succumb to
failed strategies that militarize the border, criminalize immigrants and violate
their fundamental rights. Of course, the significance of doing so reaches far beyond Mexicans entering the United States, as many other Latin American immigrants come into the United States through its southern border, and their
rights and dignity are equally deserving of recognition and protection.

Increase public awareness of the Latino/a experience and rights issues

Increased public awareness of the historical reality and characteristics of
Latinos/as in the United States, including present-day discrimination and injustices against them, is essential in the process of taking appropriate measures to protect Latino/a human rights. Too much still remains hidden, unknown, untaught, or undiscovered about Latinos/as in the United States
(Perea et al. 2000). Latino/a communities remain poorly understood, particularly as it pertains to the history of colonial conquest and domination that is
the basis for today's unequal colonial and neo-colonial relations between the

---

3. According to MALDEF, the DREAM ACT Amendment to H.R. 1585 provides "a 6-
year path to legal status starting after high school graduation for undocumented individuals brought to the U.S. as children more than 5 years ago. To qualify for legal status, they
would have to demonstrate good moral character and within the 6-year period either grad-
uate from community college, complete two years towards a four-year degree, or serve at
least two years in the U.S. military.... Over 65,000 immigrant students who have been
raised in the United States and whose families pay taxes need, but do not have, a legal
mechanism to remain here. The DREAM Act will enable them to adjust their immigration
status and contribute their education to the nation's benefit" (Mexican American Legal Defense and Education Fund 2007).

United States and Latin America—an unequal relationship that has in part shaped the lives of Latinos/as in the United States. To their detriment, Latinos/as are also kept uninformed about their own history and thereby disempowered and rendered further vulnerable to existing prejudices and discrimination. Future progress is dependent on how well we can learn from the past.

Dispel myths and challenge stereotypes

A key goal of this book has been to dispel many prevalent and resilient myths about Latinos/as in the United States and to debunk negative and widely-held stereotypes. The book attempts to shed light on the false associations made between Latinos/as and illicit drugs (Chapter 4), Latino/a immigrants and crime (Chapter 4), and Latinos/as and gangs (Chapter 5). It is hoped that the information presented will make it evident that much needs to be done to challenge myths and stereotypes about Latinos/as in the United States. Accurate information about Latinos/as must be disseminated at all levels and in many ways—including through the schools, the media and awareness training in many different institutions—and at every opportunity.

Promote respect and observance of international law abroad

Considering the impact of U.S. policies on Latin America and the long and ignominious history of U.S. interventions and violations of international law in the hemisphere discussed in Chapter 2, in all aspects of its policies toward Latin America the U.S. government should comply with its obligations under international law, such as respect for sovereignty, self-determination, and human rights. U.S. foreign policy toward Latin America continues to have an impact on the situation of human rights for Latin Americans in their countries and for Latinos/as in the United States. U.S. trade and immigration policies should be consistent with the protection of human rights, including the protection of the rights of workers in Latin America and of Latino/a immigrants in the United States. The continuing colonial status of Puerto Rico should also be resolved in conformity with international law and the right of self-determination as delineated in the Declaration on the Granting of Independence to Colonial Countries and Peoples, U.N. General Assembly resolution 1514(XV) of 1960 (United Nations 1960; Appendix B).

Address inequities in the criminal justice system

There have been many recommendations made in order that the criminal justice system's treatment of communities of color in the United States be more equitable. Among the most notable in view of the issues addressed in this book have been those made by the National Criminal Justice Commission (Donziger 1996). With specific focus of the problems encountered by Latino/a youth in the U.S. justice system, the report by Michigan State University/Building Blocks for Youth is also very important (Villarruel et al. 2002). As these and other sources point out (see, e.g., Perea et al. 2000; Haney López 2003), the elimination of racial profiling and other forms of racial and ethnic discrimination in police departments, the courts and the legal system in general requires a deeper examination of the issue of race and ethnicity in the United States, and a better understanding of Latino/a communities, their histories, culture, values, and aspirations. In addition, many of the changes recommended by the sources cited call for profound changes in the economic and social conditions at the root of many criminal justice problems (see Villarruel et al. 2002; Donziger 1996).

End racial profiling and the criminalization of youth

Racial profiling and other forms of discriminatory treatment must be addressed, not only at the local police precinct level, but as part of a larger effort that engages the grassroots up to the highest levels of government and its institutions. Indeed, as found in a study by the Vera Institute of Justice, leadership from the top has been found to be central in preventing incidents of police misconduct and abuse (Davis and Mateu-Gelabert 1999). Such leadership can have an even greater impact if applied wherever prejudice and discrimination take place throughout society.

As described in this book, youth have been unfairly depicted by law enforcement and the media as criminals. Youth crime and youth gang involvement in crime have been shown to be overblown (Greene and Pranis 2007). Nevertheless, the impetus to over-police persists, as revealed by a recent study by the New York Civil Liberties Union (2007), entitled *Criminalizing the Classroom: The Over-Policing in New York City Schools*. The report documents that New York City public school children are regularly subjected to derogatory language, intrusive searches, various forms of harassment, and physical and other abuse by police officers assigned to schools throughout the City. According to the study:

> Statistical analysis shows that all students are not equally likely to bear the brunt of over-policing in New York City schools. The burden falls primarily on the schools with permanent metal detectors, which are attended by the city's most vulnerable children. The students attending these high schools are disproportionately poor, Black, and Latino

compared to citywide averages, and they are more often confronted
by police personnel in school for 'non-criminal' incidents than their
peers citywide. These children receive grossly less per-pupil funding
on direct educational services than city averages. Their schools are
likely to be large and overcrowded, and to have unusually high sus-
pension and drop-out rates. (New York Civil Liberties Union 2007, 4)

Steps must be taken to end the over-policing of youths, including in the
schools. Adequate preventive measures and safeguards against abuse must be
implemented, and remedies in cases of abuse—including recourse to file
meaningful complaints against the police—must be established. As discussed
in Chapter 5, recommendations for promoting positive public safety strategies should be implemented in lieu of the increasingly heavy-handed and futile tactics employed against youth gangs, and those youths perceived to be in
gangs (see Greene and Pranis 2007).

Promote social and economic justice

Fundamental and systemic problems, such as economic and social inequality and residential segregation, must be addressed to open economic and social
opportunities still closed to many people of color. Indeed, 50 years after the
U.S. Supreme Court decision in *Brown v. Board of Education*, 347 U.S. 483
(1954), U.S. schools and society remain highly segregated by race and class. As
discussed in previous chapters, Latino/a communities experience disproportionately high levels of residential segregation and economic dislocation in U.S.
society; their children often attend overcrowded, poorly funded schools with
under-qualified teachers; and their communities suffer from inadequate housing, health care, and employment. The prospects for broadening economic and
social opportunities and advancement are ostensibly bleak. For example, in New
York City—where people of color comprise a majority of the population—
more than 93 percent of the Fire Department's 11,112 member force consists
of White men, according to data as recent as December 2001 (Baker 2002, B3).[4]

Moreover, in a country where the rate of child poverty surpasses that of all
other developed nations (Rainwater and Smeeding 2003), a majority of U.S.-
controlled corporations paid no taxes from 1996 to 2000 (General Accounting Office 2004, 2). In view of persistent economic and social inequalities in

---

4. In May 2007, the U.S. Justice Department filed suit against the City of New York,
claiming that the City's firefighter's exam has a discriminatory impact on African American and Latino/a applicants (Newman 2007, B1).

the United States, the recognition and protection of economic, social, and cultural rights, as discussed in Chapter 7, should be made a priority. Existing international human rights instruments—including, but not limited to, the International Covenant on Economic, Social and Cultural Rights (1966b; Appendix C)—can help form the basis and serve as a guide for the extension and protection of these rights. To assure application and enforcement of these international laws and principles, the active engagement of community-based organizations, litigation and advocacy groups and civic institutions throughout society must be encouraged and considered indispensable.

End mass imprisonment

As discussed in Chapter 4, Latinos/as have fallen prey to this country's mass imprisonment phenomenon. Specific recommendations for reversing the incarceration trends exist and merit serious consideration and implementation. For instance, Jacobson (2005) stresses the need to recognize that mass incarceration has led to many inequitable results, including the unfair treatment of certain racial and ethnic groups. He calls for the downsizing of the prison system and suggests various efficacious and cost-effective alternatives. His proposals include sentencing reform, strategies to reduce recidivism rates, job training, and increased community-based services.

Many other perspectives deserve consideration in developing strategies to end mass imprisonment. A number of scholars have looked at addressing the various social, economic, and political forces that contribute to mass incarceration (see, e.g., Garland 2001a). Others still call for challenging the entire penal system (Davis 2003). One very obvious fact remains: If not immediately and adequately addressed, mass imprisonment will continue to have a devastating impact on communities of color—including Latino/a communities.

Address the problems of recidivism and prisoner reentry

Other sensible recommendations and approaches, as advocated by Travis (2005) and Jacobson (2005), seek to address the problems of recidivism and prisoner reentry. Their recommendations include creating or enhancing educational opportunities and job training while in prison, the development of programs that help sustain and strengthen family and community ties during incarceration, and in other ways help enable incarcerated persons to reintegrate into society and become productive upon their release.

Greater dissemination of accurate information about the realities of Latinos/as in relation to the prison system could prove to be constructive and

vital in the effort to make institutions more sensitive to the problems of recidivism and mobilize communities and political support for the process of
achieving substantive change. Comprehensive efforts in Latina/o communities, similar to that proposed by Villarruel et al. (2002)—efforts that engage
parents, youths, community, law enforcement, and the political process—
provide a model for effecting needed and long overdue changes in the prison
and criminal justice systems, changes that may assist in turning around the
dangerous trend toward increased Latino/a imprisonment, recidivism, and
prisoner reentry.

Build on cultural strengths

A culture-based approach, such as *Palenque*, is among the many ways to
engage communities proactively, and at a grassroots level, in issues they are
confronting. The culture-based model offers the means through which
Latino/a culture, linguistic heritage, self-esteem, and identity among Latino/a
youth and families can be reaffirmed, potentially serving to improve their status in relation to the rest of U.S. society. Norms and principles of international human rights that recognize and promote the linguistic and cultural diversity of all persons in society lend support for this culturally-oriented model,
a model that should be replicated in many communities.

The debate about language issues must also be reframed to allow for sound
educational policies. As discussed in Chapter 7, bilingualism and multilingualism have been misunderstood. Calls for "English-only" and making English the official language have been used as a political tool against immigrants,
and particularly Latinos/as (see, e.g., Crawford 2000, 1992; Krashen 1999,
1996). Studies have repeatedly proven the value of bilingualism and the efficacy of bilingual education.[5] It is important, then, to stop politics that usurp
the implementation of sound educational and public policies that support of
bilingualism and multilingualism.

Promote meaningful Latino/a representation in policymaking

There must be efforts to insure meaningful access to the highest levels of
decision- and policy-making. Latino/a representation in all levels of author-

---

5. *The New York Times* (2005b, A22) urged the Bush administration to release a long-
waited study by the Education Department that concluded, once again, that "bilingual education was helpful to those learning English." According to the *Times*, the administration's
hesitancy in releasing this report raises suspicion of political meddling.

ity and in all aspects of law and public policy should not only be given greater priority, but those Latinos/as holding positions within law enforcement and other institutions that serve the public should be respected for the cultural knowledge and sensitivity they bring to their institutions. The concept of cultural competency should be incorporated into the efforts of public institutions to effectively serve all communities.

Inequalities, discrimination, and injustice, if tolerated in society, will invariably be mirrored by the legal and justice systems. Police departments and the judicial system often reflect the same problems found in society. The problems of prejudice and discrimination in U.S. society must not be overlooked, but addressed meaningfully and with the goal of achieving justice in all areas of the society. In this regard, vigorous steps must be taken to end a police culture that maintains a code of silence and other forms of corruption and misconduct. Trust within communities of color, including Latino/a communities, will not be restored absent comprehensive action to prevent and punish police brutality and misconduct. Strengthening the investigatory scope of civilian review agencies and increased accountability throughout the system must be made a reality. Increasing the number of Latino/a police officers should be viewed as only one step in a larger process of opening access to and acceptance of people of color in police departments. New recruits should not have to conform to a police culture that tolerates unethical practices or illegal discriminatory behavior.

Promote domestic application and observance of international human rights

Increasing public knowledge and familiarity with international human rights principles and standards should be given precedence. Principles and standards that champion respect and protection of cultural, linguistic, social, and economic rights open the possibility of advancing Latino/a rights throughout the United States. Schools, law enforcement, and the courts should be engaged in a process of learning and implementing international human rights standards, not solely in order to better serve particular groups in society, but as a way to promote greater social and economic progress for all.

International human rights norms and standards that relate to law enforcement must be considered and implemented in the process of reformulating policies that will be accepting of and fair to people of color on police forces, and in Latino/a communities. International human rights norms and standards that the United States is already obligated to observe must be enforced.

The U.S. government must enforce its existing obligations under all international human rights laws and it should also take steps to join the large number of world nations that have ratified the major human right treaties—including, but not limited to, the International Covenant on Economic, Social and Cultural Rights (1966b; Appendix C); the Convention on the Rights of the Child (1989; Appendix E), and the Convention on the Elimination of all Forms of Discrimination against Women (1979b; Appendix F). Advocacy in favor of the implementation of these standards is needed as part of a larger campaign to extend human rights protections, not simply for communities of color, including Latino/a communities, but to further the cause for equal rights and human rights for all.

LATINOS/AS IN THE POST-9/11 ERA

Changes in the law and in attitudes do not signified that the blatant forms of racial and ethnic hatred and discrimination of past decades no longer exist or that Latinos/as and other people of color are no longer vulnerable. The tragic events of September 11, 2001, while presenting an opportunity for uniting a country, also present a considerable challenge for U.S. policymakers to create effective measures to prevent future attacks by non-state actors against U.S. citizens while continuing to protect civil rights and liberties. Washington's response to September 11, unfortunately, may be doing less to avert future attacks and more to set in motion domestic and foreign policies and practices that undermine fundamental and universally-held civil and human rights. Governmental actions and legislative initiatives premised on fighting the so-called "war on terrorism" are already causing grave concerns about the loss of basic human rights protections for citizens and non-citizens alike. As persons whose rights of citizenship and other rights have long been circumscribed in the United States, Latinos/as are especially vulnerable to violations of their civil and human rights in the post-September 11 era. In view of past and present-day policies and practices in the United States that have consigned large sectors of Latinos/as to treatment as a racialized "other" in U.S. society, the post-September 11 period may be a harbinger of a return to some of the worst policies of the past.

Under international law, the terrorist acts of September 11, 2001 do not fall within the true definition of "acts of war." More accurately, they constitute crimes against humanity by non-state actors. Nevertheless, the war metaphor has been appropriated by the Bush Administration to press for policies and practices that restrict foreign and domestic human rights. These policies and practices have had the most immediate impact on the rights of persons in the United States who have long been the most marginalized and discriminated segments of the population, including Latinos/as.

History provides many examples of immigrants and law-abiding citizens considered as "foreign" or "others" who have fallen victim to extremist policies in times of war or emergency. One of the earliest instances of laws designed to have this result was the Alien and Sedition Act of 1798, designed to silence criticism of the U.S. government under President John Adams (Chang 2002, 2). Twentieth-century examples of governmental excess include actions taken during World War I and World War II. In 1919, under the direction of Attorney General A. Mitchell Palmer, the U.S. government rounded up more than 6,000 immigrants while searching for suspects of the bombing of the attorney general's home; 556 immigrants were deported, not for their involvement in the bombing, but for their political associations (Cole and Dempsey 2002, 150). During World War II, 110,000 persons of Japanese descent—over two-thirds of whom were U.S. citizens—were stripped of all rights and possessions and interned in harsh detention camps for the duration of the war (Chang 2002, 39; Cole and Dempsey 2002, 150).

Latinos/as have also been affected by policies that rely on ethnic and racial profiling—policies similar to those that led to the internment of persons of Japanese descent during World War II. The Greaser Act of 1855 used racial and ethnic identifiers to enforce a supposed anti-vagrancy campaign (Haney-López 1999, 145; Acuña 2007, 115). Other instances of profiling and government harassment of Latinos/as, include the targeting of Los Angeles zoot suiters in the 1940s (Escobar 1999) and the federal government's Operation Wetback in the 1950s, in which 3.7 million persons of Mexican ancestry were deported in the anti-immigrant hysteria of the time, despite the fact that many were U.S. citizens (Acuña 2007, 225–226; Mirandé 1987, 125–29; McWilliams 1990, 315–18).

The massive governmental infiltration and disruption campaign known as COINTELPRO of the 1960s and 1970s also infringed the basic rights of association and expression of Chicanos and Puerto Ricans in their advocacy efforts to secure rights for their respective communities (see, e.g., Haney López 2003; Morales 1998). Indeed, the willingness of the government to suspend basic constitutional and human rights of Latinos/as in the past resembles the readiness with which recent practices in New York City, Los Angeles, Chicago, New Jersey, and other parts of the United States have perpetuated police stops and searches of Latinos/as using racial and ethnic criteria, as previously discussed in this volume.

Immediately following the September 11 attacks, reports of Latinos/as having been stopped or placed in custody began to surface, including reports of a Latino detained in Providence, Rhode Island by police who were searching for persons of Middle Eastern and Indian origin (Goodstein and Niebuhr 2001, A14). Other reports also came to light about airline passengers "with dark skin or who spoke with an accent" and "any male with too much facial hair" having been detained (Levy and Rashbaum 2001, A1).

Among the U.S. citizens detained as "enemy combatants" was a Puerto Rican. In May 2002, the government detained José Padilla, a.k.a. Abdullah al Muhajir, indefinitely without charge and without the right to counsel. It was alleged in the media that he was tied to a bomb plot and that he was formerly a Chicago street gang member (Schulhofer 2002). Many legal analysts view the government's actions in cases such as Padilla's as an assault on bedrock constitutional principles (see, e.g., Schulhofer 2002; Cole and Dempsey 2002). It is especially curious that of all the U.S. citizens who have been detained only the White U.S. citizen, John Walker Lindh, was afforded immediate and complete rights to counsel, speedy criminal trial, and sentence (see Meek 2003, 14). One can reasonably infer from the John Walker Lindh case that the government is repeating its past practice of denying rights to those considered as "other" while sending a message that White U.S. citizens need not be concerned that their constitutional rights will be trampled upon in the "war on terror."

The racialized aspects of government and media portrayals of Mr. Padilla have not gone unnoticed by those analyzing his case. As Professor Ana Y. Ramos-Zayas (2004, 39) notes,

> Not unlike the so-called 'illegal aliens,' Puerto Ricans are susceptible to accusations of illegality that oftentimes span the gray area between media-produced (and officially sanctioned) images of barrios-grown criminality and the US imperialist investment in configuring racist understandings of international terrorism.

After being detained for more than three years without charge and without legal counsel for much of that time, the government brought criminal charges against José Padilla in a move to avoid Supreme Court consideration of the legality of his military detention. The Bush administration's original claim that he plotted to detonate a radioactive "dirty bomb" in the United States did not even figure in the case tried in Federal District Court in Miami. Instead, the prosecutors endeavored to show that "Jose Padilla became an Al Qaeda terrorist trainee" in support of "jihad" (Goodnough 2007, A14). Videotape of Padilla's detention in solitary confinement is highly suggestive of torture at the hands of his captors (Sontag 2006, A1).

The unsympathetic picture painted of him and his ostensibly harsh and illegal treatment by the government made it probable that he would be found guilty. Professor Frances Negrón-Muntaner (2007, 261) observes that singling Mr. Padilla out as a terrorist was as if he had been chosen "straight from central casting." He "evokes all of the worst Hollywood and popular images of a Puerto Rican who is " 'naturally' criminal and irrational, a ready-made image for public consumption" (259).

In August 2007, Mr. Padilla was found guilty of all charges, and stood the possibility of a sentence of life in prison (Goodnough and Shane 2007, A1). The Bush administration was quick to claim victory, but the Padilla case has come to represent much of what has gone wrong with the "war on terror." As the New York Times pointed out:

> On the way to this verdict, the government repeatedly trampled on the Constitution, and its prosecution of Mr. Padilla was so cynical and inept that the crime that he was convicted of—conspiracy to commit terrorism overseas—bears no relation to the ambitious plot to wreak mass destruction inside the United States, which the Justice Department loudly proclaimed. Even with the guilty verdict, this conviction remains a shining example of how not to prosecute terrorism cases. (*New York Times* 2007, A22)

Tapping into preexisting and longstanding stereotypes of Latinos/as and other persons of color as prone to criminality surely facilitated the typecasting of Mr. Padilla. But most ominously, Mr. Padilla, a Latino, became the means through which the Bush administration sought to undermine some of the most fundamental Constitutional rights—among them the right to habeas corpus; the right to counsel; the right to be free from torture, and cruel and inhuman treatment; and the right to a fair and speedy trial. Mr. Padilla also became the vehicle through which the administration could begin to deny basic rights to U.S. citizens. Mr. Padilla is a U.S. citizen of Puerto Rican descent, and in keeping with age-old stereotypes, a foreign "other," undeserving of rights. No one should lose sight of the implications for any country of having a President with the power to detain citizens and non-citizens indefinitely and without rights.

While in the aftermath of the September 11 attacks, steps to secure individual and national security were necessary,[6] it has been argued that the government has gone beyond reasonable measures. The Bush administration's disdain for the protection of fundamental civil liberties and constitutional rights as well as for international law, specifically the Geneva Conventions and

---

6. Measures to bolster security at the borders, stronger actions to prevent money laundering, and enhancing communication among government law enforcement agencies post-9/11 were not unreasonable (see Cole and Dempsey 2002, 152).

the universally-recognized prohibition against torture, undermines the civil and human rights of persons in and outside of the United States (Leone and Anrig 2003; Cole 2003)

Considering the ways in which Latinos/as have been racialized as the "other" and frequently projected as criminals, new legislation passed in Washington to fight the so-called "war on terrorism" poses additional challenges for the protection of the rights of Latinos/as. The USA PATRIOT Act, for instance, defines "domestic terrorism" so broadly as to potentially silence forms of dissent formerly protected under the constitution; it provides for the infringement of privacy through its "sneak-and-peak" and other provisions, which allow the government access to telephone and Internet communications; it eliminates many protections for immigrants; and its provisions may render suspect many nonprofit community agencies (U.S. Public Law 107-56). The Homeland Security Act, promising the government "total information access," presents additional threats to the civil liberties and civil rights of groups and individuals (U.S. House 2002).

For Latinos/as, these new legislative initiatives are reminiscent of past government practices that unduly and illegally monitored and undermined efforts to engage in lawful organizing activities to secure their rights in the United States. Sweeping governmental proposals since 9-11—including attempts to legitimize the use of torture during the interrogation of suspects—signify the lengths to which the government is willing to go in its "war on terrorism." Little doubt is left that the most vulnerable in society may likely suffer violations of their rights.

The detention of suspects, including U.S. citizens, without charge and without legal counsel; the federal government's enhanced surveillance and monitoring mechanisms without judicial oversight; and unprecedented government secrecy are aspects of the PATRIOT Act considered perilous to the preservation of constitutional rights and democratic principles (Leone and Anrig 2003; Schulhofer 2002; Chang 2002; Cole and Dempsey 2002). The lesson to be drawn from history and the Latino/a experience is that the protection of constitutional, civil, and human rights becomes more crucial in times of crisis and fear. Thus, their application and enforcement are vital to protecting the rights of all people, but especially those of people racialized as "other" and whose rights have been frequently violated in the past, including Latinos/as.

Observance of International Law and the Protection of Human Rights and Dignity

As detailed in this book, the failure to observe fundamental international laws, principles, and standards has shaped the relationship between the United

States and Latin American countries and reinforced a long history of paternalistic policies detrimental to the advancement of human rights in the region. These policies mirror the ways in which Latino/a communities in the United States are viewed and treated. Today, Latinos/as in the United States still face the challenges of prejudice and discrimination, and socioeconomic problems stemming from policies and practices rooted in longstanding biases.

Racial profiling, drug laws and drug law enforcement policies, police brutality and misconduct, and anti-immigrant and anti-bilingual initiatives directed against Latinos/as parallel U.S. globalization strategies that reinforce U.S. domination over Latin America, its peoples and its resources. Economic exploitation, through such means as the proliferation of sweatshops or *maquiladoras* throughout Latin America, emulate past U.S. policies and practices that perpetuated poverty and despair, and that resulted in the ongoing influx of persons from Latin America to the United States. In turn, their arrival provides U.S. employers with a readily available surplus of low-wage exploitable workers within U.S. borders.

Given this reality, there is a need to rethink and reframe the relationship between the United States and Latin American nations in ways that truly represent a relationship among equals as required by international law. As important is the need to reevaluate and reshape the way Latinos/as are perceived and treated in the United States. International law and, specifically, developments in international human rights law, provide a framework for respect for the political, social, economic, and cultural rights of all persons. It is a framework of rights that, if adopted in the United States, can help serve the cause of justice nationally and internationally.

In the United States, broadening the concept of human rights to include social, economic, and cultural rights appears crucial for Latinos/as in their quest for justice, equality, and dignity. Indeed, it has been observed that "whereas human dignity is the core and the foundation of human rights, it is through the operationalization of rights that dignity is protected" (Goldewijk 2002, 6). Thus, the quest for justice should not be limited to the pursuit of justice and dignity by those who suffer from a deprivation of rights and from economic and social dislocation such as Latinos/as. It should be a quest for justice embraced by all who believe in building a more just society and in protecting the inherent dignity of all humankind.

Appendices

Universal Declaration of Human Rights

Adopted and Proclaimed by General Assembly Resolution
217 A(III) of 10 December 1948

Preamble

Whereas recognition of the inherent dignity and of the equal and inalienable rights of all members of the human family is the foundation of freedom, justice and peace in the world,

Whereas disregard and contempt for human rights have resulted in barbarous acts which have outraged the conscience of mankind, and the advent of a world in which human beings shall enjoy freedom of speech and belief and freedom from fear and want has been proclaimed as the highest aspiration of the common people,

Whereas it is essential, if man is not to be compelled to have recourse, as a last resort, to rebellion against tyranny and oppression, that human rights should be protected by the rule of law,

Whereas it is essential to promote the development of friendly relations between nations,

Whereas the peoples of the United Nations have in the Charter reaffirmed their faith in fundamental human rights, in the dignity and worth of the human person and in the equal rights of men and women and have determined to promote social progress and better standards of life in larger freedom,

Whereas Member States have pledged themselves to achieve, in cooperation with the United Nations, the promotion of universal respect for and observance of human rights and fundamental freedoms,

Whereas a common understanding of these rights and freedoms is of the greatest importance for the full realization of this pledge,

Now, therefore,
The General Assembly,
Proclaims this Universal Declaration of Human Rights as a common standard of achievement for all peoples and all nations, to the end that every individual and every organ of society, keeping this Declaration constantly in mind, shall strive by teaching and education to promote respect for these rights and freedoms and by progressive measures, national and international, to secure their universal and effective recognition and observance, both among the peoples of Member States themselves and among the peoples of territories under their jurisdiction.

Article 1

All human beings are born free and equal in dignity and rights. They are endowed with reason and conscience and should act towards one another in a spirit of brotherhood.

Article 2

Everyone is entitled to all the rights and freedoms set forth in this Declaration, without distinction of any kind, such as race, colour, sex, language, religion, political or other opinion, national or social origin, property, birth or other status.

Furthermore, no distinction shall be made on the basis of the political, jurisdictional or international status of the country or territory to which a person belongs, whether it be independent, trust, non-self-governing or under any other limitation of sovereignty.

Article 3

Everyone has the right to life, liberty and security of person.

Article 4

No one shall be held in slavery or servitude; slavery and the slave trade shall be prohibited in all their forms.

Article 5

No one shall be subjected to torture or to cruel, inhuman or degrading treatment or punishment.

Article 6

Everyone has the right to recognition everywhere as a person before the law.

Article 7

All are equal before the law and are entitled without any discrimination to equal protection of the law. All are entitled to equal protection against any discrimination in violation of this Declaration and against any incitement to such discrimination.

Article 8

Everyone has the right to an effective remedy by the competent national tribunals for acts violating the fundamental rights granted him by the constitution or by law.

Article 9

No one shall be subjected to arbitrary arrest, detention or exile.

Article 10

Everyone is entitled in full equality to a fair and public hearing by an independent and impartial tribunal, in the determination of his rights and obligations and of any criminal charge against him.

Article 11

1. Everyone charged with a penal offence has the right to be presumed innocent until proved guilty according to law in a public trial at which he has had all the guarantees necessary for his defence.

2. No one shall be held guilty of any penal offence on account of any act or omission which did not constitute a penal offence, under national or international law, at the time when it was committed. Nor shall a heavier penalty be imposed than the one that was applicable at the time the penal offence was committed.

Article 12

No one shall be subjected to arbitrary interference with his privacy, family, home or correspondence, nor to attacks upon his honour and reputation. Everyone has the right to the protection of the law against such interference or attacks.

Article 13

1. Everyone has the right to freedom of movement and residence within the borders of each State.

2. Everyone has the right to leave any country, including his own, and to return to his country.

Article 14

1. Everyone has the right to seek and to enjoy in other countries asylum from persecution.

2. This right may not be invoked in the case of prosecutions genuinely arising from non-political crimes or from acts contrary to the purposes and principles of the United Nations.

Article 15

1. Everyone has the right to a nationality.

2. No one shall be arbitrarily deprived of his nationality nor denied the right to change his nationality.

Article 16

1. Men and women of full age, without any limitation due to race, nationality or religion, have the right to marry and to found a family. They are entitled to equal rights as to marriage, during marriage and at its dissolution.

2. Marriage shall be entered into only with the free and full consent of the intending spouses.

3. The family is the natural and fundamental group unit of society and is entitled to protection by society and the State.

Article 17

1. Everyone has the right to own property alone as well as in association with others.

2. No one shall be arbitrarily deprived of his property.

Article 18

Everyone has the right to freedom of thought, conscience and religion; this right includes freedom to change his religion or belief, and freedom, either alone or in community with others and in public or private, to manifest his religion or belief in teaching, practice, worship and observance.

Article 19

Everyone has the right to freedom of opinion and expression; this right includes freedom to hold opinions without interference and to seek, receive and impart information and ideas through any media and regardless of frontiers.

Article 20

1. Everyone has the right to freedom of peaceful assembly and association.

2. No one may be compelled to belong to an association.

Article 21

1. Everyone has the right to take part in the government of his country, directly or through freely chosen representatives.

2. Everyone has the right to equal access to public service in his country.

3. The will of the people shall be the basis of the authority of government; this will shall be expressed in periodic and genuine elections which shall be by universal and equal suffrage and shall be held by secret vote or by equivalent free voting procedures.

Article 22

Everyone, as a member of society, has the right to social security and is entitled to realization, through national effort and international co-operation and in accordance with the organization and resources of each State, of the economic, social and cultural rights indispensable for his dignity and the free development of his personality.

Article 23

1. Everyone has the right to work, to free choice of employment, to just and favourable conditions of work and to protection against unemployment.

2. Everyone, without any discrimination, has the right to equal pay for equal work.

3. Everyone who works has the right to just and favourable remuneration ensuring for himself and his family an existence worthy of human dignity, and supplemented, if necessary, by other means of social protection.

4. Everyone has the right to form and to join trade unions for the protection of his interests.

Article 24

Everyone has the right to rest and leisure, including reasonable limitation of working hours and periodic holidays with pay.

Article 25

1. Everyone has the right to a standard of living adequate for the health and well-being of himself and of his family, including food, clothing, housing and medical care and necessary social services, and the right to security in the event of unemployment, sickness, disability, widowhood, old age or other lack of livelihood in circumstances beyond his control.

2. Motherhood and childhood are entitled to special care and assistance. All children, whether born in or out of wedlock, shall enjoy the same social protection.

Article 26

1. Everyone has the right to education. Education shall be free, at least in the elementary and fundamental stages. Elementary education shall be compulsory. Technical and professional education shall be made generally available and higher education shall be equally accessible to all on the basis of merit.

2. Education shall be directed to the full development of the human personality and to the strengthening of respect for human rights and fundamental freedoms. It shall promote understanding, tolerance and friendship among all nations, racial or religious groups, and shall further the activities of the United Nations for the maintenance of peace.

3. Parents have a prior right to choose the kind of education that shall be given to their children.

Article 27

1. Everyone has the right freely to participate in the cultural life of the community, to enjoy the arts and to share in scientific advancement and its benefits.

2. Everyone has the right to the protection of the moral and material interests resulting from any scientific, literary or artistic production of which he is the author.

Article 28

Everyone is entitled to a social and international order in which the rights and freedoms set forth in this Declaration can be fully realized.

Article 29

1. Everyone has duties to the community in which alone the free and full development of his personality is possible.

2. In the exercise of his rights and freedoms, everyone shall be subject only to such limitations as are determined by law solely for the purpose of securing due recognition and respect for the rights and freedoms of others and of meeting the just requirements of morality, public order and the general welfare in a democratic society.

3. These rights and freedoms may in no case be exercised contrary to the purposes and principles of the United Nations.

Article 30

Nothing in this Declaration may be interpreted as implying for any State, group or person any right to engage in any activity or to perform any act aimed at the destruction of any of the rights and freedoms set forth herein.

DECLARATION ON THE GRANTING OF INDEPENDENCE TO COLONIAL COUNTRIES AND PEOPLES

Adopted by General Assembly Resolution 1514(XV) of 14 December 1960

The General Assembly,

Mindful of the determination proclaimed by the peoples of the world in the Charter of the United Nations to reaffirm faith in fundamental human rights, in the dignity and worth of the human person, in the equal rights of men and women and of nations large and small and to promote social progress and better standards of life in larger freedom,

Conscious of the need for the creation of conditions of stability and well-being and peaceful and friendly relations based on respect for the principles of equal rights and self-determination of all peoples, and of universal respect for, and observance of, human rights and fundamental freedoms for all without distinction as to race, sex, language or religion,

Recognizing the passionate yearning for freedom in all dependent peoples and the decisive role of such peoples in the attainment of their independence,

Aware of the increasing conflicts resulting from the denial of or impediments in the way of the freedom of such peoples, which constitute a serious threat to world peace,

Considering the important role of the United Nations in assisting the movement for independence in Trust and Non-Self-Governing Territories,

Recognizing that the peoples of the world ardently desire the end of colonialism in all its manifestations,

Convinced that the continued existence of colonialism prevents the development of international economic co-operation, impedes the social, cultural and economic development of dependent peoples and militates against the United Nations ideal of universal peace,

Affirming that peoples may, for their own ends, freely dispose of their natural wealth and resources without prejudice to any obligations arising out of international economic co-operation, based upon the principle of mutual benefit, and international law,

Believing that the process of liberation is irresistible and irreversible and that, in order to avoid serious crises, an end must be put to colonialism and all practices of segregation and discrimination associated therewith,

Welcoming the emergence in recent years of a large number of dependent territories into freedom and independence, and recognizing the increasingly powerful trends towards freedom in such territories which have not yet attained independence,

Convinced that all peoples have an inalienable right to complete freedom, the exercise of their sovereignty and the integrity of their national territory,

Solemnly proclaims the necessity of bringing to a speedy and unconditional end colonialism in all its forms and manifestations;

And to this end Declares that:

1. The subjection of peoples to alien subjugation, domination and exploitation constitutes a denial of fundamental human rights, is contrary to the Charter of the United Nations and is an impediment to the promotion of world peace and co-operation.

2. All peoples have the right to self-determination; by virtue of that right they freely determine their political status and freely pursue their economic, social and cultural development.

3. Inadequacy of political, economic, social or educational preparedness should never serve as a pretext for delaying independence.

4. All armed action or repressive measures of all kinds directed against dependent peoples shall cease in order to enable them to exercise peacefully and freely their right to complete independence, and the integrity of their national territory shall be respected.

5. Immediate steps shall be taken, in Trust and Non-Self-Governing Territories or all other territories which have not yet attained independence, to transfer all powers to the peoples of those territories, without any conditions or reservations, in accordance with their freely expressed will and desire, with-

out any distinction as to race, creed or colour, in order to enable them to enjoy complete independence and freedom.

6. Any attempt aimed at the partial or total disruption of the national unity and the territorial integrity of a country is incompatible with the purposes and principles of the Charter of the United Nations.

7. All States shall observe faithfully and strictly the provisions of the Charter of the United Nations, the Universal Declaration of Human Rights and the present Declaration on the basis of equality, non-interference in the internal affairs of all States, and respect for the sovereign rights of all peoples and their territorial integrity.

International Covenant on Economic, Social and Cultural Rights

Adopted and Opened for Signature, Ratification
and Accession by General Assembly Resolution 2200A(XXI)
of 16 December 1966, Entry into Force 3 January 1976,
in accordance with Article 27

(Excerpt of substantive provisions)

Article 1

1. All peoples have the right of self-determination. By virtue of that right they freely determine their political status and freely pursue their economic, social and cultural development.

2. All peoples may, for their own ends, freely dispose of their natural wealth and resources without prejudice to any obligations arising out of international economic cooperation, based upon the principle of mutual benefit, and international law. In no case may a people be deprived of its own means of subsistence.

3. The States Parties to the present Covenant, including those having responsibility for the administration of Non-Self-Governing and Trust Territories, shall promote the realization of the right of self-determination, and shall respect that right, in conformity with the provisions of the Charter of the United Nations.

Article 2

1. Each State Party to the present Covenant undertakes to take steps, individually and through international assistance and cooperation, especially eco-

nomic and technical, to the maximum of its available resources, with a view to achieving progressively the full realization of the rights recognized in the present Covenant by all appropriate means, including particularly the adoption of legislative measures.

2. The States Parties to the present Covenant undertake to guarantee that the rights enunciated in the present Covenant will be exercised without discrimination of any kind as to race, colour, sex, language, religion, political or other opinion, national or social origin property, birth or other status.

3. Developing countries, with due regard to human rights and their national economy, may determine to what extent they would guarantee the economic rights recognized in the present Covenant to non-nationals.

Article 3

The States Parties to the present Covenant undertake to ensure the equal right of men and women to the enjoyment of all economic, social and cultural rights set forth in the present Covenant.

Article 4

The States Parties to the present Covenant recognize that, in the enjoyment of those rights provided by the State in conformity with the present Covenant, the State may subject such rights only to such limitations as are determined by law only in so far as this may be compatible with the nature of these rights and solely for the purpose of promoting the general welfare in a democratic society.

Article 5

1. Nothing, in the present Covenant may be interpreted as implying for any State group or person any right to engage in any activity or to perform any act aimed at the destruction of any of the rights or freedoms recognized herein, or at their limitation to a greater extent than is provided for in the present Covenant.

2. No restriction upon or derogation from any of the fundamental human rights recognized or existing in any country in virtue of law, conventions, regulations or custom shall be admitted on the pretext that the present Covenant does not recognize such rights or that it recognizes them to a lesser extent.

Article 6

1. The States Parties to the present Covenant recognize the right to work, which includes the right of everyone to the opportunity to gain his living by

work which he freely chooses or accepts, and will take appropriate steps to safeguard this right.

2. The steps to be taken by a State Party to the present Covenant to achieve the full realization of this right shall include technical and vocational guidance and training programmes, policies and techniques to achieve steady economic, social and cultural development and full and productive employment under conditions safeguarding, fundamental political and economic freedoms to the individual.

Article 7

The States Parties to the present Covenant recognize the right of everyone to the enjoyment of just and favourable conditions of work which ensure, in particular:

(a) Remuneration which provides all workers, as a minimum, with:

(i) Fair wages and equal remuneration for work of equal value without distinction of any kind, in particular women being guaranteed conditions of work not inferior to those enjoyed by men, with equal pay for equal work;

(ii) A decent living for themselves and their families in accordance with the provisions of the present Covenant;

(b) Safe and healthy working, conditions;

(c) Equal opportunity for everyone to be promoted in his employment to an appropriate higher level, subject to no considerations other than those of seniority and competence;

(d) Rest, leisure and reasonable limitation of working hours and periodic holidays with pay, as well as remuneration for public holidays.

Article 8

1. The States Parties to the present Covenant undertake to ensure:

(a) The right of everyone to form trade unions and join the trade union of his choice, subject only to the rules of the organization concerned, for the promotion and protection of his economic and social interests. No restrictions may be placed on the exercise of this right other than those prescribed by law and which are necessary in a democratic society in the interests of national security or public order or for the protection of the rights and freedoms of others;

(b) The right of trade unions to establish national federations or confederations and the right of the latter to form or join international trade-union organizations;

(c) The right of trade unions to function freely subject to no limitations other than those prescribed by law and which are necessary in a democratic society in the interests of national security or public order or for the protection of the rights and freedoms of others;

(d) The right to strike, provided that it is exercised in conformity with the laws of the particular country.

2. This article shall not prevent the imposition of lawful restrictions on the exercise of these rights by members of the armed forces or of the police or of the administration of the State.

3. Nothing in this article shall authorize States Parties to the International Labour Organisation Convention of 1948 concerning Freedom of Association and Protection of the Right to Organize to take legislative measures which would prejudice, or apply the law in such a manner as would prejudice, the guarantees provided for in that Convention.

Article 9

The States Parties to the present Covenant recognize the right of everyone to social security, including social insurance.

Article 10

The States Parties to the present Covenant recognize that:

1. The widest possible protection and assistance should be accorded to the family, which is the natural and fundamental group unit of society, particularly for its establishment and while it is responsible for the care and education of dependent children. Marriage must be entered into with the free consent of the intending spouses.

2. Special protection should be accorded to mothers during a reasonable period before and after childbirth. During such period working mothers should be accorded paid leave or leave with adequate social security benefits.

3. Special measures of protection and assistance should be taken on behalf of all children and young persons without any discrimination for reasons of parentage or other conditions. Children and young persons should be protected from economic and social exploitation. Their employment in work harmful to their morals or health or dangerous to life or likely to hamper their normal development should be punishable by law. States should also set age limits below which the paid employment of child labour should be prohibited and punishable by law.

Article 11

1. The States Parties to the present Covenant recognize the right of everyone to an adequate standard of living for himself and his family, including adequate food, clothing and housing, and to the continuous improvement of living conditions. The States Parties will take appropriate steps to ensure the realization of this right, recognizing to this effect the essential importance of international cooperation based on free consent.

2. The States Parties to the present Covenant, recognizing the fundamental right of everyone to be free from hunger, shall take, individually and through international cooperation, the measures, including specific programmes, which are needed:

(a) To improve methods of production, conservation and distribution of food by making full use of technical and scientific knowledge, by disseminating knowledge of the principles of nutrition and by developing or reforming agrarian systems in such a way as to achieve the most efficient development and utilization of natural resources;

(b) Taking into account the problems of both food-importing and food-exporting countries, to ensure an equitable distribution of world food supplies in relation to need.

Article 12

1. The States Parties to the present Covenant recognize the right of everyone to the enjoyment of the highest attainable standard of physical and mental health.

2. The steps to be taken by the States Parties to the present Covenant to achieve the full realization of this right shall include those necessary for:

(a) The provision for the reduction of the stillbirth-rate and of infant mortality and for the healthy development of the child;

(b) The improvement of all aspects of environmental and industrial hygiene;

(c) The prevention, treatment and control of epidemic, endemic, occupational and other diseases;

(d) The creation of conditions which would assure to all medical service and medical attention in the event of sickness.

Article 13

1. The States Parties to the present Covenant recognize the right of everyone to education. They agree that education shall be directed to the full develop-

ment of the human personality and the sense of its dignity, and shall strengthen the respect for human rights and fundamental freedoms. They further agree that education shall enable all persons to participate effectively in a free society, promote understanding, tolerance and friendship among all nations and all racial, ethnic or religious groups, and further the activities of the United Nations for the maintenance of peace.

2. The States Parties to the present Covenant recognize that, with a view to achieving the full realization of this right:

(a) Primary education shall be compulsory and available free to all;

(b) Secondary education in its different forms, including technical and vocational secondary education, shall be made generally available and accessible to all by every appropriate means, and in particular by the progressive introduction of free education;

(c) Higher education shall be made equally accessible to all, on the basis of capacity, by every appropriate means, and in particular by the progressive introduction of free education;

(d) Fundamental education shall be encouraged or intensified as far as possible for those persons who have not received or completed the whole period of their primary education;

(e) The development of a system of schools at all levels shall be actively pursued, an adequate fellowship system shall be established, and the material conditions of teaching staff shall be continuously improved.

3. The States Parties to the present Covenant undertake to have respect for the liberty of parents and, when applicable, legal guardians to choose for their children schools, other than those established by the public authorities, which conform to such minimum educational standards as may be laid down or approved by the State and to ensure the religious and moral education of their children in conformity with their own convictions.

4. No part of this article shall be construed so as to interfere with the liberty of individuals and bodies to establish and direct educational institutions, subject always to the observance of the principles set forth in paragraph 1 of this article and to the requirement that the education given in such institutions shall conform to such minimum standards as may be laid down by the State.

Article 14

Each State Party to the present Covenant which, at the time of becoming a Party, has not been able to secure in its metropolitan territory or other territories under its jurisdiction compulsory primary education, free of charge, undertakes within two years, to work out and adopt a detailed plan of action for the progressive implementation, within a reasonable number of years, to be fixed in the plan, of the principle of compulsory education free of charge for all.

Article 15

1. The States Parties to the present Covenant recognize the right of everyone:

(a) To take part in cultural life;

(b) To enjoy the benefits of scientific progress and its applications;

(c) To benefit from the protection of the moral and material interests resulting from any scientific, literary or artistic production of which he is the author.

2. The steps to be taken by the States Parties to the present Covenant to achieve the full realization of this right shall include those necessary for the conservation, the development and the diffusion of science and culture.

3. The States Parties to the present Covenant undertake to respect the freedom indispensable for scientific research and creative activity.

4. The States Parties to the present Covenant recognize the benefits to be derived from the encouragement and development of international contacts and cooperation in the scientific and cultural fields.

Total Parties to the International Covenant on Economic, Social and Cultural Rights, as of 20 July 2007: 156

Declaration on the Rights of Persons Belonging to National or Ethnic, Religious and Linguistic Minorities

Adopted by General Assembly Resolution 47/135
of 18 December 1992

The General Assembly,

Reaffirming that one of the basic aims of the United Nations, as proclaimed in the Charter, is to promote and encourage respect for human rights and for fundamental freedoms for all, without distinction as to race, sex, language or religion,

Reaffirming faith in fundamental human rights, in the dignity and worth of the human person, in the equal rights of men and women and of nations large and small,

Desiring to promote the realization of the principles contained in the Charter, the Universal Declaration of Human Rights, the Convention on the Prevention and Punishment of the Crime of Genocide, the International Convention on the Elimination of All Forms of Racial Discrimination, the International Covenant on Civil and Political Rights, the International Covenant on Economic, Social and Cultural Rights, the Declaration on the Elimination of All Forms of Intolerance and of Discrimination Based on Religion or Belief, and the Convention on the Rights of the Child, as well as other relevant international instruments that have been adopted at the universal or regional level and those concluded between individual States Members of the United Nations,

Inspired by the provisions of article 27 of the International Covenant on Civil and Political Rights concerning the rights of persons belonging to ethnic, religious or linguistic minorities,

Considering that the promotion and protection of the rights of persons belonging to national or ethnic, religious and linguistic minorities contribute to the political and social stability of States in which they live,

Emphasizing that the constant promotion and realization of the rights of persons belonging to national or ethnic, religious and linguistic minorities, as an integral part of the development of society as a whole and within a democratic framework based on the rule of law, would contribute to the strengthening of friendship and cooperation among peoples and States,

Considering that the United Nations has an important role to play regarding the protection of minorities,

Bearing in mind the work done so far within the United Nations system, in particular by the Commission on Human Rights, the Sub-Commission on Prevention of Discrimination and Protection of Minorities and the bodies established pursuant to the International Covenants on Human Rights and other relevant international human rights instruments in promoting and protecting the rights of persons belonging to national or ethnic, religious and linguistic minorities,

Taking into account the important work which is done by intergovernmental and non-governmental organizations in protecting minorities and in promoting and protecting the rights of persons belonging to national or ethnic, religious and linguistic minorities,

Recognizing the need to ensure even more effective implementation of international human rights instruments with regard to the rights of persons belonging to national or ethnic, religious and linguistic minorities,

Proclaims this Declaration on the Rights of Persons Belonging to National or Ethnic, Religious and Linguistic Minorities:

Article 1

1. States shall protect the existence and the national or ethnic, cultural, religious and linguistic identity of minorities within their respective territories and shall encourage conditions for the promotion of that identity.

2. States shall adopt appropriate legislative and other measures to achieve those ends.

Article 2

1. Persons belonging to national or ethnic, religious and linguistic minorities (hereinafter referred to as persons belonging to minorities) have the right to enjoy their own culture, to profess and practice their own religion, and to use their own language, in private and in public, freely and without interference or any form of discrimination.

2. Persons belonging to minorities have the right to participate effectively in cultural, religious, social, economic and public life.

3. Persons belonging to minorities have the right to participate effectively in decisions on the national and, where appropriate, regional level concerning the minority to which they belong or the regions in which they live, in a manner not incompatible with national legislation.

4. Persons belonging to minorities have the right to establish and maintain their own associations.

5. Persons belonging to minorities have the right to establish and maintain, without any discrimination, free and peaceful contacts with other members of their group and with persons belonging to other minorities, as well as contacts across frontiers with citizens of other States to whom they are related by national or ethnic, religious or linguistic ties.

Article 3

1. Persons belonging to minorities may exercise their rights, including those set forth in the present Declaration, individually as well as community with other members of their group, without any discrimination.

2. No disadvantage shall result for any person belonging to a minority as the consequence of the exercise or non-exercise of the rights set forth in the present Declaration.

Article 4

1. States shall take measures where required to ensure that persons belonging to minorities may exercise fully and effectively all their human rights and fundamental freedoms without any discrimination and in full equality before the law.

2. States shall take measures to create favourable conditions to enable persons belonging to minorities to express their characteristics and to develop their culture, language, religion, traditions and customs, except where specific practices are in violation of national law and contrary to international standards.

3. States should take appropriate measures so that, wherever possible, persons belonging to minorities may have adequate opportunities to learn their mother tongue or to have instruction in their mother tongue.

4. States should, where appropriate, take measures in the field of education, in order to encourage knowledge of the history, traditions, language and culture of the minorities existing within their territory. Persons belonging to minorities should have adequate opportunities to gain knowledge of the society as a whole.

5. States should consider appropriate measures so that persons belonging to minorities may participate fully in the economic progress and development in their country.

Article 5

1. National policies and programmes shall be planned and implemented with due regard for the legitimate interests of persons belonging to minorities.

2. Programmes of cooperation and assistance among States should be planned and implemented with due regard for the legitimate interests of persons belonging to minorities.

Article 6

States should cooperate on questions relating to persons belonging to minorities, *inter alia*, exchanging information and experiences, in order to promote mutual understanding and confidence.

Article 7

States should cooperate in order to promote respect for the rights set forth in the present Declaration.

Article 8

1. Nothing in the present Declaration shall prevent the fulfillment of international obligations of States in relation to persons belonging to minorities. In particular, States shall fulfill in good faith the obligations and commitments they have assumed under international treaties and agreements to which they are parties.

2. The exercise of the rights set forth in the present Declaration shall not prejudice the enjoyment by all persons of universally recognized human rights and fundamental freedoms.

3. Measures taken by States to ensure the effective enjoyment of the rights set forth in the present Declaration shall not *prima facie*, be considered contrary

to the principle of equality contained in the Universal Declaration of Human Rights.

4. Nothing in the present Declaration may be construed as permitting any activity contrary to the purposes and principles of the United Nations, including sovereign equality, territorial integrity and political independence of States.

Article 9

The specialized agencies and other organizations of the United Nations system shall contribute to the full realization of the rights and principles set forth in the present Declaration, within their respective fields of competence.

Convention on the Rights of the Child

Adopted and Opened for Signature, Ratification and Accession by General Assembly Resolution 44/25
of 20 November 1989
Entry into Force 2 September 1990,
in Accordance with Article 49

Preamble

The States Parties to the present Convention,

Considering that, in accordance with the principles proclaimed in the Charter of the United Nations, recognition of the inherent dignity and of the equal and inalienable rights of all members of the human family is the foundation of freedom, justice and peace in the world,

Bearing in mind that the peoples of the United Nations have, in the Charter, reaffirmed their faith in fundamental human rights and in the dignity and worth of the human person, and have determined to promote social progress and better standards of life in larger freedom,

Recognizing that the United Nations has, in the Universal Declaration of Human Rights and in the International Covenants on Human Rights, proclaimed and agreed that everyone is entitled to all the rights and freedoms set forth therein, without distinction of any kind, such as race, colour, sex, language, religion, political or other opinion, national or social origin, property, birth or other status,

Recalling that, in the Universal Declaration of Human Rights, the United Nations has proclaimed that childhood is entitled to special care and assistance,

Convinced that the family, as the fundamental group of society and the natural environment for the growth and well-being of all its members and particularly children, should be afforded the necessary protection and assistance so that it can fully assume its responsibilities within the community,

Recognizing that the child, for the full and harmonious development of his or her personality, should grow up in a family environment, in an atmosphere of happiness, love and understanding,

Considering that the child should be fully prepared to live an individual life in society, and brought up in the spirit of the ideals proclaimed in the Charter of the United Nations, and in particular in the spirit of peace, dignity, tolerance, freedom, equality and solidarity,

Bearing in mind that the need to extend particular care to the child has been stated in the Geneva Declaration of the Rights of the Child of 1924 and in the Declaration of the Rights of the Child adopted by the General Assembly on 20 November 1959 and recognized in the Universal Declaration of Human Rights, in the International Covenant on Civil and Political Rights (in particular in articles 23 and 24), in the International Covenant on Economic, Social and Cultural Rights (in particular in article 10) and in the statutes and relevant instruments of specialized agencies and international organizations concerned with the welfare of children,

Bearing in mind that, as indicated in the Declaration of the Rights of the Child, "the child, by reason of his physical and mental immaturity, needs special safeguards and care, including appropriate legal protection, before as well as after birth",

Recalling the provisions of the Declaration on Social and Legal Principles relating to the Protection and Welfare of Children, with Special Reference to Foster Placement and Adoption Nationally and Internationally; the United Nations Standard Minimum Rules for the Administration of Juvenile Justice (The Beijing Rules); and the Declaration on the Protection of Women and Children in Emergency and Armed Conflict,

Recognizing that, in all countries in the world, there are children living in exceptionally difficult conditions, and that such children need special consideration,

Taking due account of the importance of the traditions and cultural values of each people for the protection and harmonious development of the child,

Recognizing the importance of international co-operation for improving the living conditions of children in every country, in particular in the developing countries,

Have agreed as follows:

PART I

Article 1

For the purposes of the present Convention, a child means every human being below the age of eighteen years unless under the law applicable to the child, majority is attained earlier.

Article 2

1. States Parties shall respect and ensure the rights set forth in the present Convention to each child within their jurisdiction without discrimination of any kind, irrespective of the child's or his or her parent's or legal guardian's race, colour, sex, language, religion, political or other opinion, national, ethnic or social origin, property, disability, birth or other status.

2. States Parties shall take all appropriate measures to ensure that the child is protected against all forms of discrimination or punishment on the basis of the status, activities, expressed opinions, or beliefs of the child's parents, legal guardians, or family members.

Article 3

1. In all actions concerning children, whether undertaken by public or private social welfare institutions, courts of law, administrative authorities or legislative bodies, the best interests of the child shall be a primary consideration.

2. States Parties undertake to ensure the child such protection and care as is necessary for his or her well-being, taking into account the rights and duties of his or her parents, legal guardians, or other individuals legally responsible for him or her, and, to this end, shall take all appropriate legislative and administrative measures.

3. States Parties shall ensure that the institutions, services and facilities responsible for the care or protection of children shall conform with the standards established by competent authorities, particularly in the areas of safety, health, in the number and suitability of their staff, as well as competent supervision.

Article 4

States Parties shall undertake all appropriate legislative, administrative, and other measures for the implementation of the rights recognized in the present Convention. With regard to economic, social and cultural rights, States Parties shall undertake such measures to the maximum extent of their available resources and, where needed, within the framework of international co-operation.

Article 5

States Parties shall respect the responsibilities, rights and duties of parents or, where applicable, the members of the extended family or community as provided for by local custom, legal guardians or other persons legally responsible for the child, to provide, in a manner consistent with the evolving capacities of the child, appropriate direction and guidance in the exercise by the child of the rights recognized in the present Convention.

Article 6

1. States Parties recognize that every child has the inherent right to life.

2. States Parties shall ensure to the maximum extent possible the survival and development of the child.

Article 7

1. The child shall be registered immediately after birth and shall have the right from birth to a name, the right to acquire a nationality and. as far as possible, the right to know and be cared for by his or her parents.

2. States Parties shall ensure the implementation of these rights in accordance with their national law and their obligations under the relevant international instruments in this field, in particular where the child would otherwise be stateless.

Article 8

1. States Parties undertake to respect the right of the child to preserve his or her identity, including nationality, name and family relations as recognized by law without unlawful interference.

2. Where a child is illegally deprived of some or all of the elements of his or her identity, States Parties shall provide appropriate assistance and protection, with a view to re-establishing speedily his or her identity.

Article 9

1. States Parties shall ensure that a child shall not be separated from his or her parents against their will, except when competent authorities subject to judicial review determine, in accordance with applicable law and procedures, that such separation is necessary for the best interests of the child. Such determination may be necessary in a particular case such as one involving abuse or neglect of the child by the parents, or one where the parents are living separately and a decision must be made as to the child's place of residence.

2. In any proceedings pursuant to paragraph 1 of the present article, all interested parties shall be given an opportunity to participate in the proceedings and make their views known.

3. States Parties shall respect the right of the child who is separated from one or both parents to maintain personal relations and direct contact with both parents on a regular basis, except if it is contrary to the child's best interests.

4. Where such separation results from any action initiated by a State Party, such as the detention, imprisonment, exile, deportation or death (including death arising from any cause while the person is in the custody of the State) of one or both parents or of the child, that State Party shall, upon request, provide the parents, the child or, if appropriate, another member of the family with the essential information concerning the whereabouts of the absent member(s) of the family unless the provision of the information would be detrimental to the well-being of the child. States Parties shall further ensure that the submission of such a request shall of itself entail no adverse consequences for the person(s) concerned.

Article 10

1. In accordance with the obligation of States Parties under article 9, paragraph 1, applications by a child or his or her parents to enter or leave a State Party for the purpose of family reunification shall be dealt with by States Parties in a positive, humane and expeditious manner. States Parties shall further ensure that the submission of such a request shall entail no adverse consequences for the applicants and for the members of their family.

2. A child whose parents reside in different States shall have the right to maintain on a regular basis, save in exceptional circumstances personal relations and direct contacts with both parents. Towards that end and in accordance with the obligation of States Parties under article 9, paragraph 1, States Parties shall respect the right of the child and his or her parents to leave any country, including their own, and to enter their own country. The right to leave any country shall be subject only to such restrictions as are prescribed by law and which are necessary to protect the national security, public order (ordre public), public health or morals or the rights and freedoms of others and are consistent with the other rights recognized in the present Convention.

Article 11

1. States Parties shall take measures to combat the illicit transfer and non-return of children abroad.

2. To this end, States Parties shall promote the conclusion of bilateral or multilateral agreements or accession to existing agreements.

Article 12

1. States Parties shall assure to the child who is capable of forming his or her own views the right to express those views freely in all matters affecting the child, the views of the child being given due weight in accordance with the age and maturity of the child.

2. For this purpose, the child shall in particular be provided the opportunity to be heard in any judicial and administrative proceedings affecting the child, either directly, or through a representative or an appropriate body, in a manner consistent with the procedural rules of national law.

Article 13

1. The child shall have the right to freedom of expression; this right shall include freedom to seek, receive and impart information and ideas of all kinds, regardless of frontiers, either orally, in writing or in print, in the form of art, or through any other media of the child's choice.

2. The exercise of this right may be subject to certain restrictions, but these shall only be such as are provided by law and are necessary:

(a) For respect of the rights or reputations of others; or

(b) For the protection of national security or of public order (ordre public), or of public health or morals.

Article 14

1. States Parties shall respect the right of the child to freedom of thought, conscience and religion.

2. States Parties shall respect the rights and duties of the parents and, when applicable, legal guardians, to provide direction to the child in the exercise of his or her right in a manner consistent with the evolving capacities of the child.

3. Freedom to manifest one's religion or beliefs may be subject only to such limitations as are prescribed by law and are necessary to protect public safety, order, health or morals, or the fundamental rights and freedoms of others.

Article 15

1. States Parties recognize the rights of the child to freedom of association and to freedom of peaceful assembly.

2. No restrictions may be placed on the exercise of these rights other than those imposed in conformity with the law and which are necessary in a democratic society in the interests of national security or public safety, public order (ordre public), the protection of public health or morals or the protection of the rights and freedoms of others.

Article 16

1. No child shall be subjected to arbitrary or unlawful interference with his or her privacy, family, home or correspondence, nor to unlawful attacks on his or her honour and reputation.

2. The child has the right to the protection of the law against such interference or attacks.

Article 17

States Parties recognize the important function performed by the mass media and shall ensure that the child has access to information and material from a diversity of national and international sources, especially those aimed at the promotion of his or her social, spiritual and moral well-being and physical and mental health. To this end, States Parties shall:

(a) Encourage the mass media to disseminate information and material of social and cultural benefit to the child and in accordance with the spirit of article 29;

(b) Encourage international co-operation in the production, exchange and dissemination of such information and material from a diversity of cultural, national and international sources;

(c) Encourage the production and dissemination of children's books;

(d) Encourage the mass media to have particular regard to the linguistic needs of the child who belongs to a minority group or who is indigenous;

(e) Encourage the development of appropriate guidelines for the protection of the child from information and material injurious to his or her well-being, bearing in mind the provisions of articles 13 and 18.

Article 18

1. States Parties shall use their best efforts to ensure recognition of the principle that both parents have common responsibilities for the upbringing and development of the child. Parents or, as the case may be, legal guardians, have the primary responsibility for the upbringing and development of the child. The best interests of the child will be their basic concern.

2. For the purpose of guaranteeing and promoting the rights set forth in the present Convention, States Parties shall render appropriate assistance to parents and legal guardians in the performance of their child-rearing responsibilities and shall ensure the development of institutions, facilities and services for the care of children.

3. States Parties shall take all appropriate measures to ensure that children of working parents have the right to benefit from child-care services and facilities for which they are eligible.

Article 19

1. States Parties shall take all appropriate legislative, administrative, social and educational measures to protect the child from all forms of physical or mental violence, injury or abuse, neglect or negligent treatment, maltreatment or exploitation, including sexual abuse, while in the care of parent(s), legal guardian(s) or any other person who has the care of the child.

2. Such protective measures should, as appropriate, include effective procedures for the establishment of social programmes to provide necessary support for the child and for those who have the care of the child, as well as for other forms of prevention and for identification, reporting, referral, investigation, treatment and follow-up of instances of child maltreatment described heretofore, and, as appropriate, for judicial involvement.

Article 20

1. A child temporarily or permanently deprived of his or her family environment, or in whose own best interests cannot be allowed to remain in that environment, shall be entitled to special protection and assistance provided by the State.

2. States Parties shall in accordance with their national laws ensure alternative care for such a child.

3. Such care could include, inter alia, foster placement, kafalah of Islamic law, adoption or if necessary placement in suitable institutions for the care of children. When considering solutions, due regard shall be paid to the desirability of continuity in a child's upbringing and to the child's ethnic, religious, cultural and linguistic background.

Article 21

States Parties that recognize and/or permit the system of adoption shall ensure that the best interests of the child shall be the paramount consideration and they shall:

(a) Ensure that the adoption of a child is authorized only by competent authorities who determine, in accordance with applicable law and procedures and on the basis of all pertinent and reliable information, that the adoption is permissible in view of the child's status concerning parents, relatives and legal guardians and that, if required, the persons concerned have given their informed consent to the adoption on the basis of such counselling as may be necessary;

(b) Recognize that inter-country adoption may be considered as an alternative means of child's care, if the child cannot be placed in a foster or an adoptive family or cannot in any suitable manner be cared for in the child's country of origin;

(c) Ensure that the child concerned by inter-country adoption enjoys safeguards and standards equivalent to those existing in the case of national adoption;

(d) Take all appropriate measures to ensure that, in inter-country adoption, the placement does not result in improper financial gain for those involved in it;

(e) Promote, where appropriate, the objectives of the present article by concluding bilateral or multilateral arrangements or agreements, and endeavour, within this framework, to ensure that the placement of the child in another country is carried out by competent authorities or organs.

Article 22

1. States Parties shall take appropriate measures to ensure that a child who is seeking refugee status or who is considered a refugee in accordance with applicable international or domestic law and procedures shall, whether unaccompanied or accompanied by his or her parents or by any other person, receive appropriate protection and humanitarian assistance in the enjoyment of applicable rights set forth in the present Convention and in other international human rights or humanitarian instruments to which the said States are Parties.

2. For this purpose, States Parties shall provide, as they consider appropriate, co-operation in any efforts by the United Nations and other competent intergovernmental organizations or non-governmental organizations co-operating with the United Nations to protect and assist such a child and to trace the parents or other members of the family of any refugee child in order to obtain information necessary for reunification with his or her family. In cases where no parents or other members of the family can be found, the child shall be accorded the same protection as any other child permanently or temporarily deprived of his or her family environment for any reason, as set forth in the present Convention.

Article 23

1. States Parties recognize that a mentally or physically disabled child should enjoy a full and decent life, in conditions which ensure dignity, promote self-reliance and facilitate the child's active participation in the community.

2. States Parties recognize the right of the disabled child to special care and shall encourage and ensure the extension, subject to available resources, to the eligible child and those responsible for his or her care, of assistance for which application is made and which is appropriate to the child's condition and to the circumstances of the parents or others caring for the child.

3. Recognizing the special needs of a disabled child, assistance extended in accordance with paragraph 2 of the present article shall be provided free of charge, whenever possible, taking into account the financial resources of the parents or others caring for the child, and shall be designed to ensure that the disabled child has effective access to and receives education, training, health care services, rehabilitation services, preparation for employment and recreation opportunities in a manner conducive to the child's achieving the fullest possible social integration and individual development, including his or her cultural and spiritual development

4. States Parties shall promote, in the spirit of international cooperation, the exchange of appropriate information in the field of preventive health care and of medical, psychological and functional treatment of disabled children, including dissemination of and access to information concerning methods of rehabilitation, education and vocational services, with the aim of enabling States Parties to improve their capabilities and skills and to widen their experience in these areas. In this regard, particular account shall be taken of the needs of developing countries.

Article 24

1. States Parties recognize the right of the child to the enjoyment of the highest attainable standard of health and to facilities for the treatment of illness and rehabilitation of health. States Parties shall strive to ensure that no child is deprived of his or her right of access to such health care services.

2. States Parties shall pursue full implementation of this right and, in particular, shall take appropriate measures:

(a) To diminish infant and child mortality;

(b) To ensure the provision of necessary medical assistance and health care to all children with emphasis on the development of primary health care;

(c) To combat disease and malnutrition, including within the framework of primary health care, through, inter alia, the application of readily available technology and through the provision of adequate nutritious foods and clean drinking-water, taking into consideration the dangers and risks of environmental pollution;

(d) To ensure appropriate pre-natal and post-natal health care for mothers;

(e) To ensure that all segments of society, in particular parents and children, are informed, have access to education and are supported in the use of basic knowledge of child health and nutrition, the advantages of breastfeeding, hygiene and environmental sanitation and the prevention of accidents;

(f) To develop preventive health care, guidance for parents and family planning education and services.

3. States Parties shall take all effective and appropriate measures with a view to abolishing traditional practices prejudicial to the health of children.

4. States Parties undertake to promote and encourage international co-operation with a view to achieving progressively the full realization of the right recognized in the present article. In this regard, particular account shall be taken of the needs of developing countries.

Article 25

States Parties recognize the right of a child who has been placed by the competent authorities for the purposes of care, protection or treatment of his or her physical or mental health, to a periodic review of the treatment provided to the child and all other circumstances relevant to his or her placement.

Article 26

1. States Parties shall recognize for every child the right to benefit from social security, including social insurance, and shall take the necessary measures to achieve the full realization of this right in accordance with their national law.

2. The benefits should, where appropriate, be granted, taking into account the resources and the circumstances of the child and persons having responsibility for the maintenance of the child, as well as any other consideration relevant to an application for benefits made by or on behalf of the child.

Article 27

1. States Parties recognize the right of every child to a standard of living adequate for the child's physical, mental, spiritual, moral and social development.

2. The parent(s) or others responsible for the child have the primary responsibility to secure, within their abilities and financial capacities, the conditions of living necessary for the child's development.

3. States Parties, in accordance with national conditions and within their means, shall take appropriate measures to assist parents and others responsible for the child to implement this right and shall in case of need provide material assistance and support programmes, particularly with regard to nutrition, clothing and housing.

4. States Parties shall take all appropriate measures to secure the recovery of maintenance for the child from the parents or other persons having financial responsibility for the child, both within the State Party and from abroad. In particular, where the person having financial responsibility for the child lives in a State different from that of the child, States Parties shall promote the accession to international agreements or the conclusion of such agreements, as well as the making of other appropriate arrangements.

Article 28

1. States Parties recognize the right of the child to education, and with a view to achieving this right progressively and on the basis of equal opportunity, they shall, in particular:

(a) Make primary education compulsory and available free to all;

(b) Encourage the development of different forms of secondary education, including general and vocational education, make them available and accessible to every child, and take appropriate measures such as the introduction of free education and offering financial assistance in case of need;

(c) Make higher education accessible to all on the basis of capacity by every appropriate means;

(d) Make educational and vocational information and guidance available and accessible to all children;

(e) Take measures to encourage regular attendance at schools and the reduction of drop-out rates.

2. States Parties shall take all appropriate measures to ensure that school discipline is administered in a manner consistent with the child's human dignity and in conformity with the present Convention.

3. States Parties shall promote and encourage international cooperation in matters relating to education, in particular with a view to contributing to the elimination of ignorance and illiteracy throughout the world and facilitating access to scientific and technical knowledge and modern teaching methods.

In this regard, particular account shall be taken of the needs of developing countries.

Article 29

1. States Parties agree that the education of the child shall be directed to:

(a) The development of the child's personality, talents and mental and physical abilities to their fullest potential;

(b) The development of respect for human rights and fundamental freedoms, and for the principles enshrined in the Charter of the United Nations;

(c) The development of respect for the child's parents, his or her own cultural identity, language and values, for the national values of the country in which the child is living, the country from which he or she may originate, and for civilizations different from his or her own;

(d) The preparation of the child for responsible life in a free society, in the spirit of understanding, peace, tolerance, equality of sexes, and friendship among all peoples, ethnic, national and religious groups and persons of indigenous origin;

(e) The development of respect for the natural environment.

2. No part of the present article or article 28 shall be construed so as to interfere with the liberty of individuals and bodies to establish and direct educational institutions, subject always to the observance of the principle set forth in paragraph 1 of the present article and to the requirements that the education given in such institutions shall conform to such minimum standards as may be laid down by the State.

Article 30

In those States in which ethnic, religious or linguistic minorities or persons of indigenous origin exist, a child belonging to such a minority or who is indigenous shall not be denied the right, in community with other members of his or her group, to enjoy his or her own culture, to profess and practise his or her own religion, or to use his or her own language.

Article 31

1. States Parties recognize the right of the child to rest and leisure, to engage in play and recreational activities appropriate to the age of the child and to participate freely in cultural life and the arts.

2. States Parties shall respect and promote the right of the child to participate fully in cultural and artistic life and shall encourage the provision of appropriate and equal opportunities for cultural, artistic, recreational and leisure activity.

Article 32

1. States Parties recognize the right of the child to be protected from economic exploitation and from performing any work that is likely to be hazardous or to interfere with the child's education, or to be harmful to the child's health or physical, mental, spiritual, moral or social development.

2. States Parties shall take legislative, administrative, social and educational measures to ensure the implementation of the present article. To this end, and having regard to the relevant provisions of other international instruments, States Parties shall in particular:

(a) Provide for a minimum age or minimum ages for admission to employment;

(b) Provide for appropriate regulation of the hours and conditions of employment;

(c) Provide for appropriate penalties or other sanctions to ensure the effective enforcement of the present article.

Article 33

States Parties shall take all appropriate measures, including legislative, administrative, social and educational measures, to protect children from the illicit use of narcotic drugs and psychotropic substances as defined in the relevant international treaties, and to prevent the use of children in the illicit production and trafficking of such substances.

Article 34

States Parties undertake to protect the child from all forms of sexual exploitation and sexual abuse. For these purposes, States Parties shall in particular take all appropriate national, bilateral and multilateral measures to prevent:

(a) The inducement or coercion of a child to engage in any unlawful sexual activity;

(b) The exploitative use of children in prostitution or other unlawful sexual practices;

(c) The exploitative use of children in pornographic performances and materials.

Article 35

States Parties shall take all appropriate national, bilateral and multilateral measures to prevent the abduction of, the sale of or traffic in children for any purpose or in any form.

Article 36

States Parties shall protect the child against all other forms of exploitation prejudicial to any aspects of the child's welfare.

Article 37

States Parties shall ensure that:

(a) No child shall be subjected to torture or other cruel, inhuman or degrading treatment or punishment. Neither capital punishment nor life imprisonment without possibility of release shall be imposed for offences committed by persons below eighteen years of age;

(b) No child shall be deprived of his or her liberty unlawfully or arbitrarily. The arrest, detention or imprisonment of a child shall be in conformity with the law and shall be used only as a measure of last resort and for the shortest appropriate period of time;

(c) Every child deprived of liberty shall be treated with humanity and respect for the inherent dignity of the human person, and in a manner which takes into account the needs of persons of his or her age. In particular, every child deprived of liberty shall be separated from adults unless it is considered in the child's best interest not to do so and shall have the right to maintain contact with his or her family through correspondence and visits, save in exceptional circumstances;

(d) Every child deprived of his or her liberty shall have the right to prompt access to legal and other appropriate assistance, as well as the right to challenge the legality of the deprivation of his or her liberty before a court or other competent, independent and impartial authority, and to a prompt decision on any such action.

Article 38

1. States Parties undertake to respect and to ensure respect for rules of international humanitarian law applicable to them in armed conflicts which are relevant to the child.

2. States Parties shall take all feasible measures to ensure that persons who have not attained the age of fifteen years do not take a direct part in hostilities.

3. States Parties shall refrain from recruiting any person who has not attained the age of fifteen years into their armed forces. In recruiting among those persons who have attained the age of fifteen years but who have not attained the age of eighteen years, States Parties shall endeavour to give priority to those who are oldest.

4. In accordance with their obligations under international humanitarian law to protect the civilian population in armed conflicts, States Parties shall take all feasible measures to ensure protection and care of children who are affected by an armed conflict.

Article 39

States Parties shall take all appropriate measures to promote physical and psychological recovery and social reintegration of a child victim of: any form of neglect, exploitation, or abuse; torture or any other form of cruel, inhuman or degrading treatment or punishment; or armed conflicts. Such recovery and reintegration shall take place in an environment which fosters the health, self-respect and dignity of the child.

Article 40

1. States Parties recognize the right of every child alleged as, accused of, or recognized as having infringed the penal law to be treated in a manner consistent with the promotion of the child's sense of dignity and worth, which reinforces the child's respect for the human rights and fundamental freedoms of others and which takes into account the child's age and the desirability of promoting the child's reintegration and the child's assuming a constructive role in society.

2. To this end, and having regard to the relevant provisions of international instruments, States Parties shall, in particular, ensure that:

(a) No child shall be alleged as, be accused of, or recognized as having infringed the penal law by reason of acts or omissions that were not prohibited by national or international law at the time they were committed;

(b) Every child alleged as or accused of having infringed the penal law has at least the following guarantees:

(i) To be presumed innocent until proven guilty according to law;

(ii) To be informed promptly and directly of the charges against him or her, and, if appropriate, through his or her parents or legal guardians, and to have legal or other appropriate assistance in the preparation and presentation of his or her defence;

(iii) To have the matter determined without delay by a competent, independent and impartial authority or judicial body in a fair hearing according to law, in the presence of legal or other appropriate assistance and, unless it is considered not to be in the best interest of the child, in particular, taking into account his or her age or situation, his or her parents or legal guardians;

(iv) Not to be compelled to give testimony or to confess guilt; to examine or have examined adverse witnesses and to obtain the participation and examination of witnesses on his or her behalf under conditions of equality;

(v) If considered to have infringed the penal law, to have this decision and any measures imposed in consequence thereof reviewed by a higher competent, independent and impartial authority or judicial body according to law;

(vi) To have the free assistance of an interpreter if the child cannot understand or speak the language used;

(vii) To have his or her privacy fully respected at all stages of the proceedings.

3. States Parties shall seek to promote the establishment of laws, procedures, authorities and institutions specifically applicable to children alleged as, accused of, or recognized as having infringed the penal law and in particular:

(a) The establishment of a minimum age below which children shall be presumed not to have the capacity to infringe the penal law;

(b) Whenever appropriate and desirable, measures for dealing with such children without resorting to judicial proceedings, providing that human rights and legal safeguards are fully respected.

4. A variety of dispositions, such as care, guidance and supervision orders; counselling; probation; foster care; education and vocational training programmes and other alternatives to institutional care shall be available to ensure that children are dealt with in a manner appropriate to their well-being and proportionate both to their circumstances and the offence.

Article 41

Nothing in the present Convention shall affect any provisions which are more conducive to the realization of the rights of the child and which may be contained in:

(a) The law of a State party; or

(b) International law in force for that State.

PART II

Article 42

States Parties undertake to make the principles and provisions of the Convention widely known, by appropriate and active means, to adults and children alike.

Article 43

1. For the purpose of examining the progress made by States Parties in achieving the realization of the obligations undertaken in the present Convention, there shall be established a Committee on the Rights of the Child, which shall carry out the functions hereinafter provided.

2. The Committee shall consist of ten experts of high moral standing and recognized competence in the field covered by this Convention. The members of the Committee shall be elected by States Parties from among their nationals and shall serve in their personal capacity, consideration being given to equitable geographical distribution, as well as to the principal legal systems.

3. The members of the Committee shall be elected by secret ballot from a list of persons nominated by States Parties. Each State Party may nominate one person from among its own nationals.

4. The initial election to the Committee shall be held no later than six months after the date of the entry into force of the present Convention and thereafter every second year. At least four months before the date of each election, the Secretary-General of the United Nations shall address a letter to States Parties inviting them to submit their nominations within two months. The Secretary-General shall subsequently prepare a list in alphabetical order of all persons thus nominated, indicating States Parties which have nominated them, and shall submit it to the States Parties to the present Convention.

5. The elections shall be held at meetings of States Parties convened by the Secretary-General at United Nations Headquarters. At those meetings, for which two thirds of States Parties shall constitute a quorum, the persons elected to the Committee shall be those who obtain the largest number of votes and an absolute majority of the votes of the representatives of States Parties present and voting.

6. The members of the Committee shall be elected for a term of four years. They shall be eligible for re-election if renominated. The term of five of the members elected at the first election shall expire at the end of two years; immediately after the first election, the names of these five members shall be chosen by lot by the Chairman of the meeting.

7. If a member of the Committee dies or resigns or declares that for any other cause he or she can no longer perform the duties of the Committee, the State Party which nominated the member shall appoint another expert from among its nationals to serve for the remainder of the term, subject to the approval of the Committee.

8. The Committee shall establish its own rules of procedure.

9. The Committee shall elect its officers for a period of two years.

10. The meetings of the Committee shall normally be held at United Nations Headquarters or at any other convenient place as determined by the Committee. The Committee shall normally meet annually. The duration of the meetings of the Committee shall be determined, and reviewed, if necessary, by a meeting of the States Parties to the present Convention, subject to the approval of the General Assembly.

11. The Secretary-General of the United Nations shall provide the necessary staff and facilities for the effective performance of the functions of the Committee under the present Convention.

12. With the approval of the General Assembly, the members of the Committee established under the present Convention shall receive emoluments from United Nations resources on such terms and conditions as the Assembly may decide.

Article 44

1. States Parties undertake to submit to the Committee, through the Secretary-General of the United Nations, reports on the measures they have adopted which give effect to the rights recognized herein and on the progress made on the enjoyment of those rights:

(a) Within two years of the entry into force of the Convention for the State Party concerned;

(b) Thereafter every five years.

2. Reports made under the present article shall indicate factors and difficulties, if any, affecting the degree of fulfillment of the obligations under the present Convention. Reports shall also contain sufficient information to provide the Committee with a comprehensive understanding of the implementation of the Convention in the country concerned.

3. A State Party which has submitted a comprehensive initial report to the Committee need not, in its subsequent reports submitted in accordance with paragraph 1 (b) of the present article, repeat basic information previously provided.

4. The Committee may request from States Parties further information relevant to the implementation of the Convention.

5. The Committee shall submit to the General Assembly, through the Economic and Social Council, every two years, reports on its activities.

6. States Parties shall make their reports widely available to the public in their own countries.

Article 45

In order to foster the effective implementation of the Convention and to encourage international co-operation in the field covered by the Convention:

(a) The specialized agencies, the United Nations Children's Fund, and other United Nations organs shall be entitled to be represented at the consideration of the implementation of such provisions of the present Convention as fall within the scope of their mandate. The Committee may invite the specialized agencies, the United Nations Children's Fund and other competent bodies as it may consider appropriate to provide expert advice on the implementation of the Convention in areas falling within the scope of their respective mandates. The Committee may invite the specialized agencies, the United Nations Children's Fund, and other United Nations organs to submit reports on the implementation of the Convention in areas falling within the scope of their activities;

(b) The Committee shall transmit, as it may consider appropriate, to the specialized agencies, the United Nations Children's Fund and other competent bodies, any reports from States Parties that contain a request, or indicate a need, for technical advice or assistance, along with the Committee's observations and suggestions, if any, on these requests or indications;

(c) The Committee may recommend to the General Assembly to request the Secretary-General to undertake on its behalf studies on specific issues relating to the rights of the child;

(d) The Committee may make suggestions and general recommendations based on information received pursuant to articles 44 and 45 of the present Convention. Such suggestions and general recommendations shall be transmitted to any State Party concerned and reported to the General Assembly, together with comments, if any, from States Parties.

PART III

Article 46

The present Convention shall be open for signature by all States.

Article 47

The present Convention is subject to ratification. Instruments of ratification shall be deposited with the Secretary-General of the United Nations.

Article 48

The present Convention shall remain open for accession by any State. The instruments of accession shall be deposited with the Secretary-General of the United Nations.

Article 49

1. The present Convention shall enter into force on the thirtieth day following the date of deposit with the Secretary-General of the United Nations of the twentieth instrument of ratification or accession.

2. For each State ratifying or acceding to the Convention after the deposit of the twentieth instrument of ratification or accession, the Convention shall enter into force on the thirtieth day after the deposit by such State of its instrument of ratification or accession.

Article 50

1. Any State Party may propose an amendment and file it with the Secretary-General of the United Nations. The Secretary-General shall thereupon communicate the proposed amendment to States Parties, with a request that they indicate whether they favour a conference of States Parties for the purpose of considering and voting upon the proposals. In the event that, within four months from the date of such communication, at least one third of the States Parties favour such a conference, the Secretary-General shall convene the conference under the auspices of the United Nations. Any amendment adopted by a majority of States Parties present and voting at the conference shall be submitted to the General Assembly for approval.

2. An amendment adopted in accordance with paragraph 1 of the present article shall enter into force when it has been approved by the General Assembly of the United Nations and accepted by a two-thirds majority of States Parties.

3. When an amendment enters into force, it shall be binding on those States Parties which have accepted it, other States Parties still being bound by the provisions of the present Convention and any earlier amendments which they have accepted.

Article 51

1. The Secretary-General of the United Nations shall receive and circulate to all States the text of reservations made by States at the time of ratification or accession.

2. A reservation incompatible with the object and purpose of the present Convention shall not be permitted.

3. Reservations may be withdrawn at any time by notification to that effect addressed to the Secretary-General of the United Nations, who shall then inform all States. Such notification shall take effect on the date on which it is received by the Secretary-General

Article 52

A State Party may denounce the present Convention by written notification to the Secretary-General of the United Nations. Denunciation becomes effective one year after the date of receipt of the notification by the Secretary-General.

Article 53

The Secretary-General of the United Nations is designated as the depositary of the present Convention.

Article 54

The original of the present Convention, of which the Arabic, Chinese, English, French, Russian and Spanish texts are equally authentic, shall be deposited with the Secretary-General of the United Nations.

IN WITNESS THEREOF the undersigned plenipotentiaries, being duly authorized thereto by their respective governments, have signed the present Convention.

Total parties to the Convention on the Rights of the Child, as of 13 July 2007: 193. Somalia and the United States of America were the only U.N. member states not having ratified this convention.

Convention on the Elimination of All Forms of Discrimination against Women (CEDAW)

Adopted and Opened for Signature, Ratification and Accession by General Assembly Resolution 34/180 of 18 December 1979, Entry into Force 3 September 1981, in Accordance with Article 27(1)

(Excerpt of substantive provisions)

Article 1

For the purposes of the present Convention, the term "discrimination against women" shall mean any distinction, exclusion or restriction made on the basis of sex which has the effect or purpose of impairing or nullifying the recognition, enjoyment or exercise by women, irrespective of their marital status, on a basis of equality of men and women, of human rights and fundamental freedoms in the political, economic, social, cultural, civil or any other field.

Article 2

States Parties condemn discrimination against women in all its forms, agree to pursue by all appropriate means and without delay a policy of eliminating discrimination against women and, to this end, undertake:

(a) To embody the principle of the equality of men and women in their national constitutions or other appropriate legislation if not yet incorporated therein and to ensure, through law and other appropriate means, the practical realization of this principle;

(b) To adopt appropriate legislative and other measures, including sanctions where appropriate, prohibiting all discrimination against women;

(c) To establish legal protection of the rights of women on an equal basis with men and to ensure through competent national tribunals and other public institutions the effective protection of women against any act of discrimination;

(d) To refrain from engaging in any act or practice of discrimination against women and to ensure that public authorities and institutions shall act in conformity with this obligation;

(e) To take all appropriate measures to eliminate discrimination against women by any person, organization or enterprise;

(f) To take all appropriate measures, including legislation, to modify or abolish existing laws, regulations, customs and practices which constitute discrimination against women;

(g) To repeal all national penal provisions which constitute discrimination against women.

Article 3

States Parties shall take in all fields, in particular in the political, social, economic and cultural fields, all appropriate measures, including legislation, to ensure the full development and advancement of women, for the purpose of guaranteeing them the exercise and enjoyment of human rights and fundamental freedoms on a basis of equality with men.

Article 4

1. Adoption by States Parties of temporary special measures aimed at accelerating de facto equality between men and women shall not be considered discrimination as defined in the present Convention, but shall in no way entail as a consequence the maintenance of unequal or separate standards; these measures shall be discontinued when the objectives of equality of opportunity and treatment have been achieved.

2. Adoption by States Parties of special measures, including those measures contained in the present Convention, aimed at protecting maternity shall not be considered discriminatory.

Article 5

States Parties shall take all appropriate measures:

(a) To modify the social and cultural patterns of conduct of men and women, with a view to achieving the elimination of prejudices and customary and all other practices which are based on the idea of the inferiority or the superiority of either of the sexes or on stereotyped roles for men and women;

(b) To ensure that family education includes a proper understanding of maternity as a social function and the recognition of the common responsibility of men and women in the upbringing and development of their children, it being understood that the interest of the children is the primordial consideration in all cases.

Article 6

States Parties shall take all appropriate measures, including legislation, to suppress all forms of traffic in women and exploitation of prostitution of women.

Article 7

States Parties shall take all appropriate measures to eliminate discrimination against women in the political and public life of the country and, in particular, shall ensure to women, on equal terms with men, the right:

(a) To vote in all elections and public referenda and to be eligible for election to all publicly elected bodies;

(b) To participate in the formulation of government policy and the implementation thereof and to hold public office and perform all public functions at all levels of government;

(c) To participate in non-governmental organizations and associations concerned with the public and political life of the country.

Article 8

States Parties shall take all appropriate measures to ensure to women, on equal terms with men and without any discrimination, the opportunity to represent their Governments at the international level and to participate in the work of international organizations.

Article 9

1. States Parties shall grant women equal rights with men to acquire, change or retain their nationality. They shall ensure in particular that neither marriage to an alien nor change of nationality by the husband during marriage shall automatically change the nationality of the wife, render her stateless or force upon her the nationality of the husband.

2. States Parties shall grant women equal rights with men with respect to the nationality of their children.

Article 10

States Parties shall take all appropriate measures to eliminate discrimination against women in order to ensure to them equal rights with men in the field of education and in particular to ensure, on a basis of equality of men and women:

(a) The same conditions for career and vocational guidance, for access to studies and for the achievement of diplomas in educational establishments of all categories in rural as well as in urban areas; this equality shall be ensured in preschool, general, technical, professional and higher technical education, as well as in all types of vocational training;

(b) Access to the same curricula, the same examinations, teaching staff with qualifications of the same standard and school premises and equipment of the same quality;

(c) The elimination of any stereotyped concept of the roles of men and women at all levels and in all forms of education by encouraging coeducation and other types of education which will help to achieve this aim and, in particular, by the revision of textbooks and school programmes and the adaptation of teaching methods;

(d) The same opportunities to benefit from scholarships and other study grants;

(e) The same opportunities for access to programmes of continuing education, including adult and functional literacy programmes, particularly those aimed at reducing, at the earliest possible time, any gap in education existing between men and women;

(f) The reduction of female student drop-out rates and the organization of programmes for girls and women who have left school prematurely;

(g) The same opportunities to participate actively in sports and physical education;

(h) Access to specific educational information to help to ensure the health and well-being of families, including information and advice on family planning.

Article 11

1. States Parties shall take all appropriate measures to eliminate discrimination against women in the field of employment in order to ensure, on a basis of equality of men and women, the same rights, in particular:

(a) The right to work as an inalienable right of all human beings;

(b) The right to the same employment opportunities, including the application of the same criteria for selection in matters of employment;

(c) The right to free choice of profession and employment, the right to promotion, job security and all benefits and conditions of service and the right to receive vocational training and retraining, including apprenticeships, advanced vocational training and recurrent training;

(d) The right to equal remuneration, including benefits, and to equal treatment in respect of work of equal value, as well as equality of treatment in the evaluation of the quality of work;

(e) The right to social security, particularly in cases of retirement, unemployment, sickness, invalidity and old age and other incapacity to work, as well as the right to paid leave;

(f) The right to protection of health and to safety in working conditions, including the safeguarding of the function of reproduction.

2. In order to prevent discrimination against women on the grounds of marriage or maternity and to ensure their effective right to work, States Parties shall take appropriate measures:

(a) To prohibit, subject to the imposition of sanctions, dismissal on the grounds of pregnancy or of maternity leave and discrimination in dismissals on the basis of marital status;

(b) To introduce maternity leave with pay or with comparable social benefits without loss of former employment, seniority or social allowances;

(c) To encourage the provision of the necessary supporting social services to enable parents to combine family obligations with work responsibilities and participation in public life, in particular through promoting the establishment and development of a network of child-care facilities;

(d) To provide special protection to women during pregnancy in types of work proved to be harmful to them.

3. Protective legislation relating to matters covered in this article shall be reviewed periodically in the light of scientific and technological knowledge and shall be revised, repealed or extended as necessary.

Article 12

1. States Parties shall take all appropriate measures to eliminate discrimination against women in the field of health care in order to ensure, on a basis of equality of men and women, access to health care services, including those related to family planning.

2. Notwithstanding the provisions of paragraph 1 of this article, States Parties shall ensure to women appropriate services in connection with pregnancy,

confinement and the post-natal period, granting free services where necessary, as well as adequate nutrition during pregnancy and lactation.

Article 13

States Parties shall take all appropriate measures to eliminate discrimination against women in other areas of economic and social life in order to ensure, on a basis of equality of men and women, the same rights, in particular:

(a) The right to family benefits;

(b) The right to bank loans, mortgages and other forms of financial credit;

(c) The right to participate in recreational activities, sports and all aspects of cultural life.

Article 14

1. States Parties shall take into account the particular problems faced by rural women and the significant roles which rural women play in the economic survival of their families, including their work in the non-monetized sectors of the economy, and shall take all appropriate measures to ensure the application of the provisions of the present Convention to women in rural areas.

2. States Parties shall take all appropriate measures to eliminate discrimination against women in rural areas in order to ensure, on a basis of equality of men and women, that they participate in and benefit from rural development and, in particular, shall ensure to such women the right:

(a) To participate in the elaboration and implementation of development planning at all levels;

(b) To have access to adequate health care facilities, including information, counselling and services in family planning;

(c) To benefit directly from social security programmes;

(d) To obtain all types of training and education, formal and non-formal, including that relating to functional literacy, as well as, inter alia, the benefit of all community and extension services in order to increase their technical proficiency;

(e) To organize self-help groups and cooperatives in order to obtain equal access to economic opportunities through employment or self-employment;

(f) To participate in all community activities;

(g) To have access to agricultural credit and loans, marketing facilities, appropriate technology and equal treatment in land and agrarian reform as well as in land resettlement schemes;

(h) To enjoy adequate living conditions, particularly in relation to housing, sanitation, electricity and water supply, transport and communications.

Article 15

1. States Parties shall accord to women equality with men before the law.

2. States Parties shall accord to women, in civil matters, a legal capacity identical to that of men and the same opportunities to exercise that capacity. In particular, they shall give women equal rights to conclude contracts and to administer property and shall treat them equally in all stages of procedure in courts and tribunals.

3. States Parties agree that all contracts and all other private instruments of any kind with a legal effect which is directed at restricting the legal capacity of women shall be deemed null and void.

4. States Parties shall accord to men and women the same rights with regard to the law relating to the movement of persons and the freedom to choose their residence and domicile.

Article 16

1. States Parties shall take all appropriate measures to eliminate discrimination against women in all matters relating to marriage and family relations and in particular shall ensure, on a basis of equality of men and women:

(a) The same right to enter into marriage;

(b) The same right freely to choose a spouse and to enter into marriage only with their free and full consent;

(c) The same rights and responsibilities during marriage and at its dissolution;

(d) The same rights and responsibilities as parents, irrespective of their marital status, in matters relating to their children; in all cases the interests of the children shall be paramount;

(e) The same rights to decide freely and responsibly on the number and spacing of their children and to have access to the information, education and means to enable them to exercise these rights;

(f) The same rights and responsibilities with regard to guardianship, wardship, trusteeship and adoption of children, or similar institutions where these concepts exist in national legislation; in all cases the interests of the children shall be paramount;

(g) The same personal rights as husband and wife, including the right to choose a family name, a profession and an occupation;

(h) The same rights for both spouses in respect of the ownership, acquisition, management, administration, enjoyment and disposition of property, whether free of charge or for a valuable consideration.

2. The betrothal and the marriage of a child shall have no legal effect, and all necessary action, including legislation, shall be taken to specify a minimum age for marriage and to make the registration of marriages in an official registry compulsory.

* * *

Article 28 (para. 2):

A reservation incompatible with the object and purpose of the present Convention shall not be permitted.

* * *

Total Parties to the Convention on the Elimination of All Forms of Discrimination against Women, as of 19 April 2007: 185

APPENDIX G

INTERNATIONAL CONVENTION ON THE PROTECTION OF THE RIGHTS OF ALL MIGRANT WORKERS AND MEMBERS OF THEIR FAMILIES

Adopted by General Assembly Resolution 45/158 of 18 December 1990, Entry into Force 1 July 2003

Preamble

The States Parties to the present Convention,

Taking into account the principles embodied in the basic instruments of the United Nations concerning human rights, in particular the Universal Declaration of Human Rights, the International Covenant on Economic, Social and Cultural Rights, the International Covenant on Civil and Political Rights, the International Convention on the Elimination of All Forms of Racial Discrimination, the Convention on the Elimination of All Forms of Discrimination against Women and the Convention on the Rights of the Child,

Taking into account also the principles and standards set forth in the relevant instruments elaborated within the framework of the International Labour Organisation, especially the Convention concerning Migration for Employment (No. 97), the Convention concerning Migrations in Abusive Conditions and the Promotion of Equality of Opportunity and Treatment of Migrant Workers (No.143), the Recommendation concerning Migration for Employment (No. 86), the Recommendation concerning Migrant Workers (No.151), the

Convention concerning Forced or Compulsory Labour (No. 29) and the Convention concerning Abolition of Forced Labour (No. 105),

Reaffirming the importance of the principles contained in the Convention against Discrimination in Education of the United Nations Educational, Scientific and Cultural Organization,

Recalling the Convention against Torture and Other Cruel, Inhuman or Degrading Treatment or Punishment, the Declaration of the Fourth United Nations Congress on the Prevention of Crime and the Treatment of Offenders, the Code of Conduct for Law Enforcement Officials, and the Slavery Conventions,

Recalling that one of the objectives of the International Labour Organisation, as stated in its Constitution, is the protection of the interests of workers when employed in countries other than their own, and bearing in mind the expertise and experience of that organization in matters related to migrant workers and members of their families,

Recognizing the importance of the work done in connection with migrant workers and members of their families in various organs of the United Nations, in particular in the Commission on Human Rights and the Commission for Social Development, and in the Food and Agriculture Organization of the United Nations, the United Nations Educational, Scientific and Cultural Organization and the World Health Organization, as well as in other international organizations,

Recognizing also the progress made by certain States on a regional or bilateral basis towards the protection of the rights of migrant workers and members of their families, as well as the importance and usefulness of bilateral and multilateral agreements in this field,

Realizing the importance and extent of the migration phenomenon, which involves millions of people and affects a large number of States in the international community,

Aware of the impact of the flows of migrant workers on States and people concerned, and desiring to establish norms which may contribute to the harmonization of the attitudes of States through the acceptance of basic principles concerning the treatment of migrant workers and members of their families,

Considering the situation of vulnerability in which migrant workers and members of their families frequently-find themselves owing, among other things, to their absence from their State of origin and to the difficulties they may encounter arising from their presence in the State of employment,

Convinced that the rights of migrant workers and members of their families have not been sufficiently recognized everywhere and therefore require appropriate international protection,

Taking into account the fact that migration is often the cause of serious problems for the members of the families of migrant workers as well as for the workers themselves, in particular because of the scattering of the family,

Bearing in mind that the human problems involved in migration are even more serious in the case of irregular migration and convinced therefore that appropriate action should be encouraged in order to prevent and eliminate clandestine movements and trafficking in migrant workers, while at the same time assuring the protection of their fundamental human rights,

Considering that workers who are non-documented or in an irregular situation are frequently employed under less favourable conditions of work than other workers and that certain employers find this an inducement to seek such labour in order to reap the benefits of unfair competition,

Considering also that recourse to the employment of migrant workers who are in an irregular situation will be discouraged if the fundamental human rights of all migrant workers are more widely recognized and, moreover, that granting certain additional rights to migrant workers and members of their families in a regular situation will encourage all migrants and employers to respect and comply with the laws and procedures established by the States concerned,

Convinced, therefore, of the need to bring about the international protection of the rights of all migrant workers and members of their families, reaffirming and establishing basic norms in a comprehensive convention which could be applied universally,

Have agreed as follows:

PART I: SCOPE AND DEFINITIONS

Article 1

1. The present Convention is applicable, except as otherwise provided hereafter, to all migrant workers and members of their families without distinction of any kind such as sex, race, colour, language, religion or conviction, political or other opinion, national, ethnic or social origin, nationality, age, economic position, property, marital status, birth or other status.

2. The present Convention shall apply during the entire migration process of migrant workers and members of their families, which comprises preparation for migration, departure, transit and the entire period of stay and remuner-

ated activity in the State of employment as well as return to the State of origin or the State of habitual residence.

Article 2

For the purposes of the present Convention:

1. The term "migrant worker" refers to a person who is to be engaged, is engaged or has been engaged in a remunerated activity in a State of which he or she is not a national.

2. (a) The term "frontier worker" refers to a migrant worker who retains his or her habitual residence in a neighbouring State to which he or she normally returns every day or at least once a week;

(b) The term "seasonal worker" refers to a migrant worker whose work by its character is dependent on seasonal conditions and is performed only during part of the year;

(c) The term "seafarer", which includes a fisherman, refers to a migrant worker employed on board a vessel registered in a State of which he or she is not a national;

(d) The term "worker on an offshore installation" refers to a migrant worker employed on an offshore installation that is under the jurisdiction of a State of which he or she is not a national;

(e) The term "itinerant worker" refers to a migrant worker who, having his or her habitual residence in one State, has to travel to another State or States for short periods, owing to the nature of his or her occupation;

(f) The term "project-tied worker" refers to a migrant worker admitted to a State of employment for a defined period to work solely on a specific project being carried out in that State by his or her employer;

(g) The term "specified-employment worker" refers to a migrant worker:

(i) Who has been sent by his or her employer for a restricted and defined period of time to a State of employment to undertake a specific assignment or duty; or

(ii) Who engages for a restricted and defined period of time in work that requires professional, commercial, technical or other highly specialized skill; or

(iii) Who, upon the request of his or her employer in the State of employment, engages for a restricted and defined period of time in work whose nature is transitory or brief; and who is required to depart from the State of employment either at the expiration of his or her authorized period of stay, or earlier if he or she no longer undertakes that specific assignment or duty or engages in that work;

(h) The term "self-employed worker" refers to a migrant worker who is engaged in a remunerated activity otherwise than under a contract of employment and who earns his or her living through this activity normally working alone or together with members of his or her family, and to any other migrant worker recognized as self-employed by applicable legislation of the State of employment or bilateral or multilateral agreements.

Article 3

The present Convention shall not apply to:

(a) Persons sent or employed by international organizations and agencies or persons sent or employed by a State outside its territory to perform official functions, whose admission and status are regulated by general international law or by specific international agreements or conventions;

(b) Persons sent or employed by a State or on its behalf outside its territory who participate in development programmes and other co-operation programmes, whose admission and status are regulated by agreement with the State of employment and who, in accordance with that agreement, are not considered migrant workers;

(c) Persons taking up residence in a State different from their State of origin as investors;

(d) Refugees and stateless persons, unless such application is provided for in the relevant national legislation of, or international instruments in force for, the State Party concerned;

(e) Students and trainees;

(f) Seafarers and workers on an offshore installation who have not been admitted to take up residence and engage in a remunerated activity in the State of employment.

Article 4

For the purposes of the present Convention the term "members of the family" refers to persons married to migrant workers or having with them a relationship that, according to applicable law, produces effects equivalent to marriage, as well as their dependent children and other dependent persons who are recognized as members of the family by applicable legislation or applicable bilateral or multilateral agreements between the States concerned.

Article 5

For the purposes of the present Convention, migrant workers and members of their families:

(a) Are considered as documented or in a regular situation if they are authorized to enter, to stay and to engage in a remunerated activity in the State of employment pursuant to the law of that State and to international agreements to which that State is a party;

(b) Are considered as non-documented or in an irregular situation if they do not comply with the conditions provided for in subparagraph (a) of the present article.

Article 6

For the purposes of the present Convention:

(a) The term "State of origin" means the State of which the person concerned is a national;

(b) The term "State of employment" means a State where the migrant worker is to be engaged, is engaged or has been engaged in a remunerated activity, as the case may be;

(c) The term "State of transit," means any State through which the person concerned passes on any journey to the State of employment or from the State of employment to the State of origin or the State of habitual residence.

PART II: NON-DISCRIMINATION WITH RESPECT TO RIGHTS

Article 7

States Parties undertake, in accordance with the international instruments concerning human rights, to respect and to ensure to all migrant workers and members of their families within their territory or subject to their jurisdiction the rights provided for in the present Convention without distinction of any kind such as to sex, race, colour, language, religion or conviction, political or other opinion, national, ethnic or social origin, nationality, age, economic position, property, marital status, birth or other status.

PART III: HUMAN RIGHTS OF ALL MIGRANT WORKERS AND MEMBERS OF THEIR FAMILIES

Article 8

1. Migrant workers and members of their families shall be free to leave any State, including their State of origin. This right shall not be subject to any re-

strictions except those that are provided by law, are necessary to protect national security, public order (ordre public), public health or morals or the rights and freedoms of others and are consistent with the other rights recognized in the present part of the Convention.

2. Migrant workers and members of their families shall have the right at any time to enter and remain in their State of origin.

Article 9

The right to life of migrant workers and members of their families shall be protected by law.

Article 10

No migrant worker or member of his or her family shall be subjected to torture or to cruel, inhuman or degrading treatment or punishment.

Article 11

1. No migrant worker or member of his or her family shall be held in slavery or servitude.

2. No migrant worker or member of his or her family shall be required to perform forced or compulsory labour.

3. Paragraph 2 of the present article shall not be held to preclude, in States where imprisonment with hard labour may be imposed as a punishment for a crime, the performance of hard labour in pursuance of a sentence to such punishment by a competent court.

4. For the purpose of the present article the term "forced or compulsory labour" shall not include:

(a) Any work or service not referred to in paragraph 3 of the present article normally required of a person who is under detention in consequence of a lawful order of a court or of a person during conditional release from such detention;

(b) Any service exacted in cases of emergency or clamity threatening the life or well-being of the community;

(c) Any work or service that forms part of normal civil obligations so far as it is imposed also on citizens of the State concerned.

Article 12

1. Migrant workers and members of their families shall have the right to freedom of thought, conscience and religion. This right shall include freedom to

have or to adopt a religion or belief of their choice and freedom either individually or in community with others and in public or private to manifest their religion or belief in worship, observance, practice and teaching.

2. Migrant workers and members of their families shall not be subject to coercion that would impair their freedom to have or to adopt a religion or belief of their choice.

3. Freedom to manifest one's religion or belief may be subject only to such limitations as are prescribed by law and are necessary to protect public safety, order, health or morals or the fundamental rights and freedoms of others.

4. States Parties to the present Convention undertake to have respect for the liberty of parents, at least one of whom is a migrant worker, and, when applicable, legal guardians to ensure the religious and moral education of their children in conformity with their own convictions.

Article 13

1. Migrant workers and members of their families shall have the right to hold opinions without interference.

2. Migrant workers and members of their families shall have the right to freedom of expression; this right shall include freedom to seek, receive and impart information and ideas of all kinds, regardless of frontiers, either orally, in writing or in print, in the form of art or through any other media of their choice.

3. The exercise of the right provided for in paragraph 2 of the present article carries with it special duties and responsibilities. It may therefore be subject to certain restrictions, but these shall only be such as are provided by law and are necessary:

(a) For respect of the rights or reputation of others;

(b) For the protection of the national security of the States concerned or of public order (ordre public) or of public health or morals;

(c) For the purpose of preventing any propaganda for war;

(d) For the purpose of preventing any advocacy of national, racial or religious hatred that constitutes incitement to discrimination, hostility or violence.

Article 14

No migrant worker or member of his or her family shall be subjected to arbitrary or unlawful interference with his or her privacy, family, home, correspondence or other communications, or to unlawful attacks on his or her honour and reputation. Each migrant worker and member of his or her family shall have the right to the protection of the law against such interference or attacks.

Article 15

No migrant worker or member of his or her family shall be arbitrarily deprived of property, whether owned individually or in association with others. Where, under the legislation in force in the State of employment, the assets of a migrant worker or a member of his or her family are expropriated in whole or in part, the person concerned shall have the right to fair and adequate compensation.

Article 16

1. Migrant workers and members of their families shall have the right to liberty and security of person.

2. Migrant workers and members of their families shall be entitled to effective protection by the State against violence, physical injury, threats and intimidation, whether by public officials or by private individuals, groups or institutions.

3. Any verification by law enforcement officials of the identity of migrant workers or members of their families shall be carried out in accordance with procedure established by law.

4. Migrant workers and members of their families shall not be subjected individually or collectively to arbitrary arrest or detention; they shall not be deprived o their liberty except on such grounds and in accordance with such procedures as are established by law.

5. Migrant workers and members of their families who are arrested shall be informed at the time of arrest as far as possible in a language they understand of the reasons for their arrest and they shall be promptly informed in a language they understand of any charges against them.

6. Migrant workers and members of their families who are arrested or detained on a criminal charge shall be brought promptly before a judge or other officer authorized by law to exercise judicial power and shall be entitled to trial within a reasonable time or to release. It shall not be the general rule that while awaiting trial they shall be detained in custody, but release may be subject to guarantees to appear for trial, at any other stage of the judicial proceedings and, should the occasion arise, for the execution of the judgment.

7. When a migrant worker or a member of his or her family is arrested or committed to prison or custody pending trial or is detained in any other manner:

(a) The consular or diplomatic authorities of his or her State of origin or of a State representing the interests of that State shall, if he or she so requests, be informed without delay of his or her arrest or detention and of the reasons therefore;

(b) The person concerned shall have the right to communicate with the said authorities. Any communication by the person concerned to the said authorities shall be forwarded without delay, and he or she shall also have the right to receive communications sent by the said authorities without delay;

(c) The person concerned shall be informed without delay of this right and of rights deriving from relevant treaties, if any, applicable between the States concerned, to correspond and to meet with representatives of the said authorities and to make arrangements with them for his or her legal representation.

8. Migrant workers and members of their families who are deprived of their liberty by arrest or detention shall be entitled to take proceedings before a court, in order that that court may decide without delay on the lawfulness of their detention and order their release if the detention is not lawful. When they attend such proceedings, they shall have the assistance, if necessary without cost to them, of an interpreter, if they cannot understand or speak the language used.

9. Migrant workers and members of their families who have been victims of unlawful arrest or detention shall have an enforceable right to compensation.

Article 17

1. Migrant workers and members of their families who are deprived of their liberty shall be treated with humanity and with respect for the inherent dignity of the human person and for their cultural identity.

2. Accused migrant workers and members of their families shall, save in exceptional circumstances, be separated from convicted persons and shall be subject to separate treatment appropriate to their status as unconvicted persons. Accused juvenile persons shall be separated from adults and brought as speedily as possible for adjudication.

3. Any migrant worker or member of his or her family who is detained in a State of transit or in a State of employment for violation of provisions relating to migration shall be held, in so far as practicable, separately from convicted persons or persons detained pending trial.

4. During any period of imprisonment in pursuance of a sentence imposed by a court of law, the essential aim of the treatment of a migrant worker or a member of his or her family shall be his or her reformation and social reha-

bilitation. Juvenile offenders shall be separated from adults and be accorded treatment appropriate to their age and legal status.

5. During detention or imprisonment, migrant workers and members of their families shall enjoy the same rights as nationals to visits by members of their families.

6. Whenever a migrant worker is deprived of his or her liberty, the competent authorities of the State concerned shall pay attention to the problems that may be posed for members of his or her family, in particular for spouses and minor children.

7. Migrant workers and members of their families who are subjected to any form of detention or imprisonment in accordance with the law in force in the State of employment or in the State of transit shall enjoy the same rights as nationals of those States who are in the same situation.

8. If a migrant worker or a member of his or her family is detained for the purpose of verifying any infraction of provisions related to migration, he or she shall not bear any costs arising therefrom.

Article 18

1. Migrant workers and members of their families shall have the right to equality with nationals of the State concerned before the courts and tribunals. In the determination of any criminal charge against them or of their rights and obligations in a suit of law, they shall be entitled to a fair and public hearing by a competent, independent and impartial tribunal established by law.

2. Migrant workers and members of their families who are charged with a criminal offence shall have the right to be presumed innocent until proven guilty according to law.

3. In the determination of any criminal charge against them, migrant workers and members of their families shall be entitled to the following minimum guarantees:

(a) To be informed promptly and in detail in a language they understand of the nature and cause of the charge against them;

(b) To have adequate time and facilities for the preparation of their defence and to communicate with counsel of their own choosing;

(c) To be tried without undue delay;

(d) To be tried in their presence and to defend themselves in person or through legal assistance of their own choosing; to be informed, if they do not have legal assistance, of this right; and to have legal assistance assigned to them, in any case where the interests of justice so require and without payment by them in any such case if they do not have sufficient means to pay;

(e) To examine or have examined the witnesses against them and to obtain the attendance and examination of witnesses on their behalf under the same conditions as witnesses against them;

(f) To have the free assistance of an interpreter if they cannot understand or speak the language used in court;

(g) Not to be compelled to testify against themselves or to confess guilt.

4. In the case of juvenile persons, the procedure shall be such as will take account of their age and the desirability of promoting their rehabilitation.

5. Migrant workers and members of their families convicted of a crime shall have the right to their conviction and sentence being reviewed by a higher tribunal according to law.

6. When a migrant worker or a member of his or her family has, by a final decision, been convicted of a criminal offence and when subsequently his or her conviction has been reversed or he or she has been pardoned on the ground that a new or newly discovered fact shows conclusively that there has been a miscarriage of justice, the person who has suffered punishment as a result of such conviction shall be compensated according to law, unless it is proved that the non-disclosure of the unknown fact in time is wholly or partly attributable to that person.

7. No migrant worker or member of his or her family shall be liable to be tried or punished again for an offence for which he or she has already been finally convicted or acquitted in accordance with the law and penal procedure of the State concerned.

Article 19

1. No migrant worker or member of his or her family shall be held guilty of any criminal offence on account of any act or omission that did not constitute a criminal offence under national or international law at the time when the criminal offence was committed, nor shall a heavier penalty be imposed than the one that was applicable at the time when it was committed. If, subsequent to the commission of the offence, provision is made by law for the imposition of a lighter penalty, he or she shall benefit thereby.

2. Humanitarian considerations related to the status of a migrant worker, in particular with respect to his or her right of residence or work, should be taken

into account in imposing a sentence for a criminal offence committed by a migrant worker or a member of his or her family.

Article 20

1. No migrant worker or member of his or her family shall be imprisoned merely on the ground of failure to fulfill a contractual obligation.

2. No migrant worker or member of his or her family shall be deprived of his or her authorization of residence or work permit or expelled merely on the ground of failure to fulfill an obligation arising out of a work contract unless fulfillment of that obligation constitutes a condition for such authorization or permit.

Article 21

It shall be unlawful for anyone, other than a public official duly authorized by law, to confiscate, destroy or attempt to destroy identity documents, documents authorizing entry to or stay, residence or establishment in the national territory or work permits. No authorized confiscation of such documents shall take place without delivery of a detailed receipt. In no case shall it be permitted to destroy the passport or equivalent document of a migrant worker or a member of his or her family.

Article 22

1. Migrant workers and members of their families shall not be subject to measures of collective expulsion. Each case of expulsion shall be examined and decided individually.

2. Migrant workers and members of their families may be expelled from the territory of a State Party only in pursuance of a decision taken by the competent authority in accordance with law.

3. The decision shall be communicated to them in a language they understand. Upon their request where not otherwise mandatory, the decision shall be communicated to them in writing and, save in exceptional circumstances on account of national security, the reasons for the decision likewise stated. The persons concerned shall be informed of these rights before or at the latest at the time the decision is rendered.

4. Except where a final decision is pronounced by a judicial authority, the person concerned shall have the right to submit the reason he or she should not be expelled and to have his or her case reviewed by the competent authority, unless compelling reasons of national security require otherwise. Pending such review, the person concerned shall have the right to seek a stay of the decision of expulsion.

5. If a decision of expulsion that has already been executed is subsequently annulled, the person concerned shall have the right to seek compensation according to law and the earlier decision shall not be used to prevent him or her from re-entering the State concerned.

6. In case of expulsion, the person concerned shall have a reasonable opportunity before or after departure to settle any claims for wages and other entitlements due to him or her and any pending liabilities.

7. Without prejudice to the execution of a decision of expulsion, a migrant worker or a member of his or her family who is subject to such a decision may seek entry into a State other than his or her State of origin.

8. In case of expulsion of a migrant worker or a member of his or her family the costs of expulsion shall not be borne by him or her. The person concerned may be required to pay his or her own travel costs.

9. Expulsion from the State of employment shall not in itself prejudice any rights of a migrant worker or a member of his or her family acquired in accordance with the law of that State, including the right to receive wages and other entitlements due to him or her.

Article 23

Migrant workers and members of their families shall have the right to have recourse to the protection and assistance of the consular or diplomatic authorities of their State of origin or of a State representing the interests of that State whenever the rights recognized in the present Convention are impaired. In particular, in case of expulsion, the person concerned shall be informed of this right without delay and the authorities of the expelling State shall facilitate the exercise of such right.

Article 24

Every migrant worker and every member of his or her family shall have the right to recognition everywhere as a person before the law.

Article 25

1. Migrant workers shall enjoy treatment not less favourable than that which applies to nationals of the State of employment in respect of remuneration and:

(a) Other conditions of work, that is to say, overtime, hours of work, weekly rest, holidays with pay, safety, health, termination of the employment relationship and any other conditions of work which, according to national law and practice, are covered by these terms;

(b) Other terms of employment, that is to say, minimum age of employment, restriction on home work and any other matters which, according to national law and practice, are considered a term of employment.

2. It shall not be lawful to derogate in private contracts of employment from the principle of equality of treatment referred to in paragraph 1 of the present article.

3. States Parties shall take all appropriate measures to ensure that migrant workers are not deprived of any rights derived from this principle by reason of any irregularity in their stay or employment. In particular, employers shall not be relieved of any legal or contractual obligations, nor shall their obligations be limited in any manner by reason of such irregularity.

Article 26

1. States Parties recognize the right of migrant workers and members of their families:

(a) To take part in meetings and activities of trade unions and of any other associations established in accordance with law, with a view to protecting their economic, social, cultural and other interests, subject only to the rules of the organization concerned;

(b) To join freely any trade union and any such association as aforesaid, subject only to the rules of the organization concerned;

(c) To seek the aid and assistance of any trade union and of any such association as aforesaid.

2. No restrictions may be placed on the exercise of these rights other than those that are prescribed by law and which are necessary in a democratic society in the interests of national security, public order (ordre public) or the protection of the rights and freedoms of others.

Article 27

1. With respect to social security, migrant workers and members of their families shall enjoy in the State of employment the same treatment granted to nationals in so far as they fulfill the requirements provided for by the applicable legislation of that State and the applicable bilateral and multilateral treaties. The competent authorities of the State of origin and the State of employment can at any time establish the necessary arrangements to determine the modalities of application of this norm.

2. Where the applicable legislation does not allow migrant workers and members of their families a benefit, the States concerned shall examine the possi-

bility of reimbursing interested persons the amount of contributions made by them with respect to that benefit on the basis of the treatment granted to nationals who are in similar circumstances.

Article 28

Migrant workers and members of their families shall have the right to receive any medical care that is urgently required for the preservation of their life or the avoidance of irreparable harm to their health on the basis of equality of treatment with nationals of the State concerned. Such emergency medical care shall not be refused them by reason of any irregularity with regard to stay or employment.

Article 29

Each child of a migrant worker shall have the right to a name, to registration of birth and to a nationality.

Article 30

Each child of a migrant worker shall have the basic right of access to education on the basis of equality of treatment with nationals of the State concerned. Access to public pre-school educational institutions or schools shall not be refused or limited by reason of the irregular situation with respect to stay or employment of either parent or by reason of the irregularity of the child's stay in the State of employment.

Article 31

1. States Parties shall ensure respect for the cultural identity of migrant workers and members of their families and shall not prevent them from maintaining their cultural links with their State of origin.

2. States Parties may take appropriate measures to assist and encourage efforts in this respect.

Article 32

Upon the termination of their stay in the State of employment, migrant workers and members of their families shall have the right to transfer their earnings and savings and, in accordance with the applicable legislation of the States concerned, their personal effects and belongings.

Article 33

1. Migrant workers and members of their families shall have the right to be informed by the State of origin, the State of employment or the State of transit as the case may be concerning:

(a) Their rights arising out of the present Convention;

(b) The conditions of their admission, their rights and obligations under the law and practice of the State concerned and such other matters as will enable them to comply with administrative or other formalities in that State.

2. States Parties shall take all measures they deem appropriate to disseminate the said information or to ensure that it is provided by employers, trade unions or other appropriate bodies or institutions. As appropriate, they shall co-operate with other States concerned.

3. Such adequate information shall be provided upon request to migrant workers and members of their families, free of charge, and, as far as possible, in a language they are able to understand.

Article 34

Nothing in the present part of the Convention shall have the effect of relieving migrant workers and the members of their families from either the obligation to comply with the laws and regulations of any State of transit and the State of employment or the obligation to respect the cultural identity of the inhabitants of such States.

Article 35

Nothing in the present part of the Convention shall be interpreted as implying the regularization of the situation of migrant workers or members of their families who are non-documented or in an irregular situation or any right to such regularization of their situation, nor shall it prejudice the measures intended to ensure sound and equitable-conditions for international migration as provided in part VI of the present Convention.

PART IV: OTHER RIGHTS OF MIGRANT WORKERS AND MEMBERS OF THEIR FAMILIES WHO ARE DOCUMENTED OR IN A REGULAR SITUATION

Article 36

Migrant workers and members of their families who are documented or in a regular situation in the State of employment shall enjoy the rights set forth in the present part of the Convention in addition to those set forth in part III.

Article 37

Before their departure, or at the latest at the time of their admission to the State of employment, migrant workers and members of their families shall have the right to be fully informed by the State of origin or the State of employment, as appropriate, of all conditions applicable to their admission and particularly those concerning their stay and the remunerated activities in which they may engage as well as of the requirements they must satisfy in the State of employment and the authority to which they must address themselves for any modification of those conditions.

Article 38

1. States of employment shall make every effort to authorize migrant workers and members of the families to be temporarily absent without effect upon their authorization to stay or to work, as the case may be. In doing so, States of employment shall take into account the special needs and obligations of migrant workers and members of their families, in particular in their States of origin.

2. Migrant workers and members of their families shall have the right to be fully informed of the terms on which such temporary absences are authorized.

Article 39

1. Migrant workers and members of their families shall have the right to liberty of movement in the territory of the State of employment and freedom to choose their residence there.

2. The rights mentioned in paragraph 1 of the present article shall not be subject to any restrictions except those that are provided by law, are necessary to protect national security, public order (ordre public), public health or morals, or the rights and freedoms of others and are consistent with the other rights recognized in the present Convention.

Article 40

1. Migrant workers and members of their families shall have the right to form associations and trade unions in the State of employment for the promotion and protection of their economic, social, cultural and other interests.

2. No restrictions may be placed on the exercise of this right other than those that are prescribed by law and are necessary in a democratic society in the in-

terests of national security, public order (ordre public) or the protection of the rights and freedoms of others.

Article 41

1. Migrant workers and members of their families shall have the right to participate in public affairs of their State of origin and to vote and to be elected at elections of that State, in accordance with its legislation.

2. The States concerned shall, as appropriate and in accordance with their legislation, facilitate the exercise of these rights.

Article 42

1. States Parties shall consider the establishment of procedures or institutions through which account may be taken, both in States of origin and in States of employment, of special needs, aspirations and obligations of migrant workers and members of their families and shall envisage, as appropriate, the possibility for migrant workers and members of their families to have their freely chosen representatives in those institutions.

2. States of employment shall facilitate, in accordance with their national legislation, the consultation or participation of migrant workers and members of their families in decisions concerning the life and administration of local communities.

3. Migrant workers may enjoy political rights in the State of employment if that State, in the exercise of its sovereignty, grants them such rights.

Article 43

1. Migrant workers shall enjoy equality of treatment with nationals of the State of employment in relation to:

(a) Access to educational institutions and services subject to the admission requirements and other regulations of the institutions and services concerned;

(b) Access to vocational guidance and placement services;

(c) Access to vocational training and retraining facilities and institutions;

(d) Access to housing, including social housing schemes, and protection against exploitation in respect of rents;

(e) Access to social and health services, provided that the requirements for participation in the respective schemes are met;

(f) Access to co-operatives and self-managed enterprises, which shall not imply a change of their migration status and shall be subject to the rules and regulations of the bodies concerned;

(g) Access to and participation in cultural life.

2. States Parties shall promote conditions to ensure effective equality of treatment to enable migrant workers to enjoy the rights mentioned in paragraph 1 of the present article whenever the terms of their stay, as authorized by the State of employment, meet the appropriate requirements.

3. States of employment shall not prevent an employer of migrant workers from establishing housing or social or cultural facilities for them. Subject to article 70 of the present Convention, a State of employment may make the establishment of such facilities subject to the requirements generally applied in that State concerning their installation.

Article 44

1. States Parties, recognizing that the family is the natural and fundamental group unit of society and is entitled to protection by society and the State, shall take appropriate measures to ensure the protection of the unity of the families of migrant workers.

2. States Parties shall take measures that they deem appropriate and that fall within their competence to facilitate the reunification of migrant workers with their spouses or persons who have with the migrant worker a relationship that, according to applicable law, produces effects equivalent to marriage, as well as with their minor dependent unmarried children.

3. States of employment, on humanitarian grounds, shall favourably consider granting equal treatment, as set forth in paragraph 2 of the present article, to other family members of migrant workers.

Article 45

1. Members of the families of migrant workers shall, in the State of employment, enjoy equality of treatment with nationals of that State in relation to:

(a) Access to educational institutions and services, subject to the admission requirements and other regulations of the institutions and services concerned;

(b) Access to vocational guidance and training institutions and services, provided that requirements for participation are met;

(c) Access to social and health services, provided that requirements for participation in the respective schemes are met;

(d) Access to and participation in cultural life.

2. States of employment shall pursue a policy, where appropriate in collaboration with the States of origin, aimed at facilitating the integration of children of migrant workers in the local school system, particularly in respect of teaching them the local language.

3. States of employment shall endeavour to facilitate for the children of migrant workers the teaching of their mother tongue and culture and, in this regard, States of origin shall collaborate whenever appropriate.

4. States of employment may provide special schemes of education in the mother tongue of children of migrant workers, if necessary in collaboration with the States of origin.

Article 46

Migrant workers and members of their families shall, subject to the applicable legislation of the States concerned, as well as relevant international agreements and the obligations of the States concerned arising out of their participation in customs unions, enjoy exemption from import and export duties and taxes in respect of their personal and household effects as well as the equipment necessary to engage in the remunerated activity for which they were admitted to the State of employment:

(a) Upon departure from the State of origin or State of habitual residence;

(b) Upon initial admission to the State of employment;

(c) Upon final departure from the State of employment;

(d) Upon final return to the State of origin or State of habitual residence.

Article 47

1. Migrant workers shall have the right to transfer their earnings and savings, in particular those funds necessary for the support of their families, from the State of employment to their State of origin or any other State. Such transfers shall be made in conformity with procedures established by applicable legislation of the State concerned and in conformity with applicable international agreements.

2. States concerned shall take appropriate measures to facilitate such transfers.

Article 48

1. Without prejudice to applicable double taxation agreements, migrant workers and members of their families shall, in the matter of earnings in the State of employment:

(a) Not be liable to taxes, duties or charges of any description higher or more onerous than those imposed on nationals in similar circumstances;

(b) Be entitled to deductions or exemptions from taxes of any description and to any tax allowances applicable to nationals in similar circumstances, including tax allowances for dependent members of their families.

2. States Parties shall endeavour to adopt appropriate measures to avoid double taxation of the earnings and savings of migrant workers and members of their families.

Article 49

1. Where separate authorizations to reside and to engage in employment are required by national legislation, the States of employment shall issue to migrant workers authorization of residence for at least the same period of time as their authorization to engage in remunerated activity.

2. Migrant workers who in the State of employment are allowed freely to choose their remunerated activity shall neither be regarded as in an irregular situation nor shall they lose their authorization of residence by the mere fact of the termination of their remunerated activity prior to the expiration of their work permits or similar authorizations.

3. In order to allow migrant workers referred to in paragraph 2 of the present article sufficient time to find alternative remunerated activities, the authorization of residence shall not be withdrawn at least for a period corresponding to that during which they may be entitled to unemployment benefits.

Article 50

1. In the case of death of a migrant worker or dissolution of marriage, the State of employment shall favourably consider granting family members of that migrant worker residing in that State on the basis of family reunion an authorization to stay; the State of employment shall take into account the length of time they have already resided in that State.

2. Members of the family to whom such authorization is not granted shall be allowed before departure a reasonable period of time in order to enable them to settle their affairs in the State of employment.

3. The provisions of paragraphs 1 and 2 of the present article may not be interpreted as adversely affecting any right to stay and work otherwise granted to such family members by the legislation of the State of employment or by bilateral and multilateral treaties applicable to that State.

Article 51

Migrant workers who in the State of employment are not permitted freely to choose their remunerated activity shall neither be regarded as in an irregular situation nor shall they lose their authorization of residence by the mere fact of the termination of their remunerated activity prior to the expiration of their work permit, except where the authorization of residence is expressly dependent upon the specific remunerated activity for which they were admitted. Such migrant workers shall have the right to seek alternative employment, participation in public work schemes and retraining during the remaining period of their authorization to work, subject to such conditions and limitations as are specified in the authorization to work.

Article 52

1. Migrant workers in the State of employment shall have the right freely to choose their remunerated activity, subject to the following restrictions or conditions.

2. For any migrant worker a State of employment may:

(a) Restrict access to limited categories of employment, functions, services or activities where this is necessary in the interests of this State and provided for by national legislation;

(b) Restrict free choice of remunerated activity in accordance with its legislation concerning recognition of occupational qualifications acquired outside its territory. However, States Parties concerned shall endeavour to provide for recognition of such qualifications.

3. For migrant workers whose permission to work is limited in time, a State of employment may also:

(a) Make the right freely to choose their remunerated activities subject to the condition that the migrant worker has resided lawfully in its territory for the purpose of remunerated activity for a period of time prescribed in its national legislation that should not exceed two years;

(b) Limit access by a migrant worker to remunerated activities in pursuance of a policy of granting priority to its nationals or to persons who are assimilated to them for these purposes by virtue of legislation or bilateral or multilateral agreements. Any such limitation shall cease to apply to a migrant worker who has resided lawfully in its territory for the purpose of remunerated activity for a period of time prescribed in its national legislation that should not exceed five years.

4. States of employment shall prescribe the conditions under which a migrant worker who has been admitted to take up employment may be au-

thorized to engage in work on his or her own account. Account shall be taken of the period during which the worker has already been lawfully in the State of employment.

Article 53

1. Members of a migrant worker's family who have themselves an authorization of residence or admission that is without limit of time or is automatically renewable shall be permitted freely to choose their remunerated activity under the same conditions as are applicable to the said migrant worker in accordance with article 52 of the present Convention.

2. With respect to members of a migrant worker's family who are not permitted freely to choose their remunerated activity, States Parties shall consider favourably granting them priority in obtaining permission to engage in a remunerated activity over other workers who seek admission to the State of employment, subject to applicable bilateral and multilateral agreements.

Article 54

1. Without prejudice to the terms of their authorization of residence or their permission to work and the rights provided for in articles 25 and 27 of the present Convention, migrant workers shall enjoy equality of treatment with nationals of the State of employment in respect of:

(a) Protection against dismissal;

(b) Unemployment benefits;

(c) Access to public work schemes intended to combat unemployment;

(d) Access to alternative employment in the event of loss of work or termination of other remunerated activity, subject to article 52 of the present Convention.

2. If a migrant worker claims that the terms of his or her work contract have been violated by his or her employer, he or she shall have the right to address his or her case to the competent authorities of the State of employment, on terms provided for in article 18, paragraph 1, of the present Convention.

Article 55

Migrant workers who have been granted permission to engage in a remunerated activity, subject to the conditions attached to such permission, shall be entitled to equality of treatment with nationals of the State of employment in the exercise of that remunerated activity.

Article 56

1. Migrant workers and members of their families referred to in the present part of the Convention may not be expelled from a State of employment, except for reasons defined in the national legislation of that State, and subject to the safeguards established in part III.

2. Expulsion shall not be resorted to for the purpose of depriving a migrant worker or a member of his or her family of the rights arising out of the authorization of residence and the work permit.

3. In considering whether to expel a migrant worker or a member of his or her family, account should be taken of humanitarian considerations and of the length of time that the person concerned has already resided in the State of employment.

PART V: PROVISIONS APPLICABLE TO PARTICULAR CATEGORIES OF MIGRANT WORKERS AND OF THEIR FAMILIES

Article 57

The particular categories of migrant workers and members of their families specified in the present part of the Convention who are documented or in a regular situation shall enjoy the rights set forth in part m and, except as modified below, the rights set forth in part IV.

Article 58

1. Frontier workers, as defined in article 2, paragraph 2 (a), of the present Convention, shall be entitled to the rights provided for in part IV that can be applied to them by reason of their presence and work in the territory of the State of employment, taking into account that they do not have their habitual residence in that State.

2. States of employment shall consider favourably granting frontier workers the right freely to choose their remunerated activity after a specified period of time. The granting of that right shall not affect their status as frontier workers.

Article 59

1. Seasonal workers, as defined in article 2, paragraph 2 (b), of the present Convention, shall be entitled to the rights provided for in part IV that can be applied to them by reason of their presence and work in the territory of the State of employment and that are compatible with their status in that State as seasonal workers, taking into account the fact that they are present in that State for only part of the year.

2. The State of employment shall, subject to paragraph 1 of the present article, consider granting seasonal workers who have been employed in its territory for a significant period of time the possibility of taking up other remunerated activities and giving them priority over other workers who seek admission to that State, subject to applicable bilateral and multilateral agreements.

Article 60

Itinerant workers, as defined in article 2, paragraph 2 (e), of the present Convention, shall be entitled to the rights provided for in part IV that can be granted to them by reason of their presence and work in the territory of the State of employment and that are compatible with their status as itinerant workers in that State.

Article 61

1. Project-tied workers, as defined in article 2, paragraph 2 (f), of the present Convention, and members of their families shall be entitled to the rights provided for in part IV except the provisions of article 43, paragraphs 1 (b) and (c), article 43, paragraph 1 (d), as it pertains to social housing schemes, article 45, paragraph 1 (b), and articles 52 to 55.

2. If a project-tied worker claims that the terms of his or her work contract have been violated by his or her employer, he or she shall have the right to address his or her case to the competent authorities of the State which has jurisdiction over that employer, on terms provided for in article 18, paragraph 1, of the present Convention.

3. Subject to bilateral or multilateral agreements in force for them, the States Parties concerned shall endeavour to enable project-tied workers to remain adequately protected by the social security systems of their States of origin or habitual residence during their engagement in the project. States Parties concerned shall take appropriate measures with the aim of avoiding any denial of rights or duplication of payments in this respect.

4. Without prejudice to the provisions of article 47 of the present Convention and to relevant bilateral or multilateral agreements, States Parties concerned shall permit payment of the earnings of project-tied workers in their State of origin or habitual residence.

Article 62

1. Specified-employment workers as defined in article 2, paragraph 2 (g), of the present Convention, shall be entitled to the rights provided for in part IV, except the provisions of article 43, paragraphs 1 (b) and (c), article 43, para-

graph 1 (d), as it pertains to social housing schemes, article 52, and article 54, paragraph 1 (d).

2. Members of the families of specified-employment workers shall be entitled to the rights relating to family members of migrant workers provided for in part IV of the present Convention, except the provisions of article 53.

Article 63

1. Self-employed workers, as defined in article 2, paragraph 2 (h), of the pre sent Convention, shall be entitled to the rights provided for in part IV with the exception of those rights which are exclusively applicable to workers having a contract of employment.

2. Without prejudice to articles 52 and 79 of the present Convention, the termination of the economic activity of the self-employed workers shall not in itself imply the withdrawal of the authorization for them or for the members of their families to stay or to engage in a remunerated activity in the State of employment except where the authorization of residence is expressly dependent upon the specific remunerated activity for which they were admitted.

PART VI: PROMOTION OF SOUND, EQUITABLE, HUMANE AND LAWFUL CONDITIONS CONNECTION WITH INTERNATIONAL MIGRATION OF WORKERS AND MEMBERS OF THEIR FAMILIES

Article 64

1. Without prejudice to article 79 of the present Convention, the States Parties concerned shall as appropriate consult and co-operate with a view to promoting sound, equitable and humane conditions in connection with international migration of workers and members of their families.

2. In this respect, due regard shall be paid not only to labour needs and resources, but also to the social, economic, cultural and other needs of migrant workers and members of their families involved, as well as to the consequences of such migration for the communities concerned.

Article 65

1. States Parties shall maintain appropriate services to deal with questions concerning international migration of workers and members of their families. Their functions shall include, *inter alia*:

(a) The formulation and implementation of policies regarding such migration;

(b) An exchange of information. consultation and co-operation with the competent authorities of other States Parties involved in such migration;

(c) The provision of appropriate information, particularly to employers, workers and their organizations on policies, laws and regulations relating to migration and employment, on agreements concluded with other States concerning migration and on other relevant matters;

(d) The provision of information and appropriate assistance to migrant workers and members of their families regarding requisite authorizations and formalities and arrangements for departure, travel, arrival, stay, remunerated activities, exit and return, as well as on conditions of work and life in the State of employment and on customs, currency, tax and other relevant laws and regulations.

2. States Parties shall facilitate as appropriate the provision of adequate consular and other services that are necessary to meet the social, cultural and other needs of migrant workers and members of their families.

Article 66

1. Subject to paragraph 2 of the present article, the right to undertake operations with a view to the recruitment of workers for employment in another State shall be restricted to:

(a) Public services or bodies of the State in which such operations take place;

(b) Public services or bodies of the State of employment on the basis of agreement between the States concerned;

(c) A body established by virtue of a bilateral or multilateral agreement.

2. Subject to any authorization, approval and supervision by the public authorities of the States Parties concerned as may be established pursuant to the legislation and practice of those States, agencies, prospective employers or persons acting on their behalf may also be permitted to undertake the said operations.

Article 67

1. States Parties concerned shall co-operate as appropriate in the adoption of measures regarding the orderly return of migrant workers and members of their families to the State of origin when they decide to return or their authorization of residence or employment expires or when they are in the State of employment in an irregular situation.

2. Concerning migrant workers and members of their families in a regular situation, States Parties concerned shall co-operate as appropriate, on terms agreed upon by those States, with a view to promoting adequate economic

conditions for their resettlement and to facilitating their durable social and cultural reintegration in the State of origin.

Article 68

1. States Parties, including States of transit, shall collaborate with a view to preventing and eliminating illegal or clandestine movements and employment of migrant workers in an irregular situation. The measures to be taken to this end within the jurisdiction of each State concerned shall include:

(a) Appropriate measures against the dissemination of misleading information relating to emigration and immigration;

(b) Measures to detect and eradicate illegal or clandestine movements of migrant workers and members of their families and to impose effective sanctions on persons, groups or entities which organize, operate or assist in organizing or operating such movements;

(c) Measures to impose effective sanctions on persons, groups or entities which use violence, threats or intimidation against migrant workers or members of their families in an irregular situation.

2. States of employment shall take all adequate and effective measures to eliminate employment in their territory of migrant workers in an irregular situation, including, whenever appropriate, sanctions on employers of such workers. The rights of migrant workers vis-à-vis their employer arising from employment shall not be impaired by these measures.

Article 69

1. States Parties shall, when there are migrant workers and members of their families within their territory in an irregular situation, take appropriate measures to ensure that such a situation does not persist.

2. Whenever States Parties concerned consider the possibility of regularizing the situation of such persons in accordance with applicable national legislation and bilateral or multilateral agreements, appropriate account shall be taken of the circumstances of their entry, the duration of their stay in the States of employment and other relevant considerations, in particular those relating to their family situation.

Article 70

States Parties shall take measures not less favourable than those applied to nationals to ensure that working and living conditions of migrant workers and members of their families in a regular situation are in keeping with the standards of fitness, safety, health and principles of human dignity.

Article 71

1. States Parties shall facilitate, whenever necessary, the repatriation to the State of origin of the bodies of deceased migrant workers or members of their families.

2. As regards compensation matters relating to the death of a migrant worker or a member of his or her family, States Parties shall, as appropriate, provide assistance to the persons concerned with a view to the prompt settlement of such matters. Settlement of these matters shall be carried out on the basis of applicable national law in accordance with the provisions of the present Convention and any relevant bilateral or multilateral agreements.

PART VII: APPLICATION OF THE CONVENTION

Article 72

1. (a) For the purpose of reviewing the application of the present Convention, there shall be established a Committee on the Protection of the Rights of All Migrant Workers and Members of Their Families (hereinafter referred to as "the Committee");

(b) The Committee shall consist, at the time of entry into force of the present Convention, of ten and, after the entry into force of the Convention for the forty-first State Party, of fourteen experts of high moral standing, impartiality and recognized competence in the field covered by the Convention.

2. (a) Members of the Committee shall be elected by secret ballot by the States Parties from a list of persons nominated by the States Parties, due consideration being given to equitable geographical distribution, including both States of origin and States of employment, and to the representation of the principal legal system. Each State Party may nominate one person from among its own nationals;

(b) Members shall be elected and shall serve in their personal capacity.

3. The initial election shall be held no later than six months after the date of the entry into force of the present Convention and subsequent elections every second year. At least four months before the date of each election, the Secretary-General of the United Nations shall address a letter to all States Parties inviting them to submit their nominations within two months. The Secretary-General shall prepare a list in alphabetical order of all persons thus nominated, indicating the States Parties that have nominated them, and shall

submit it to the States Parties not later than one month before the date of the corresponding election, together with the curricula vitae of the persons thus nominated.

4. Elections of members of the Committee shall be held at a meeting of States Parties convened by the Secretary-General at United Nations Headquarters. At that meeting, for which two thirds of the States Parties shall constitute a quorum, the persons elected to the Committee shall be those nominees who obtain the largest number of votes and an absolute majority of the votes of the States Parties present and voting.

5. (a) The members of the Committee shall serve for a term of four years. However, the terms of five of the members elected in the first election shall expire at the end of two years; immediately after the first election, the names of these five members shall be chosen by lot by the Chairman of the meeting of States Parties;

(b) The election of the four additional members of the Committee shall be held in accordance with the provisions of paragraphs 2, 3 and 4 of the present article, following the entry into force of the Convention for the forty-first State Party. The term of two of the additional members elected on this occasion shall expire at the end of two years; the names of these members shall be chosen by lot by the Chairman of the meeting of States Parties;

(c) The members of the Committee shall be eligible for re-election if renominated.

6. If a member of the Committee dies or resigns or declares that for any other cause he or she can no longer perform the duties of the Committee, the State Party that nominated the expert shall appoint another expert from among its own nationals for the remaining part of the term. The new appointment is subject to the approval of the Committee.

7. The Secretary-General of the United Nations shall provide the necessary staff and facilities for the effective performance of the functions of the Committee.

8. The members of the Committee shall receive emoluments from United Nations resources on such terms and conditions as the General Assembly may decide.

9. The members of the Committee shall be entitled to the facilities, privileges and immunities of experts on mission for the United Nations as laid down in the relevant sections of the Convention on the Privileges and Immunities of the United Nations.

Article 73

1. States Parties undertake to submit to the Secretary-General of the United Nations for consideration by the Committee a report on the legislative, judicial, administrative and other measures they have taken to give effect to the provisions of the present Convention:

(a) Within one year after the entry into force of the Convention for the State Party concerned;

(b) Thereafter every five years and whenever the Committee so requests.

2. Reports prepared under the present article shall also indicate factors and difficulties, if any, affecting the implementation of the Convention and shall include information on the characteristics of migration flows in which the State Party concerned is involved.

3. The Committee shall decide any further guidelines applicable to the content of the reports.

4. States Parties shall make their reports widely available to the public in their own countries.

Article 74

1. The Committee shall examine the reports submitted by each State Party and shall transmit such comments as it may consider appropriate to the State Party concerned. This State Party may submit to the Committee observations on any comment made by the Committee in accordance with the present article. The Committee may request supplementary information from States Parties when considering these reports.

2. The Secretary-General of the United Nations shall, in due time before the opening of each regular session of the Committee, transmit to the Director-General of the International Labour Office copies of the reports submitted by States Parties concerned and information relevant to the consideration of these reports, in order to enable the Office to assist the Committee with the expertise the Office may provide regarding those matters dealt with by the present Convention that fall within the sphere of competence of the International Labour Organisation. The Committee shall consider in its deliberations such comments and materials as the Office may provide.

3. The Secretary-General of the United Nations may also, after consultation with the Committee, transmit to other specialized agencies as well as to intergovernmental organizations, copies of such parts of these reports as may fall within their competence.

4. The Committee may invite the specialized agencies and organs of the United Nations, as well as intergovernmental organizations and other concerned bodies to submit, for consideration by the Committee, written information on such matters dealt with in the present Convention as fall within the scope of their activities.

5. The International Labour Office shall be invited by the Committee to appoint representatives to participate, in a consultative capacity, in the meetings of the Committee.

6. The Committee may invite representatives of other specialized agencies and organs of the United Nations, as well as of intergovernmental organizations, to be present and to be heard in its meetings whenever matters falling within their field of competence are considered.

7. The Committee shall present an annual report to the General Assembly of the United Nations on the implementation of the present Convention, containing its own considerations and recommendations, based, in particular, on the examination of the reports and any observations presented by States Parties.

8. The Secretary-General of the United Nations shall transmit the annual reports of the Committee to the States Parties to the present Convention, the Economic and Social Council, the Commission on Human Rights of the United Nations, the Director-General of the International Labour Office and other relevant organizations.

Article 75

1. The Committee shall adopt its own rules of procedure.

2. The Committee shall elect its officers for a term of two years.

3. The Committee shall normally meet annually.

4. The meetings of the Committee shall normally be held at United Nations Headquarters.

Article 76

1. A State Party to the present Convention may at any time declare under this article that it recognizes the competence of the Committee to receive and consider communications to the effect that a State Party claims that another State Party is not fulfilling its obligations under the present Convention. Communications under this article may be received and considered only if submitted by a State Party that has made a declaration recognizing in regard to itself the competence of the Committee. No communication shall be received by the

Committee if it concerns a State Party which has not made such a declaration. Communications received under this article shall be dealt with in accordance with the following procedure:

(a) If a State Party to the present Convention considers that another State Party is not fulfilling its obligations under the present Convention, it may, by written communication, bring the matter to the attention of that State Party. The State Party may also inform the Committee of the matter. Within three months after the receipt of the communication the receiving State shall afford the State that sent the communication an explanation, or any other statement in writing clarifying the matter which should include, to the extent possible and pertinent, reference to domestic procedures and remedies taken, pending or available in the matter;

(b) If the matter is not adjusted to the satisfaction of both States Parties concerned within six months after the receipt by the receiving State of the initial communication, either State shall have the right to refer the matter to the Committee, by notice given to the Committee and to the other State;

(c) The Committee shall deal with a matter referred to it only after it has ascertained that all available domestic remedies have been invoked and exhausted in the matter, in conformity with the generally recognized principles of international law. This shall not be the rule where, in the view of the Committee, the application of the remedies is unreasonably prolonged;

(d) Subject to the provisions of subparagraph (c) of the present paragraph, the Committee shall make available its good offices to the States Parties concerned with a view to a friendly solution of the matter on the basis of the respect for the obligations set forth in the present Convention;

(e) The Committee shall hold closed meetings when examining communications under the present article;

(f) In any matter referred to it in accordance with subparagraph (b) of the present paragraph, the Committee may call upon the States Parties concerned, referred to in subparagraph (b), to supply any relevant information;

(g) The States Parties concerned, referred to in subparagraph (b) of the present paragraph, shall have the right to be represented when the matter is being considered by the Committee and to make submissions orally and/or in writing;

(h) The Committee shall, within twelve months after the date of receipt of notice under subparagraph (b) of the present paragraph, submit a report, as follows:

(i) If a solution within the terms of subparagraph (d) of the present paragraph is reached, the Committee shall confine its report to a brief statement of the facts and of the solution reached;

(ii) If a solution within the terms of subparagraph (d) is not reached, the Committee shall, in its report, set forth the relevant facts concerning the issue between the States Parties concerned. The written submissions and record of the oral submissions made by the States Parties concerned shall be attached to the report. The Committee may also communicate only to the States Parties concerned any views that it may consider relevant to the issue between them.

In every matter, the report shall be communicated to the States Parties concerned.

2. The provisions of the present article shall come into force when ten States Parties to the present Convention have made a declaration under paragraph 1 of the present article. Such declarations shall be deposited by the States Parties with the Secretary-General of the United Nations, who shall transmit copies thereof to the other States Parties. A declaration may be withdrawn at any time by notification to the Secretary-General. Such a withdrawal shall not prejudice the consideration of any matter that is the subject of a communication already transmitted under the present article; no further communication by any State Party shall be received under the present article after the notification of withdrawal of the declaration has been received by the Secretary-General, unless the State Party concerned has made a new declaration.

Article 77

1. A State Party to the present Convention may at any time declare under the present article that it recognizes the competence of the Committee to receive and consider communications from or on behalf of individuals subject to its jurisdiction who claim that their individual rights as established by the present Convention have been violated by that State Party. No communication shall be received by the Committee if it concerns a State Party that has not made such a declaration.

2. The Committee shall consider inadmissible any communication under the present article which is anonymous or which it considers to be an abuse of the right of submission of such communications or to be incompatible with the provisions of the present Convention.

3. The Committee shall not consider any communication from an individual under the present article unless it has ascertained that:

(a) The same matter has not been, and is not being, examined under another procedure of international investigation or settlement;

(b) The individual has exhausted all available domestic remedies; this shall not be the rule where, in the view of the Committee, the application of the remedies is unreasonably prolonged or is unlikely to bring effective relief to that individual.

4. Subject to the provisions of paragraph 2 of the present article, the Committee shall bring any communications submitted to it under this article to the attention of the State Party to the present Convention that has made a declaration under paragraph 1 and is alleged to be violating any provisions of the Convention. Within six months, the receiving State shall submit to the Committee written explanations or statements clarifying the matter and the remedy, if any, that may have been taken by that State.

5. The Committee shall consider communications received under the present article in the light of all information made available to it by or on behalf of the individual and by the State Party concerned.

6. The Committee shall hold closed meetings when examining communications under the present article.

7. The Committee shall forward its views to the State Party concerned and to the individual.

8. The provisions of the present article shall come into force when ten States Parties to the present Convention have made declarations under paragraph 1 of the present article. Such declarations shall be deposited by the States Parties with the Secretary-General of the United Nations, who shall transmit copies thereof to the other States Parties. A declaration may be withdrawn at any time by notification to the Secretary-General. Such a withdrawal shall not prejudice the consideration of any matter that is the subject of a communication already transmitted under the present article; no further communication by or on behalf of an individual shall be received under the present article after the notification of withdrawal of the declaration has been received by the Secretary-General, unless the State Party has made a new declaration.

Article 78

The provisions of article 76 of the present Convention shall be applied without prejudice to any procedures for settling disputes or complaints in the field covered by the present Convention laid down in the constituent instruments of, or in conventions adopted by, the United Nations and the specialized agencies and shall not prevent the States Parties from having recourse to any procedures for settling a dispute in accordance with international agreements in force between them.

PART VIII: GENERAL PROVISIONS

Article 79

Nothing in the present Convention shall affect the right of each State Party to establish the criteria governing admission of migrant workers and members of their families. Concerning other matters related to their legal situation and treatment as migrant workers and members of their families, States Parties shall be subject to the limitations set forth in the present Convention.

Article 80

Nothing in the present Convention shall be interpreted as impairing the provisions of the Charter of the United Nations and of the constitutions of the specialized agencies which define the respective responsibilities of the various organs of the United Nations and of the specialized agencies in regard to the matters dealt with in the present Convention.

Article 81

1. Nothing in the present Convention shall affect more favourable rights or freedoms granted to migrant workers and members of their families by virtue of:

(a) The law or practice of a State Party; or

(b) Any bilateral or multilateral treaty in force for the State Party concerned.

2. Nothing in the present Convention may be interpreted as implying for any State, group or person any right to engage in any activity or perform any act that would impair any of the rights and freedoms as set forth in the present Convention.

Article 82

The rights of migrant workers and members of their families provided for in the present Convention may not be renounced. It shall not be permissible to exert any form of pressure upon migrant workers and members of their families with a view to their relinquishing or foregoing any of the said rights. It shall not be possible to derogate by contract from rights recognized in the present Convention. States Parties shall take appropriate measures to ensure that these principles are respected.

Article 83

Each State Party to the present Convention undertakes:

(a) To ensure that any person whose rights or freedoms as herein recognized are violated shall have an effective remedy, notwithstanding that the violation has been committed by persons acting in an official capacity;

(b) To ensure that any persons seeking such a remedy shall have his or her claim reviewed and decided by competent judicial, administrative or legislative authorities, or by any other competent authority provided for by the legal system of the State, and to develop the possibilities of judicial remedy;

(c) To ensure that the competent authorities shall enforce such remedies when granted.

Article 84

Each State Party undertakes to adopt the legislative and other measures that are necessary to implement the provisions of the present Convention.

PART IX: FINAL PROVISIONS

Article 85

The Secretary-General of the United Nations is designated as the depositary of the present Convention.

Article 86

1. The present Convention shall be open for signature by all States. It is subject to ratification.

2. The present Convention shall be open to accession by any State.

3. Instruments of ratification or accession shall be deposited with the Secretary-General of the United Nations.

Article 87

1. The present Convention shall enter into force on the first day of the month following a period of three months after the date of the deposit of the twentieth instrument of ratification or accession.

2. For each State ratifying or acceding to the present Convention after its entry into force, the Convention shall enter into force on the first day of the month following a period of three months after the date of the deposit of its own instrument of ratification or accession.

Article 88

A State ratifying or acceding to the present Convention may not exclude the application of any Part of it, or, without prejudice to article 3, exclude any particular category of migrant workers from its application.

Article 89

1. Any State Party may denounce the present Convention, not earlier than five years after the Convention has entered into force for the State concerned, by means of a notification writing addressed to the Secretary-General of the United Nations.

2. Such denunciation shall become effective on the first day of the month following the expiration of a period of twelve months after the date of the receipt of the notification by the Secretary-General of the United Nations.

3. Such a denunciation shall not have the effect of releasing the State Party from its obligations under the present Convention in regard to any act or omission which occurs prior to the date at which the denunciation becomes effective, nor shall denunciation prejudice in any way the continued consideration of any matter which is already under consideration by the Committee prior to the date at which the denunciation becomes effective.

4. Following the date at which the denunciation of a State Party becomes effective, the Committee shall not commence consideration of any new matter regarding that State.

Article 90

1. After five years from the entry into force of the Convention a request for the revision of the Convention may be made at any time by any State Party by means of a notification in writing addressed to the Secretary-General of the United Nations. The Secretary-General shall thereupon communicate any proposed amendments to the States Parties with a request that they notify him whether the favour a conference of States Parties for the purpose of considering and voting upon the proposals. In the event that within four months from the date of such communication at least one third of the States Parties favours such a conference, the Secretary-General shall convene the conference under the auspices of the United Nations. Any amendment adopted by a majority of the States Parties present and voting shall be submitted to the General Assembly for approval.

2. Amendments shall come into force when they have been approved by the General Assembly of the United Nations and accepted by a two-thirds major-

ity of the States Parties in accordance with their respective constitutional processes.

3. When amendments come into force, they shall be binding on those States Parties that have accepted them, other States Parties still being bound by the provisions of the present Convention and any earlier amendment that they have accepted.

Article 91

1. The Secretary-General of the United Nations shall receive and circulate to all States the text of reservations made by States at the time of signature, ratification or accession.

2. A reservation incompatible with the object and purpose of the present Convention shall not be permitted.

3. Reservations may be withdrawn at any time by notification to this effect addressed to the Secretary-General of the United Nations, who shall then inform all States thereof. Such notification shall take effect on the date on which it is received.

Article 92

1. Any dispute between two or more States Parties concerning the interpretation or application of the present Convention that is not settled by negotiation shall, at the request of one of them, be submitted to arbitration. If within six months from the date of the request for arbitration the Parties are unable to agree on the organization of the arbitration, any one of those Parties may refer the dispute to the International Court of Justice by request in conformity with the Statute of the Court.

2. Each State Party may at the time of signature or ratification of the present Convention or accession thereto declare that it does not consider itself bound by paragraph 1 of the present article. The other States Parties shall not be bound by that paragraph with respect to any State Party that has made such a declaration.

3. Any State Party that has made a declaration in accordance with paragraph 2 of the present article may at any time withdraw that declaration by notification to the Secretary-General of the United Nations.

Article 93

1. The present Convention, of which the Arabic, Chinese, English, French, Russian and Spanish texts are equally authentic, shall be deposited with the Secretary-General of the United Nations.

2. The Secretary-General of the United Nations shall transmit certified copies of the present Convention to all States.

IN WITNESS WHEREOF the undersigned plenipotentiaries, being duly authorized thereto by their respective Governments, have signed the present Convention.

Status of ratification of the International Convention on the Protection of the Rights of All Migrant Workers and Members of Their Families: Number of parties as of 18 July 2007: 37

REFERENCES

Acuña, Rodolfo. 2007. *Occupied America: A history of Chicanos.* 6th ed. New York: Pearson Longman.

Albonetti, Celesta A. 1997. "Sentencing under the Federal Sentencing Guidelines: Effects of defendant characteristics, guilty pleas, and departures on sentence outcomes for drug offenses, 1991–92." *Law and Society Review* 31: 789–822.

Amnesty International. 1998. *United States of America: Rights for all.* New York: Amnesty International Publications.

_____. 2003. *United States of America: Death by discrimination—the continuing role of race in capital cases.* New York: Amnesty International Publications. http://www.amnestyusa.org/abolish/reports/dp_discrimination.html.

Arriola, Christopher. 1997. Mendez v. Westminster (1947). *Los Angeles Times, 14 April,* http://mendezvwestminster.com/_wsn/page3.html (accessed July 21, 2007).

Audley, John J., Demetrios G. Papademetriou, Sandra Polaski, and Scott Vaughan. 2003. *NAFTA's promise and reality: Lessons from Mexico for the hemisphere.* Washington, D.C.: Carnegie Endowment for International Peace.

Audre Lorde Project. 2000. *Silent screams: Police brutality against lesbian, gay, bisexual, two spirit, and transgender communities of color in New York City.* New York: Audre Lorde Project.

Bacon, David. 2004. *The children of NAFTA: Labor wars on the U.S./Mexico border.* Berkeley: University of California Press.

Báez, Iris. 2002. Interview by author. Bronx, New York, 13 August.

Baker, Al. 2002. Fire Department looks to diversify the ranks. *New York Times,* 3 April.

Barrios, Luis. 1998. "'Santa María' as a liberating zone: A community church in search of restorative justice." *Humanity and Society* 22, 1 (February): 55–78.

Bayley, David H., and Harold Mendelsohn. 1969. *Minorities and the police: Confrontation in America.* New York: Free Press.

Baynes, Leonard M. 2006. "The LSAT, *U.S. News & World Report*, and Minority admissions." *St. John's Law Review* 80, 1: 1–14.

———. 2007. "Abandoning *Brown* and '[race]ing' backwards on K-12 education." *Diverse Online*, http://www.diverseeducation.com/artman/publish/article_8791.shtml (accessed July 27, 2007).

Beckett, Katherine. 1997. *Making crime pay: Law and order in contemporary American politics.* Oxford: Oxford University Press.

Beckett, Katherine, and Theodore Sasson. 2004. *The politics of injustice: Crime and punishment in America.* New York: Sage.

Bell, Derrick. 2007. Desegregation's demise. *Chronicle of Higher Education,* 13 July.

Bender, Steven W. 2003. *Greasers and gringos: Latinos, law, and the American imagination.* New York: New York University Press.

Berg, Charles Ramírez. 2002. *Latino images in film: Stereotypes, subversion, resistance.* Austin, Texas: University of Texas Press.

Bernstein, Ilene Nagel, Edward Kick, Jan T. Leung, and Barbara Schultz. 1977. "Charge reduction: An intermediary state in the process of labeling criminal defendants." *Social Forces* 56: 362–84.

Black, Donald. 1980. *The manners and customs of the police.* New York: Academic Press.

Blauner, Robert. 1972. *Racial oppression in America.* New York: Harper & Row.

Blumstein, Alfred, and Joel Wallman, eds. 2000. *The crime drop in America.* New York: Cambridge University Press.

Bourgois, Philippe. 1995. *In search of respect: Selling crack in El Barrio.* Cambridge, United Kingdom: Cambridge University Press.

Broyles-González, Yolanda. 1994. *El Teatro Campesino: Theater in the Chicano movement.* Austin, Texas: University of Texas Press.

Buergenthal, Thomas, Dinah Shelton, and David Stewart. 2002. *International human rights in a nutshell.* 3d ed. St. Paul, Minnesota: West Group.

Bureau of Justice Statistics. 1999. *Truth in sentencing in state prisons: Bureau of Justice Statistics special report (January 1999)*, NCJ 170032, by Paula M. Ditton, and Doris James Wilson. Washington, D.C.: U.S. Department of Justice.

_____. 2000. *Criminal victimization in the United States, 1995(May 2000)*, NCJ 171129. Washington, D.C.: U.S. Department of Justice.

_____. 2002. *Hispanic victims of violent crime, 1993–2000: Bureau of Justice Statistics special report (April 2002)*, NCJ 191208, by Callie Marie Rennison. Washington, D.C.: U.S. Department of Justice.

_____. 2003a. *Criminal victimization in the United States, 2002, Statistical Tables (December 2003)*, NCJ 200561. Washington, D.C.: U.S. Department of Justice.

_____. 2003b. *Criminal Victimization, 2002: Bureau of Justice Statistics National Crime Victimization Survey (August 2003)*, NCJ 199994, by Callie Marie Rennison, and Michael R. Rand. Washington, D.C.: U.S. Department of Justice.

_____. 2003c. *Local police departments: Bureau of Justice Statistics law enforcement management and administrative statistics (January 2003)*, NCJ 196002, by Matthew J. Hickman, and Brian A. Reaves. Washington, D.C.: U.S. Department of Justice.

_____. 2003d. *Prisoners in 2002: Bureau of Justice Statistics bulletin (July 2003)*, NCJ 200248, by Paige M. Harrison, and Allen J. Beck. Washington, D.C.: U.S. Department of Justice.

_____. 2005. *Prisoners in 2004*. NCJ 210677, by Paige M. Harrison, and Allen J. Beck. Washington, D.C.: U.S. Department of Justice.

_____. 2006a. *Criminal victimization in the United States, 2005, Statistical Tables (December 2006)*, NCJ 215244. Washington, D.C.: U.S. Department of Justice.

_____. 2006b. *Prisoners in 2005*. NCJ 215092, by Paige M. Harrison, and Allen J. Beck. Washington, D.C.: U.S. Department of Justice.

_____. 2006c. *Prison and Jail Inmates at Midyear 2005*. NCJ 213133, by Paige M. Harrison, and Allen J. Beck. Washington, D.C.: U.S. Department of Justice.

_____. 2007a. *Contacts between police and the public, 2005*, NCJ 215243. Washington, D.C.: U.S. Department of Justice.

_____. 2007b. *Prison and Jail Inmates at Midyear 2005*. NCJ 217675, by William J. Sabol, Todd D. Minton, and Paige M. Harrison. Washington, D.C.: U.S. Department of Justice.

Butcher, Kristen F., and Anne Morrison Piehl. 2005. "Why are immigrants' incarceration rates so low? Evidence on selective immigration deterrence, and deportation." Working Papers 2005-19. Chicago: Federal Reserve Bank of Chicago, http://www.chicagofed.org/publications/workingpapers/wp2005_19.pdf (accessed June 17, 2007).

Butler, Smedley D. [1935] 2003. *War is a racket*. Los Angeles: Feral House.

Cabán, Pedro A. 1999. *Construction a colonial people: Puerto Rico and the United States, 1898–1932*. Boulder, Colorado: Westview Press.

Cabranes, José, A. 1979. *Citizenship and the American Empire*. New Haven: Yale University Press.

Canedy, Dana. 2001. Troubling label for Hispanics: 'Girls most likely to drop out.' *New York Times*, 25 March.

Cannon, Lou. 2000. One bad cop. *New York Times Magazine*, 1 October.

Carrasco, Gilbert Paul. 1997. Latinos in the United States: Invitation and exile. In *Immigrants out! The new nativism and the anti-immigrant impulse in the United States*, ed. J. F. Perea, 190–204. New York: New York University Press.

Cassese, Antonio. 1996. *Self-determination of peoples: A legal reappraisal*. Cambridge, Great Britain: Cambridge University Press.

Césaire, Aimé. 2000. *Discourse on colonialism*. New York: Monthly Review Press.

Chambliss, Elizabeth. 2000. *Miles to go 2000: Progress of minorities in the legal profession*. Chicago: American Bar Association Commission on Racial and Ethnic Diversity in the Profession, American Bar Association.

Chang, Nancy. 2002. *Silencing political dissent: How post-September 11 anti-terrorist measures threaten our civil liberties*. New York: Seven Stories Press.

Chapman, Francisco. 2002. *Race, identity and myth in the Spanish-speaking Caribbean: Essays on biculturalism as a contested terrain of difference*. New York: Diaspora Publishing.

Chemerinsky, Erwin. 2001. "Symposium: The Rampart scandal: Policing the criminal justice system: An independent analysis of the Los Angeles Police Department's Board of Inquiry Report on the Rampart scandal."

Loyola of Los Angeles Law Review 34: 545–655.

Chemerinsky, Erwin, with Paul Hoffman, Laurie Levenson, R. Samuel Paz, Connie Rice, and Carol Sobel. 2000. *An independent analysis of the Los Angeles Police Department's Board of Inquiry Report on the Rampart scandal, Los Angeles, California.* Los Angeles, California.

Chevingny, Paul. 1995. *Edge of the knife: Police violence in the Americas.* New York: New Press.

Citizens' Committee for Children of New York. 2000. *Keeping track of New York City's children: A Citizens' Committee for Children status report.* New York: Citizens Committee for Children of New York, Inc.

_____. 2002. *Keeping track of New York City's children: A Citizens' Committee for Children status report.* New York: Citizens Committee for Children of New York, Inc.

Clark, Ramsey. 1991. We never heard the truth, In *The U.S. invasion of Panama: The truth behind Operation "Just Cause,"* ed. The Independent Commission of Inquiry on the U.S. Invasion of Panama, 9–14. Boston: South End Press.

Cohn, D'Vera. 2003. Hispanics declared largest minority; Blacks overtaken in census update. *Washington Post,* 19 June.

Cole, David. 1999. *No equal justice: Race and class in the American criminal justice system.* New York: New Press.

_____. 2001. Formalism, realism, and the war on drugs. *Suffolk University Law Review* 35:241–55.

_____. 2003. *Enemy aliens: Double standards and constitutional freedoms in the war on terrorism.* The New Press.

Cole, David, and James X. Dempsey. 2002. *Terror and the constitution: Sacrificing civil liberties in the name of national security.* New York: New Press.

Collins, Susan M., Barry P. Bosworth, and Miguel A. Soto-Class, eds. 2006. *The economy of Puerto Rico: Restoring growth.* San Juan, Puerto Rico: Center for the New Economy/Brookings Institution Press.

Commission for Historical Clarification. 1999. *Guatemala, Memory of silence: Report of the Commission for Historical Clarification (Conclusions and recommendations).* Guatemala: Commission for Historical Clarification.

Commission on Racial and Ethnic Diversity in the Profession. (n.d.) Executive summary: *Miles to go 2000: The progress of minorities in the legal profes-*

sion. Washington, D.C.: American Bar Association, http://www.abanet
.org/minorities/publications/milesummary.html (accessed July 24, 2007).

Convention on the Rights and Duties of States. 1933. Done at Montevideo,
Dec. 26, 1933. Entered into force, Dec. 26, 1934; for the United States,
Dec. 26, 1934. 49 Stat. 3097, T.S. No. 881, Bevans 145, 165 L.N.T.S. 19.

Cooper, Marc. 2007. Lockdown in Greeley: How immigration raids terrorized a Colorado town. *The Nation,* 26 February.

Crawford, James, ed. 1992. *Language loyalties: A source book on the official
English controversy.* Chicago: University of Chicago Press.

_____. 2000. *At war with diversity: U.S. language policy in an age of anxiety.*
Clevedon, England: Multilingual Matters, Ltd.

Crutchfield, Robert, Joseph G. Weis, Rodney L. Engen, and Randy R.
Gainey. 1995. *Racial and ethnic disparities in the prosecution of felony
cases in King County.* Olympia Washington State Minority and Justice
Commission.

Cummins, Jim. 1993. Empowering minority students: A framework for in-
tervention. In *Beyond silenced voices: Class, race, and gender in United
States schools,* ed. L. W. and M. Fine, 101–17. Albany, New York: State
University of New York Press.

_____. 2000. *Language, power and pedagogy: Bilingual children in the cross-
fire.* Clevedon, England: Multilingual Matters.

Danner, Mark. 1993. *The massacre at El Mozote.* New York: Vintage Books.

Dávila, Arlene. 2001. *Latinos, Inc.: The marketing and making of a people.*
Berkeley: University of California Press.

Davis, Kenneth C. 2003. *Don't know much about history: Everything you
need to know about American history but never learned.* New York:
HarperCollins.

Davis, Robert C., and Pedro Mateu-Gelabert. 1999. *Respectful and effective
policing: Two examples in the South Bronx.* New York: Vera Institute of
Justice.

DeCesare, Donna. 2003. From civil war to gang war: The tragedy of Edgar
Bolanos. In *Gangs and society: Alternative perspectives,* ed. L. Kontos, D.
Brotherton, and L. Barrios, 283–313. New York: Columbia University
Press.

Delgado, Richard, and Jean Stefancic. 1992. "Images of the outsider in

American law and culture: Can free expression remedy systemic social ills?" *Cornell Law Review* 77: 1258–97.

_____, eds. 1998. *The Latino/a condition: A critical reader.* New York: New York University Press.

Delpit, Lisa. 1995. *Other people's children: Cultural conflict in the classroom.* New York: The New Press.

Del Valle, Sandra. 2003. *Language rights and the law in the United States: Finding our voices.* Clevedon, England: Multilingual Matters.

Demuth, Stephen, and Darrell Steffensmeier. 2004. Ethnicity Effects on Sentencing Outcomes in Large Urban Courts: Comparisons among White, Black and Hispanic Defendants. *Social Science Quarterly* 85: 994–1011.

DeNavas-Walt, Carmen, Robert W. Cleveland, and Marc I. Roemer. 2001. *Money Income in the United States: 2000.* Current Population Reports, Consumer Income, P60–213, U.S. Census Bureau, Washington, D.C.

Díaz-Stevens, Ana María. 1996. Aspects of Puerto Rican religious experience: A socio-historical overview. In *Latinos in New York: Communities in transition,* ed. G. Haslip-Viera and S. L. Baver, 147–86. Notre Dame, Indiana: University of Notre Dame Press.

Donziger, Steven R., ed. 1996. *The real war on crime: The report of the National Criminal Justice Commission.* New York: HarperPerrenial.

Dorfman, Ariel, and Armand Mattelart. 1984. *How to read Donald Duck: Imperialist ideology in the Disney comic.* Trans. David Kunzle. New York: International General.

Dorfman, Lori, and Vincent Schiraldi. 2001. *Off balance: Youth, race and crime in the news.* Washington, D.C.: Building Blocks for Youth.

Dow, Mark. 2004. *American Gulag: Inside U.S. Immigration Prisons.* Berkeley: University of California Press.

Ebright, Malcolm. 1994. *Land grants and law suits in Northern New Mexico.* Albuquerque, New Mexico: University of New Mexico Press.

Ehlers, Scott, Vincent Schiraldi, and Jason Ziedenberg. 2004. *Still striking out: Ten years of California's three strikes.* Washington, D.C.: Justice Policy Institute.

Ellis, Edwin. 1993. *The non-traditional approach to criminal justice and social justice.* Harlem: Community Justice Center, mimeographed, 8 pages.

Engle, Charles Donald. 1971. Criminal justice in the city: A study of sentence severity and variation in the Philadelphia court system. Ph.D. diss., Temple University.

Eron, Leonard D., and L. Rowell Huesmann. 1990. The stability of aggressive behavior—even unto the third generation. In *Handbook of developmental psychopathology,* ed. M. Lewis and S. M. Miller, 147–56. New York: Plenum.

Escobar, Edward J. 1999. *Race, police, and the making of a political identity: Mexican Americans and the Los Angeles Police Department 1900–1945.* Berkeley: University of California Press.

Falcón, Angelo. 2002. *Opening up the courthouse doors: The need for more Hispanic judges.* New York: Puerto Rican Legal Defense and Education Fund.

Fanon, Frantz. [1963] 1986. *The wretched of the earth.* New York: Grove Press.

Feagin, Joe E., and Clairece Booher Feagin. 1996. *Racial and ethnic relations.* Upper Saddle River, New Jersey: Prentice-Hall.

Fellner, Jamie, and Marc Mauer. 1998. Losing the Vote: The Impact of felony disenfranchisement laws in the United States. New York: Human Rights Watch, The Sentencing Project, http://sentencingproject.org/tmp/File/FVR/fd_losingthevote.pdf (accessed July 24, 2007).

Fernandez, Manny. 2007. Remembrance, and Protest, for a Man Slain by an Officer. *New York Times,* 27 May.

Fernandez, Ronald. 1994. *Prisoners of colonialism: The struggle for justice in Puerto Rico.* Monroe, Maine: Common Courage Press.

Fernandez-Kelly, Patricia, and Douglas S. Massey. 2007. "Borders for whom? The role of NAFTA in Mexico-U.S. migration." *Annals of the American Academy of Political and Social Science* 610: 98–116.

Ferrante, Joan, and Prince Browne, Jr., eds. 2001. *The social construction of race and ethnicity in the United States.* 2d ed. Upper Saddle River, New Jersey: Prentice Hall.

Feuer, Alan. 2003. Little but language in common; Mexicans and Puerto Ricans quarrel in East Harlem. *New York Times,* 6 September.

Flores, Glenn et al. 2002. "The health of Latino children: Urgent priorities, unanswered questions, and research agenda." *Journal of the American Medical Association* 288, 1 (July): 82–90.

Flores, Juan. 2000. *From bomba to hip-hop: Puerto Rican Culture and Latino identity.* New York: Columbia University Press.

Flores-González, Nilda, Matthew Rodríguez, and Michael Rodríguez-Muñiz. 2006. From hip-hop to humanization: Batey Urbano as a space for Latino youth culture and community action. In *Beyond resistance: Youth activism and community change*, eds. Shawn Ginwright, Pedro Noguera, and Julio Cammarota. New York: Routledge.

Flynn, Kevin. 1999. Record payout in settlements against police. *New York Times*, 1 October.

Forero, Juan. 2005. Report criticizes labor standards in Central America. *New York Times*, 1 July.

Fountain, John W. with Jim Yardley. 2002. Skeletons Tell Tale of Gamble by Immigrants. *New York Times*, 16 October.

Franklin, Benjamin. 1959. *The papers of Benjamin Franklin*, ed. L. W. Labarre. New Haven: Yale University Press.

Freedman, Samuel G. 2007. English Language Learners as Pawns in the School System's Overhaul. *New York Times*, 9 May.

Freidman, Warren, and Martha Hott. 1995. *Young people and the police: Respect, fear and the future of community policing in Chicago*. Chicago: Chicago Alliance for Neighborhood Safety.

Freire, Paulo. 1994. *Pedagogy of the oppressed*. New York: Continuum.

Fyfe, James J. 1981. "Who shoots? A look at officer race and police shooting." *Journal of Police Science and Administration* 9: 367–82.

Galeano, Eduardo. [1973] 1997. *Open veins of Latin America: Five centuries of the pillage of a continent*. New York: Monthly Review.

García, John A. 2001. The Chicano Movement: Its legacy for politics and policy. In *Chicano studies: Survey and analysis*, 2nd ed., ed. D. J. Bixler-Márquez, C. F. Ortega, R. Solórzano Torres, and L. G. LaFarelle, 165–75. Dubuque, Iowa: Kendall/Hunt Publishing.

García, Mario T. 1994. *Memories of Chicano history: The life and narrative of Bert Corona*. Berkeley: University of California Press.

García Martínez, Alfonso. 1989. *Puerto Rico: Leyes fundamentales*. Río Piedras, Puerto Rico: Editorial Edil.

Garland, David, ed. 2001a. *Mass imprisonment: Social causes and consequences*. London: Sage.

_____. 2001b. *The culture of control: Crime and social order in contemporary society*. Chicago: University of Chicago Press.

Gautier Mayoral, Carmen, and María Del Pilar Argüelles. 1978. *Puerto Rico y la ONU*. Río Piedras, Puerto Rico: Editorial Edil.

General Accounting Office. 1991. *The war on drugs: Narcotics control efforts in Panama*. GAO/NSIAD-91-233. Washington, D.C.

———. 2004. *Tax administration: Comparison of the tax liabilities of foreign- and U.S.-controlled corporations, 1996–2000*. GAO-04-358. Washington, D.C.

Gereffi, Gary, David Spener, and Jennifer Bair, eds. 2002. *Free trade and uneven development: The North American apparel industry after NAFTA*. Philadelphia: Temple University Press.

Gleach, Frederic W. 2002. "Images of empire: Representations of the 1898 war." *Latino(a) Research Review* 5, 1 (Spring): 51–79.

Goldberg, Jeffrey. 1999. What cops talk about when they talk about race: The color of suspicion. *New York Times Magazine*, 20 June.

Goldewijk, Berma Klein. 2002. From Seattle to Porto Alegre: Emergence of a new focus on dignity and the implementation of economic, social and cultural rights. In *Dignity and human rights: The implementation of economic, social and cultural rights*, ed. B. K. Goldewijk, A. C. Baspineiro, and P. C. Carbonari, 3–16. Antwerp, Belgium: Intersentia/Transnational Publishers.

Goldewijk, Berma Klein, Adalid Contreras Baspineiro, and Paolo César Carbonari, eds. 2002. *Dignity and human rights: The implementation of economic, social and cultural rights*. Antwerp, Belgium: Intersentia/Transnational Publishers.

Gómez Quiñones, Juan. 1990. *Chicano politics: Reality and promise, 1940–1990*. Albuquerque, New Mexico: University of New Mexico.

Gonzalez, Juan. 1996. Her bravery shatters blue wall. *New York Daily News*, 27 September, 21.

———. 2000. *Harvest of Empire: A history of Latinos in America*. New York: Viking.

Goodnough, Abby. 2007. After 5 years, Padilla goes on trial in terror case. *New York Times Magazine*, 15 May.

Goodnough, Abby, and Scott Shane. 2007. Padilla is guilty on all charges in terror trial. *New York Times Magazine*, 17 August.

Goodstein, Laurie, and Gustav Niebuhr. 2001. Attacks and harassment of

Middle Eastern Americans rising. *New York Times*, 14 September.

Gootman, Elissa. 2003. Old tensions over immigrants surface after fire-bombing. *New York Times*, 14 July.

———. 2006. In elite schools, A dip in Blacks And Hispanics, *New York Times*, 18 August.

Grasmuck, Sherri, and Patricia R. Pessar. 1991. *Between two islands: Dominican international migration*. Berkeley: University of California Press.

———. 1996. Dominicans in the United States: First- and second generation settlement, 1960–1990. In *Origins and destinies: Immigration, race, and ethnicity in America*, ed. S. Pedraza and R. G. Rumbaut, 280–301. Belmont, California: Wadsworth Publishing Company.

Green, Mark. 1999. *Investigation of the New York City Police Department's response to civilian complains of police misconduct: Interim report*. New York: Office of the Public Advocate.

Greene, Judith, and Kevin Pranis. 2007. *Gang wars: The failure of enforcement tactics and the need for effective public safety strategies*. Washington, D.C.: Justice Policy Institute.

Greenhouse, Steven. 2003a. Immigrants rally in city, seeking rights. *New York Times*, 5 October.

———. 2003b. Wal-Mart raids by U.S. aimed at illegal aliens. *New York Times*, 24 October.

Hadden, Bob. 2003a. Government leaders crack down on gangs in Central America. *National Public Radio, Morning Edition*, 9 September.

———. 2003b. Latino migration to the United States. *National Public Radio, Morning Edition*, 29 September.

Hagan, John, and Alberto Palloni. 1999. "Sociological Criminology and the mythology of Hispanic immigration and crime." *Social Problems* 46 (4): 617–32.

Hakim, Danny. 2006, Breathing room for Spitzer in decision on the schools. *New York Times*, 21 November.

Hall, Kermit, L., William M. Wiecek, and Paul Finkelman. 1996. *American Legal History: Cases and Materials*, 2nd ed. New York: Oxford University Press.

Haney López, Ian F. 1996. *White by Law: The Legal Construction of Race*.

New York: New York University Press.

_____. 2003. *Racism on trial: The Chicano fight for justice.* Cambridge, Massachusetts: Belknap/Harvard University Press.

Hannum, Hurst. 1990. *Autonomy, sovereignty and self-determination: The accommodation of conflicting rights.* Philadelphia, Pennsylvania: University of Pennsylvania Press.

Harris, David A. 2002. *Profiles in injustice: Why racial profiling cannot work.* New York: the New Press.

Harris, Fred R., and Roger W. Wilkins. 1988. *Quiet riots: Race and poverty in the United States—The Kerner Report twenty years later.* New York: Pantheon Books.

Hayden, Tom. 2000. We need peacemakers like Alex Sanchez. *Los Angeles Times*, 26 January.

Hayes-Bautista, David E., and Chapa, Jorge. 1987. "Latino terminology: Conceptual basis for standardized terminology." *American Journal of Public Health* 77: 61–68.

Healey, Joseph F. 2006. *Race, ethnicity, gender, and class in the United States: Inequality, group conflict, and power.* 4th ed. Thousand Oaks, CA: Pine Forge Press.

Hendricks, Tyche. 2007. An early blow for equality. *San Francisco Chronicle*, 9 May.

Henkin, Louis. 1990. *The age of rights.* New York: Columbia University Press.

Herbert, Bob. 2007. American Cities and the Great Divide. *New York Times*, 22 May.

Hernández, Ramona. 2002. *The mobility of workers under advanced capitalism: Dominican migration to the United States.* New York: Columbia University Press.

Hernández, Ramona, and Silvio Torres-Saillant. 1996. Dominicans in New York: Men, women, and prospects. In *Latinos in New York: Communities in transition*, ed. G. Haslip-Viera, and S. L. Baver, 30–56. Notre Dame, Indiana: Notre Dame University Press.

Hernández-Chávez, Eduardo. 1995. Language policy in the United States: A history of cultural genocide. In *Linguistic human rights: Overcoming linguistic discrimination*, ed. T. Skutnabb-Kangas, and R. Phillipson, 141–77. Berlin: Mouton de Gruyter.

Hernández-Truyol, Berta Esperanza. 1997. Reconciling rights in collision: An international human rights strategy. In *Immigrants out! The new nativism and the anti-immigrant impulse in the United States*, ed. J. F. Perea, 254–76. New York: New York University Press.

———. 1998. Bringing international human rights home. In *The Latino/a condition: A critical reader*, ed. R. Delgado, and J. Stefancic, 381–86. New York: New York University Press.

Herrnstein, Richard, and Murray, Charles. 1994. *The bell curve*. New York: Free Press.

Herszenhorn, David M. 2003. City English scores show marked gain. *New York Times*, 21 May.

———. 2007a, Eighth graders show big gain in reading test, *New York Times*, 23 May.

———. 2007b. Higher graduation rates in City, but 'more work to do.' *New York Times*, 21 May.

Hing, Bill Ong. 2004. *Defining America through immigration policy*. Philadelphia: Temple University Press.

Hirschi, Travis, and Michael J. Hindelang. 1977. "Intelligence and delinquency: a revisionist review." *American Sociological Review*, 42: 571–87.

Hitchens, Christopher. 2001. *The trial of Henry Kissinger*. London: Verso.

Hoffman, Alison. 2003. *Looking for Latino regulars on prime-time television: The fall 2002 season*. Los Angeles, California: Chicano Research Report/UCLA Chicano Studies Research Center. Also available online at http//www.sscnet.ucla.edu/csrc/.

Holden, Robert H., and Eric Zolov, eds. 2000. *Latin America and the United States: A documentary history*. New York: Oxford University Press.

Holmes, Malcolm D., Harmon M. Hosch, Howard C. Daudistel, Dolores A. Perez, and Joseph B. Graves. 1993. "Judges' ethnicity and minority sentencing: Evidence concerning Hispanics." *Social Science Quarterly* 74: 496–506.

Hood, Roger. 1992. *Race and sentencing*. Oxford, England: Clarendon.

Horsman, Reginald, 1981. *Race and Manifest Destiny: The origins of American racial Anglo-Saxsonism*. Cambridge Massachusetts: Harvard University Press.

Hostos, Eugenio María de. 1999. *Estímulos de vida para cada día.* 2d ed., ed. V. Quiles-Calderín. San Juan, Puerto Rico: Instituto de Cultura Puertorriqueña.

Hsiao, Andrew. 2001. Mothers of invention: The families of police-brutality victims and the movement they've built. In *Zero tolerance: Quality of life and the new police brutality in New York City,* ed. A. McArdle and T. Erzen, 179–95. New York: New York University Press.

Human Rights Watch. 1998. *Shielded from justice: Police brutality and accountability in the United States.* New York: Human Rights Watch.

_____. 2002. *Race and incarceration in the United States: Human Rights Watch briefing.* New York: Human Rights Watch. Also available online at http://hrw.org/backgrounder/usa/race/ pdf/race-bck.pdf.

_____. 2003. *Incarcerated America: Human Rights Watch backgrounder.* New York: Human Rights Watch. Also available online at http://hrw.org/backgrounder/usa/ incarceration/us042903.pdf.

Independent Commission on the Los Angeles Police Department. 1991. *Report of Independent Commission on the Los Angeles Police Department.* Los Angeles: California, 9 July.

Institute of Medicine of the National Academy of Sciences. 2004a. *Insuring America's health: Principles and recommendations.* Washington, D.C.: The National Academies Press. Also available online at http://www.nap.edu.

_____. 2004b. *IOM report calls for universal health coverage by 2010; Offers principles to judge, compare proposed solutions*(Press Release). Washington, D.C.: The National Academies. Also available online at http://www4.nationalacademies.org/ news.nsf.

Jacobson, Michael. 2005. *Downsizing Prisons: How to Reduce Crime and End Mass Incarceration.* New York: New York University Press.

Jay, John. [1788] 2003. Federalist No. 2. In *The Federalist Papers,* ed. C. Rossiter, 31–35. New York: Signet Classic.

Johnson, Kevin R. 2003. "Law and the border: Open borders?" *UCLA Law Review* 51: 193–265.

_____. 2004. "International human rights class actions: New frontiers for group litigation." *Michigan State Law Review* 2004: 643–70.

Johnson, Marilynn S. 2003. *Street justice: A history of police violence in New York City.* Boston: Beacon Press.

Jordan, Mary, and Kevin Sullivan. 2003. Trade brings riches, but not to Mexico's poor. *Washington Post,* 22 March.

Journal of el Centro de Estudios Puertorriqueños. 1998. "Focus/en foco: 1898–1998, Part I." *CENTRO Journal of the Center for Puerto Rican Studies* 10, 1–2 (Fall): 5–223.

Justice Policy Institute. 2007. *Press Release: Groundbreaking New Report: Gang suppression tactics fail to reduce crime, can worsen problem; Pervasive myths about gang members and gang crime debunked,* http://www.justicepolicy.org/reports_jl/7-10-07_gangs/press_release.htm (accessed July 30, 2007).

Karman, Andrew. 2000. *New York murder mystery: The true story behind the crime crash of the 1990s.* New York: New York University Press.

Kennedy, Randall. 1997. *Race, crime, and the law.* New York: Vintage Books.

Kessler, Judi. 2002. The impact of North American economic integration on the Los Angeles apparel industry. In *Free trade and uneven development: The North American apparel industry after NAFTA,* ed. G. Gereffi, D. Spener, and J. Bair, 74–99. Philadelphia: Temple University Press.

Kocieniewski, David and Robert Hanley. 2000. Racial profiling was routine. *New York Times,* 28 November.

Kontos, Louis, David Brotherton, and Luis Barrios, eds. 2003. *Gangs and society: Alternative perspectives.* New York: Colombia University Press.

Kontra, Miklós, Robert Phillipson, Tove Skutnabb-Kangas and Tibor Várady, eds. 1999. *Language: A right and a resource: Approaching linguistic human rights.* Budapest, Hungary: Central European University Press.

Kornbluh, Peter. 2003a. "Opening up the files Chile declassified." *NACLA Report on the Americas* 37, 1 (July/August): 25–31.

————. 2003b. *The Pinochet file: A declassified dossier on atrocity and accountability.* New York: New Press.

Koss-Chioino, Joan D., and Luis A. Vargas. 1999. *Working with Latino youth: Culture, development, and context.* San Francisco, California: Jossey-Bass Publishers.

Krashen, Stephen D. 1996. *Under attack: The case against bilingual education.* Culver City, California: Language Education Associates.

_____. 1999. *Condemned without a trial: Bogus arguments against bilingual education.* Portsmouth, New Hampshire: Heinemann.

Lacey, Marc. 2007. Bush to press free trade in a place where young children still cut the cane. *New York Times,* March 12, 2007.

LaFeber, Walter. [1963] 1998. *The new empire: An interpretation of American expansionism, 1860–1898,* Reprint, with a new preface by W. LaFeber, Ithaca, New York: Cornell University Press.

_____. 1993. *Inevitable revolutions: The United States in Central America.* 2d ed. New York: W. W. Norton.

LaFree, Gary, K. Drass and P. O'Day. 1992. "Race and Crime in Post-war America: Determinants of African American and white rates, 1957–1988." *Criminology* 30: 157–188.

Larsen, Solana. 2007. "The anti-immigrant movement: From shovels to suits." *NACLA Report on the Americas* 40, 3 (May/June): 14–18.

Lauren, Paul Gordon. 1998. *The evolution of international human rights: Visions seen.* Philadelphia, Pennsylvania: University of Pennsylvania Press.

Lee, Matthew. 2003. *Crime on the border: Immigration and homicide in urban communities.* New York: LFB Scholarly Publishing.

Leo Grande, William, M. 1998. *Our own backyard: The United States in Central America, 1977–1992.* Chapel Hill, North Carolina: University of North Carolina Press.

Leone, Richard C., and Greg Anrig, Jr., eds. 2003. *The war on our freedoms: Civil liberties in an age of terrorism.* New York: Century Foundation.

Leonhardt, David. 2007a. "Immigrants and Prison," *New York Times,* 30 May. http://www.nytimes.com/2007/05/30/business/30leonside.html?ex =1184299200&en=e350a7f3a7435f38&ei=5070 (accessed: July 8, 2007).

_____. 2007b. "Truth, fiction and Lou Dobbs," *New York Times,* 30 May.

Levy, Clifford J., and William K. Rashbaum. 2001. After the attacks: The airports. *New York Times,* 14 September.

Lewin, Tamar. 2007. States found to vary widely on education. *New York Times,* 8 June.

Lewin, Tamar, and David M. Herszenhorn. 2007. Money, not race, is fueling new push to bolster schools. *New York Times,* 30 June.

Lewis, Gordon K. 1963. *Puerto Rico: Freedom and power in the Caribbean.* New York: Monthly Review.

López, Gerald P. 1981. "Undocumented Mexican Migration: In search of a just immigration law and policy." *UCLA Law Review* 28: 615–714.

Los Angeles Times. 2007. School bias exhibit to join parade in Surf City, 22 June.

Louima, Gariot. 2002. *Bracero protest "caravan" comes to L.A. The Los Angeles Times*, 11 April.

Lyall, Sarah. 1988. 'Blunt force' is cited in a death in police custody. *New York Times*, 21 February.

Maldonado-Denis, Manuel. 1972. *Puerto Rico: A socio-historic interpretation.* New York: Vintage.

Martin, Elizabeth A., ed. 2002. *A Dictionary of Law: Oxford Reference Online.* Oxford University Press. http://www.oxfordreference.com/views/ENTRY.html?subview= Main&entry=t49.001994 (accessed July 2, 2003).

Martínez, Elizabeth. 1993. "Beyond black/white: The racisms of our time." *Social Justice* 20 (1–2): 22–34.

Martinez, Jr., Ramiro. 2002. *Latino homicide: Immigration, violence and community.* New York: Routledge.

Matsuda, Mari 1991. "Voices of America: Accent, antidiscrimination law, and a jurisprudence for the last Reconstruction." *Yale Law Journal* 100: 1329–1404.

Maxfield, Linda Drazga, and John H. Kramer. 1998. *Substantial assistance: An empirical yardstick gauging equity in current federal policy and practice.* Washington, D.C.: U.S. Sentencing Commission.

McArdle, Andrea. 2001. Introduction. In *Zero tolerance: Quality of life and the new police brutality in New York City*, ed. A. McArdle and T. Erzen, 1–16. New York: New York University Press.

McArdle, Andrea, and Tanya Erzen, eds. 2001. *Zero tolerance: Quality of life and the new police brutality in New York City.* New York: New York University Press.

McKinley, Jr., James C. 2004. Killings deepen the family's drama. *New York Times*, 10 December.

McLeod, Aman, Ismail K.White, and Amelia Gavin. 2003. "The locked ballot box: The impact of state criminal disenfranchisement laws on African American voting behavior and implications for reform." *Virginia Journal of Social Policy and Law* 11:66–87.

McWilliams, Carey. 1990. *North from Mexico: The Spanish-speaking people of the United States.* New York: Praeger.

Medina, Jennifer. 2007a. Chancellor answers critics on school financing data. *New York Times,* 18 July.

_____. , Jennifer. 2007b. City students lead big rise on math tests. *New York Times,* 13 June.

Meek, James. 2003. Inside Guantánamo: People the law forgot. *The Guardian,* 12 March.

Meeks, Kenneth. 2000. *Driving while Black.* New York: Broadway Books.

Meléndez, Miguel. 2003. *We took the streets: Fighting for Latino rights with the Young Lords.* New York: St. Martin's Press.

Memmi, Albert. [1965] 1991. *The colonizer and the colonized.* Boston: Beacon Press.

Menchaca, Martha. 1993. Chicano Indianism: A historical account of racial repression in the United States. *American Ethnologist* 20:583–603.

Méndez, Miguel A. 1993. "Hernandez: The wrong message at the wrong time." *Stanford Law and Policy Review* 4: 193–202.

_____. 1997. "Lawyers, linguists, story-tellers, and limited English-speaking witnesses." *New Mexico Law Review* 27: 77–99.

Méndez-Méndez, Serafín, and Diana Alverio. 2003. *Network brownout 2003: The portrayal of Latinos in network television news, 2002.* Washington, D.C.: National Association of Hispanic Journalists.

Mexican American Legal Defense and Education Fund. 2007. Press Release: Department of Defense (DoD) authorization bill pulled from Senate floor: *Vote on DREAM Act postponed,* http://maldef.org/news/press.cfm (accessed July 18, 2007).

Miranda, Anthony. 2002. Interview by author. New York, 30 September.

Mirandé, Alfredo. 1987. *Gringo justice.* Notre Dame, Indiana: University of Notre Dame Press.

Montalvo, Daniela. 2006. *Network brownout 2006: The portrayal of Latinos and Latino issues on network television news, 2005.* Washington, D.C.: National Association of Hispanic Journalists, http://www.nahj.org/resources/2006Brownout.pdf (accessed July 14, 2007).

Montoya, Margaret E. 2001. A Brief History of Chicana/o School Segregation: One Rationale for Affirmative Action. *La Raza Law Journal.* 12: 159–72.

Moore, Joan and Harry Pachon. 1985. *Hispanics in the United States.* Englewood Cliffs, New Jersey: Prentice-Hall.

Morales, Iris. 1998. ¡PALANTE, SIEMPRE PALANTE! The Young Lords. In *The Puerto Rican movement: Voices from the diaspora,* ed. A. Torres and J. E. Velázquez, 210–27. Philadelphia: Temple University Press.

Morín, José Luis. 2000. "Indigenous Hawaiians under statehood: Lessons for Puerto Rico." *CENTRO Journal of the Center for Puerto Rican Studies* 11 (Spring): 4–25.

Morín, José Luis, and Manuel del Valle. 1990. Racially motivated violence: International remedies for human rights violations in the United States, *International Review of Contemporary Law,* 1: 61–68.

Mosisa, Abraham. 2002. "The role of foreign-born workers in the U.S. economy." *Monthly Labor Review* (May): 3–14.

Moya Pons, Frank. 1995. *The Dominican Republic: A national history.* New Rochelle, New York: Hispaniola Books.

Moynihan, Colin. 2004. Latino police officers and city settle suit. *New York Times,* 1 February, late edition.

Mumford Center. 2001. *Ethnic diversity grows, neighborhood integration lags behind.* Albany, New York: University at Albany. Also available online at www.albany.edu/ mumford/census.

_____. 2002. *Hispanic populations and their residential patterns in the metropolis.* Albany, New York: University at Albany. Also available online at www.albany.edu/ mumford/census.

NACLA Report on the Americas. 2007. In the name of Democracy: U.S. intervention in the Americas today. Special issue. *NACLA Report on the Americas* 40, 1 (January/February).

National Advisory Commission on Civil Disorder. [1968] 1988. *The Kerner Report: The 1968 report of the National Advisory Commission on Civil Disorders.* Reprint, with new introductions by Fred R. Harris and Tom Wicker, New York: Pantheon Books.

Navarro, Mireya, and Marjorie Connelly. 2003. Hispanics in New York hold bleaker views. *New York Times,* 8 August.

Negrón-Muntaner, Frances, ed. 2007. *None of the above: Puerto Ricans in the global era*. Palgrave Macmillan.

New Jersey Black and Latino Caucus. 2002. "Report on discriminatory practices within the New Jersey State Police." *Seton Hall Legislative Journal* 26: 273–313.

Newman, Andy. 2007. Justice Dept. sues New York City, calling firefighter hiring biased. *New York Times*, 22 May.

New York City Civilian Complaint Review Board. 2003. *Status report: January–June 2003*. New York: New York City Civilian Complaint Review Board, http://www.nyc.gov/html/ccrb/pdf/ccrbann2006.pdf (accessed July 19, 2007).

_____. 2007. *Status report: January–December 2006*. New York: New York City Civilian Complaint Review Board, http://www.nyc.gov/html/ccrb/pdf/ccrbann2006.pdf (accessed July 19, 2007).

New York Civil Liberties Union. 2007. *Criminalizing the classroom: The over-policing of New York City schools*. New York: NYCLU.

New York Times. 1997. 2 police officers' groups file U.S. bias complaint, 18 April.

_____. 1999. Former police officer sues over dismissal, 7 April.

_____. 2003a. Harvesting poverty: The great catfish war. Editorial, 22 July.

_____. 2003b. Harvesting poverty: The long reach of king cotton. Editorial, 5 August.

_____. 2003c. Harvesting poverty: The rigged trade game. Editorial, 20 July.

_____. 2003d. Harvesting poverty: The unkept promise. Editorial, 30 December.

_____. 2005a. Applauding the CAFTA 15. Editorial, 29 July.

_____. 2005b. Tongue-Tied on Bilingual Education. Editorial, 2 September.

_____. 2007a, A bad report card. Editorial, 27 February.

_____. 2007b, Humanity v. Hazleton. Editorial, 28 July.

_____. 2007c, The Padilla conviction. Editorial, 17 August.

Ngũgĩ, Wa Thiong'o. 1986. *Decolonising the mind: The politics of language in African literature*. Portsmouth, New Hampshire: Heinemann.

Noel, Donald. 1968. "A theory of the origin of ethnic stratification." *Social Problems* 16: 157–72.

Noguera, Pedro A. 2001. Youth perspectives on violence and the implications for public policy. *In Motion Magazine*, 30 September. Also available online at http://inmotionmagazine.com/er/pnypref.html.

Oboler, Suzanne. 1995. *Ethnic labels, Latino lives: Identity and the politics of re-presentation in the United States.* Minneapolis, Minnesota: University of Minnesota Press.

_____, ed. 2006. *Latinos and citizenship: The dilemma of belonging.* New York: Palgrave Macmillan.

Olivas, Michael A., ed. 2006. *"Colored Men" and "Hombres Aquí": Hernandez v. Texas and the emergence of Mexican-American lawyering.* Houston, Texas: Arte Público Press.

Office of National Drug Control Policy. 2003. *Minorities and drugs.* Also available online at http://www.whitehousedrugpolicy.gov/drugfact/minorities/index.html.

Omi, Michael, and Howard Winant. 1994. *Racial formations in the United States: From the 1960s to the 1990s.* 2d ed. New York: Routledge.

Oquendo, Angel R. 1995. "Re-imagining the Latino/a race." *Harvard Blackletter Law Journal* 12: 93–129.

Pagán, Eduardo Obregón. 2003. *Murder at the Sleepy Lagoon: Zoot suits, race, and riot in Wartime L.A.* Chapel Hill, North Carolina: University of North Carolina Press.

Palpacuer, Florence. 2002. Subcontracting networks in the New York City garment industry: Changing characteristics in a global era. In *Free trade and uneven development: The North American apparel industry after NAFTA*, ed. G. Gereffi, D. Spener, and J. Bair 53–73. Philadelphia: Temple University Press.

Pantoja, Antonia. 2002. *Memoir of a visionary: Antonia Pantoja.* Houston, Texas: Arte Público Press.

Passel, Jeffrey S., and Rebecca Clark. 1998. *Immigrants in New York: Their legal status, incomes, and taxes.* Washington, D.C.: Urban Institute. Also available online at http:// www.urban.org.

Pastor, Manuel, Jr. 1993. *Latinos and the L.A. Uprising.* Tomás Rivera Study Center, Occidental College, California.

Patterson, Gerald, John B. Reid, and Thomas J. Dishion. 1997. *Antisocial boys.* Eugene, Oregon: Castalia.

Pedraza, Sylvia. 1996. Cuba's refugees: Manifold migrations. In *Origins and destinies: Immigration, race, and ethnicity in America,* ed. S. Pedraza and R. G. Rumbaut, 263–79. Belmont, California: Wadsworth Publishing Company.

Perea, Juan F. 1990. "English-only rules and the right to speak one's primary language in the workplace." *University of Michigan Journal of Law Reform* 23: 265–318.

———. 1995. "Los Olvidados: On the making of invisible people." *New York University Law Review* 70: 965–91.

———. 1997a. *Immigrants out! The new nativism and the anti-immigrant impulse in the United States.* New York: New York University Press.

———. 1997b. "The Black/White binary paradigm of race: The 'normal science' of American racial thought." *California Law Review* 85: 1213–58.

Perea, Juan F., Richard Delgado, Angela P. Harris, and Stephanie M. Wildman. 2000. *Race and races: Cases and resources for a diverse America.* St. Paul, Minnesota: West Group.

Pérez, Luis. 2004. Cops' work bias suit settled. *New York Newsday,* 31 January, Queens edition.

Pérez, Jr., Louis A. 1995. *Cuba: Between reform and revolution.* 2d ed. New York: Oxford University Press.

Petersilia, Joan, and Susan Turner. 1986. *Prison versus probation in California.* Santa Monica, California: Rand.

Pew Hispanic Center. 2006. *Fact sheet: Hispanic attitudes toward learning English.* Washington, D.C., Pew Hispanic Center, http://pewhispanic .org/files/factsheets/20.pdf (accessed July 29, 2007).

Pew Hispanic Center/Kaiser Family Foundation. 2002. *2002 National Survey of Latinos.* Washington, D.C.: Pew Hispanic Center/Kaiser Family Foundation.

Piatt, Bill. 1990. "Attorney as interpreter: A return to babble." *New Mexico Law Review* 20: 1–16.

Police Officer David. 2002. Interview by author. New York, 24 September.

Pollan, Michael. 2003. The (agri)cultural contradictions of obesity: A generation of U.S. farm policy promoting overproduction of corn has made us fat—and made Big Food happy. *New York Times Magazine,* 12 October.

Portes, Alejandro, and Rubén G. Rumbaut. 2006. *Immigrant America: A portrait.* Berkeley, California: University of California Press.

Portes, Alejandro, and Richard Schauffler. 1996. Language acquisition and loss among children of immigrants. In *Origins and Destinies: Immigration, race, and ethnicity in America*, ed. S. Pedraza and R. G. Rumbaut, 432–43. Belmont, California: Wadsworth Publishing Company.

President's Task Force on Puerto Rico's Status. 2005. *Report of President's Task Force on Puerto Rico's Status*. Washington D.C.: White House, http://iprac.aspira.org/PDF's/PR_status_report_05.pdf (accessed July 16, 2007).

Rainwater, Lee, and Timothy M. Smeeding. 2003. *Poor kids in a rich country: America's children in comparative perspective*. New York: Russell Sage Foundation.

Ramos-Zayas, Ana Y. 2004. "Delinquent citizenship, national performances: Racialization, surveillance, and the politics of "worthiness" in Puerto Rican Chicago." *Latino Studies* 2(1): 26–44.

Rappleye, Charles. 2000. Harassing Homies: LAPD campaigns against a church-based gang-peace project. *LA Weekly*, 11–17 February.

Reiman, Jeffrey. 2001. *The rich get richer and the poor get prison: Ideology, class, and criminal justice*. Boston: Allyn and Bacon.

Reynoso, Cruz. 2000. Hispanics and the criminal justice system. In *Hispanics in the United States: An agenda for the twenty-first century*, ed. P. San Juan Cafferty and D. W. Engstrom, 277–315. New Brunswick, New Jersey: Transaction Publishers.

Riley, K. Jack. 1997. *Crack, powder cocaine, and heroin: Drug purchase and use patterns in six U.S. cities*. Washington D.C.: U.S. Department of Justice, National Institute of Justice.

Rivera, Raquel Z. 2003. *New York Ricans from the hip hop zone*. New York: Palgrave.

Rivera Ramos, Efrén. 2001. *The legal construction of identity: The judicial and social legacy of American colonialism in Puerto Rico*. Washington, D.C.: American Psychological Association.

Roach, Ronald. 2007. Cause for action. *Diverse Issues in Higher Education*, 12 July.

Robles, Frances. 2007. Court win fuels Puerto Rican citizenship debate. *Miami Herald*, 13 July, http://www.lexisnexis.com/us/lnacademic/auth/checkbrowser.do?ipcounter=1&cookieState=0&rand=0.6264436205512268&bhcp=1(accessed August 25, 2007).

Rodriguez, Orlando. 1996. *The new immigrant Hispanic population: An integrated approach to preventing delinquency and crime.* National Institute of Justice, Research Review: U.S. Department of Justice.

Romaine, Suzanne. [1989] 1992. *Bilingualism.* Oxford, United Kingdom: Blackwell Publishers.

Román, Ediberto. 2006. *The other American colonies: An international and constitutional law examination of the United States' nineteenth and twentieth century island conquests.* Durham, North Carolina: Carolina Academic Press.

Roorda, Eric Paul. 1998. *The dictator next door: The Good Neighbor Policy and the Trujillo regime in the Dominican Republic, 1930–1945.* Durham, North Carolina: Duke University Press.

Rosen, Fred, and Diedre McFadyen, eds. 1995. *Free trade and economic restructuring in Latin America.* New York: Monthly Review.

Rosenbaum, Robert J. 1998. *Mexicano resistance in the Southwest.* Dallas, Texas: Southern Methodist University Press.

Rosenberg, Tina. 2003. The taint of the greased palm. *New York Times Magazine,* 10 August.

Rumbaut, Rubén, Roberto G. Gonzales, Golnaz Komaie, Charlie V. Morgan and Rosaura Tafoya-Estrada. 2006. Immigration and incarceration: Patterns and predictors of imprisonment among first- and second generation young adults. In *Immigration and Crime: Race, Ethnicity, and Violence.* eds. Ramiro Martínez, Jr., and Abel Valenzuela, Jr., 64–89. New York: New York University Press.

Said, Edward. 1993. *Culture and imperialism.* New York: Vintage Books.

Sampson, Robert J. and Janet L. Lauritsen. 1997. Racial and ethnic disparities in crime and criminal justice in the United States. In *Ethnicity, crime, and immigration: Comparative and cross-national perspectives,* ed. Michael Tonry, 311–74. Chicago: University of Chicago Press.

Sánchez, Alex. 2001. Interview by author. Los Angeles, California, 18 July.

Sánchez, Marcela. 2003. Immigration reform growing at the grassroots. *Washington Post,* 2 October.

Santos, Fernanda. 2007. Demand for English lessons outstrips supply. New York Times, 27 February.

Sassen, Saskia. 1998. *Globalization and its discontents: Essays on the new mobility of people and money.* New York: The New Press.

Schaefer, Richard T. 2001. *Race and ethnicity in the United States.* 2d ed. Upper Saddle River, New Jersey: Prentice Hall.

———. 2004. *Racial and ethnic groups.* 9th ed. Upper Saddle River, New Jersey: Pearson/Prentice Hall.

Schmidt, Hans. 1995. *The United States occupation of Haiti, 1915–1934.* New Brunswick, New Jersey: Rutgers University Press.

Schmitz, David F. 1999. *Thank God they're on our side: The United States and right-wing dictatorships, 1921–1965.* Chapel Hill, North Carolina: University of North Carolina Press.

Schoultz, Lars. 1998. *Beneath the United States: A history of U.S. policy toward Latin America.* Cambridge, Massachusetts: Harvard University Press.

Schulhofer, Stephen J. 2002. *The enemy within: Intelligence gathering, law enforcement, and civil liberties in the wake of September 11.* New York: Century Foundation.

Schweber, Nate. 2007. Arrests of illegal immigrants doubled in the last year, *New York Times,* 10 June.

Scott, Janny. 2001. Races still tend to live apart in New York, census shows. *New York Times,* 23 March.

Scott, Dale Peter, and Jonathan Marshall. 1991. *Cocaine politics: Drugs, armies, and the CIA in Central America.* Berkeley: University of California Press.

Sentencing Project. 2003. *Hispanic prisoners in the United States.* Washington, D.C.: Sentencing Project. Also available online at http://www.sentencingproject.org/ pdfs/1051.pdf.

———. 2007a. Felony disenfranchisement laws in the United States. Washington, D.C.: Sentencing Project, http://sentencingproject.org/Admin %5CDocuments%5Cpublications%5Cfd_bs_fdlawsinus.pdf (accessed July 24, 2007).

———. 2007b. Uneven justice: State rates of incarceration by race and ethnicity. Washington, D.C.: Sentencing Project, http://sentencingproject .org/Admin/Documents/publications/rd_stateratesofincbyraceandethnic ity.pdf (accessed July 25, 2007).

Silverman, Eli B. 1999. *NYPD battles crime: Innovative strategies in policing.* Boston: Northeastern University Press.

Simon, Jonathan. 2007. *Governing Through Crime: How the War on Crime*

Transformed American Democracy and Created a Culture of Fear. Oxford: Oxford University Press.

Sklar, Holly. 1995. *Chaos or community: Seeking solutions, not scapegoats for bad economics.* Boston: South End Press.

Skutnabb-Kangas, Tove. 2000. *Linguistic Genocide in education—or worldwide diversity and human rights?* Mahwah, New Jersey: Lawrence Erlbaum Associate, Publishers.

Skutnabb-Kangas, Tove, and Robert Phillipson, eds. 1995. *Linguistic human rights: Overcoming linguistic discrimination.* Berlin: Mouton de Gruyter.

Smith, Robert C. 1996. Mexicans in New York: Membership and incorporation in a new immigrant community. In *Latinos in New York: Communities in transition,* ed. G. Haslip-Viera, and S. L. Baver, 57–103. Notre Dame, Indiana: Notre Dame University Press.

Smith, Peter H. 2000. *Talons of the eagle: Dynamics of U.S.-Latin American relations.* 2d ed. New York: Oxford University Press.

Sohn, Louis B., and Thomas Buergernthal. 1974. *International Protection of Human Rights.* New York: Bobbs-Merrill Company.

Soltero, Carlos R. 2006. *Latinos and American law: Landmark Supreme Court cases.* Austin, Texas: University of Texas Press.

Sontag, Deborah. 2006. A videotape offers a window into a terror suspect's isolation: Leg shackles, blinders and 3 years in solitary, *New York Times,* 4 December.

Sotomayor, Sonia. 2002. "Raising the bar: Latino and Latina presence in the judiciary and the struggle for representation: Judge Mario G. Olmos memorial lecture: Latina judge's voice." *La Raza Law Journal* 13 (Spring): 87–93.

Spears, Jeffrey W. 1999. Diversity in the courtroom: A comparison of the sentencing decisions of black and white judges and male and female judges in Cook County Circuit Court. Ph.D. diss., University of Nebraska at Omaha.

Spitzer, Elliot. 1999. *The New York City Police Department's "Stop and Frisk" Practices: a Report to the People of the State of New York from the Attorney General.* New York: Civil Rights Bureau.

Spohn, Cassia. 1990. "The sentencing decisions of black and white judges: Expected and unexpected similarities." *Law & Society Review* 24: 1197–1216.

_____. 2000. Thirty years of sentencing reform: The quest for a racially neutral sentencing process. In *Criminal Justice 2000, Vol. 3*, 427–80. Washington, D.C.: U.S. Department of Justice.

Spohn, Cassia, John Gruhl, and Susan Welch. 1987. The impact of the ethnicity and gender of defendants on the decision to reject or dismiss felony charges. *Criminology* 25: 175–91.

Steffensmeier, Darrell, and Stephen Demuth. 2000. Ethnicity and Sentencing in U.S. Federal Courts: Who Is Punished More Harshly? *American Sociological Review* 65:705–29.

Steffensmeier, Darrell, and Stephen Demuth. 2001. Ethnicity and Judges' Sentencing Decisions: Hispanic-Black-White Comparisons. *Criminology* 39:145–78.

Stephanson, Anders. 1995. *Manifest Destiny: American expansion and the empire of right*. New York: Hill and Wang.

Stiglitz, Joseph E. 2002. *Globalization and its discontents*. New York: W.W. Norton & Company.

Substance Abuse and Mental Health Services Administration. 2002. *Results from the 2001 National Household Survey on Drug Abuse: Volume 1. Summary of national findings*. Rockville, Maryland: Office of Applied Studies, NHSDA Series H-17, DHHS Publication No. SMA 02-3758.

_____. 2003. *The NHSDA report*, 15 August.

Tomlinson, John. 1991. *Cultural imperialism: A critical introduction*. Baltimore: Maryland: Johns Hopkins University Press.

Tonry, Michael. 1995. *Maligned Neglect: Race, Crime and Punishment in America*. New York: Oxford University Press.

Torres, Andrés, and José E. Velázquez. 1998. *The Puerto Rican movement: Voices from the diaspora*. Philadelphia: Temple University Press.

Torruella, Juan R. 1988. *The Supreme Court and Puerto Rico: The doctrine of separate and unequal*. Río Piedras, Puerto Rico: Universidad de Puerto Rico.

Treaty of Guadalupe Hidalgo. 1848. *Treaty of peace, friendship, limits, and settlement*. Done at Guadalupe Hidalgo, February 2, 1848. Entered into force May 30, 1848. 9 Stat. 922; T.S. No. 207; 9 Bevans 791.

Trías Monge, José 1997. *Puerto Rico: The trials of the oldest colony in the world*. New Haven: Yale University Press.

Trubeck, David M. 1984. Economic, social and cultural rights in the Third World: Human rights and human needs. In *Human rights in interna-*

tional law, ed. T. Meron, 205–71. New York: Oxford University Press.

Tse, Lucy. 2001. *Why don't they learn English?": Separating fact from fallacy in the U.S. language debate*, New York: Teachers College Press.

Uhlman, Thomas M. 1978. "Black elite decision Making: The case of trial judges." *American Journal of Political Science* 22: 884–95.

United Nations. 1945. Charter of the United Nations. Adopted 26 June 1945, entered into force 24 Oct. 1945, as amended by G.A. Res. 1991 (XVIII) 17 Dec. 1963, entered into force 31 Aug. 1965 (557 UNTS 143); 2101 of 20 Dec. 1965, entered into force 12 June 1968 (638 UNTS 308); 2847(XXVI) of 20 Dec. 1971, entered into force 24 Sept. 1973 (892 UNTS 119).

_____. 1948. Universal Declaration of Human Rights. Adopted by the U.N. General Assembly, Dec. 10, 1948. U.N.G.A. Res. 217 A(III), U.N. A/810, at 71 (1948).

_____. 1951. Convention Relating to the Status of Refugees. Done at Geneva, July 28, 1951. Entered into force, Apr. 22, 1954. 189 U.N.T.S. 137.

_____. 1960. Declaration on the Granting of Independence to Colonial Countries and Peoples, G.A. Res. 1514, U.N. GAOR, 15th Sess., Supp. No.16, at 66, U.N. Doc. A /4684 (1960).

_____. 1966a. International Covenant on Civil and Political Rights. Done at New York, Dec. 16, 1966. Entered into force, Mar. 23, 1976. U.N.G.A. Res. 2200(XXI), 21 U.N. GAOR, Supp. (No. 16) 52, U.N. Doc. A/RES/6316 (1967), *reprinted in* 6 I.L.M. 368 (1967).

_____. 1966b. International Covenant on Economic, Social and Cultural Rights. Done at New York, Dec. 16, 1966. Entered into force, Jan. 3, 1976. U.N.G.A. Res. 2200(XXI), 21 U.N. GAOR, Supp. (No. 16) 49, U.N. Doc. A/RES/6316 (1967), *reprinted in* 6 I.L.M. 360 (1967).

_____. 1966c. International Convention on the Elimination of All Forms of Racial Discrimination. Done at New York, Mar. 7, 1966. Entered into force, Jan. 4, 1969. 660 U.N.T.S. 195, *reprinted in* 5 I.L.M. 352 (1966).

_____. 1977. United Nations General Assembly resolution 32/130. Adopted 16 December 1977, G.A. Res. 32/130 (1977).

_____. 1979a. Code of Conduct for Law Enforcement Officials. Adopted 7 December 1979, G.A. Res. 34/169 (1979).

_____. 1979b. Convention on the Elimination of all Forms of Discrimination against Women. Done at New York, Dec. 18, 1979. Entered into force,

Sept. 3, 1981. U.N.G.A. Res. 34/180(XXXIV), 34 U.N. GAOR. Supp. (No. 46) 194, U.N. Doc. A/34/830 (1979), reprinted in 19 I.L.M. 33 (1980).

_____. 1984. Convention against Torture and Other Cruel, Inhuman or Degrading Treatment or Punishment. Done at New York, Dec. 10, 1984. Entered into force, June 26, 1987. U.N.G.A. Res. 39/46 Annex, 39 U.N. GAOR, Supp. (No. 51) 197, U.N. Doc. E/CN.4/1884/72, Annex (1984), *reprinted in* 23 I.L.M. 1027 (1984).

_____. 1989. Convention on the Rights of the Child. Done at New York, Nov. 20, 1989. A/Res/44/25 (1989) *reprinted in* 28 I.L.M. 1457 (1989).

_____. 1990. International Convention on the Protection of the Rights of All Migrant Workers and Members of Their Families. Adopted 18 December 1990, G.A. Res. 45/158, (1990).

_____. 1991. *Fact Sheet No. 16 (Rev.1), The Committee on Economic, Social and Cultural Rights.* Geneva, Switzerland: United Nations. Also available online at http://www.unhchr.ch/html/menu6/2/fs16.htm.

_____. 1992. Declaration on the Rights of Persons Belonging to National or Ethnic, Religious and Linguistic Minorities. Adopted 18 Dec. 1992, G.A. Res. 47/135, reprinted in 32 ILM 911 (1993), 14 HRLJ 54 (1993).

_____. 1994a. Agreement on the establishment of the commission to clarify past human rights violations and acts of violence that have caused the Guatemalan population to suffer, U.N. Doc. A/48/954/S/1994/751, Annex II, Done at Oslo, June 23, 1994.

_____. 1994b. *Human rights: A compilation of international instruments, volume 1 (part 1), Universal instruments.* New York: United Nations.

_____. 2003a. *Report of the Special Committee on the Situation with regard to the Implementation of the Declaration of the Granting of Independence to Countries and Peoples for 2003*, U.N. Doc. A/58/23 (Part I), 3 July 2003.

_____. 2003b. *Special Committee decision of 10 June 2003 concerning Puerto Rico. Special Committee on the Situation with regard to the Implementation of the Declaration of the Granting of Independence to Countries and Peoples for 2003*, U.N. Doc. A/AC.109/2003/22, 10 June 2003.

_____. 2007. *Special Committee decision of 12 June 2007 concerning Puerto Rico. Special Committee on the Situation with regard to the Implementation of the Declaration of the Granting of Independence to Countries and Peoples*, U.N. Doc. A/AC.109/2007/L.7, 11 June 2007.

United Nations Development Programme. 2003. *Human development report 2003.* New York: Oxford University Press.

United Nations Human Rights Committee. 1994. *General comment no. 24 (52) on issues relating to reservations*, U.N. Doc. CCPR/C/21/Rev.1/Add. 6 (1994).

Urban Institute. 2002. *Immigrants in nation's two largest cities report extensive unmet food needs: Greatest hardship among those who speak limited English.* Washington, D.C.: Urban Institute. Also available online at http://www.urban.org/url.cfm?ID= 900483.

Urbina, Martin G. 2003. *Capital punishment and Latino offenders: Racial and ethnic differences in death sentences.* New York: LFB Scholarly Publishing.

U.S. Bureau of the Census. 2001a. *Money Income in the United States: 2000.* Current Population Reports, Consumer Income, P60–213. Prepared by Carmen DeNavas-Walt, Robert W. Cleveland, and Marc I. Roemer, Bureau of the Census. Washington, D.C.

_____. 2001b. *The Hispanic population: Census 2000 Brief.* Publication No. C2KBR/01-3. Prepared by Betsy Guzmán, Bureau of the Census. Washington, D.C.

_____. 2002a. *Poverty in the United States: 2001.* Current Population Reports, Consumer Income, P60–219. Prepared by Bernadette D. Procter, and Joseph Dalaker, Bureau of the Census. Washington, D.C.

_____. 2002b. *The Hispanic population in the United Status: March 2002.* Current Population Reports, P20–545. Prepared by Roberto R. Ramirez and G. Patricia de la Cruz, Bureau of the Census. Washington, D.C.

_____. 2003a. *Health insurance coverage in the United States: 2002.* Current Population Reports, Consumer Income, P60–223. Prepared by Mills, Robert J., and Shailesh Bhandari, Bureau of the Census. Washington, D.C.

_____. 2003b. *Hispanic population reaches all-time high of 38.8 million, new census estimates show.* United States Commerce News, Economics and Statistics Administration, Bureau of the Census. Washington, D.C. Also available online at www.census.gov/Press-Release/www/2003/cb03-1000.html.

_____. 2003c. *Net worth and asset ownership of households: 1998–2000.* Household Economic Studies, P70–88. Prepared by Shawna Orzechowski, and Peter Sepielli, Bureau of the Census. Washington, D.C.

_____. 2003d. *Poverty in the United States: 2002.* Current Population Reports, Consumer Income, P60–222. Prepared by Bernadette D. Procter, and Joseph Dalaker, Bureau of the Census. Washington, D.C.

_____. 2003e. *Young, diverse, urban: Hispanic population reaches all-time high of 38.8 million, new Census Bureau estimates show* (Press Release No. CB03-100). Washington, D.C.: Public Information Office, B. Bernstein and M. Bergman.

_____. 2007. *Minority population tops 100 million* (Press Release No. CB07-70). Washington, D.C.: Public Information Office, B. Bernstein, http://www.census.gov/Press-Release/www/releases/archives/population/010048.html (accessed July 15, 2007).

U.S. Commission on Civil Rights. 2000. *Police practices and civil rights in New York City: A report of the United States Commission on Civil Rights,* Washington, D.C.

U.S. Department of Health and Human Services. 2003. *Monitoring the Future National Survey Results on Drug Use, 1975–2002, Volume II: College Students & Adults Ages 19–40,* by Lloyd D. Johnston, Patrick M. O'Malley, and Jerald G. Bachman, National Institute on Drug Abuse and University of Michigan. Bethesda, Maryland.

U.S. Department of Justice. 2001. *Crime in the United States, 2000, Uniform Crime Reports.* Washington, D.C.: U.S. Department of Justice.

_____. 2002. *Crime in the United States, 2001, Uniform Crime Reports.* Washington, D.C.: U.S. Department of Justice.

_____. 2003. *Crime in the United States, 2003, Uniform Crime Reports.* Washington, D.C.: U.S. Department of Justice.

_____. 2005. *Crime in the United States, 2005, Uniform Crime Reports.* Washington, D.C.: U.S. Department of Justice, http://www.fbi.gov/ucr/05cius/arrests/index.html (accessed July 22, 2007).

U.S. Department of State. 1898. *Treaties and other international agreements of the United States of America, 1776–1949,* Treaty of Peace (Treaty of Paris), 30 Stat. 1754; T.S. 343.

_____. 1905. *Papers relating to the foreign policy of the United States, with the annual message of the President transmitted to Congress, 6 December 1904.* Washington, D.C.: GPO.

U.S. House. 2002. *Homeland Security Act of 2002.* 107th Cong., 2nd sess., H.R. 5005.

U.S. News and World Report. 2003. Did you know? http://www.usnews.com/usnews/edu/grad/rankings/law/lawindex_brief.php (accessed December

18, 2003).

U.S. Public Law 107-56. 170th Cong., 1st sess., 3 January 2001. *Uniting and Strengthening America by Providing Appropriate Tools Required to Intercept and Obstruct Terrorism (USA PATRIOT) Act of 2001.*

U.S. Senate. 1900. *Congressional Record*, 56th Cong., 1st sess., 30 April. Washington, D.C.

_____.1975a. Select Committee to Study Governmental Operations with Respect to Intelligence Activities. *Alleged assassination plots involving foreign leaders: An interim report, November 20, 1975.* Washington, D.C.: GPO.

_____.1975b. Select Committee to Study Governmental Operations with Respect to Intelligence Activities. *Covert action in Chile, 1963–1973: Staff report.* Washington, D.C.: GPO.

U.S. Sentencing Commission. 2001. *2001 Sourcebook of Federal Sentencing Statistics.* Washington, D.C.: U.S. Sentencing Commission.

Villarruel, Francisco A., and Nancy E. Walker, with Pamela Minifree, Omara Rivera-Vázquez, Susan Peterson, and Kristen Perry. 2002. *¿Dónde está la justicia? A call to action on behalf of Latino and Latina youth in the U.S. justice system.* Washington, D.C.: Michigan State University/Building Blocks for Youth.

Wacquant, Loïc. 2001. Deadly symbiosis: When ghetto and prison meet and mesh. In *Mass imprisonment: Social causes and consequences*, ed. Garland, David, 82–120. London: Sage.

Wagner, Peter. 2007. *Prisoners in the Census skew county government in New York.* New York: Prison Policy Initiative, http://www.prisonersofthecensus.org/news/2007/07/18/nycounties/ (accessed July 23, 2007).

Wagner, Peter, Meghan Rudy, Ellie Happel, and Will Goldberg. 2007. *Phantom constituents in the Empire State: How outdated Census Bureau methodology burdens New York counties.* New York: Prison Policy Initiative, http://www.prisonersofthecensus.org/nycounties/nycounties.pdf (accessed July 23, 2007).

Walker, Nancy, E., J. Michael Senger, Francisco A. Villarruel, and Angela M. Arboleda. 2004. *Lost Opportunities: The reality of Latinos in the U.S. criminal justice system.* Washington, D.C.: National Council of La Raza.

Walker, Samuel, Miriam Delone, and Cassia Spohn. 2007. *The color of justice: Race, ethnicity, and crime in America.* 4th ed. Belmont, California:

Thomson/Wadsworth.

Wallach, Lori, and Michelle Sforza. 1999. *The WTO: Five years of reasons to resist corporate globalization.* New York: Seven Stories Press. Quoting United Nations Development Program (UNDP), Human Development Report 1999, Geneva: UNDP (1999): 3.

Weiser Benjamin. 1999a. 14 minority officers sue police force, alleging bias in disciplinary practices. *New York Times,* 10 September.

_____. 1999b. City violated officers' right to free speech, judges rule. *New York Times,* 19 November.

_____. 1998. U.S. asserts police officer planned to lie. *New York Times,* 25 June.

Weitzer, Ronald. 1999. "Citizens' Perceptions of Police Misconduct: Race and Neighborhood Context." *Justice Quarterly* 16:819–846.

Weitzer, Ronald, and Steven A. Tuch. 2006. *Race and Policing in America: Conflict and Reform.* New York: Cambridge University Press.

Welch, Susan, Michael Combs, and John Gruhl. 1988. "Do black judges make a difference?" *American Journal of Political Science* 32: 126–36.

Western, Bruce. 2006. *Punishment and inequality in America.* New York: Russell Sage Foundation.

Wilbanks, William. 1987. *The myth of a racist criminal justice system.* Belmont California: Wadsworth.

Wright, Bruce. 1987. *Black robes, white justice.* Secaucus, New Jersey: Lyle Stewart Inc.

Zea, María, Virginia A. Diehl, and Katherine S. Porterfield. 1997. Central American youth exposed to war violence. In *Psychological interventions and research with Latino populations,* ed. J. G. García and M. C. Zea, 39–55. Boston: Allyn and Bacon.

Zentella, Ana Celia. 1999. Language policy/planning and U.S. colonialism: The Puerto Rican thorn in the English-only's side. In *Sociopolitical perspectives on language policy and planning in the USA,* ed. T. Huebner and K. D. Davis, 155–71. Amsterdam: John Benjamins.

Zernike, Kate. 2003. Woman accused of leading smuggling in which 19 died. *New York Times,* 17 June.

Zinn, Howard. 2003. *People's history of the United States: 1492–present.* New

Acknowledgments

An endeavor of this kind typically draws on many sources of support, and the second edition of *Latino Rights and Justice in the United States* is no exception. There are many who were instrumental in supporting the first edition who I wish to thank again, including my colleagues at the Puerto Rican/Latin American Studies Department at John Jay College of Criminal Justice, City University of New York; the department's office assistant, Christopher Aviles; and my research assistant, Rafael Torruella.

The research and other tasks involved in the production of this book would not have been possible without the support of two PSC/CUNY Research Grant Awards, along with the institutional support given by John Jay College's administration, and Jacob Marini of the college's Office of Sponsored Programs. Other colleagues at John Jay College who lent direct or indirect support for this project include Professors Dorothy Moses Schulz, David Brotherton, and Michael Blitz. I am especially grateful for the efforts and support given by Timothy Stevens, Marta Morales, Charles Frederick, Edgar Rivera Colón, and Yolanda Martín.

At John Jay College, I have also been fortunate to have been part of an important and dynamic initiative discussed in this book, the John Jay College-Family Life Center/*Palenque*. I wish to thank the many people who have served as part of the staff of the program for their contributions and dedication to its success, including Luis Barrios, Marta Morales, Rafael Torruella, Claudia De La Cruz, Reynaldo García-Pantaleón, Diógenes Abréu, Héctor Rivera, Sandra María Esteves, Dagoberto López, Luisa Sánchez, Randol Contreras, and the John Jay College students who participated as mentors/facilitators. I also wish to acknowledge the support of the program's community-based partnership agencies, including *Alianza Dominicana* and the Dominican Women's Development Center, as well as the funding assistance provided by the Family and Community Violence Prevention Program (FCVP) headed by Dr. Laxley W. Rodney at Central States University in Ohio and the Office of Minority Health, Department of Health and Human Services. Most importantly, I thank the youth of the *Palenque* program, who have consistently proven that

Latina and Latino youth have much to offer to their communities and the greater society.

My appreciation is also extended to those who provided an array of information and assistance at different points during this project, including attorneys Jorge González, Michael Zinzum of the Coalition against Police Abuse, Vina Camper of Police Watch, Elizabeth Schroeder of the American Civil Liberties Union Foundation of Southern California, Anthony Miranda, the Latino Officers Association, Iris Báez, the Anthony Báez Foundation, Alex Sánchez, Homies Unidos, Ralph Rivera, Klaudia M. Rivera, and Raul Añorve of the *Instituto de Educación Popular del Sur de California.*

I am grateful to the many Latina and Latino law enforcement personnel and Latina and Latino youth who have provided insights and encouragement for this work. This book was written in the hope of improving the lives of our Latina and Latino youth and communities.

I thank Richard Delgado, not just for his contribution to this second edition, but for his leadership and inspiration.

Key to the completion of this second edition was Olga Sanabria. I thank her for her recommendations and assistance, but most of all, for her dedication and her appreciation of the significance of this project. I also thank Reynaldo García-Pantaleón for contributing the cover artwork for the second edition.

I am deeply indebted to my students at John Jay College, who are an endless source of reflection and inspiration. As I embark upon my new role as undergraduate dean, I look forward to working to advance their educational success.

A special final word of gratitude is reserved for my wife, Jeanette Guillén-Morín, who has been steadfast in assisting and supporting me through both editions. I dedicate this second edition to her.

ABOUT THE AUTHOR

José Luis Morín is the Interim Dean for Undergraduate Studies at John Jay College of Criminal Justice, City University of New York. He is also Professor in the Latin American and Latina/o Studies Department (formerly the Puerto Rican/Latin American Studies Department) and a member of the faculty in the Ph.D. Program in Criminal Justice at the college. His areas of specialization include domestic and international criminal justice, civil rights and international human rights, race and ethnicity in the United States, Latina/o studies, and U.S.-Latin America relations. Prior to joining the faculty at John Jay College in 1998, he was a Visiting Professor at the University of Hawai'i at Mānoa, where he taught courses on international law and Indigenous Peoples' rights. For many years he has also worked as a civil rights and international human rights attorney. He holds a Bachelor of Arts in political science from Columbia University and a Juris Doctor degree from New York University School of Law.

INDEX